DOCUMENTING FIRST WAVE FEMINISMS
Volume I: Transnational Collaborations and Crosscurrents

STUDIES IN GENDER AND HISTORY

General Editors: Franca Iacovetta and Karen Dubinsky

Documenting First Wave Feminisms

Volume I:
Transnational Collaborations and Crosscurrents

Edited by
Maureen Moynagh
with Nancy Forestell

UNIVERSITY OF TORONTO PRESS
Toronto Buffalo London

Toronto Buffalo London
www.utppublishing.com
Printed in Canada

ISBN 978-0-8020-9134-5

Printed on acid-free, 100% post-consumer recycled paper with vegetable-based
inks.

Library and Archives Canada Cataloguing in Publication

Documenting first wave feminism : transnational collaborations and
crosscurrents / edited by Maureen Moynagh ; with Nancy Forestell.

(Studies in gender and history)
Includes bibliographical references and index.
ISBN 978-0-8020-9134-5 (v.1)

1. Feminism – History – 19th century – Sources. 2. Feminism – History – 20th
century – Sources. 3. Women's rights – History – 19th century – Sources.
4. Women's rights – History – 20th century – Sources. I. Forestell, Nancy M.
(Nancy Margaret), 1960– II. Moynagh, Maureen Anne, 1963– III. Series:
Studies in gender and history

HQ1154.D63 2012   305.4209′034   C2011-906612-2

University of Toronto Press acknowledges the financial assistance to its publishing
program of the Canada Council for the Arts and the Ontario Arts Council.

 Canada Council Conseil des Arts  ONTARIO ARTS COUNCIL
for the Arts   du Canada   CONSEIL DES ARTS DE L'ONTARIO

University of Toronto Press acknowledges the financial support of the Government
of Canada through the Canada Book Fund for its publishing activities.

For our mothers,
Frances (Jenkins) Moynagh
Alice (O'Leary) Forestell

Contents

PART TWO: IMPERIAL FEMINISMS

PART THREE: SUFFRAGE

PART FOUR: NATIONALISM / INTERNATIONALISM

PART FIVE: CITIZENSHIP

PART SIX: MORAL REFORM, SEXUALITY, AND BIRTH CONTROL

PART SEVEN: WORK

PART EIGHT: PEACE

Acknowledgments

We owe a debt of gratitude to several people and institutions for the support they have given to us and to this project. The Dean of Arts and the Academic Vice President and Provost at St Francis Xavier University offered vital funding when it was most needed. The University Council for Research of St Francis Xavier University provided research funding that enabled us to visit archives and hire research assistants. The librarians and staff at the Women's Library, London Metropolitan University, were welcoming and helpful. For Volume I, Janette Fecteau and Clare Mulcahy offered terrific research assistance, helping with permissions and literature searches, scanning and proofing documents, all the while sharing in our enthusiasm for the project. Additional research assistance was ably provided by Brandy McDougall, who searched the archives of the Pacific Collection at the University of Hawaii at Manoa for materials related to the Pan-Pacific Women's Association. For Volume II, thanks are due to Ryan Eyford, for his translation of Margaret Benedictsson from Icelandic; to Alison Norman for providing the Emily Grant document and biographical information about Grant; to Cecilia Morgan for assisting with Lally Bernard; to Peter Campbell for biographical information on Rose Henderson; to Jennifer Steel for her research on Québécois nationalism; and to Lynne Marks, Clare Fawcett, Rhonda Semple, and Cecilia Morgan for reading portions of the manuscript. We are also grateful for technical assistance from Marie Gillis, secretary of the Department of English, Anne-Marie McPherson, secretary of the Department of History, and Betty MacNeil, secretary of the Women's Studies Program at St Francis Xavier University. Finally, without the encouragement, enthusiasm, and unflagging support of our series editors Franca Iacovetta and Karen Dubinksy, this documents book would not have been published. Franca and Karen, thank you.

Permissions

Nazira Zain al-Din, 'Unveiling and Veiling: On the Liberation of the Women and Social Renewal in the Islamic World,' in *Opening the Gates*, ed. Margot Badran and Miriam Cooke (Bloomington: Indiana UP, 1990). Reprinted with the permission of Indiana University Press.

Mary Austin, 'Sex Emancipation through War,' in *American Feminisms: Key Source Documents 1848–1920*, vol. 4, *Women's Clubs and Settlements*, ed. Janet Beer, Anne-Marie Ford, and Katherine Joslin (London and New York: Routledge, 2003), 453–63. Reproduced by permission of Taylor & Francis Books UK.

Annette Akroyd Beveridge, 'Letter to *The Englishman* about the Ilbert Bill,' in *India Called Them* by Lord Beveridge (London : George Allen and Unwin, 1947), 228. Reprinted by permission.

Vera Brittain, 'Married Women and Surnames,' *Time and Tide*, 15 January 1926. Vera Brittain material is reproduced by permission of Mark Bostridge and Timothy Brittain-Catlin, Literary Executors for the Estate of Vera Brittain, 1970.

F.W. Stella Browne, 'The Right to Abortion,' *Sexual Reform Congress, London, 8–14 September, 1929 (World Social League for Sexual Reform), Proceedings of the Third Congress*, ed. Norman Haire (London: Kegan Paul, Trench, Trubner, 1930), 178–81. Reprinted by permission.

Josephine Butler, 'The Modern Slave Trade' – Letter to the Editor of *The Shield*, from *Josephine Butler and the Prostitution Campaigns*, volume 4, ed.

Jane Jordan and Ingrid Sharpe (London: Routledge Curzon, 2003) 63–5. Reprinted by permission.

Adelaide Casely-Hayford, 'A Girl's School in West Africa,' *The Southern Workman* (1926). Reprinted with the permission of Kobina Hunter.

Mabel Dove, [On Suffrage in West Africa], in *Selected Writings of a Pioneer West African Feminist*, ed. Audrey Gadzekpo and Stephanie Newell (Nottingham: Trent Editions, 2004), 7–8. Reprinted by permission of Trent Editions.

Frances Ellen Watkins Harper, 'The Colored People in America,' in *American Feminism: Key Source Documents 1848–1920*, vol. 1, ed. Janet Beer, Anne-Marie Ford, and Katherine Joslin (London and New York: Routledge, 2002), 77–8. Reproduced by permission of Taylor & Francis Books UK.

Eleanor Hinder, 'Pan-Pacific Women's Conference in Relation to World Conferences,' *Bulletin of the Pan-Pacific Union* (July 1928). Reprinted with the permission of Rosslyn Fraser and Ron Fraser.

Alexandre Kollontai, 'Resolution on the Role of Working Women,' in *Theses, Resolutions and Manifestos of the First Four Congresses of the Third International*, ed. Alan Adler (London: Ink Links, Atlantic Highlands: Humanities Press, 1980), 46–7. Reprinted by permission of Pluto Press.

'The Lima Declaration in Favor of Women's Rights,' in *The International Conferences of American States: First Supplement, 1933–1940* (Washington, DC: Carnegie Endowment for International Peace, 1940). Reprinted by permission.

Paulina Luisi, 'International Woman Suffrage Alliance: Committee on Equal Moral Standard and Against the Traffic in Women' – from the Report of the Chairman (1926). Reprinted with the permission of the International Alliance of Women.

Najiye Hanīm, 'Address to the First Congress of the Peoples of the East,' in *To See the Dawn: Baku, 1920 – First Congress of the Peoples of the East*, ed. John Riddell (Pathfinder Press, 1993). Copyright © 1993 by Pathfinder Press. Reprinted by permission.

Emmeline Pankhurst, 'The Importance of the Vote,' in *Speeches and Trials of the Militant Suffragettes*, ed. Cheryl R. Jorgensen-Earp (Madison: Farleigh-Dickinson UP, 1999), 31–3, 34–41. Reprinted by permission.

Sarah Parker Remond, 'Lecture at the Lion Hotel,' *Warrington Times*, 4 February 1859. Copyright held by The Black Abolitionist Archive, University of Detroit Mercy.

'Resolution on the Problem of the Indigenous Woman,' in *The International Conferences of American States: First Supplement, 1933–1940* (Washington, DC: Carnegie Endowment for International Peace, 1940). Reprinted by permission.

Huda Shaarawi, 'Pan-Arab Feminism,' in *Opening the Gates*, ed. Margot Badran and Miriam Cooke (Bloomington: Indiana UP, 1990, 2004). Reprinted with the permission of Indiana University Press.

'Women of the Working People!' International Conference of Socialist Women in Berne (1915), in *Lenin's Struggle for a Revolutionary International*, ed. John Riddell (Pathfinder Press, 1984). Copyright © 1984 by Pathfinder Press. Reprinted by permission.

Virginia Woolf, from *Three Guineas* (San Diego, New York, London: Harcourt, Brace World, 1938), 106–9. Reprinted by permission of the Society of Authors, Literary Representative of the Estate of Virginia Woolf.

Illustrations

Jus cartoons no. XI, 'Guidance in the Choice of a Career,' *International Women's News: Jus Sufragii* 25.5 (1931): 73. Image published with permission of ProQuest. Further reproduction is prohibited without permission.

'Sample of Suffragist Logic as Shown in Their Cartoons,' *The Woman's Protest against Woman Suffrage* 1.2 (1912): 9. Image published with permission of ProQuest. Further reproduction is prohibited without permission.

Jus cartoons no. VII, 'The Assembly of the League of Nations: 1930,' *International Women's News: Jus Suffragii* 24:12 (1930): 193. Image published with permission of ProQuest. Further reproduction is prohibited without permission.

These images reproduced by permission of the Spencer Research Library,

University of Kansas. Images produced by ProQuest as part of the *Gerritsen Collection of Aletta H. Jacobs*. Inquiries may be made to:

ProQuest
The Quorum
Barnwell Road
Cambridge, CB5 8SW
UK
Tel. +44 (0) 1223 215512
Web page: http://www.proquest.co.uk

Every effort has been made to secure permissions for the material published in this book. Any errors or omissions brought to the attention of the publisher will be rectified in the next printing.

General Introduction

MAUREEN MOYNAGH AND NANCY FORESTELL

Documenting First Wave Feminisms is a two-volume collection of essays, pamphlets, manifestos, memoirs, petitions, reports, and resolutions documenting the multiple forms of engagement and organizing within first wave feminism. Our project is not primarily about recuperation, an undertaking that cannot be embarked upon blithely given the deep implication of many first wave women in structures of privilege and empire building. Rather, we seek to make more readily available some of the documents of first wave feminism that make especially evident its international linkages and its engagement with categories of social location other than gender that were and continue to be so central to women's organizing and feminist theorizing. Needless to say, the contours of debates on questions of race, sexuality, nation, and so on were significantly different at the turn of the last century than those which characterize the beginning of the twenty-first, but we anticipate that precisely those differences may prove instructive.

The story of first wave feminism, as Christine Bolt has pointed out, is 'one of national distinctiveness within an international cause.'[1] Our volumes emphasize the international cause and an underrepresented national case, respectively, and in making the 'feminism' of our title plural we aim to signal our conviction that there are multiple, overlapping stories of the first wave to take account of. The emergence of 'woman's rights' movements over the course of the nineteenth century, concerned as they were with broadly similar social and political goals – higher education, political enfranchisement, legal reforms, moral reforms – made for the possibility of international collaboration. At the same time, the distinctiveness of feminist social movements within different national and sub-national spheres means that any attempt to chart the international can only be partial. Finally, accounts of national movements can elide important ways in which key events were as international as they were local or national, as is the case, for example, with the Seneca Falls Convention.

The primary focus of the first volume, *Transnational Collaborations and Crosscurrents*, is to document international feminist organizing, the overlapping and conflicting aims of feminists across the globe, and the largely unacknowledged influence of minority women and women from the south on international feminist thought. Our aim in this volume has not been to abstract feminist organizing from the material, political circumstances and embedded social relationships of specific localities, but rather to emphasize the ways that 'local' feminist organizing was most often informed by what feminists were doing elsewhere, and the ways 'local' issues frequently became international ones. Beyond specific instances of transnational collaboration like the financial assistance English and Irish women provided to US and Canadian women abolitionists, or the support some British feminists loaned to Indian women who were in London to petition the colonial government, or the mentoring relationships forged between Uruguayan and other Latin American women, feminists also created formal international organizations to further their aims and pursued international legislation when that seemed the most fruitful course of action. Volume 2, *Canada: National and Transnational Contexts*, recognizes the participation of Canadian women in international feminist networks as well as the parallels and divergences between Canadian feminists and their counterparts around the world. The Canadian volume, moreover, will address and in some respects *redress* significant gaps in the historiography on first wave feminism in Canada. Certainly the situation of Canada as a white settler colony with a significant French-language minority had potentially far-reaching implications for international feminist political activism.

Our volumes also strive to document the first wave in ways that enable a critical apprehension of the dominant roles played by elite white women, and thus to reorient the scholarly focus by presenting evidence of a more diverse social movement than is conventionally associated with the first wave. The work of decentring first wave feminism entails attending not only to the usual dominance of Britain and the United States in the literature, but avoiding envisioning the peripheries as merely 'writing back' – yet another way of placing the British Empire or the United States in the centre. Instead, we need to look at 'south–south' relations, to use contemporary terminology, and to consider, for instance, alliances among Latin American feminists, organizations like the Pan-Pacific Women's Association, or Second-World alliances. Equally important are the ways that indigenous and other racialized women, within particular national contexts, contested dominant constructions of feminism that excluded them or positioned them as the objects of white feminist intervention. The transnational focus in particular enables us to take account of the dynamic interplay of individuals, organizations, and debates across a wide range of geographical centres. There are nonetheless significant gaps in our anthology, despite our aim to decentre the first wave. A documents book is inherently biased against oral sources, and in favour of those more privileged sectors of any culture that produced written texts. In our volume introductions and in our introductions to the thematic sections of each volume, we strive to make apparent the silences that persist and to historicize them.

While 1848 is often the starting point of accounts of the first wave, because the Seneca Falls Convention took place in that year, we have included texts that pre-date that moment as a means of recognizing texts and activism that resonated internationally in ways that were consequential for women activists in different national contexts. Our cut-off point, for the most part, is the Second World War. There was a significant expansion of internationalism after 1920, and a significant increase in the participation in feminist and nationalist movements of women in colonial settings that an earlier, more conventional cut-off date would elide. The Second World War not only interrupted transnational feminist organizing for a significant period of time, the world that emerged from the conflict was a much altered place, and feminist organizing was significantly transformed as a consequence. Suffrage, for instance, receded as a leading principle of transnational feminist politics, even if it continued to matter in many national spheres. In the context of widespread decolonization around the globe, human rights arguably came to displace women's rights for a time in international spheres of organizing; transnational solidarity also arguably took new forms and acquired new objectives for many women in the global south. The Cold War that followed the Second World War also altered the terrain of international collaboration, making communication across 'blocs' all but impossible.

We are, at the same time, conscious of the fact that thinking in terms of 'waves' is not unproblematic, but we retain the term to distinguish the feminisms we are documenting from post-war feminism, which departs in significant ways from what went before. It is always problematic to establish a 'beginning' and an 'endpoint' for women's movements. While feminist historians once conceived of 'waves' in these terms, more recent scholars have recognized the extent to which it makes more sense to trace patterns of continuity or transformation, and have argued that in fact the more established chronologies neglect the ongoing activism of some groups of women. Dorothy Sue Cobble, for instance, points out that women in the US labour movement were very active from the late 1930s through the 1960s, suggesting more continuity between the first wave and the second.[2] Another difficulty in a collection such as ours has to do with the tension between chronologies generated out of national women's movements and the international struggles in which many of these activists participated. While cut-off points are always somewhat arbitrary, the Second World War, in our estimation, constituted a significant enough interruption of the transnational collaborations we are attempting to track to warrant designating as different what came after the war.

Our use of the term 'feminism' to encompass the thought and activism of many women around the world may well be perceived as problematic. Certainly many of the activists whose voices are documented here used different terminology. In the early nineteenth century 'woman's rights' was the term most commonly in use; 'feminism' was not used until the late nineteenth century, and even then was not embraced by all the activists involved in organizing for social change. We use 'feminism' to indicate an awareness, on the part of women, that they are oppressed at least in part because of their sex, and to designate the analyses of oppression and the struggles for liberation conducted by and for women, whether or not the women in question used the term 'feminism.' In other words, we mean to designate as 'feminist' concepts that manifest a critical, gendered consciousness. Where possible, we will indicate when alternative terminology was in use or where the term 'feminist' was itself explicitly rejected or critiqued. For instance, socialist women were among those reluctant to use the term feminism because of its associations with the particular preoccupations of bourgeois women. Indian women were also reluctant to identify as feminists or suffragettes because of their sense that feminists were inclined to separatism, whereas Indian women saw themselves working together with men in the nationalist movement.

Our aim has been to produce collections of documents that reflect the more nuanced picture of the first wave that has been emerging in the recent work of feminist historians, literary critics, and political theorists. The influence of critical race and postcolonial studies, as well as efforts to consider links between feminism and globalization and an awareness of the need to be attentive to nationalism and transnationalism inform our anthology just as they inform the current secondary literature. Rather than constituting an anachronism, this approach promises to make more visible some of the features of the first wave that had been obscured in studies exclusively focused on gender as a category of analysis and dominated by attention to the work of European and Euro-American women, especially feminists in Britain and the United States. Although there have been editions that make more widely available material published in particular journals or documents pertinent to a given nation, or even collections focused on a particular theme, there has not yet been a first wave documents book that is transnational in scope. Estelle Friedman's important collection *The Essential Feminist Reader*,[3] while transnational, is not focused on the first wave women's movement, but encompasses feminist documents ranging from the late Middle Ages to the present. In the case of Canada, a number of document books have been published, but with the exception of several impressive works that focus on Quebec, none have incorporated texts by both anglophone and francophone first wave feminists. Nor has there been any attempt thus far to contextualize Canadian feminism within the overlapping frameworks of imperialism, internationalism, and transnationalism. Both of our volumes are intended to be used by researchers as well as in undergraduate and graduate classrooms as a complement to current historiographic, literary, and political studies.

Working on *Documenting First Wave Feminisms* has taught us a great deal about the ways earlier feminists understood their social worlds. While there is no denying that the first wave was dominated by privileged Euro-American women, these documents also suggest that feminist politics in this period were far more complex and interesting than this important acknowledgment betrays. The effort to organize transnationally, fraught and contradictory as it often was, exposed these women to other ways of conceiving feminism, other strategies for pursuing their goals, and other ways of understanding the world, even if many were not always open to the possibilities they encountered. We hope our readers will find these documents similarly engaging.

NOTES

1 Christine Bolt, *The Women's Movements in the United States and Britain from the 1790s to the 1920s* (Amherst: University of Massachusetts Press, 1993), 5.
2 Dorothy Sue Cobble, *The Other Women's Movement: Workplace Justice and Social Rights in Modern America* (Princeton: Princeton University Press, 2004).
3 Estelle Friedman, *The Essential Feminist Reader* (New York: Modern Library, 2007).

DOCUMENTING FIRST WAVE FEMINISMS
Volume I: Transnational Collaborations and Crosscurrents

Volume Introduction: Transnational Collaborations and Crosscurrents

MAUREEN MOYNAGH

As contemporary feminists around the world strive to negotiate competing and conflicting affiliations based on imperialism or globalization, nation, race, class, sexuality, and religion, it is useful to take another look at the ways first wave feminists negotiated – or failed to negotiate – similar tensions in their international organizing. Feminism has long been recognized as one of the first international social movements. In the first part of the nineteenth century, women involved with the abolition movement in the United Kingdom and the United States, utopian socialists, and members of dissenting religious groups began to read one another's work, to correspond, to travel, and to support one another transnationally.[1] Long before the first international organizations were founded late in the century, feminists were persuaded of the value of combining their forces to emancipate women across the globe. That this meant working across and often reinforcing asymmetries of power has been a matter of concern to contemporary scholars, particularly those working in the area of colonial and postcolonial studies. The overriding global practice that facilitated travel by women (chiefly, though not exclusively, by privileged white women), that enabled a global imaginary, and that provided ready-made international linkages was of course imperialism. The 'imperial feminisms,' to borrow Antoinette Burton's coinage, that emerged as a consequence of these material frameworks operated both with and against the grain of imperial ideology, as scholars as diverse as Burton, Sara Mills, Anne McClintock, and Ann Laura Stoler have shown.[2] Any account of transnational linkages within first wave feminism must reckon with this imperial legacy, and with the other kinds of geopolitical and ideological tensions that either marked or thwarted transnational collaborations. A critical reassessment of the first wave women's movement, then, is best approached through a collection of documents that lays out both the bases for collaboration and the conflicts and debates that ensued.

The Discourse of Global Sisterhood

Despite the evident challenges of working across the boundaries of nation, race, language, and religion, many feminists active in the early women's movement believed in a fundamental common ground among women across the world. As Josephine Butler would put it in the suffrage periodical *Common Cause*, 'the womanhood of the world is *solidaire*.'[3] Elizabeth Cady Stanton pointed to the 'universal sense of injustice, that forms a common bond of union' among 'women of all nationalities' at the founding meeting of the International Council of Women (ICW).[4] Addressing an audience of German women in 1907, Annie Kenney declared: 'No nationality, no political creed, no class distinction, no difference of any sort divides us women.'[5] That often very real distinctions of precisely these sorts did divide women around the world is made poignantly clear in African American Sarah Parker Remond's emotional response to being hailed as a 'sister' by an Englishwoman while she travelled through England on an abolitionist lecture tour.[6] International meetings frequently reinforced a sense of commonality and kinship among women; in a notice about the International Woman Suffrage Alliance (IWSA) meeting in Budapest, Mary Sheepshanks affirmed that 'every country and every individual gains in inspiration and knowledge by these meetings with women of all countries, all bound together in a common movement for liberty.'[7] Yet 'sisterhood' was in practice much less global, and international gatherings could just as easily aggravate differences.

The international harmony Sheepshanks claims for the IWSA meetings was arguably at least partly an effect of the relative homogeneity of the participants. If nothing else, the time and travel demands of international organizing presupposed women with sufficient leisure and income at their disposal, and thus automatically excluded most women around the world. The location of most international meetings in Europe or the United States made attendance prohibitive for all but the most wealthy of women from Asia, Africa, and Latin America, and the languages in which most of these organizations operated (English, French, and German) enacted another order of Eurocentric exclusion. What Leila Rupp has aptly characterized as the 'tension between the ideal of inclusiveness and the reality of exclusiveness' was the often unacknowledged subtext of the discourse of global sisterhood.[8]

With few exceptions, the membership of the international women's movement was drawn from the privileged classes. Long-time ICW president Lady Ishbel Aberdeen may have been more privileged than most, but there were more aristocrats among the overwhelmingly middle-class members of mainstream first wave women's organizations than there were working-class women. That these were often women with political influence as well as the financial where-withal to travel and to contribute to institutional coffers meant that organizations often came to rely upon the contributions of elite women, and this situation thus perpetuated the exclusion of participants from a broader range of class backgrounds. Similarly, the largely European and Christian composition of the major organizations meant that they came to be informed by sets of assumptions that also excluded large numbers of women, and this despite the efforts of some organizations in the early twentieth century to widen and diversify their membership. Clearly, the class and race privilege that marked the membership of these organizations does not paint the whole picture; it is important to stress that feminist political identifications cannot be reduced to categories of social location. Yet, as feminist historiography has made evident for several decades now, the participation of women of colour and working-class women in the mainstream women's organizations, and the alliances these organizations forged with other groups, cannot belie the ways in which whiteness and class privilege were formative for the mainstream organizations in North America, Europe, Australia, and New Zealand.[9]

The Socialist International and the Communist International afforded more working-class women leadership opportunities and were of course explicitly conceived around the interests of working-class women. While the Socialist International remained almost exclusively European, at least as far as the women's congresses were concerned, the Communist International was able to draw on women in the Soviet Republics of Asia and encouraged the building of bridges with working women in colonial contexts as well. Socialist and communist women were much less inclined to invoke a global sisterhood predicated on gender alone, clearly aware as they were of what separated them from the interests of bourgeois women. While there was a certain amount of collaboration between liberal and socialist feminists in some European contexts, particularly in Britain and France, the different political ideologies frequently made for sharp divisions and breaks.

The ideology of global sisterhood articulated by the mainstream women's organizations was undeniably marked by the imperial divide, even as feminists collaborated across it. Many of the European and American feminists who articulated their conviction in universal womanhood also gave evidence of a conviction in the superiority of Western political institutions, values, and beliefs, and in the notion that feminism itself originated in the West. As Fiona Paisley puts it, 'Interest in liberating Oriental women has been a founding feature of Euro-American international feminism.'[10] These attitudes did not go unchallenged, however. Speaking to a proposed resolution on East–West cooperation at the Istanbul meeting of the International Alliance of Women (IAW) in 1935, Shareefeh Hamid Ali of India warned women 'of the west that any arrogant assumption of superiority or of patronage on the part of Europe or America, any undue pressure of enforcement of religion or government or of trade or economic "spheres of influence" will alienate Asia and Africa and with it the womanhood of Asia and Africa.'[11] For Ali, clearly, the terms of East–West cooperation must not simply mask geopolitical asymmetries of power, but had to enable genuine cooperation; feminists ought not to be complicit with the imperial machinations of their respective polities. At its 1936 meeting, the All-India Women's Conference endorsed the IAW resolution on the basis of the general principle that 'the women of every country must advance on the lines of equality and justice,'[12] wording that seems particularly significant in light of Ali's intervention at the Istanbul congress.

Women outside of Europe and what Leila Rupp calls the 'neo-Europes' did participate in international women's organizations, and did sometimes also invoke the language of global womanhood. At the 1933 ICW Congress in Chicago, for instance, Muthulakshmi Reddi spoke of the political disenfranchisement of women as a 'world problem' and praised the extent to which the women's movement was 'international in character, crossing all barriers of caste, color, creed, or race,'[13] even as she addressed the specificity of the Indian women's movement. Similarly, Siao-Mei Djang, a Chinese member of the Women's International League for Peace and Freedom (WILPF), referred to 'the problems which are universal to womanhood' in a letter to Mary Sheepshanks.[14] Occasionally this discourse was even placed in the service of antiimperialism. Collaboration in Paris between black radical intellectuals and white feminists like Marguerite Martin offers an instance where the language of sisterhood forged bonds across racial divides. Jennifer Boittin argues that Jane and Paulette Nardal's 'initiation of interracial alliances led to connections between radical black organizations such as the UTN [Union des Travailleurs Nègres] and white bourgeois women whose primary concerns were suffrage and an international humanitarianism that fit well with anti-imperialism.'[15] Speaking at a rally in Brussels in 1935 protesting the Italian invasion of Ethiopia, Paulette Nardal used the discourse of sisterhood to urge women around the world to anti-imperial and anti-fascist action: 'We hold out our hands to the women of the whole world, without distinction of race or nationality, to defend a common ideal.'[16] She exhorted women to demand that sanctions be imposed on Italy, and to devote their energies to ending the invasion. Collaborations like this were more the exception than the rule, however, and the major international organizations remained US- and European-dominated. Whatever the genuine value of crossing barriers of caste, colour, creed, and race, it remained far more difficult in practice than in theory.

Transnational Organizations

The institutionalizing of feminist internationalism can be traced to the 1870s with the founding of the Women's Christian Temperance Union, whose international ethos led to the emergence of the World WCTU in 1884. Leila Rupp's important scholarship has been focused on what she regards as the three major international organizations, whose secular orientation and global vision meant that they were, theoretically at least, open to 'women from every corner of the globe.'[17] They were the International Council of Women (ICW), founded in 1888; the International Alliance of Women (IAW), founded in 1904 as the International Woman Suffrage Alliance (IWSA) and also briefly known as the International Alliance of Women for Suffrage and Equal Citizenship; and the Women's International League for Peace and Freedom (WILPF), founded in 1915. Many of the documents assembled in this volume were produced under the auspices of one of these three organizations, and many of the feminists around the world who engaged in internationalism at the end of the nineteenth century and during the early decades of the twentieth were affiliated with one of these organizations in addition to whatever national or local organizations they also belonged to. Yet an important part of the narrative of transnational collaboration among feminists involves the creation of regional alliances or organizations, particularly as in some instances these organizations were not quite as dominated by European and US feminists as the ICW, the IAW, and the WILPF.

One of these organizations, the British Commonwealth League, while it 'presents distinct evidence of continuity with the nineteenth- and early twentieth-century British imperial feminism,' was also the product of changing relations within empire, including between Britain and dominions like Canada, Australia, and New Zealand, but more importantly between Britain and India and, to a lesser degree, between Britain and South Africa.[18] Angela Woolacott argues that while it, too, was dominated by privileged white, English-speaking women and held its conferences in London, the BCL 'presented a significant challenge to the European and American hegemony of the larger three organizations.'[19] It was, for one thing, more racially inclusive: at its July 1925 conference (the first after the organization's inauguration in February of that year), speakers on the program included representatives from Bermuda, the British West Indies, Kenya, Ireland, and India. For another, it afforded women united, albeit unequally, by the history of British colonialism a venue through which they could devote themselves to the specific concerns of 'empire feminists' and, in some cases, critique the colonial policies of the settler-dominions or Britain itself.

The Pan-Pacific Women's Association (1930) grew out of a series of Pan-Pacific Women's Conferences that also, despite the very active role taken by American feminists, largely bypassed the European-American axis of feminist internationalism. Australians, New Zealanders, and Canadians played prominent roles here as in the BCL, but the Pacific geographical focus drew in significant numbers of women from China and Japan, as well as the Philippines, Samoa, Fiji, and India. This is not to say that there were not significant gaps. Fiona Paisley points out that 'Pacific Islander women, although at times the objects of Pan-Pacific women's concerns, were largely marginalized from conferences as women unable to represent themselves.'[20] Similarly, although the first three conferences were held in Hawaii, native Hawaiian women were largely silent, appearing on the conference programs chiefly in the entertainments offered by the Hawaiian hosts. Emerging out of a sense that the Pacific region was of increasing importance internationally, in view of the 'modernizing' of China and Japan and the perception of a need for social-welfare work in the region, the Pan-Pacific Women's Conferences aimed at enabling greater communication among women of the East and West. According to Paisley, most of the delegates 'were members of various urban-based welfare, health or education professions,' and through the focus on social-welfare feminism in the Pan-Pacific region, the PPWA 'continued to provide a privileged space for white woman's civilising mission.'[21] Increasingly, though, such attitudes met with resistance. Australian Eleanor Hinder's offer to host the second Pan-Pacific Women's Conference in Shanghai, where she then resided, met with a sharp rebuke from Me Iung Ting of the Chinese delegation, who objected that 'the women of China had not been consulted' and that Hinder had usurped a right that was not hers in issuing the invitation.[22] The second conference was in the end held in Hawaii, but unlike BCL conferences, Pan-Pacific Women's conferences did move around the region to Canada, New Zealand, the Philippines, Japan, and Australia among other places. In this way, it created an organizational structure that, as Woollacott puts it, took 'the global decentralisation of feminist international organisation even further.'[23]

In the Americas there were several attempts among feminists to collaborate across national boundaries, including organizations meant to unite them right across the hemisphere. In practice, of course, matters were more complicated. Canadians were largely absent from this collaboration until after the Second World War, and there were frequent tensions between Latin American and US feminists. Argentine feminists hosted several International Women's Congresses, beginning in 1910, that brought together women from across Latin America. The Uruguayan women's movement, under the leadership of Paulina Luisi, subsequently served as inspiration and 'godmother' to many other feminist movements across the continent as well as Cuba and Mexico.[24] Following the First World War, US feminists increasingly turned their attention to the South. Two organizations tried to build bridges between US and Latin American feminists. The Pan-American Women's Association, founded in 1922, focused on cultural exchanges and forging ties among US and Latin American women. When Carrie Chapman Catt travelled through South America under the auspices of the PAWA, however, she succeeded in alienating many of the Latin American feminists she met and her written accounts of her journey betray a decided ethnocentrism. The second hemispheric organization was the Inter-American Commission of Women, established in 1928 in Havana, and, under the leadership of US feminist Doris Stevens, it was responsible for the establishment of an Equal Rights Treaty and, in 1938, the Lima Declaration in Favour of Women's Rights. One indication, though, of Latin American feminists' resentment of the US domination of these organizations was the creation of the Liga Internacional de Mujeres Ibéricas e Hispanoamericanas. Little is known about the impetus for the founding of this organization, but according to Christine Ehrick, 'in later years the Iberian and Hispano-American Women's League existed in part as an alternative to the Inter-American Commission of Women.'[25]

Another kind of feminist internationalism was to be found among socialist and communist women, for whom the principle of internationalism formed a key part of their revolutionary ideology as well as the organizational practice of the Second and Third Internationals. While feminists found in socialism a political ideology suited to their desires for social and political emancipation, feminism was not necessarily well received by the male leadership of socialist parties. By the late nineteenth century, however, feminists began to gain some ground within the ranks of European socialists. At the founding meeting of the Second International in 1889, Clara Zetkin spoke out against the antagonism towards working women among socialists, and over the course of the 1890s, she worked at forging 'a socialist women's programme and practice within the German Social Democratic Party that became the prototype for women in socialist parties around the world.'[26] By 1907, what had been an unofficial transnational socialist women's network within the Socialist International emerged as an autonomous organization with the first women's international socialist conference at Stuttgart in 1907. The Third, or Communist, International was founded in 1919, and in contrast with the Second International, it 'gave assistance and encouragement to revolutionists in building parties in the colonial world. Its parties in the imperialist countries began to orient to recruiting Black and Asian working people, and toilers of other oppressed countries.'[27] In this respect, then, the feminism of the Communist International was oriented towards a decidedly more diverse membership. In a move reminiscent of Clara Zetkin, whom she knew, Alexandre Kollontai submitted a resolution on working women at the first Congress of the Third International, encouraging the recruitment of women to the Party and endorsing the importance of the role they might play in the development of communism.[28] While the Communist International was officially opposed to separate women's associations, it recognized the need for 'special methods' and 'special apparatuses' to facilitate communist work among women, and so the first International Conference of Communist Women was held in the summer of 1920, and by the Third Congress of the Third International, the International Women's Secretariat was organizing meetings twice a year. The first objective of the communist women's movement was to educate the masses of working women and draw them into the movement (and away from bourgeois women's organizations).[29] The 'masses of passive working women ... who are still under the influence of the bourgeois world-view' were seen as a threat to the communist revolution, and only *the victory of Communism* could bring about women's emancipation.[30]

Organization of the Volume

We have organized the source documents into thematic rubrics that address the central issues that brought feminists together internationally and that encompass the key debates and struggles within first wave feminism. While we clearly cannot hope to address all the issues associated with first wave feminism any more than we can hope, given constraints of space, to be comprehensive in our selection of documents, we are persuaded that the eight categories we have chosen are broadly representative.

The close historical linkage between the international movement for the abolition of slavery and the early women's movement dictates that we begin with a unit entitled *Slavery, Abolition, and Woman's Rights*. As Bonnie Anderson, Clare Midgley, and others have shown, the cause of abolition and both the experience and the idea of slavery informed the writing of first wave feminists throughout the British Empire, the United States, and Europe and occasioned much travel and collaboration back and forth across the Atlantic. Comparisons between the social conditions of women (implicitly white) and slaves labouring in the colonies of the Americas relied upon an imperial imaginary that made itself felt in a variety of ways in the thinking, writing, and activism of first wave feminists. At the same time, the broadly emancipatory character of this discourse did enable important, even formative, alliances across the boundaries of gender and race.

Although imperialist sentiment will be evident in documents collected under several different rubrics in this book, we felt it imperative to create a section devoted to examining *imperial feminisms* more specifically. Imperialism authorized feminist activism in imperial centres like Britain, it provided careers abroad for Western women who went as missionaries, teachers, and doctors to colonies around the globe, and it provided key images of what Western women might be were they to fail in their feminist ambitions. Women speaking from colonial contexts, by contrast, were frequently critical of the assumptions held by their European 'sisters,' and demonstrated they were quite capable of pursuing their own social and political goals.

Suffrage is of course a central category of first wave feminist organizing and theorizing, but as a consideration of the international literature on suffrage suggests, conceptions of suffrage, the nature of the struggle, and strategies varied broadly. Ellen Dubois points out that suffrage movements were fundamentally marked by internationalism; not only did women's movements cooperate transnationally, influencing one another across national borders, but they also often shared resources in ways that enabled suffrage movements to resist political marginalization within particular national contexts.[31]

Nationalism and internationalism were not necessarily opposing ideological positions for first wave feminist organizers, many of whom engaged in both at once, or felt that national organizing was a prerequisite for international organizing. Nationalism and feminism went hand-in-hand in many countries where efforts to decolonize were under way: Ireland, India, Egypt, and Palestine, to name a few. At the same time, the role of feminists in nationalist movements made for a key point of tension between nationalist feminists and feminists who insisted on a more transcendent vision of unity among women, often at the expense of non-European women whose understanding of gender and women's rights were not necessarily the same. It is important, consequently, to take account of the ways these different positions informed transnational debates among women. As well, some feminists came to feel that international organizing and international legislation were the only avenues for addressing certain kinds of issues, while still others found nations and nationalism antithetical to feminism.

Both through their participation in nationalist movements and international feminist organizations, first wave women came to redefine conceptions of *citizenship* in ways that had implications not only at 'home,' but abroad. Collaboration on the question of the nationality of married women is a case in point. Of particular significance is the extent to which the question of citizenship emerged at international meetings, offering, among other outcomes, an opportunity for minority women in the United States to alert the international community of feminists to discrimination on the basis of race, as well as gender.

Implicitly, if not explicitly, such statements pointed out tensions and inequities within a given national women's movement, while transnational organizing made another constituency of women available for solidarity and support.

Several themes that may be regarded as aspects of citizenship warrant fuller treatment in units of their own because of their centrality to first wave feminist organizing. *Moral reform* became an important facet of organizing among feminists in many nations, and there were several efforts to collaborate internationally, not least around temperance. The regulation of prostitution, which was linked to efforts to control the spread of venereal disease, became the focus of international campaigns, reports, surveys, and resolutions on the part of feminist organizations, who understood the ways efforts to regulate sexually transmitted diseases were fundamentally efforts to regulate women and women's *sexuality*, thereby entrenching the sexual double standard feminists sought to overturn. There was also significant transnational collaboration among the major *birth control* activists, supporters of the work of Margaret Sanger and Marie Stopes, among others, who argued women could be better mothers if they were not forced to wed too early or have too many children, a discourse of social reform marked by eugenics that was particularly directed at working-class and immigrant women.

From international labour legislation 'protecting' women and children, to campaigns for equal access to employment, equal pay for equal work, and maternity-leave benefits, feminists also found tremendous scope for collaborating internationally around the issue of *work*. There were also tensions. The women who belonged to the Communist International were concerned to recruit working women away from organizations led by bourgeois feminists; some socialist feminists approved of protective legislation while others did not; women in China argued against the legislation excluding women from night work that their European and North American counterparts pursued.

Pacifism emerged as a point of debate and tension within the international women's movement in the nineteenth century, but gained increasing numbers of adherents leading up to the First World War. Socialist women, many women in colonial settings, and many European and North American feminists adopted an anti-militarist stance. Feminists identified with imperialism, or those for whom war represented an opportunity for women to enter non-traditional fields of work, or, indeed, for whom the war was perceived as just, on the other hand, were vociferous in their critiques of their pacifist colleagues. These debates often took place at international meetings, but were also important contributions to debate on a national scale. Eventually, new international organizations like the Women's International League for Peace and Freedom would emerge as a consequence of these pacifist critiques.

In selecting specific documents for a given thematic unit, preference has been given to less readily available materials on the principle that the more canonical texts can be found in most libraries. In some cases, however, short excerpts from canonical texts have been included because they are so central to the issue(s) in question. Where possible we have avoided abridging archival documents or materials from out-of-print books, but we have been forced in one or two instances, again because of space considerations, to depart from this policy. We have been limited in our selection of documents from the global South in a more profound way, and that is by the greater difficulty of accessing documents in distant archives and by the limited availability of documents that have been translated into the European languages we can claim to be competent in. The tremendously important work being done by scholars like Margot Badran and Miriam Cooke compiling and translating the documents of Arab feminists, and by Tuzyline Jita Allan, Abena Busia, and Florence Howe with the Women Writing Africa Project, has helped us beyond measure. The ideal documents book of the international women's movement would itself be an endeavour of transnational collaboration.

A Note on the Text

The original spelling conventions have been retained for all of the documents collected in this volume. The texts I have translated from French follow the British convention. Errors in punctuation and obvious typographical errors have been silently corrected. Square brackets indicate an editorial intervention, whether to abridge or emend.

NOTES

1 See Bonnie Anderson, *Joyous Greetings: The First International Women's Movement, 1830–1860* (Oxford; New York: Oxford UP, 2000); Nancy Hewitt, 'Origin Stories: Remapping First Wave Feminism,' Sisterhood and Slavery: Transatlantic Antislavery and Women's Rights, Proceedings of the Third Annual Gilder Lehrman Center International Conference at Yale University, 25–8 October 2001, http://www.yale.edu/glc/conference/index.htm; Clare Midgley, *Women against Slavery: The British Campaigns 1780–1870* (New York, London: Routledge, 1992).

2 Sara Mills, *Discourses of Difference: An Analysis of Women's Travel Writing and Colonialism* (New York and London: Routledge, 1993); Antoinette Burton, *Burdens of History: British Feminists, Indian Women, and Imperial Culture, 1865–1915* (Chapel Hill: U of North Carolina P, 1994); Anne McClintock, *Impe-*

rial Leather: Race, Gender and Sexuality in the Colonial Closet (New York: Routledge, 1995); Ann Laura Stoler, *Carnal Knowledge and Imperial Power: Race and the Intimate in Colonial Rule* (Berkeley: U of California P, 2002).

3 Josephine Butler, 'Solidaire,' *Common Cause*, 6 June 1913, 131.

4 Quoted in Leila Rupp, *Worlds of Women: The Making of an International Movement* (Princeton: Princeton UP, 1997), 87.

5 Annie Kenney, 'To the Women of Germany,' *Votes for Women*, October 1907, 3.

6 See the account of this moment in 'Lecture at the Lion Hotel,' this volume, pp. 46–7.

7 Mary Sheepshanks, 'Notice of the IWSA-Budapest,' *Common Cause*, 13 February 1913, 770.

8 Rupp, *Worlds of Women*, 52.

9 See, for instance, Louise Michele Newman, *White Women's Rights: The Racial Origins of Feminism in the United States* (Oxford: Oxford University Press, 1999).

10 Fiona Paisley, 'Cultivating Modernity: Culture and Internationalism in Australian Feminism's Pacific Age,' *Journal of Women's History* 14.3 (2002): 107.

11 Quoted in Rupp, *Worlds of Women*, 80.

12 AIWC, 'Resolution on East–West Co-Operation,' this volume, p. 208.

13 Muthulakshmi Reddi, 'Creative Citizenship,' this volume, pp. 202–4.

14 Siao-Mei Djang to Mary Sheepshanks, 30 July 1929, WILPF papers, reel 19.

15 Jennifer Anne Boittin, 'In Black and White: Gender, Race Relations, and the Nardal Sisters in Interwar Paris,' *French Colonial History* 6 (2005): 123.

16 Nardal's speech was reported in *Le Cri des Nègres* 4.23 (December 1935): 1, newspaper of the radical black working-class organization UTN. Quoted in Boittin, 'In Black and White,' 128.

17 Rupp, *Worlds of Women*, 4.

18 Angela Woollacott, 'Inventing Commonwealth and Pan-Pacific Feminisms: Australian Women's Internationalist Activism in the 1920s and 1930s,' in *Feminisms and Internationalism*, ed. Mrinalini Sinha, Donna Guy, and Angela Woollancott (London: Palgrave, 2001), 81–2.

19 Ibid., 82.

20 Paisley, 'Cultivating Modernity,' 106.

21 Ibid., 110, 112.

22 Quoted in Paisley, 'Cultivating Modernity,' 125.

23 Woollacott, 'Inventing Commonwealth and Pan-Pacific Feminisms,' 82.

24 Christine Ehrick, '*Madrinas* and Missionaries: Uruguay and the Pan-American Women's Movement,' in *Feminisms and Internationalism*, ed. Mrinalini Sinha, Donna Guy, and Angela Woollacott (Oxford: Blackwell, 1999), 71.

25 Ibid., 75.

26 Ellen Carol Dubois, 'Woman Suffrage and the Left: An International Socialist-Feminist Perspective,' *New Left Review* 186 (1991): 29.

27 John Riddell, 'Introduction,' in *Lenin's Struggle for a Revolutionary International*, ed. John Riddell (New York, London, Sydney: Monad Press,1986), xii.

28 See Kollontai, 'Resolution on the Role of Working Women,' this volume, p. 340.

29 'Forms and Methods of Communist Work among Women,' Third Congress of the Communist International, 8 July 1921, in *Theses, Resolutions and Manifestos of the First Four Congresses of the Third International*, ed. Alan Adler (London: Ink Links, 1980; Atlantic Highlands, NJ: Humanities Press, 1980), 212.

30 'Methods and Forms of Work among Communist Party Women: Theses,' Third Congress of the Communist International, 8 July 1921, 215.

31 Ellen Carol Dubois, 'Woman Suffrage around the World: Three Phases of Suffragist Internationalism,' in *Suffrage and Beyond: International Feminist Perspectives*, ed. Caroline Daley and Melanie Nolan (New York: New York UP, 1994), 254.

PART ONE
Slavery, Abolition, and Woman's Rights

The links between slavery, abolition, and the early women's movement present ample evidence of both transnational activity and what we might think of as a transnational imagination among first wave feminists. In the late eighteenth century, the beginnings of the abolition movement in England spread not merely awareness among social reformers of the horrors of the slave trade and of the terrible and unjust conditions under which African slaves in the West Indies lived and worked, but the sense that something should and could be done to bring an end to the system. Thus, Mary Wollstonecraft cites the abolition movement as an instance of revolutionary possibility for achieving equality among 'men' and for linking governmental policy with justice under a liberal political system in her response to Edmund Burke's critique of the French Revolution. A more specific linkage between the condition of women and the condition of slaves had been evident in European and especially British letters for some time, as Moira Ferguson has shown. The use of colonial slavery as 'a specific referent applied to the circumstances of contemporary British women' dates to about 1670.[1] By the late eighteenth and early nineteenth centuries, this analogy became a pervasive trope in feminist tracts, two of the best known of which are Wollstonecraft's *A Vindication of the Rights of Woman* and William Thompson and Anna Wheeler's *An Appeal from One Half of the Human Race* ... This imperial imaginary, by means of which comparisons could be made between the conditions lived by slaves in the colonies and the social lives of women in the heart of empire, is thus a key element of the early women's movement.

While in the seventeenth and eighteenth centuries women frequently compared their situation to slavery without necessarily condemning colonial slavery itself,[2] by the end of the eighteenth century women were increasingly involved in the anti-slavery movement. The international linkages and travels among early feminists, particularly between Britain, the United States, and France, owed a great deal to the already extant international networks established by the movement for abolition, according to Bonnie Anderson.[3] Not only did anti-slavery women correspond with one another, and meet through their travels, they also exchanged financial support. Clare Midgley reports that English and Irish women sent a great deal of money to their US counterparts in the 1840s and 1850s, and in the 1850s they also donated to groups in Canada and the United States working with fugitive slaves.[4] Harriet Martineau was one of the key members of the 'transatlantic anti-slavery sisterhood,' to borrow a phrase from Midgley. While Martineau had published 'Negro Slavery' in 1830, it was particularly during her two-year sojourn in the United States, beginning in 1834, that she came to be involved in the anti-slavery movement, and to meet with women involved in the movement, such as the members of the Boston Female Anti-Slavery Society.[5] Martineau also wrote a series of articles about US abolitionists for the *London and Westminster Review*, to elicit support for the movement among Britons; the series was eventually published in book form under the title *The Martyr Age of the United States*.

The emblem of the woman slave that anti-slavery women circulated to mobilize support for the cause also crossed the Atlantic from Britain to the United States, and its variants, including a French one, were regularly exchanged internationally in publications, on letterhead, coins, crockery, and other folk art created to raise money for anti-slavery activism. The version reproduced here, taken from Lydia Maria Child's *Authentic Anecdotes of American Slavery* (1838), adds to the figure of the supplicant slave inviting first identification and then liberty from her free sisters the figure of justice responding to this call for emancipation at once from slavery and patriarchy. The biblical quotation speaks to the free beholder of the emblem, reminding her that she too is in bondage as long as her sisters are enslaved.[6] Anti-slavery feminists like Angelina Grimké argued for the importance of these emblems as a propaganda tool in the abolitionist struggle, and, as Jean Fagin Yellin has argued, drew on the emblem's codes in their own rhetorical positioning in their anti-slavery work: 'They recoded and re-recoded the emblem of the female supplicant, picturing themselves as chain-breaking liberators and as slaves pleading for their own liberty, then asserting it and freeing themselves.'[7]

One of the best-known narratives about the birth of the US women's movement is centred around the experiences of Elizabeth Cady Stanton and Lucretia Mott at the World Anti-Slavery Convention in London in 1840, where they met for the first time. The refusal of the British and Foreign Anti-Slavery Society to admit them and other women as delegates is, according to Stanton's autobiography, what sowed the seed that germinated in the Seneca Falls convention eight years later. Lucretia Mott's diary of her journey to the London convention, published under the title *Slavery and the 'Woman Question,'* gives evidence of the support and sympathy the women delegates received outside of the convention as well as of the circumstances of their refusal. Nancy Hewitt has pointed out that the world of 1848, when the Seneca Falls Convention on Woman's Rights took place, was one profoundly shaped by revolutions in Europe, the Mexican-American war, immigration to the United States, and the abolitionist movement – shaped, in other words, by the kind of transnational imagination as well as transnational linkages among women that these events entailed. The 'Declaration of Sentiments' that Elizabeth Cady Stanton present- ed, while it explicitly engages in a rewriting of the US constitution, begins by speaking of the 'family of man,' in decidedly universal terms.

Some of the black women involved in the anti-slavery movement worked and travelled internationally as well. Sarah Parker Remond, a free black wom- an, toured Britain lecturing about slavery on behalf of the American Anti-Slav- ery Society. As this account of her lecture in Warrington indicates, she also met with women's anti-slavery groups there, extending the 'transnational anti- slavery sisterhood' across race lines. Mary Ann Shadd Cary was born in Wilm- ington, Delaware, but moved to Windsor, Ontario, in 1850 after the passage of the Fugitive Slave Act, which she and others understood to pose a threat to free blacks like herself as well as to fugitive slaves. There she founded a newspaper, *The Provincial Freeman*, and while working for black civil rights in Ontario, she maintained contacts with abolitionists and the women's movement in the United States, as these editorials from her newspaper attest.

Sojourner Truth may not have travelled outside of the United States, but her participation in women's rights conventions and her lecturing against slavery in the United States made her an internationally renowned figure nonetheless. Most importantly, as Yellin points out, women like Sojourner Truth 'redefined the antislavery feminists' definitions of womanhood' and refused the silent and passive role in the 'sisterhood' that they were often accorded by white anti- slavery feminists. For Truth, the emblematic appeal 'Am I Not a Woman and a Sister?' became 'Ain't I a Woman?' Here, in her address to the American Equal Rights Association in 1868, she calls for equal rights specifically between black men and women in the wake of the passage of the fifteenth amendment, which gave suffrage to black men. In so doing, she implicitly counters the con- flations white anti-slavery feminists made of their condition and that of their black slave sisters.

NOTES

1 Moira Ferguson, *Subject to Others: British Women Writers and Colonial Slavery, 1670–1834* (New York, London: Routledge, 1992), 23.
2 Ibid., 25.

3 Bonnie Anderson, *Joyous Greetings: The First International Women's Movement, 1830–1860* (Oxford, New York: Oxford UP, 2000), 115.
4 Clare Midgley, *Women against Slavery: The British Campaigns 1780–1870* (New York, London: Routledge, 1992), 126–7.
5 Ibid., 130ff.
6 See Jean Fagin Yellin's extended treatment of the abolitionist emblem in *Women and Sisters: The Antislavery Feminists in American Culture* (New Haven, London: Yale UP, 1989).
7 Ibid., 25.

Mary Wollstonecraft (1759–97) was a tremendously important figure for the nineteenth-century women's movement because of her foundational feminist philosophical works. Best known today for *A Vindication of the Rights of Woman* (1792), Wollstonecraft wrote several political treatises, novels, a travel narrative, a history of the French Revolution, and a children's book, as well as *Thoughts on the Education of Daughters* (1787). *A Vindication of the Rights of Men* (1790) was Wollstonecraft's response to Edmund Burke's conservative *Reflections on the Revolution in France* (1790). It takes the form of an open letter, directly addressing Burke and taking up the various elements of his argument in order to counter them.

Mary Wollstonecraft

From *A Vindication of the Rights of Men, a Letter to the Right Honourable Edmund Burke; Occasioned by his Reflections on the Revolution in France* (1790)

You find it very difficult to separate policy from justice: in the political world they have frequently been separated with shameful dexterity. To mention a recent instance. According to the limited views of timid, or interested politicians, an abolition of the infernal slave trade would not only be unfound policy, but a flagrant infringement of the laws (which are allowed to have been infamous) that induced the planters to purchase their estates. But is it not consonant with justice, with the common principles of humanity, not to mention Christianity, to abolish this abominable mischief? There is not one argument, one invective, levelled by you at the confiscators of the church revenue, which could not, with the strictest propriety, be applied by the planters and negro-drivers to our Parliament, if it gloriously dared to shew the world that British senators were men: if the natural feelings of humanity silenced the cold cautions of timidity, till this stigma on our nature was wiped off, and all men were allowed to enjoy their birth-right – liberty, till by their crimes they had authorized society to deprive them of the blessing they had abused.

The same arguments might be used in India, if any attempt were made to bring back things to nature, to prove that a man ought never to quit the cast that confined him to the profession of his lineal forefathers. The Bramins would doubtless find many ingenious reasons to justify this debasing, though venerable prejudice; and would not, it is to be supposed, forget to observe that time, by interweaving the oppressive law with many useful customs, had rendered it for the present very convenient, and consequently legal. Almost every vice that has degraded our nature might be justified by shewing that it had been productive of *some* benefit to society: for it would be as difficult to point out positive evil as unalloyed good, in this imperfect state. What indeed would become of morals, if they had no other test than prescription? The manners of men may change without end; but, wherever reason receives the least cultivation – wherever men rise above brutes, morality must rest on the same base.

[Source: *A Vindication of the Rights of Men, in a Letter to the Right Honourable Edmund Burke, Occasioned by his Reflections on the Revolution in France,* 2nd ed. (London: Printed for J. Johnson, 1790), 46.]

Mary Wollstonecraft
From A Vindication of the Rights of Woman with Strictures on Political and Moral Subjects (1792)

It appears to me necessary to dwell on these obvious truths, because females have been insulated, as it were; and while they have been stripped of the virtues that should clothe humanity, they have been decked with artificial graces that enable them to exercise a short-lived tyranny. Love, in their bosoms, taking place of every nobler passion, their sole ambition is to be fair, to raise emotion instead of inspiring respect; and this ignoble desire, like the servility in absolute monarchies, destroys all strength of character. Liberty is the mother of virtue, and if women be, by their very constitution, slaves, and not allowed to breathe the sharp invigorating air of freedom, they must ever languish like exotics, and be reckoned beautiful flaws in nature [...]

A truly benevolent legislator always endeavours to make it the interest of each individual to be virtuous; and thus private virtue becoming the cement of public happiness, an orderly whole is consolidated by the tendency of all the parts towards a common centre. But, the private or public virtue of woman is very problematical; for Rousseau, and a numerous list of male writers, insist that she should all her life be subjected to a severe restraint, that of propriety. Why subject her to propriety – blind propriety, if she be capable of acting from a nobler spring, if she be an heir of immortality? Is sugar always to be produced by vital blood? Is one half of the human species, like the poor African slaves, to be subject to prejudices that brutalize them, when principles would be a surer guard, only to sweeten the cup of man? Is not this indirectly to deny woman reason? for a gift is a mockery, if it be unfit for use.

[Source: *A Vindication of the Rights of Woman with Strictures on Political and Moral Subjects* (Boston: Peter Edes for Thomas and Andrews, 1792).]

William Thompson (1775–1833) met Anna Wheeler (1785–1848) while staying with Jeremy Bentham, an early proponent of birth control. Already an advocate of contraceptives himself, Thompson's progressive ideas took on an overtly feminist tone after he became close friends with Wheeler, who had left her husband to travel throughout Europe, spreading the news of the women's movement. In response to James Mill's 'On Government,' which declared that only men had a right to the vote, Thompson wrote *Appeal of One Half the Human Race* ... As is made clear by the introduction, 'Introductory Letter to Mrs Wheeler,' Thompson credits Wheeler for many of the ideas and inspiration for the book.

William Thompson with Anna Wheeler

From *Appeal of One Half the Human Race, Women, against the Pretensions of the Other Half, Men, To Retain Them in Political, and Thence in Civil and Domestic, Slavery* (1825)

By way of distinguishing and honoring this class of the proscribed half of the human race, man condescends to enter into what he calls a *contract* with certain women, for certain purposes, the most important of which is, the producing and rearing of children to maturity. Each man yokes a woman to his establishment, and calls it a *contract*. Audacious falsehood! A contract! where are any of the attributes of contracts, of equal and just contracts, to be found in this transaction? A contract implies the voluntary assent of both the contracting parties. Can even both the parties, man and woman, by agreement alter the terms, as to *indissolubility* and *inequality*, of this pretended contract? No. Can any individual man divest himself, were he even so inclined, of his power of despotic control? He cannot. Have women been consulted as to the terms of this pretended contract? A contract, all of whose enjoyments – wherever nature has not imposed a physical bar on the depravity of selfishness – are on one side, while all of its pains and privations are on the other! A contract, giving all power, arbitrary will and unbridled enjoyment to the one side; to the other, unqualified obedience, and enjoyments meted out or withheld at the caprice of the ruling and enjoying party. Such a contract, as the owners of *slaves* in the West Indies and every other slave-polluted soil, enter into with their slaves – the law of the stronger imposed on the weaker, *in contempt* of the interests and wishes of the weaker. As little as slaves have had to do in any part of the world in the enacting of slave-codes, have women in any part of the world had to do with the partial codes of selfishness and ignorance, which every where dispose of their right over their own actions and all their other enjoyments, in favor of those who made the regulations; particularly that most unequal and debasing code, absurdly called the *contract* of marriage. This, alas! the best boon that the selfishness and ignorance of men have permitted them to grant to women – compelling at least the waywardness of man to provide, till adult age, for the children he begat – this pretended contract is, as to the women, in every other respect the law of restraint and exclusion, the law of the stronger, enacted with reference to the enjoyments of that stronger alone; and no more consulting the interests of women, the other pretended contracting party, than the interests of bullocks are consulted in the police regulations that precede and follow their slaughter. From regulating the terms of this pretended contract, women have been as completely excluded as bullocks, or sheep, or any other animals sub-jugated to man, have been from determining the regulations of commons or slaughter-houses. Men enacted, that is to say, *willed* the terms, let women like them or not: man to be the owner, master, and ruler of every thing, even to the minutest action, and most trifling article of property brought into the common stock by the woman; woman to be the moveable property, and ever-obedient servant, to the bidding of man [...]

Man, by law, superstition, and opinion, commands: woman, in marriage, by law, superstition, and opinion, obeys. The happiness of both is sacrificed. Not only does woman obey; the despotism of man demands another sacrifice. Woman must cast nature, or feign to cast it, from her breast. She is not per-mitted to appear to feel, or desire. The whole of what is called her education training her to be the obedient instrument of men's sensual gratification, she is not permitted even to wish for any gratification for herself. She must have no desires: she must always yield, must submit as a matter of duty; not repose upon her equal for the sake of happiness: she must blush to own that she joys in his generous caresses, were such by chance ever given. This engrafted duplicity of character still further increases, and to an incalculable extent, the dependence of woman in marriage on man; his slave for what nature has implanted as the most innocent and useful of human desires, when not gratified at the expense of ulterior mischief or of any fellow-creature's happiness; doubly his slave, from the necessity of concealing these natural desires, and from the heartless insult with which the brutal male sensualist is wont to repress the gentlest, the humblest, the most kindly overflowings of them.

But if, from the balance of mere sexual feelings, the dependence of woman on the pernicious despotism of man, is increased instead of being mitigated, how deplorable is and must be her situation every where, when we consider that wealth and knowledge are reserved exclusively for the male as additional stays of despotism! Not satisfied with superiority of strength, man makes it but the basis on which to erect his system of sexual exclusions to gratify his unhallowed lust of domination. To secure what seem to his ignorance the advantages of superiority of strength, he makes the mind of his victim as feeble as nature, but particularly as artificial circumstances, have rendered her body, by excluding from her, and reserving to himself, all sources of knowledge and skill; by vesting in himself all power to create, all right to possess and control, property; by excluding her from all those offices, actions, and incidents, which afford opportunities for exercising the judgement, and calling into life all the higher and more useful intellectual powers; and lastly, by making her swear, when about to enter on life and assist in producing and rearing a family, to renounce the exercise of that reason of which his vile practices have deprived her, to surrender the control over her voluntary actions, to be in all things, going out and coming in, in the minutest incidents of life, *obedient* to his will, be it wise or capricious. Black slaves are not insulted with the requisition to swear or vow obedience to their masters: the compulsion of the slave-code is sufficient without unnecessary childish insult. For white slaves parcelled out amongst men (as if to compensate them for their own cowardly submission almost every where to the chains of political power), the uninquiring instruments first of their voluptuousness, and, when that is sated, of their caprice of command, was and is reserved this gratuitous degradation of swearing to be slaves, of kissing the rod of domestic despotism, and of devoting themselves to its worship. Was it not enough to deprive women, by the iniquitous inequality of the marriage, or white-slave, code, of all the attributes of personal liberty? to invest in the hands of another human being all the attributes of despotism backed by the possession of wealth, knowledge, and strength, without the cruel mockery of exacting from her trained obsequiousness the semblance of a *voluntary* obedience, of devotedness to her degradation? What need of this heartless insult? Are not the laws, supported first by the individual strength of every individual man despotic in his own right, and next supported by the united strength of all men, sufficient to control, to compel submission from, this helpless creature? Would not the pleasure of commanding the actions and the body be complete, without the luxury and banquet of despotism, of laying prostrate the mind? would not the simple pleasure of commanding be sufficient, without the gratification of the additional power of taunting the victim with her pretended *voluntary* surrender of the control over her own actions?

Woman is then compelled, in marriage, by the possession of superior strength on the part of men, by the want of knowledge, skill and wealth, by the positive, cruel, partial, and cowardly enactments of law, by the terrors of superstition, by the mockery of a pretended vow of obedience, and to crown all, and as the result of all, by the force of an unrelenting, unreasoning, unfeeling, public opinion, to be the literal unequivocal *slave* of the man who may be styled her husband. I say emphatically the slave; for a slave is a person whose actions and earnings, instead of being under his own control, liable only to equal laws, to public opinion, and to his own calculations, under these, of his own interest, are under the arbitrary control of any other human being, by whatever called. This is the essence of slavery, and what distinguishes it from freedom.

[Original source: *Appeal of One Half the Human Race, Women, Against the Pretensions of the Other Half, Men, To Retain Them in Political, and Thence in Civil and Domestic, Slavery* (London: Longman, Hurst Rees, Orme, Brown & Green, 1825); History of Women Microfilm, Gale International Ltd., reel 945.]

Harriet Martineau (1802–76) was an author, a feminist, and an abolitionist who travelled throughout the United States, Europe, and the Middle East, writing of her journeys. In her own estimation, she was something of a political economist from a young age, and indeed, she attacked slavery as both an unchristian, immoral system and one that wasted capital and labour. She was similarly vocal when it came to women's rights, calling for the vote and for higher education for women, and fighting against the Contagious Diseases Act.

Harriet Martineau
Negro Slavery (1830)

If a spirit from some higher region were moved by curiosity to visit our planet what, in the circuit of the globe, would most excite his wonder and dismay? There is much in every inhabited clime which to a celestial mind must appear 'most strange, most pitiful'; much which cannot but draw down 'tears such as angels weep.' Here, oppression and answering degradation; there, lawlessness and violence; here, abject superstition; there, rebellion against the common Father. In one country, the heavenly visitant would behold how the natives of the soil are driven back into the wastes to perish, not by destitution merely, but by the vices and diseases imparted by their usurping conquerors. In another, he would mourn to see how the imperishable mind is shrouded in thick darkness, and the immortal soul buried in sensual degradation. In a third, he would wonder at the dominion of an idolatry, whose rites, too impure to meet the eye of day, are lighted by the unholy fires of human sacrifice. But he would remember that these slaves, these sufferers, these agonized victims, have not yet been offered the liberty, the security and the peace of the gospel. He would joyfully anticipate the hour when the announcement of these glad tidings should be the signal for universal emancipation. He would count the days till the influences of Christianity should protect the Indian in his forest glades, spiritualize the relations of savage society, exalt the apathy of the Hindoo into heroism, and tame the ferocity of the Tartar into gentleness. He would expect with confidence that wherever this influence was acknowledged, freedom and purity would prevail. He would expect to see the limbs set free from chains, and the mind only subjected to that mild yoke which was not imposed by human hands. He would suppose that common rights would be respected, universal gifts equally shared, and domestic relations sanctified by the benignant operation of a power adequate to these purposes, and ultimately destined to fulfil them; and with this hope he would turn to Christian lands. What would he see there? Much to disappoint, and much to encourage. Much external inconsistency, weakness, and depravity; but also much internal purity and strength; many abuses, but a secret power of rectification; great cause for mourning, but more for hope. But if he should at length arrive at a region where all the degradation, all the cruelty, all the sensuality, all the impiety of the worst heathen lands prevail, notwithstanding the influences of Christianity, and under its pretended sanction, what would he think of such an anomaly? If he found that this region was closely connected with one more powerful, where a continual war is waged with oppression and vice, would not his wonder increase? If he further saw that the oppressed were many, the oppressors few, and that these few were under the control of a power which professed to advocate truth and justice, how could he account for the existence of such an abomination? If England is free, how can she countenance slavery in her West Indian dependencies? If England loves justice, why does she permit oppression? If England is Christian, why does she encourage the temporal and spiritual degradation of her brethren? The anomaly has long appeared no less strange to mortal than celestial eyes, and the question has been rung in the ears of men till many are heart-sick and some are weary; but it must be asked again and again, till the insolent bravado, the irrelevant complaint, the contemptible excuse, are silenced; till not a single minister of the gospel can be found (we hope there is but one) to declare that slavery is sanctioned by the law of liberty; till the indignant remonstrance of millions ceases to be withstood by the puny insults of individuals; till appeals to the heart are no longer answered by appeals to the purse. Let us not be told that enough has been said already, that men are disgusted with details of barbarity, and wearied with the repetition of facts which every body knows, and arguments which there are few to dispute. It is true, we *are* thus weary and disgusted, and therefore should we labour the more diligently till the abuses are removed of which we complain. It *is* most painful to think on the condition of our Negro brethren; of their tortured bodies, their stunted intellects, their perverted affections, their extorted labour, their violated homes: but the more painful such thoughts, the more rapid and energetic should be our exertions to banish them for ever by extinguishing the evils which suggest them. Are the friends of the slave less disgusted than ourselves? Having struggled for years against this enormous evil, are they less weary of it than we? Have we a right to complain of discouragement, while they have persevered amidst difficulty, and hoped almost against hope? They have pursued this pest of humanity with unremitting watchfulness, they have grappled with it, brought it to light and justice, and now, we are told, have prepared its death warrant. We hope it is so, for it is full time. We believe that it is so; for if human prejudice can gainsay the arguments of such upright minds, if selfishness can withstand such appeals to natural sympathy, if the love of power can long maintain a struggle with such a holy spirit of justice, as have been employed in this cause, we shall not know where to repose our confidence, and our trust in the triumph of righteousness will be shaken. The time is, we trust, arrived, for which patriots and philanthropists have so long watched in vain. Many eyes have of late been opened; many sleeping energies aroused; many perverted views rectified; and what wonder, when the subject has been presented to them as in the pamphlet before us?

This pamphlet consists of a republication of two articles of review on the topic of Colonial Slavery. The first of these articles appeared in the *Edinburgh Review* of October 1824, and the other in the *Westminster Review* of October 1829. They are of the first order of excellence both as to style and matter; and a more efficacious service to the cause of the slave could not, we conceive, have been rendered, than by reissuing them in such a form as may make them accessible to every reader in the kingdom. Their object is not so much to set forth the wrongs and woes of the slave (which had before been done sufficiently,) as to shew with whom lies the power of taming the tyrants and reinstating the oppressed, to point out how easily such a power may be exercised, and how contemptible is the utmost opposition which can be anticipated.

There is not a heart actuated by the common feelings of humanity – we will not say in a Christian country, but in any country, which would not be moved by a recital of the wrongs of the slaves in our colonies, and therefore a bare statement of the facts which have been persevering adduced by their advocates form a strong and universal appeal. Every man in every country feels that it can never be right to torture women, to condemn men to exile and toil, to separate children from their mothers, to subject the helpless to the violence of the strong, to make life one scene of hardship, pain, and degradation. The debased Hindoo and the contemplative Indian would here be of one mind with the British philanthropist. Men in civilized countries who regard only the temporal condition of their race (if such men there be) are ready to join in the universal cry against the abuse of unlawful power, and though they look no further than the toil and sufferings of a day, though they believe that the consequences of the oppression extend no further than the grave, they burn with indignation that the day of life should be embittered beyond endurance, and that the grave become the resting-place of beings more degraded and less happy than the brutes. But to those who know any thing of the life and beauty of religion, to those especially who have been made free in the liberty of the gospel, the whole matter assumes a new form and appears in different proportions. Like others, they burn to unlock the fetters which enchain the limbs, to restore the exile to his home, and the freeborn to his rights; but they feel that there are worse fetters than those which confine the limbs – the iron which enters into the soul. They feel that the oppressed are, by oppression, rendered unfit for a better home than the hut beneath the plantain; that the highest rights are those which constitute man a citizen of heaven. Thus feels every Christian. If he feels not thus, he usurps the name. But there are other considerations which occur to those who believe themselves to be possessed of divine truth in its purity: there are obligations which press peculiarly upon them.

To the most enlightened is confided a charge of surpassing importance. To them is appointed the care of the universal mind of their race. Every spiritual privilege which they enjoy involves an obligation; every gift imposes a corresponding responsibility. The same radiance of truth which displays the glories of the world of mind, lights their path to the darkest abodes of ignorance and vice. The same hand which presents the lever by which they are to move the moral world, points out the spot where they may plant their foot. The celestial life, by which their own frame is animated, they are enabled and commissioned to impart to all who are fainting under oppression or dead in ignorance and guilt. In proportion as truth is discovered to be beautiful, should fellow minds be awakened to its contemplation; as virtuous pleasures swell high in the heart, should their overflowings be poured into the bosoms of others. For this cause is it that human sympathies are imparted; for this cause is it that they become tenderer and warmer as the mind is more fully informed by the wisdom which is from above. For this cause is it that 'as face answereth to face in water, so is the heart of man'; and that the tumults of passion which agitate the bosoms of our Negro brethren, awaken an answering throb in our own; and that the deadness of their despair casts a chill over our hopes on their behalf. To us (for we must not, while appropriating the privileges of pure religion, evade the responsibility which it imposes), to us is confided the task of watching over whatever is feeble in intellect – of animating whatever is dull, of cherishing whatever is weak, of informing whatever is vacant in the mind of man, wherever our influence extends; and we know not that that influence has any boundary short of the limits of the globe. We are told that the world has become one vast whispering gallery, and that the faintest accents of science are heard from the remotest regions of the earth. If this be true of science, in which the multitude of every country have no interest, how much more true must it be of that which is better than science; of that which already finds an echo in every bosom, and will, in time, make a herald of every tongue! The law of liberty is engraved on every heart, and conscience is its universal exponent: if the interpreter sleep, or if he interpret unfaithfully, it is given to those who have the power, to rouse him from indolence and to expose his deceptions. We are bound to warn, to oppose, to disarm all who despise and break through this unnatural law; and, in behalf of the oppressed, to carry on against the oppressors a war which admits neither peace nor truce.

It is appointed to us to mark the movements of the universal human soul; to direct its powers, to controul its tendencies, to develop its capabilities, to animate its exertions, while we present to it ample scope and adequate objects. If we see any portion of it cramped, blinded, and deadened, it is our part to remove the evil influence, or to resist if we cannot remove it. And in what portion of the human race is mind more debased and intellect more stunted than in the slaves of the West Indies? Some are still inspired by a love of liberty; some would still, if they dared, sing, by the streams of their captivity, the songs of their own land; some yet retain sufficient sense of their rights to mutter deep curses against their tyrants, and to long for one moment's freedom that they might dash his little ones against the stones: but many are sunk into a state of apathy more hopeless even than vice, a despair more painful than the tumult of revengeful passions. Such beings advance a claim upon us which we cannot resist. We are as much bound to interpose on their behalf as to afford bread to our dependents, and instruction to the children of our families. If they loudly call upon us for our alliance, we cannot refuse it. If they do not, we must bend our ear to catch the faintest breathings of their complaint. If none such are heard, the double duty devolves upon us of warring against the tyrant and arousing the slave to the contest. The more insensible the slave, the stronger is the proof of his degradation; the deeper the apathy which we have to dispel, the more withering must have been the gripe of tyranny. This gripe must be loosened by the friends of the slave, for the slave has himself no power. In this case, force must be opposed by force, and usurpation by authority; brute force must be met by the might of reason; and usurpation put down by the authority of justice. Knowledge is power, and wisdom confers authority; and if we really believe (as we have often deliberately asserted) that, by the blessing of the universal Father, the highest knowledge and the purest wisdom have been placed within our reach, we must accept the office connected with their possession, and fulfil the conditions on which they are communicated. In the primeval days, when the earth shone in its newly created beauty, and the human race was in its infancy, God himself vouchsafed to be the visible guardian of his people. By visible signs, by audible communion, he guided and warned and sustained them. In later times, he withdrew himself in part from the cognizance of the external senses, and spoke by prophets and righteous men. Now the eye sees him not, the ear hears him not, and no external manifestations of his presence are given; yet the eye of the mind has been so far purified, the ear of the understanding may be so intently fixed, that his presence cannot be doubted nor his commissions refused. There are now no prophets among men, but there are still delegates from the Most High; and every man who accepts his revelation is bound to announce his judgments, and to assert his will; and the more distinct the revelation, the more awful should be the announcement, the more steadfast the assertion. He was pleased himself to release the Israelites from their captivity to Pharaoh; and if he has now appointed us to lead out our brethren from a worse than Egyptian bondage to a state of higher privilege than any under the old dispensation, we must not protract the work; for the time has been already too long delayed. Their bodily slavery at an end, a long and difficult task has to be accomplished in teaching them to enjoy their freedom, and in making them understand to whose mercy they owe it, and to whose gentle yoke they ought to offer themselves.

These things cannot be taught them while they remain in their present state. We who are free know nothing of a morality or a religion of which freedom is not the basis. We can teach only what we have learned, and we have learned from the Bible; and what is there in that volume which a slave can appropriate? A new Bible must be made for him if he wants a manual of duty suitable to his present state; for no changing, no cutting out, no suppression, no interdiction can make our gospel a book for the slave. In the first chapter we read, that God made man in his own image and blessed him; in the last, that the leaves of the tree of life are for the healing of the nations, and that all who are athirst may drink freely of the water of life. But who can discern the image of God in the slave; and what is it but mockery to invite him to the tree and the waters of life? In every intermediate chapter, in every dispensation by which the mind of man is led on to larger views and loftier expectations, in the intrepidity of prophets, the fervour of saints, the heroism of martyrs, the sanctity of apostles, and above all, in the serene majesty of the prince of our salvation, we find a truth which is veiled from the eye of a slave, a promise in which he cannot participate, and a beauty which, as a slave, he will never perceive. The motives of the gospel cannot be urged upon minds which have no share in its promises, and can form no estimate of its privileges.

> The immortality and irreligion of the slaves are the necessary consequences of their political and personal degradation. They are not considered by the law as human beings, and they have, therefore, in some measure, ceased to be human beings. They must become men before they can become Christians. A great effect may, under fortunate circumstances, have been wrought on particular individuals; but those who believe that any extensive effect can be produced by religious instruction on this miserable race, may believe in the famous conversion wrought by St Anthony on the fish. Can a preacher prevail on his hearers strictly to fulfil their conjugal duties, in a country where no protection is given to their conjugal rights; in a country where the husband and wife may, at the pleasure of the master, or by a process of law, be, in an instant, separated for ever? Can he persuade them to rest on the Sunday, in colonies where the law appoints that time for the markets? Is there any lesson which a Christian minister is more solemnly bound to teach, is there any lesson which it is, in a religious point of view, more important for a convert to learn, than that it is a duty to refuse obedience to the unlawful commands of superiors? Are the new pastors of the slaves to inculcate this principle or not? In other words, are the slaves to remain uninstructed in the fundamental laws of Christian morality, or are their teachers to be hanged? This is the alternative. We all remember that it was made a charge against Mr Smith that he had read an inflammatory chapter of the Bible to his congregation! Excellent encouragement for their future teachers 'to declare unto them,' according to the expression of an old divine, far too Methodistical to be considered as an authority in the West Indies, 'the whole counsel of God!' – P.7.

Nor is there more hope that we can agree with the master on the most important questions of morality than that we can teach the slave.

> The people of the West Indies seem to labour under an utter ignorance of the light in which their system is altogether viewed in England. When West Indian magistrates apply the term 'wretch' to a Negro who is put to death for having failed in an attempt at resistance, the people of England do not consider him as a 'wretch,' but as a good and gallant man, dying in the best of causes, – the resistance to oppression, by which themselves hold all the good that they enjoy. They consider him as a soldier fallen in the advance guard of that combat, which is only kept from themselves, because somebody else is exposed to it further off. If the murdered Negro is a 'wretch,' then an Englishman is a 'wretch' for not bowing his head to

slavery whenever it invites him. The same reason that makes the white English-man's resistance virtuous and honourable, makes the black one's too; it is only a regiment with different facings, fighting in the same cause. Will these men never know the ground on which they stand? Can nothing make them find out, that the universal British people would stand by and cheer on their dusky brethren to the assault, if it was not for the solitary hope that the end may be obtained more effec-tually by other means? It is not true that the people of England believe that any set of men, here or any where, can, by any act of theirs, alter the nature of slavery, or make that not robbery which was robbery before. They can make it robbery according to law – the more is the pity that the power of law-making should be in such hands; but this is the only inference. All moral respect for such laws – all submission of the mind, as to a rule which it is desirable to obey and honourable to support – is as much out of the question, as if a freebooter were to lay down a scale of punishment for those who should be found guilty of having lifted a hand against his power. – P.35.

Our only method of teaching morality to master and slave is by removing the obstacles in the way of those truths which must be learned by all, some time or other, in this world or the next. We must shew the masters that they are culprits, and the slaves that they are men. We must lighten the burden which weighs down the soul yet more than the body: we must loosen the chains which con-fine the limbs, before we can induce the captive to cast off the fetters, as sub-stantial, though intangible, which bind down the intellect and the affections. The spirit cannot escape from its thralldom till the death-warrant of slavery be not only signed, but executed.

And how far does it rest with us to effect this? What powers have we to assist in this righteous work? We have the power conferred by a swelling heart and a willing spirit to quicken other minds, and to bring them into sympathy with our own. We have power to relate facts to those who know them not; to keep alive the interest of those who do; to spread our own convictions while we strengthen them; and, from the centre of influence, to which all, even the least influential, are placed, to send out to the remotest points where we can act, tidings from the land of freedom, and threatenings of the downfall of oppres-sion. We have inquired of the oracles of truth, and we know that this abode of the idolatrous worship of Mammon shall be yielded up. It may not be ours to go forth to the fight, or to mount the breach; but having patiently compassed its extent for the appointed time, we may raise our voices in the general shout before which its bulwarks shall fall, and its strength be forever overthrown.

[Source: *Monthly Repository* no. 4 (1830): 4–9.]

Angelina E. Grimké (1805–79) was a staunch feminist and an early white abolitionist. She was one of fourteen children, both white and black, fathered by Judge John Grimké, a member of the ruling elite in her hometown, Charleston, South Carolina. Both Angelina and her sister Sarah Moore Grimké rejected the lives of wealthy Southern aristocrats and travelled to Philadelphia, becoming Quakers and lecturing on slavery. Angelina was the first woman to address a legislative body when she presented a petition of 20,000 women supporting the abolition cause to the Massachusetts state legislature. While Grimké delivered her speech to the Anti-Slavery Convention in Philadelphia, the audience remained enthralled despite the mob gathering strength outside. The following evening, the same mob ransacked and set fire to the building.

Angelina E. Grimké
Address to the Anti-Slavery Convention, Philadelphia (1838)

Do you ask, 'What has the North to do with slavery?' Hear it, hear it! Those voices without tell us that the spirit of slavery is *here*, and has been roused to wrath by our Conventions; for surely liberty would not foam and tear herself with rage, because her friends are multiplied daily, and meetings are held in quick succession to set forth her virtues and extend her peaceful kingdom. This opposition shows that slavery has done its deadliest work in the hearts of our citizens. Do you ask, then, 'What has the North to do?' I answer, cast out first the spirit of slavery from your own hearts, and then lend your aid to convert the South. Each one present has a work to do, be his or her situation what it may, however limited their means or insignificant their supposed influence. The great men of this country will not do this work; the Church will never do it. A desire to please the world, to keep the favor of all parties and of all conditions, makes them dumb on this and every other unpopular subject.

As a Southerner, I feel that it is my duty to stand up here tonight and bear testimony against slavery. I have seen it! I have seen it! I know it has horrors that can never be described. I was brought up under its wing. I witnessed for many years its demoralizing influences and its destructiveness to human happiness. I have never seen a happy slave. I have seen him dance in his chains, it is true, but he was not happy. There is a wide difference between happiness and mirth. Man can not enjoy happiness while his manhood is destroyed. Slaves, however, may be, and sometimes are mirthful. When hope is extinguished, they say, 'Let us eat and drink, for tomorrow we die.' [Here stones were thrown at the windows – a great noise without and commotion within.]

What is a mob? What would the breaking of every window be? What would the leveling of this hall be? Any evidence that we are wrong, or that slavery is a good and wholesome institution? What if the mob should now burst in upon us, break up our meeting, and commit violence upon our persons, would that be anything compared with what the slaves endure? No, no; and we do not remember them, 'as bound with them,' if we shrink in the time of peril, or feel unwilling to sacrifice ourselves, if need be, for their sake. [Great noise]. I thank the Lord that there is yet enough left to feel the truth, even though it rages at it; that conscience is not so completely seared as to be unmoved by the truth of the living God. [Another outbreak of the mob and confusion in the house.]

How wonderfully constituted is the human mind! How it resists, as long as it can, all efforts to reclaim it from error! I feel that all this disturbance is but an evidence that our efforts are the best that could have been adopted, or else the friends of slavery would not care for what we say and do. The South know what we do. I am thankful that they are reached by our efforts. Many times have I wept in the land of my birth over the system of slavery. I knew of none who sympathized in my feelings; I was unaware that any efforts were made to deliver the oppressed; no voice in the wilderness was heard calling on the people to repent and do works meet for repentance, and my heart sickened within me. Oh, how should I have rejoiced to know that such efforts as these were being made. I only wonder that I had such feelings. But in the midst of temptation I was preserved, and my sympathy grew warmer, and my hatred of slavery more inveterate, until at last I have exiled myself from my native land, because I could no longer endure to hear the wailing of the slave.

I fled to the land of Penn; for here, thought I, sympathy for the slave will surely be found. But I found it not. The people were kind and hospitable, but the slave had no place in their thoughts. I therefore shut up my grief in my own heart. I remembered that I was a Carolinian, from a State which framed this iniquity by law. Every Southern breeze wafted to me the discordant tones of weeping and wailing, shrieks and groans, mingled with prayers and blasphemous curses. My heart sank within me at the abominations in the midst of which I had been born and educated. What will it avail, cried I, in bitterness of spirit, to expose to the gaze of strangers the horrors and pollutions of slavery, when there is no ear to hear nor heart to feel and pray for the slave? But how different do I feel now! Animated with hope, nay, with an assurance of the triumph of liberty and good-will to man, I will lift up my voice like a trumpet, and show this people what they can do to influence the Southern mind and overthrow slavery. [Shouting. And stones against the windows.]

We often hear the question asked, 'What shall we do?' Here is an opportunity. Every man and every woman present may do something, by showing that we fear not a mob, and in the midst of revilings and threatenings, pleading the cause of those who are ready to perish. Let me urge everyone to buy the books written on this subject; read them, and lend them to your neighbors. Give your money no longer for things which pander to pride and lust, but aid in scattering 'the living coals of truth upon the naked heart of the nation'; in circulating appeals to the sympathies of Christians in behalf of the outraged slave.

But it is said by some, our 'books and papers do not speak the truth'; why, then, do they not contradict what we say? They can not. Moreover, the South has entreated, nay, commanded us, to be silent; and what greater evidence of the truth of our publications could be desired?

Women of Philadelphia! allow me as a Southern woman, with much attachment to the land of my birth, to entreat you to come up to this work. Especially, let me urge you to petition. Men may settle this and other questions at the ballot-box, but you have no such right. It is only through petitions that you can reach the Legislature. It is, therefore, peculiarly your duty to petition. Do you say, 'It does no good!' The South already turns pale at the number sent. They have read the reports of the proceedings of Congress, and there have seen that among other petitions were very many from the women of the North on the subject of slavery. Men who hold the rod over slaves rule in the councils of the nation; and they deny our right to petition and remonstrate against abuses of our sex and our kind. We have these rights, however, from our God. Only let us exercise them, and, though often turned away unanswered, let us remember the influence of importunity upon the unjust judge, and act accordingly. The fact that the South looks jealously upon our measures shows that they are effectual. There is, therefore, no cause for doubting or despair.

It was remarked in England that women did much to abolish slavery in her colonies. Nor are they now idle. Numerous petitions from them have recently been presented to the Queen to abolish apprenticeship, with its cruelties, nearly equal to those of the system whose place it supplies. One petition, two miles and a quarter long, has been presented. And do you think these labors will be in vain? Let the history of the past answer. When the women of these States send up to Congress such a petition our legislators will arise, as did those of England, and say: 'When all the maids and matrons of the land are knocking at our doors we must legislate.' Let the zeal and love, the faith and works of our English sisters quicken ours; that while the slaves continue to suffer, and when they shout for deliverance, we may feel the satisfaction of 'having done what we could.'

[Source: Vol. 1 of *History of Woman Suffrage*, ed. Elizabeth Cady Stanton, Susan B. Anthony, and Matilda Joslyn Gage (Rochester, NY: Charles Mann, 1889), 334–6.]

AM I NOT A WOMAN AND A SISTER?

Remember them that are in bonds as bound with them. Heb. 13:3.

[Source: Lydia Maria Child, *Authentic Anecdotes of American Slavery* (Newburyport: Charles Whipple, 1838)]

Lucretia Mott (1793–1880) was one of the first Quaker women to advocate the abolition of slavery, and one of the earliest advocates of women's rights in the United States. She was also interested in Native American peoples, visiting the Seneca in New York State on several occasions. Her meeting with Elizabeth Cady Stanton at the World Anti-Slavery Convention in London in 1940 is one of the best-known stories about the early US women's movement.

Lucretia Mott

From *Slavery and 'The Woman Question': Lucretia Mott's Diary of Her Visit to Great Britain to Attend the World's Anti-Slavery Convention of 1840* (1840)

5th day [June] 11th. […] Met again about our exclusion – William Boultbee wished to have our decision – talked much with him, liked him – agreed on the following Protest:

The American Women Delegates from Pennsylvania to the World's Convention would present to the Committee of the British & Foreign Anti-Slavery Society their grateful acknowledgements for the kind attentions received by them since their arrival in London. But while as individuals they return thanks for these favors, as delegates from the bodies appointing them, they deeply regret to learn by a series of resolutions passed at a Meeting of your Committee, bearing reference to credentials from the Mass. Society, that it is contemplated to exclude women from a seat in the convention, as co-equals in the advocacy of Universal Liberty. The Delegates will duly communicate to their constituents the intimation which these resolutions convey: in the mean time they stand prepared to co-operate to any extent, and in any form, consistent with their instructions, in promoting the just objects of the Convention, to whom it is presumed will belong the power of determining the validity of any claim to a seat in that body.

On behalf of the Delegates

Very respectfully

Sarah Pugh

6 Mo. 11th. 40

H. Grew – J. Mott – & Joseph Sturge with many others waited on Lord Brougham with a box presented him by Managers of Pennsylvania Hall – the company of Women not desired.

Evening. Several sent to us to persuade us not to offer ourselves to the Convention – Colver rather bold in his suggestions – answered & of course offended him. W. Morgan & Scales informed us 'it wasn't designed as a *World* Convention – that was a mere Poetical license,' & that all power would rest with the 'London Committee of Arrangements.' Prescod of Jamaica (colored) thought it would lower the dignity of the Convention and bring ridicule on the whole thing if ladies were admitted – he was told that similar reasons were urged in Pennsylvania for the exclusion of colored people from our meetings – but had we yielded on such flimsy arguments, we might as well have abandoned our enterprise. Colver thought Women constitutionally unfit for public or business meetings – he was told that the colored man too was said to be *constitutionally* unfit to mingle with the white man. He left the room angry.

6th day 6 Mo. 12th. The World's Convention – *alias* the 'Conference of the British and Foreign Anti-Slavery Society,' with such guests as they chose to invite, assembled. We were kindly admitted behind the bar – politely conducted to our seats and introduced to many, whom we had not before met – Dr Bowering – William Ashurst – a Mrs Thompson, grand-daughter of Lady

Middleton who first suggested to Wilberforce some action in Parliament on slavery. Samuel King also appeared – made kind inquiries after children & friends. William Forster spoke to us. Introduced him to S. Pugh as orthodox – he begged there might be no allusion to differences between us, – said, 'thou touches me on a tender spot – I remember thee with much affection in Baltimore in 1820.' Afterward invited us to his house at Norwich – not merely to call but to make a visit. E. Neall delighted with all she saw – particularly with meeting with Dr Bowring. Meeting opened in a dignified manner – silence observed. Those who wished prayer informed the next room was appropriated for them. Thomas Clarkson's entrance deeply interesting – accompanied by his daughter-in-law and her little son, his only representative. Most of the speeches &c. being reported in the papers &c. renders it unnecessary to record any part here. S. Prescod was warned that his conduct would be watched & he must be on his guard not to compromise 'the dignity of the convention.' He was the first however to bring ridicule on himself & to throw the meeting into confusion by improper mention of the 'Goddess Delegates.' Friends present – nearly all opposed to women's admission which was well introduced by Wendell Phillips – J.C. Fuller told us the secret of it was that so many of us were not of their faith – that it was announced in London Yearly Meeting that we were coming and they were put on their guard. George Stacey made some remarks on the subject, exposing his apostacy as a Quaker. He & others were answered nicely by Dr Bowring – William Ashurst – George Bradburn and William Adam. George Thompson too & several others spoke well for us. Col. Miller amusing. Dr B. said it was 'a custom more honored in the breach than in the observance' – William Ashurst pointed them to the inconsistency of calling a 'World's Convention' to abolish Slavery – and at its threshold depriving half the world their liberty. H. Grew betrayed some inconsistency – discussion very animated – rather noisy – the result cheered, unworthily – were told it was common in England. Several beautiful speeches on Clarkson's presence. J.A. James alluding to him & his little grandson called them the evening and morning stars. John Burnet, one of the most eloquent men of the day. Made impressive remarks on the importance of laying aside every passion, but a well directed, well controlled zeal. O'Connell's entrance greatly cheered. Beckford's address to Clarkson impressive. He was a liberated slave from the West Indies – said to the audience 'look at me and work on.' O'Connell took off his hat & bowed to him when he closed.

[Source: *Slavery and 'The Woman Question': Lucretia Mott's Diary of Her Visit to Great Britain to Attend the World's Anti-Slavery Convention of 1840*, ed. Frederick B. Tolles (London and Haverford: Friends' Historical Association and Friends' Historical Society, 1952), 28–31.]

The Seneca Falls Convention (19–20 July 1848), held in Seneca Falls, New York, was organized by Elizabeth Cady Stanton, Lucretia Mott, and other pioneer feminists. Approximately three hundred people of both sexes discussed the oppression and legal limitations of women; it was the first large-scale public meeting to address these issues. The Declaration of Sentiments, modelled after the Declaration of Independence, set out the rights to which women were entitled.

Seneca Falls Convention

The First Convention Ever Called to Discuss the Civil and Political Rights of Women, Seneca Falls, NY, July 19, 20, 1848

Woman's Rights Convention

A Convention to discuss the social, civil, and religious condition and rights of woman will be held in the Wesleyan Chapel, at Seneca Falls, N.Y., on Wednesday and Thursday, the 19th and 20th of July current; commencing at 10 o'clock A.M. During the first day the meeting will be exclusively for women, who are earnestly invited to attend. The public generally are invited to be present on the second day, when Lucretia Mott, of Philadelphia, and other ladies and gentlemen, will address the convention.

Declaration of Sentiments

When, in the course of human events, it becomes necessary for one portion of the family of man to assume among the people of the earth a position different from that which they have hitherto occupied, but one to which the laws of nature and of nature's God entitle them, a decent respect to the opinions of mankind requires that they should declare the causes that impel them to such a course.

We hold these truths to be self-evident: that all men and women are created equal; that they are endowed by their Creator with certain inalienable rights, that among these are life, liberty, and the pursuit of happiness; that to secure these rights governments are instituted, deriving their just powers from the consent of the governed. Whenever any form of government becomes destructive of these ends, it is the right of those who suffer from it to refuse allegiance to it, and to insist upon the institution of a new government, laying its foundation on such principles, and organizing its powers in such form as to them shall seem most likely to effect their safety and happiness. Prudence, indeed, will dictate that governments long established should not be changed for light and transient causes; and accordingly, all experience hath shown that mankind are more disposed to suffer, while evils are sufferable, than to right themselves by abolishing the forms to which they were accustomed. But when a long trail of abuses and usurpations, pursuing invariably the same object evinces a design to reduce them under absolute despotism, it is their duty to throw off such government, and to provide new guard for their future security. Such has been the patient sufferance of the women under this government, and such is now the necessity which constrains them to demand the equal station to which they are entitled.

The history of mankind is a history of repeated injuries and usurpations on the part of man toward woman, having in direct object the establishment of an absolute tyranny over her. To prove this, let facts be submitted to a candid world.

He has never permitted her to exercise her inalienable right to the elective franchise.

He has compelled her to submit to laws, in the formation of which she had no voice.

He has withheld from her rights which are given to the most ignorant and degraded men – both natives and foreigners.

Having deprived her of this first right of a citizen, the elective franchise, thereby leaving her without representation in the halls of legislation, he has oppressed her on all sides.

He has made her, if married, in the eye of the law, civilly dead.

He has taken from her all right in property, even to the wages she earns.

He has made her, morally, an irresponsible being, as she can commit many crimes with impunity, provided they be done in the presence of her husband. In the covenant of marriage, she is compelled to promise obedience to her husband, he becoming, to all intents and purposes, her master – the law giving him power to deprive her of her liberty, and to administer chastisement.

He has so framed the laws of divorce, as to what shall be the proper causes of divorce; in case of separation, to whom the guardianship of the children shall be given; as to be wholly regardless of the happiness of women – the law, in all cases, going upon a false supposition of the supremacy of man, and giving all power into his hands.

After depriving her of all rights as a married woman, if single and the owner of property, he has taxed her to support a government which recognizes her only when her property can be made profitable to it.

He has monopolized nearly all the profitable employments, and from those she is permitted to follow, she receives but a scanty remuneration. He closes against her all the avenues to wealth and distinction, which he considers most honorable to himself. As a teacher of theology, medicine, or law, she is not known.

He has denied her the facilities for obtaining a thorough education – all colleges being closed against her.

He allows her in Church, as well as State, but a subordinate position, claiming Apostolic authority for her exclusion from the ministry, and, with some exceptions, from any public participation in title affairs of the Church.

He has created a false public sentiment, by giving to the world a different code of morals for men and women, by which moral delinquencies which exclude women from society, are not only tolerated but deemed of little account in man.

He has usurped the prerogative of Jehovah himself, claiming it as his right to assign for her a sphere of action, when that belongs to her conscience and to her God.

He has endeavored, in every way that he could, to destroy her confidence in her own powers, to lessen her self-respect, and to make her willing to lead a dependent and abject life.

Now, in view of this entire disfranchisement of one half the people of this country, their social and religious degradation, – in view of the unjust laws above mentioned, and because women do feel themselves aggrieved, oppressed, and fraudulently deprived of their most sacred rights, we insist that they have immediate admission to all the rights and privileges which belong to them as citizens of the United States.

In entering upon the great work before us, we anticipate no small amount of misconception, misrepresentation, and ridicule; but we shall use every instrumentality within our power to effect our object. We shall employ agents, circulate tracts, petition the state and national legislatures, and endeavor to enlist the pulpit and the press in our behalf. We hope this Convention will be followed by a series of Conventions, embracing every part of the country ...

Whereas the great precept of Nature is conceded to be, 'that man shall pursue his own true and substantial happiness.' Blackstone, in his Commentaries remarks, that this law of Nature being coeval with mankind, and dictated by God himself, is of course superior in obligation to any other. It is binding over all the globe, in all countries, and at all times; no human laws are of any validity if contrary to this, and such of them as are valid, derive all their force, and all their validity, and all their authority, mediately and immediately, from this original: therefore,

Resolved, That such laws as conflict, in any way, with the true and substantial happiness of woman are contrary to the great precept of nature, and therefore of no validity; for this is 'superior in obligation to any other.'

Resolved, That all laws which prevent woman from occupying such a station in society as her conscience shall dictate, or which place her in a position inferior to that of man, are contrary to the great precept of nature, and therefore of no force or authority.

Resolved, That woman is man's equal – was intended to be so by the Creator – and the highest good of the race demands that she should be recognized as such.

Resolved, That the women of this country ought to be enlightened in regard to the laws under which they live, that they may no longer publish their degradation, by declaring themselves satisfied with their present position, nor their ignorance, by asserting that they have all the rights they want.

Resolved, That inasmuch as man, while claiming for himself intellectual superiority, does accord to woman moral superiority, it is pre-eminently his duty to encourage her to speak, and teach, as she has an opportunity, in all religious assemblies.

Resolved, That the same amount of virtue, delicacy, and refinement of behavior, that is required of woman in the social state, should also be required of man, and the same transgressions should be visited with equal severity on both man and woman.

Resolved, That the objection of indelicacy and impropriety, which is so often brought against woman when she addresses a public audience, comes with a very ill grace from those who encourage, by their attendance, her appearance on the stage, in the concert, or in feats of the circus.

Resolved, That woman has too long rested satisfied in the circumscribed limits which corrupt customs and a perverted application of the Scriptures have marked out for her, and that it is time she should move in the enlarged sphere which her great Creator has assigned her.

Resolved, That it is the duty of the women of this country to secure to themselves their sacred right to the elective franchise.

Resolved, That the equality of human rights results necessarily from the fact of the identity of the race in capabilities and responsibilities.

Resolved, therefore, That, being invested by the Creator with the same capabilities, and the same consciousness of responsibility for their exercise, it is demonstrably the right and duty of woman, equally with man, to promote every righteous cause, by every righteous means, and especially in regard to the great subjects of morals and religion, it is self-evidently her right to participate with her brother in teaching them, both in private and in public, by writing and by speaking, by any instrumentalities proper to be used, and in any assemblies proper to be held; and this being a self-evident truth, growing out of the divinely implanted principles of human nature, any custom or authority adverse to it, whether modern or wearing the hoary sanction of antiquity, is to be regarded as a self-evident falsehood, and at war with the interests of mankind ...

Resolved, That the speedy success of our cause depends upon the zealous and untiring efforts of both men and women, for the overthrow of the monopoly of the pulpit, and for the securing to woman an equal participation with men in the various trades, professions, and commerce.

The only resolution which met opposition was the 9th, demanding the right of suffrage which, however, after a prolonged discussion was adopted. All of the meetings throughout the two days were largely attended, but this, like every step in progress, was ridiculed from Maine to Louisiana.

[Note: This call was published in the *Seneca County Courier*, 14 July 1848, without any signatures. The movers of this Convention, who drafted the call, the declaration and resolutions were Elizabeth Cady Stanton, Lucretia Mott, Martha C. Wright, Mary Ann McClintock, and Jane C. Hunt.

Source: Vol. 1 of *History of Woman Suffrage*, ed. Elizabeth Cady Stanton, Susan B. Anthony, and Matilda Joslyn Gage (Rochester, NY: Charles Mann, 1889), 67, 70–3.]

Mary Ann Shadd Cary (1823–93) was born to free blacks in Wilmington, Delaware, but moved to Canada in 1850 after the Fugitive Slave Law was passed by Congress, making it the responsibility of all law-enforcement officials to capture all blacks who were suspected to be escaped slaves. Settling in Windsor, Shadd Cary made waves in the black community by championing integration, eventually establishing the first integrated school in Canada, and becoming the first female newspaper editor in Canada. *The Provincial Freeman* was one of the longest-running black newspapers before the Civil War, and addressed such issues as moral reform, civil rights, and racism.

Mary Ann Shadd Cary

Editorials from the *Provincial Freeman* (1857)

Anti-Slavery Meetings in Chatham

M. R. Hull, Esq., well known to Eastern and Western Anti-slavery men, completed a series of meetings on the subject of slavery, on Monday evening last, to the satisfaction of the hundreds who were eager listeners. The first meeting was held in the Town Hall, but owing to the weather, was not as numerously attended as it would otherwise have been; however, there was a respectable attendance.

The speaker who is of Virginia birth and of German and Irish parentage, discoursed powerfully upon the bearings of slavery upon Canadians, and all free and Christian nations; and called upon them to make it a national question, and to fight if need be for its overthrow. Though suffering at the time, severely from the effects of an accident by runaway horses in the morning, the subject was handled in a new and eminently attractive way to a British audience. The encroachments of the Institution – its voracious, horse-leach-like cry of give! give! – its contaminating influence, and pestiferous breath being felt from American intercourse here in Canada; its demoralizing and degrading influence upon the whites, making of the master a tyrant, and of the poor white man a creature, infinitely below the slave in intellect, and all else, except the liberty to leave the slave states if he knew how to go and had the means to go with, were all dwelt upon in a masterly and forcible manner. The different abolition schools were then adverted to, and though of the Radical Abolitionists, handsome reference was made to the Garrisonians. The political parties were next brought in review, and the Know Nothings and the Democrats were so ably handled, as to frighten a pair of live Buchananites quite away.

Mr Hull, very properly rebuked our Canadian churches for their silent fellowship with American slaveholding churches. At the Indiana Methodist conference, at which he attempted to exercise the church for its great sin, our British Wesleyan delegates 'were like Isaiah's pupps, dum dogs.'

The other meetings held in the churches, though consisting mostly of colored people, were densely crowded by eager listeners, who showed their appreciation of the speaker, by a large voluntary contribution. Mr Hull will lecture in the Province yet further, and will set sail for England in June next.

Meetings at Philadelphia

We beg to call attention to the proceedings of a meeting held in Philadelphia lately, to express condemnation of the Dred Scott decision, &c. Mrs Mott, Messrs Still, Remond, Purvis, McKimm and many others, white and colored participated.

The resolutions are strong and pointed, but why not go farther? This is not the time for strong words only; when all realize the yoke so forcibly as now why not act? Protests are well enough in their way, but to be of effect, they must point to determined action. Do the Purvises, Remonds, and others, who took part in the meeting intend to stay in the U[nited] States? if so, the resolutions amount to nothing, if not why not say so friends? Your national ship is rotten sinking, why not leave it, and why not say so boldly, manfully?

Canada is a good country – we have British freedom and an abundance of it – equal political rights of course, and if you covet it, social intercourse with those in your position in life. We here give you facts. If Canada should be distasteful, British Europe, or the Isles may be more to your mind; at all events, leave that slavery-cursed republic. Another meeting of respectable free and independent colored citizens was held previously, as they claim to believe in the United States Constitution. We shall wait with patience to see what it will do for them. We hope, however, that they too, will look at facts instead of everlastingly theorising.

[Source: 'Anti-Slavery Meetings in Chatham' and 'Meetings at Philadelphia,' editorials, *Provincial Freeman*, 18 April 1857, 134.]

Sarah Parker Remond (1826–94), an African American abolitionist, grew up surrounded by both black and white abolitionists, attending anti-slavery lectures and eventually giving them herself. Her entire family actively participated in the abolition movement, her brother Charles joining her on the anti-slavery circuit, along with speakers like Susan B. Anthony. In her lectures, Remond spoke not only of the horrors of slavery, with particular emphasis on the sexual exploitation of female slaves, but also of the continued racism free blacks endured.

Sarah Parker Remond
Lecture at the Lion Hotel, Warrington (1859)

Miss Remond then spoke, and her remarks chiefly bore on the sufferings and indignities which were perpetrated on her sisters in America, and the fearful amount of licentiousness which everywhere pervaded the Southern States. This fact would be best realised when she stated that there were 800,000 mulattoes in the Southern States of America – the fruits of licentiousness – bringing nothing but desolation in the hearts of the mother who bore them, and it ought to have brought shame to the fathers; but there was no respect for morality while the ministers of the gospel and statesmen of the south did not set an example which even the slaves could follow. She preferred, however, giving them unquestionable facts instead of personal statements which she might offer, and to this end read several extracts from books, all proving that the system of slavery and the immorality it engenders is eating out the vitals of the country, and destroying domestic happiness, not only amongst the subject race, but amongst the families of slaveholders. She then read a graphic description of a young and beautiful girl at a slave sale. The auctioneer was offered 1,000 dollars for her at first. He then expatiated on the superior education she possessed, and 600 dollars more were offered, and hastily he commented on the religious and moral principles she held, when she rose to 2,000 dollars, at which she was knocked down. Thus 1,000 were paid for her blood, bone, and sinew, 600 for her improved intellect, and 400 more for the profession of the religion of God! Miss Remond further treated her subject, and in concluding said she intended to have said more, but her strength failed her.

At the conclusion, Mrs Ashton advanced towards Miss Remond, and after addressing her in a few most affectionate sentiments, said she felt proud to acknowledge her as a sister, and she, in common with her sex present, entertained the most heartfelt sympathy with her in the object she proposed to herself to endeavor to carry out. As a slight expression of their sympathy and esteem, she begged, on the part of the ladies of Warrington, to present her with a watch, on which was inscribed, –

'Presented to S. P. Remond by Englishwomen,
her sisters, in Warrington. February 2nd, 1859.'

Miss Remond was so taken by surprise at this manifestation of feeling towards her that her utterance was for some moments prevented by her emotions. At length she said 'I do not need this testimonial. I have been received here as a sister by white women for the first time in my life. I have been removed from the degradation which overhangs all persons of my complexion; and I have felt most deeply that since I have been in Warrington and in England that I have received a sympathy I never was offered before. I had therefore no need of this testimonial of sympathy, but I receive it as the representative of my race with pleasure. In this spirit I accept it, and I believe I shall be faithful to that race now and forever. Miss Remond then sat down.

[Source: 'Lecture at the Lion Hotel,' *Warrington Times*, 4 February 1859. Available through the Black Abolitionist Archives, Doc. no. 20242.]

Sojourner Truth (c. 1797–1883), originally known as Isabella Baumfree, was born into slavery in New York. She came to be owned by a man named Dumont who promised to free her after a year's service, but later reneged, claiming she had not been productive enough that year. She eventually escaped to freedom in 1836, able to bring only one of her children with her. In 1843 she changed her name to Sojourner Truth, and from then on she spent her life working with abolitionists and women's rights activists, delivering anti-slavery speeches, and travelling.

Sojourner Truth

Address to the American Equal Rights Association (1868)

My friends, I am rejoiced that you are glad, but I don't know how you will feel when I get through. I come from another field – the country of the slave. They have got their liberty – so much good luck to have slavery partly destroyed; not entirely. I want it root and branch destroyed. Then we will all be free indeed. I feel that if I have to answer for the deeds done in my body just as much as a man, I have a right to have just as much as a man. There is a great stir about colored men getting their rights, but not a word about the colored women; and if colored men get their rights, and not colored women theirs, you see the colored men will be masters over the women, and it will be just as bad as it was before. So I am for keeping the thing going while things are stirring; because if we wait 'til it is still, it will take a great while to get it going again. White women are a great deal smarter, and know more than colored women, while colored women do not know scarcely anything. They go out washing, which is about as high as a colored woman gets, and their men go about idle, strutting up and down; and when the women come home, they ask for their money and take it all, and then scold because there is no food. I want you to consider on that, children. I call you children; you are somebody's children, and I am old enough to be mother of all that is here. I want women to have their rights. In the courts women have no right, no voice; nobody speaks for them. I wish woman to have her voice there among the pettifoggers. If it is not a fit place for women, it is unfit for men to be there, too.

I am above eighty years old; it is about time for me to be going. I have been forty years a slave and forty years free, and would be here forty years more to have equal rights for all. I suppose I am kept here because something remains for me to do; I suppose I am yet to help to break the chain. I have done a great deal of work; as much as a man, but did not get so much pay. I used to work in the field and bind grain, keeping up with the cradler, but men doing no more, got twice as much pay; so with the German women. They work in the field and do as much work, but do not get the pay. We do as much, we eat as much, we want as much. I suppose I am about the only colored woman that goes about to speak for the rights of the colored women. I want to keep the thing stirring, now that the ice is cracked. What we want is a little money. You men know that you get as much again as women when you write, or for what you do. When we get our rights we shall not have to come to you for money, for then we shall have money enough in our own pockets; and maybe you will ask us for money. But help us now until we get it. It is a good consolation to know that when we have got this battle once fought we shall not be coming to you any more. You have been having our rights so long, that you think, like a slaveholder, that you own us. I know that it is hard for one who has held the reins for so long to give up; it cuts like a knife. It will feel all the better when it closes up again. I have been in Washington about three years, seeing about these colored people. Now colored men have the right to vote. There ought to be equal rights now more than ever, since colored people have got their freedom.

[Source: Vol. 2 of *History of Woman Suffrage*, ed. Elizabeth Cady Stanton, Susan B. Anthony, and Matilda Joslyn Gage (Rochester, NY: Charles Mann, 1889), 193–4.]

PART TWO
Imperial Feminisms

Hear the wail of India's women:
    Millions, millions to us cry,
They, to us for aid appealing,
Are their sorest griefs revealing,
    Calling for our sympathy:
'Come to us!' with hands uplifted
And with streaming eyes they plead.[1]

So goes the opening stanza of a poem titled 'India's Call,' published in 1882 in *India's Women*, the journal of the Church of England Zenana Missionary Society. Its melodramatic representation of the plight of Indian women and their need of rescuing by their English (Christian) sisters neatly authorizes the missionary zeal of the Englishwomen. The poem encapsulates, in a rather extreme way, the imperialist sensibility of many British first wave feminists who found an outlet for their own desires for careers and independence through missionary work in India, China, Ceylon (Sri Lanka), and elsewhere in the East. As Antoinette Burton puts it, 'Indian women appeared [in the British feminist periodical press] as a colonial clientele that defined and authorized British feminists' imperial saving role.'[2] Burton points out that the impetus of British feminists to work on behalf of their 'Oriental' sisters had a great deal to do with their need to represent their own feminist aspirations in imperial terms. Suffrage for British women, for instance, was frequently represented as necessary so that they might more effectively intervene on behalf of their Indian 'sisters': Helena Swanwick, a member of the National Union of Women's Suffrage Societies and editor of its journal *Common Cause*, wrote in its pages in

1913: 'If it were only for our responsibilities in India we women must not rest until we have the vote.'[3]

Indian women in particular and other women from Eastern cultures more generally figured in British, US, and European feminist discourse in another way. Orientalist depictions of Indian women as passive and silenced, captives of the *zenana*, led imperial feminists to construct their Indian 'sisters' as the image of what they might themselves be were they to fail in their struggles for emancipation.[4] As Clare Midgley points out, this sort of comparison between British women and their 'enslaved' sisters puts imperial feminists on a kind of continuum with their anti-slavery forbears.[5] Many British women striving to intervene in India either directly or from afar undoubtedly felt authorized to do so by the lecture tours in England of Indian reformers like Keshub Chunder Sen, who invites Englishwomen to take an interest in the women of India, although he cautions against imposing Western ways. Annette Akroyd Beveridge was one who took up the invitation, and travelled to India in order to establish a girls' school. Her experiences in India clearly did not dislodge a decidedly orientalist view of Indian men, as her letter to *The Englishman* protesting a bill that accorded senior Indian magistrates the right to hear the same types of cases as their British colonial counterparts.

The potential for identification between Western and Eastern women was frequently disrupted by European notions of racial superiority; feminist orientalists insisted on their cultural differences from Eastern women, and often wrote disparagingly and condescendingly about Eastern cultures and religions. Priscilla Chapman's book *Hindoo Female Education* (1839) offers a key example of this sort of thinking. Not only does she insist that Indian women require the intervention of English women, she also argues that Indian women need Western education and Christianity, too. Kate Mayo's *Mother India* (1927), although it was written much later, offers a very similar critique of Indian religious and cultural traditions. At the time that it was published it met with a great deal of criticism from Indians, including Gandhi. Mayo's conclusion that the treatment of Indian women was evidence that Indians were not capable of self-government justifiably outraged the adherents of the Indian nationalist movement, among whom numbered a great many Indian feminists.[6] The controversy around Mayo's book reveals that the imperial gaze of many European and US feminists did not go uncontested. Ananda Coomaraswamy, writing in the Women's Social and Political Union journal *Votes for Women*, explicitly counters the view that Eastern women are less well treated in Eastern religions and cultures than Western women are in theirs, and offers an important reminder that Western women do not occupy a particularly good position in their own societies. The social and political activism of Indian feminists, particularly by the early twentieth century, made the claims of British and US feminists seem increasingly hollow. In many respects imperial feminists needed their 'Oriental' sisters a good deal more than the latter needed them.

Still, it is important to acknowledge that white women had a variety of motives for travelling to the East and coming to be involved with the women's movement in places like India or Turkey. Margaret Cousins, for instance, an Irish suffragette and nationalist, was drawn to India by fellow theosophist Annie Besant, and once there co-founded the Women's Indian Association and the All-Indian Women's Conference, working in close collaboration with Indian women like Sarojini Naidu, Kamaladevi Chattopadhyaya, and Muthulakshmi Reddi. Cousins's emphasis in the excerpt from *The Awakening of Asian Womanhood* (1922) is on the activism that not only Indian women but women across Asia are engaged in, an implicit contradiction of Western assumptions about their passivity and need of assistance. On the other hand, the title of her book still echoes a dominant strain in European discourse about non-European women in the early twentieth century. Rosamund Blomfield, in her contribution to *The Nineteenth Century*, attempts to counter some of the conventional misperceptions about Muslim women from her experiences and contacts in Turkey, yet her ventriloquizing of an unnamed Turkish 'princess' is discomfiting.

It was not until the early twentieth century, and most especially after the First World War, that the main international women's organizations, the ICW, the IWSA, and the WILPF, made efforts to expand their memberships beyond Europe, the United States, and settler colonies like Australia and Canada.[7] One of the efforts in this direction was the world tour undertaken in 1911 by Carrie Chapman Catt and Aletta Jacobs of the International Women's Suffrage Alliance. Efforts such as these were only partly successful, however; while women from Asia, the Middle East, Latin America, and Africa came increasingly to participate in international organizations like the IWSA, tensions remained owing to their very different conceptions of feminism, the residual Eurocentrism of the organizations which continued to operate chiefly in English, French, and German and to hold conferences in Europe and occasionally in the United States, and conflict over the links many non-European feminists had with nationalist struggles. If Carrie Chapman Catt's observations on veiling in Egypt represent a departure from the conventional Western wisdom on the meaning of the veil, her understanding and that of many Western feminists about the necessary connection between feminist emancipation and entry into the public sphere impeded much of the understanding between European feminists and feminists in the Middle East.[8]

The ideology of 'global sisterhood' that marked these European-dominated international organizations emerged from an imperial vision of the globe that linked women in a nominally universal set of goals while implicitly maintaining asymmetries of power between them. Within this broad ideology, however, there were also those who challenged the asymmetries of power forged by colonialism. Edith Jones was among a small group of white Australian women who were critical of Australian policies towards Aboriginal peoples, and who challenged the dominant racial ideology of the day. These were women who travelled internationally and attended international congresses, including those of the British Commonwealth League, an organization that, while it often echoed the imperial feminist critique of the 'native' treatment of women and children in many cultures colonized by the British Empire, had members who 'were equally critical of British colonial administrations.'[9] Australian women agitating for reform of Australia's Aboriginal policies used the BCL as a key forum for their activism during the 1920s and 1930s. Adelaide Casely Hayford, a participant in the Pan-African movement in this period, points to the ways colonial missionary education perpetuated disparaging views of African culture in her bid to create a girls' school in Sierra Leone that would offer an alternative. Alice Kandaleft's presentation at the International Congress of Women meeting in Chicago in 1933 directly challenged imperialism and the inequalities it fostered in her critique of the Mandate system, a critique that was not well received by a French delegate to the conference who felt compelled to defend France as the Mandate power in Syria.[10]

The documents in this section attest to what the author of the report of the 1920 IWSA congress in Geneva described as the difficulty of achieving 'understanding between East and West.' The report acknowledges that the speakers from India, Turkey, and Japan who addressed the congress represented 'a feminist movement that is both like and unlike our own,' and offered hopefully the suggestion that 'if the ideas that the audience gleaned from the most eloquent and moving speeches were a little vague and illusive, the sympathy and goodwill remain tangible and concrete facts.'[11]

NOTES

1 Anonymous, 'India's Call,' *India's Women* 2, no. 9 (1882): 129–33.
2 Antoinette Burton, *Burdens of History: British Feminists, Indian Women, and Imperial Culture, 1865–1915* (Chapel Hill: U of North Carolina P, 1994), 101.
3 Quoted ibid., 10.

4 See ibid., 184.

5 Clare Midgley, 'Anti-Slavery and the Roots of "Imperial Feminism,"' in *Gender and Imperialism*, ed. Clare Midgley (Manchester: Manchester UP, 1998), 164–5.

6 According to Catherine Candy, the British government sponsored the publication of *Mother India*, so its conclusions on India's lack of preparedness for self-government may be read as propaganda for British colonial rule. See 'The Inscrutable Irish-Indian Feminist Management of Anglo-American Hegemony,' *Journal of Colonialism and Colonial History* 2, no.1 (2001).

7 See Leila Rupp, 'Challenging Imperialism in International Women's Organizations, 1888–1945,' *NWSA Journal* 8, no. 1 (1996): 8.

8 Charlotte Weber, 'Unveiling Sheherazade,' *Feminist Studies* 27, no. 1 (2002): 132.

9 Fiona Paisley, *Loving Protection? Australian Feminism and Aboriginal Women's Rights, 1919–1939* (Melbourne: Melbourne UP, 2000), 41.

10 See *Our Common Cause: Civilization: Report of the National Council of Women of the United States. Including the Series of Round Tables, July 16–22, 1933, Chicago, Illinois* (New York: National Council of Women of the United States, 1973).

11 'The Eighth Congress of the IWSA,' *Jus Suffragii: The International Woman Suffrage News* 14, no. 9 (1920): 147.

Priscilla Chapman
Preface to *Hindoo Female Education* (1839)

It was an appeal to the ladies of Liverpool in 1821, from the Rev. H. Ward, Baptist Missionary, which first excited attention to the degraded and neglected state of the females in India. The most limited insight into the state of the Hindoo Female population, brings to view so much misery and wretchedness, that it is impossible for the Christian mind not to feel impatient that the moral condition of the many millions of females existing in our dominions in the east, should be well understood, that they may promptly receive their share of sympathy from those possessing the means of ministering to their necessities. It will be shown that the difficulties in the way of benefiting the Hindoo female are great; but in exact proportion to their very formidable character, exertion and assistance become the more urgent.

The attempts which have been making for the last seventeen years, to introduce Christianity and education among the Native Females of Hindostan are here described;– though progress in the work has been slow, and success very limited, it will be evident that real good has been done, and that the way is now opened and prepared for more extended efforts.

Had it fallen to the lot of any European to penetrate the abyss of female degradation, the best of feelings would forbid the recital; it is rather to the obvious consequences of the neglect they suffer, and to their unhappy exclusion from all the precious gifts of God which we enjoy, that attention is directed:– whilst the manners, customs, and superstitions of the people are noticed, as explaining the sources of existing evils.

The Society for Promoting Native Female Education in China and the East, has already prominently brought this subject to the consideration of the Christian public, and affords valuable assistance to the cause.

The Efforts of European females are alluded to with a humiliating consciousness of how few there are, who can speak upon the subject; we feel thankful, however, that an example of singular devotion, to the promotion of this cause especially, is before us – Mrs Wilson, who was first led to embark for India, by Mr Ward's appeal. After seventeen years unceasing labor, she continues to find the Lord's blessing resting upon, and extending her benevolent designs. It is the result of Mrs Wilson's endeavours in the two institutions in Calcutta, designated the Native Female Orphan refuge and the Central School, which this sketch principally embraces.

Such Institutions or Schools as the Author is acquainted with, are mentioned; but in the absence of correct information from the Presidencies of Madras and

Bombay, in both of which, schools for native females have been formed, our notices are confined to the state of the work in Bengal.

The profits that may ensue from this little work, will be devoted to the benefit of the Female Orphan Refuge, and the Central School.

[Source: Preface to *Hindoo Female Education* (London: R.B. Seeley and W. Burnside, 1839), v–vii.]

Keshub Chunder Sen (also spelled Keshab Chandra Sen) (1838–84) was a Bengali intellectual and a religious reformer. His primary quest was for a universal religion or belief-system. Keshub Chunder Sen was for several decades a leader of the Brahmo Samaj, which advocated education and social reform for women. In later life, he established a syncretic school of spiritualism, called the Nabo Bidhan or 'New Dispensation,' which he intended to amalgamate the best principles of the Western spiritual tradition with Hinduism.

Keshub Chunder Sen
Speech to the Victoria Discussion Society (1870)

At the monthly meeting of the Victoria Discussion Society, held at the Architectural Gallery, Conduit Street, London, on Monday, August 1, 1870, the chair was taken by BABOO KESHUB CHUNDER SEN. [...]

The CHAIRMAN, who was warmly received, said:–

It may appear somewhat singular that a Hindu should preside on the present occasion. It has been said that my countrymen altogether deny the rights and privileges of women. Now I do not think that such statements are true, although I believe there are certain facts connected with the present state of Hindu society, which may justify some measure of reproach of this kind. India to-day is not what she was in ancient times, and if we see anything in India which is sad, painful, or discouraging, we must not rush to the conclusion that Indian society is altogether depraved. Time was when men and women freely mixed with each other in society in India, when celebrated ladies solved mathematical problems, and evinced the deepest interest in mathematics and science generally; when Hindu ladies entered into interesting conversations with their husbands on religious and moral questions, and when not only men chose for themselves, but even ladies came forward and selected husbands for themselves. (Laughter.) But those days are gone. However, it is quite clear that in ancient times in India, women sometimes enjoyed an amount of liberty which would not be considered quite warrantable in civilized England at the present moment. Hindu society is now in a sad condition owing to idolatry and caste, and a number of most demoralizing and mischievous social customs and institutions. The people, both men and women, have fallen into a low state, so much so that it is impossible to recognise in the modern Indian the noble soul of the ancient Hindu. What do we see in India at the present moment? Some men having more than seventy wives. There is a beautiful popular drama in Bengal, in which one of those husbands of seventy wives is represented as passing through the streets one day, and meeting a boy, who approaches him and addresses him as 'father.' The man, confounded and somewhat indignant, denies his fatherhood, but the boy perseveres in his statement. At last it strikes this learned man that it may after all be true, and he instantly refers to a bundle of papers which he always carries about with him, and goes through the long list of his wives, until he finds out that the statement made by the boy turns out to be true.

There is another injurious custom, which makes an old man of eighty marry a little girl of five years of age. This is shocking and pernicious in the extreme, but such things are common in Bengal, and in other parts of the country.

There is another custom which prevents a widow from remarrying. Once a widow, the Hindu woman is not only forced to remain so, but has to pass through endless mortifications, and penances of the most painful character. Her condition is really pitiable, and excites the commiseration of every feeling heart. Thus the marriage customs which prevail in India are injurious in a variety of ways. An immediate reform and purification are therefore required. Widows must be allowed to remarry, and to have the privileges which are accorded to them in other countries. They must not be made to submit by force and pressure to a state of things which they do not themselves like, but which, for the sake of attaining a false heaven, they so often submit to. The custom of early marriages ought to be abolished, and men and women should be permitted to marry only when they are of marriageable age. Bigamy and polygamy should be suppressed, if possible, by legislative enactment. But there are other things that can only be put down by the operation of personal influence, and by the publication of books, pointing out the evils which must result from objectionable customs. The root of the mischief is the want of enlightenment. If Hindu ladies received a proper amount of enlightenment, they would themselves raise a voice powerful enough to suppress those great evils. The victims not only suffer, but they suffer oftentimes with great patience and forbearance, and with willing hearts. When a widow is doomed not to remarry, she thinks it is the will of Heaven that she must be assigned to perpetual widowhood. When women do not receive the blessings of true enlightenment, they think they ought not to aspire to enjoy those blessings, because they are taught it is Heaven's wish that they should remain in the midst of the darkness of ignorance. It is necessary, therefore, to raise up the spirit of Hindu women, and stimulate their curiosity, and excite their taste for nobler and higher things. When we succeed in dispelling the gloom of ignorance which now broods over the length and breadth of the country, when we succeed in uprooting all those prejudices and superstitious notions which keep the women of India in a state of moral, spiritual, social, and intellectual subjection, we shall succeed, indirectly though it may be, in opening ten thousand flood-gates through which the stream of truth will flow, diffusing the blessings of purity and peace. If it be said that what we see in India at the present moment is the normal state of things, and that the Hindu ladies submit to ignorance because they have always been told by their own Scriptures to do so, I can only say there are passages in those Scriptures which inculcate other principles. It is there said that the husband should always try to please his wife, 'with wealth, dress, love, respect, and sweet words.' The Hindu husband you see is enjoined, not only to love, but to respect his wife, and love and respect are the proper feelings which men everywhere should cherish towards women.

It had been said that Hindu legislators in ancient times did not show any anxiety for the education of girls. Now it is written in the Hindu Scriptures that parents should train up not only their boys, but also their girls, with great care. I have only to quote another passage in order to refute the charge which has oftentimes been made against the Hindu nation. It has been said that early marriage has been inculcated in the Hindu Scriptures. Here is a passage that will show the inaccuracy of that statement:– 'So long as the girl does not know how to respect the husband, so long as she is not acquainted with true moral discipline, so long the father should not think of getting her married.' These passages clearly and distinctly show that Hindu society, as it at present exists in India, is not what it ought to be according to the religious books of the nation. There can be no doubt that the country has fallen from the high position which it occupied centuries ago. It is not true that absolute and severe seclusion of the female sex prevails in all parts of India. We see it to a lamentable extent in Bengal, but in the Punjab, and Bombay, and to some extent in Madras, the women enjoy a large amount of liberty. Though there are some very sad things connected with the condition of female society in India, I am bound to say that with all its degradation there are some good things to be found even in the relics of a past fabric of society. There are arts and sciences which prove that that society has been truly great and noble. As regards devotion to her husband, I do not think the Hindu lady yields to any nation on earth, and in regard to modesty, gentleness, serenity of temper, and absolute devotion to the interests of her husband, even at the present moment in India those characteristics are still preserved. In conducting our reform of Indian female character it is necessary then that we should gather together, and not overlook, these good materials. With all my respect and admiration for civilization as it prevails in England, I have always been foremost in protesting against the demoralization of India by importing English customs into it. (Cheers.) Though I can respect learned, intelligent, philanthropic and generous-hearted ladies in England, I could not for one moment persuade myself to believe that for the interest of India I ought to introduce their customs and institutions. The growth of society must be indigenous, native, and natural. (Hear, hear.) Foreign customs must not be forced upon us. Our women have elements of character which are really noble and good, and these ought to constitute the basis upon which we should spread a superstructure of reformed female Indian society. (Cheers.) It has been said that women in England should not have what are called women's rights, and this evening I have had the opportunity of listening to the arguments on both sides. I feel puzzled, and, perhaps, like Sir Roger de Coverley, I may say that much might be said on behalf of either party. We should not certainly keep up that unpleasant agitation which many people seem to delight in. We should express our feelings without bitterness or animosity. If women think it is their duty to do certain things, why should men seek to prevent them? (Cheers.) Men do not like men to interfere with their freedom of action, and why should women allow men to interfere with theirs? As to the question whether men are morally superior to women, or women morally superior to men, I say still, much may be said on both sides. Let us settle the matter by admitting that men are superior in some respects, and women superior in others. (Laughter.) That I think would be an amicable settlement of the whole matter. In all that is manly and vigorous men excel, and must continue to excel, but in all that is soft, and tender, and gentle, women must continue to surpass men. It is the combination of the various elements that constitutes true manhood. It is in the union of these qualities that true moral excellence is to be found. (Applause.) I would proscribe and denounce class legislation and class agitation. Why should we need an exclusive movement to be got up for the purpose of obtaining women's rights, so-called? If women are fit, they must have their rights and privileges. I do not see why they should be excluded from positions which they are entitled to, and which they are fitted to occupy. If they are not fit, they ought not to occupy them, but if they are fit, then let their fitness be held up, and vindicated and declared throughout the length and breadth of the land. It has been said that in theory sometimes man is a noun, and woman simply an adjective that agrees with the noun. I believe, however, the case is otherwise. In practice man is a noun, and a noun of the masculine gender; and he is also a noun in the objective case governed by the verb woman. (Laughter.) Practically women govern men all over the world. You or I may not admit it openly, and some of you may make vehement protestations to the contrary, but what is the actual state of things? In India, ninety-nine husbands out of every hundred are practically governed by their wives. Is not that the case in England too, and in all civilized and refined countries? From early infancy to mature age, the influence of mother, sister, or wife, and female society generally, has always continued to be felt and prized. By their gentle, soft, sweet tempers, women exercise an irresistible influence over men. If, then, we must be governed by women, are we to govern absolutely in all matters? No. In those things wherein man excels woman, let man's voice be heard; where woman excels man, let her voice be heard. The true prosperity of society depends on the harmony of the sexes. It is necessary, therefore, whether we look to India or to England, that we should always try to bring the two together, and allow them to consult each other's interests, so that in the end we may have the valuable suggestions and the active philanthropic labours of both. I wish to say a few words more about India before I resume my seat. I am glad you have given me the opportunity of addressing you, for this is a ladies' society. I want your help. I have addressed meetings of men in various parts of the country, and have besought them as humbly as I could possibly do to help India. I now have the honour to make an urgent yet humble appeal to you English-women – I may say English sisters. I sincerely and earnestly call upon you to do all in your power to effect the elevation of the Hindu women. I dare say many of you have read in books in what way Hindu women may be helped by you. The best way in which that help can be given is for some of you to embark on the grand and noble enterprise of going over personally to that great country, and looking after the state of things there. A noble-minded and kind-hearted lady went to India a few years ago in order to promote the work of female education. Miss Carpenter's name is familiar to you all. Why should not some of you follow her praiseworthy example? I say this because the work that requires your aid and co-operation is urgent. At the present moment a thousand Hindu houses are open to receive and welcome English governesses – well-trained, accomplished English ladies, capable of doing good to their Indian sisters, both by instruction and personal example. And what sort of education do we expect and wish from you? An unsectarian, liberal, sound, useful education. (Cheers.) An education that will not patronize any particular church, that will not be subservient or subordinated to the views of any particular religious community, an education free, and liberal, and comprehensive in its character, an education calculated to make Indian women good wives, mothers, sisters, and daughters. Such an education we want for our ladies, and are there no feeling hearts in England capable of responding to this exhortation and invitation? I speak to you not for one, not for fifty, but for millions of Indian sisters, whose lamentations and wails penetrate the skies, and seem to come over to England at the present moment to stir up the hearts of their English sisters. Shall we hear those cries and lamentations with hearts of steel? Shall we not weep over this scene of spiritual and intellectual desolation that spreads far and wide over that once glorious country? Will you not come forward and say – 'We will part with our substance if we cannot go over personally, but we who can go over personally shall go, for our Heavenly Father calls upon us to undertake this noble mission'? A noble mission decidedly it is, to go across the ocean and scale hills and mountains, to surmount difficulties and to risk health, in order to wipe the tears from the eyes of weeping Indian sisters, to rescue them from widowhood, from the evil customs of premature marriage, and to induce them to feel that there is something higher and nobler for them to aspire to.

My business this evening is to tell you, that in her distress India bids you come over and help her. Governments are trying to do what improved legislation can to crush and exterminate the bad customs. Philanthropic men have gone there to promote a liberal education amongst the males, and now if Englishwomen are ready to vindicate what are called women's rights in England, if they have to make platform speeches, let them show that their views and sympathies are not confined within the limits of this small island. This is a Society where I am especially entitled to bring forward this appeal. I trust that I have not spoken to the walls, but to the generous hearts of men and women, who will combine to do what they can to help forward their Indian sisters. Religiously we are doing a great work by giving a better and purer religion to the people. Many of our ladies are giving up idolatrous superstitions. In many Hindu houses the idols have been beaten to the ground, and the ten thousand gods and goddesses of the Hindoo Pantheon are no longer treated with respect. This is cheering, and encourages us to hope that though India to-day is a fallen nation, higher and higher it will ascend until she arrives at that high position which has been destined for her. When you have given us the help for which I ask, England will have done her duty towards India, and the people of both lands will assist each other in pressing forward to the goal which we all desire to keep in view. (Cheers.)

[Source: *Keshub Chunder Sen's English Visit*, ed. Sophia Dobson Collet (London: Strahan Publishers, 1871), 465–76.]

A medical doctor, Clara Swain (1834–1910) graduated from Woman's Medical College of Pennsylvania in 1869. She became one of the first single female missionaries to India from the Woman's Foreign Missionary Society of the Methodist Episcopal Church in the United States. She arrived in India on 7 January 1870 and began medical work in Bareilly, India. In 1874, the Clara Swain Hospital opened, the first hospital for women in all of Asia.

Dr Clara Swain
Letter to her sister (8 June 1873)

My Dear Sister:

The dispensary building was completed early last month and formally opened on the tenth of the month. The friends who have visited it are much pleased with the arrangements and congratulate me on having so desirable a place to receive patients.

The dispensary opens for work at six o'clock every morning except Sunday, and some mornings we have as many as sixty patients. We have cards on which the prescriptions are written and numbered and these cards are printed in three different characters, Hindi, Persian and Roman-Urdu, and on the back of each is a text of Scripture so that every new patient receives with her prescription a portion of the Word of Life. She may not be able to read it but possibly some one of her family can read it for her. This is one of the very simple methods of circulating the Word of God in the families of those who come to us, and by His blessing it may be the means of bringing some one into the truth. A passage of Scripture on a card given to a patient is often the subject of our morning lesson for all who come and are willing to listen a while until their prescriptions are ready for them.

Two of my medical class are valuable assistants in the dispensary, Emma, who married one of the students in the theological school, and Jane Paul, so with my faithful Rebecca at the head everything goes smoothly.

The hospital buildings will probably be completed this year. Much care has been taken in the arrangement of them that the taste and convenience of native ladies may be suited and their seclusion, according to their custom, be ensured. Our plan was to build just what we needed and no more and we have followed native ideas as far as possible, so that patients may feel perfectly at home and be enabled to carry on their plan of cooking and living the same as in their own houses. The plan is much like that of an Eastern *Sarai* or inn only with more of a view to home comfort. A piece of ground two hundred and fifty feet by one hundred and seventy-five is enclosed by a wall eight feet high; at the front of this stands the dispensary buildings. The front entrance is from the general compound and the back veranda opens into the hospital grounds, thus making the dispensary a part of the general plan. At the right of the dispensary within the enclosure is a row of dormitories one story high, extending nearly the whole length of the wall, and across the end, opposite the dispensary is another row, more commodious, designed for patients requiring larger rooms. Dormitories will be built on the other side of the enclosure when needed. A front veranda extends the whole length of the dormitories, and another at the back will serve as kitchens as there are partitions arranged so that the occupants of each room can cook their food outside their living room. The rooms are twelve by fourteen feet. In the centre of the enclosure is a fine large well where each modern Rebecca who comes to us can draw water for herself, with her own bucket and rope as is the custom of people of caste in India. The grounds are tastefully laid out and in due time will be beautified with some of India's lovely roses, flowers and shrubbery.

[Source: *A Glimpse of India: Being a Collection of Extracts from the Letters of Dr. Clara A. Swain, First Medical Missionary to India of the Women's Foreign Missionary Society of the Methodist Episcopal Church in America* (New York: L.J. Pott, 1909).]

Annette Susannah Akroyd Beveridge (1844–1929), an educationalist and social reformer, is remembered primarily for her early efforts at women's education in India. Inspired by the speeches Keshub Chunder Sen gave in England, Akroyd decided to go to India herself where she met with members of the progressive Brahmo Samaj, who led the campaign for women's education. Once in India, however, Akroyd found herself in frequent disagreement with Sen, who was critical of the Westernized model of education Akroyd introduced.

Annette Akroyd Beveridge
Letter to *The Englishman* about the Ilbert Bill (3 March 1883)

I am not afraid to assert that I speak the feeling of all English-women in India when I say that we regard the proposal to subject us to the jurisdiction of native Judges as an insult.

It is not pride of race which dictates this feeling, which is the outcome of something far deeper – it is the pride of womanhood. This is a form of respect which we are not ready to abrogate in order to give such advantages to others as are offered by Mr Ilbert's Bill to its beneficiaries.

In this discussion as in most 'il y a question de femmes' – and in this discussion the ignorant and neglected women of India rise up from their enslavement in evidence against their masters. They testify to the justice of the resentment which Englishmen feel at Mr Ilbert's proposal to subject civilised women to the jurisdiction of men who have done little or nothing to redeem the women of their own races, and whose social ideas are still on the outer verge of civilization.

[Source: Lord Beveridge, *India Called Them* (London: George Allen & Unwin, 1947), 228.]

Born in Colombo, Sri Lanka, the son of a Tamil man and an English woman, Ananda Coomaraswamy (1877–1947) spent his childhood in Kent and studied geology at the University of London. In 1902 he married Ethel Partridge and together they moved to Sri Lanka, where Coomaraswamy took up the post of director of geology. The couple studied folklore and the arts and crafts of Sri Lanka, and wrote critically about the encroaching Westernization in South Asian education, advocating the study of South Asian languages and literatures rather than European ones for both women and men. Coomaraswamy's conservatism on women's social roles can be linked to his anti-imperialist stance on Western influences in South Asia.

Ananda K. Coomaraswamy
The Oriental View of Woman (1910)

It is frequently assumed, by speakers and writers on the present and past position of woman in the West, that the Oriental view of woman is lower than the Western; and statements involving this assumption are often made, as if the assumption were an admitted fact. It must in the first place be observed that there is no 'absolute Western' and no 'absolute Eastern' point of view. It is a mistake to assume that 'East is East and West is West, and never the twain shall meet'; attitudes of reverence, comradeship, or contempt towards women find expression at various times in the history of civilisation alike in the West and in the East.

It is not therefore possible in a short article to expound the whole Oriental view of woman. I shall only endeavour to correct the prevalent misconception – largely of missionary inspiration – by showing how the matter may present itself to any person who is not quite ignorant of Oriental thought and Oriental civilisations.

It is sometimes suggested that Christianity, an Oriental religion, has imposed upon European women a position of inferiority. But it was certainly not Christ, who was an Oriental, who treated women as inferior beings. It was Paul, a Greek, who was primarily responsible for the low spiritual status of woman in the Christian Church. From this position she only temporarily emerged in that Oriental period of post-classic European culture when the Church first accepted marriage as a sacrament, and men worshipped God in the form of woman – as they still do in the East.

It is noteworthy that we find in the writings of some of those Oriental philosophers whose work had so much influence in Europe at that time pronouncements in favour of the social emancipation of women which are almost verbally identical with those of modern Suffragists. 'Our social condition,' wrote Ibn-Rushd, 'does not permit women to unfold all the resources that are in them; it seems as if they were only meant to bear children and to suckle them. And it is this state of servitude that has destroyed in them the capacity for great things. That is the reason why we seldom find among us women endowed with any great moral qualities; their lives pass away like those of plants, and they are a burden to their husbands. From this cause arises the misery that devours our cities, since there are twice as many women as men, and they are unable to procure their means of livelihood by their own industry.'

It is true that the early Germans honoured women; but the later Germans thought that they knew better. It was the essentially Western materialism of Luther that had the main share in the degradation of woman accompanying the Reformation. 'If a woman becomes weary and at last dead from bearing,' says Luther, 'that matters not. Let her only die from bearing; she is there to do it.' And, again, she 'must neither begin nor complete anything without the man; where he is, there must she be, and bend before him as before her master, whom she shall fear, and to whom she shall be subject and obedient.'[1]

It is not, indeed, by contrasting the religious standpoints of the East and the West that the supposed inferior position of woman in the East can be demonstrated. At the present day there are millions of Orientals who worship the

---

1 See the chapters on Luther in Karl Pearson's 'Ethic of Freethought.'

Divine life in the image of a woman. Woman is honoured in religious literature and art. Mahàdev, addressing Umà, in the Mahàbhàrata, says, 'Thou, O
Lady, knowest both the Self and the Not-Self, ... Thou art skilled in every
work. Thou art endued with self-restraint and with perfect same-sightedness in
respect of every creature ... Thy energy and power are equal to My own, and
Thou hast not shrunk from the most severe austerities.' In Sufi mysticism, the
Beloved (feminine) is 'all that lives' – God: the Lover (masculine), is 'a dead
thing' – the individual soul lacking the Divine Life. These lines were written
by Jalàlud-din Rùmi:

> Woman is a ray of God, not a mere mistress,
> The Creator's Self, as it were, not a mere creature!

One must consider also the representation of Divinity symbolised as feminine
in Hindu and Buddhist art; there are forms ranging from the dread image of
Kàli, Destroyer of Time, to the compassionate, tender forms of Umà and of
Tàrà. We must remember that the gods are shaped by human beings in their
own image; the status of women on earth is reflected in the status of a goddess.

On the other hand one might point out how the whole history of mythology
and art in Greece reflects the gradual degradation from an ancient ideal of high
companionship (exactly corresponding to the Indian conception of the feminine principle in the cosmos as Sakti) to that of the Hausfrau in a patriarchal
community.[2]

If we turn from this question of the inner attitude to that of social status,
we shall find that the Oriental woman has always enjoyed certain advantages
which the Western woman has, at the best, very lately won: e.g., the universal
right of Muhammadan women to hold and inherit property in their own names.
The Oriental woman has also more real power of control in her own home than
most Western women; her word is law even to her grown-up sons. It is very
well known that in Burma women are more independent and more happy than
in perhaps any other country in the world; and, indeed, one has only to return
to London from any Oriental country and contrast the facial expression of most
women there with the facial expression of most women in the East to realise
that the latter are the happiest.

Both in the East and in the West the social position of woman needs reformation of a drastic character. When one reflects, however, upon the opposition

---

2 See Jane E. Harrison, 'Prolegomena to Greek Religion,' 273, 285.

to woman's advance characteristic of Western universities, legal and medical associations, and of Parliament, and still more the manner than the fact of it, it is difficult to feel that the Western woman is so much to be envied.

It is surely a tragedy that out of all the women in England between the ages of fifteen and fifty scarcely more than half are married. In all that this implies lies the comparative wickedness of modern Western industrial civilisation, which sets a premium on vice by saying, 'Seek indulgence, but beware of children.' Neither this, nor sweated labour, nor its result – street solicitation – are of the East.

I would admit women to absolute equality of opportunity with men in all respects. But I think that State most fortunate wherein most women between the ages of twenty and forty are primarily concerned with the making of children, beautiful in every sense. To this end women must obtain economic security, either from individuals or from the State. There can be no freedom for women which does not include the freedom to have, as well as not to have children. It is ultimately I conceive – at least, I hope – for the right to be themselves, rather than for the right to become more like men, that Suffragettes are, however unconsciously, fighting. There can be no freedom for women till good motherhood is regarded as an intrinsic glory.

The East has always recognised the fundamental difference in the psychology of men and women. I do not think that any attempt to minimise or to ignore these differences can be successful. It is because men and women *are* different that they need each other. What is needed at present is that women should be allowed to discover for themselves what is their 'sphere,' rather than that they should continue to perforce occupy the sphere which men (rightly or wrongly) have at various times allowed to them in the patriarchal ages. This necessity is as much a necessity for the West as for the East.

Social status, as I have said, needs reformation both in the East and in the West. But the West far more than the East needs a change of heart. The Western view of sex is degraded and material contrasted with the Eastern. Women are not lightly spoken of, or written of, in the East as they are so often in the West. Sex for the Oriental is a sacrament. For the European it is a pleasure.

With the consciousness of this, and much more that might be added to it, I feel that the West has at least as much to learn from the East of reverence to women as the East has to learn from the West. And it is better for reformers, whether in East or West, to work together for a common end than to pride themselves upon their own supposedly superior achievement.

[Source 'The Oriental View of Woman,' *Votes for Women* 4 (1910): 531.]

Rosamund Blomfield (?–?) is not specifically identified.

Rosamund F. Blomfield
Our Moslem Sisters (1911)

At the present moment when the affairs of Turkey are occupying a prominent place in the public mind, it might not be uninteresting to bring before the English public some account of the thoughts and feelings of the Turkish woman, who, surely, as well as her countryman, deserves a measure of consideration. Having lived in Egypt for more than a quarter of a century and having had opportunities there of forming acquaintances with many Turkish ladies, I feel that I must bring to the notice of the women readers of this Review my experience relating to their position. Now, when the feminist movement is making headway here, it seems to be a peculiarly appropriate occasion to ask the women of Great Britain to support the efforts of their Moslem sisters, efforts which are going on, slowly and silently, behind the closed *mushrabeyehs* of the Turkish harems; and when I have laid the case before them, I feel confident that it will enlist the sympathy of all sections of British women, both those who think the feminist champions here at home have done enough for their cause, and those whose desire it is to urge it on still further.

It is the duty of Englishwomen to recognize the moral and intellectual needs of their Eastern sisters. Perhaps their seeming lack of sympathy may be due to ignorance of the actual state of affairs. They may not realise that there are cultivated ladies who, though brought up in strict seclusion, cherish sentiments which are pure and high, and who, under the greatest possible difficulties, are trying to effect a change in their midst which may raise them and their co-religionists from their sadly fallen position and set them once more, as they were many centuries ago, by the side of their husbands and male relatives as companions and helpmeets in private and social life. In this matter I do not wish to put forward my own arguments, but simply to give an inside opinion, a voice which should appeal with double eloquence coming, as it does, from within the walls of those very harems where the veiled leaders of their sex's cause live a life of ineffectual idleness. The letter from which I propose to quote freely in this paper is a touching appeal addressed by a Turkish Princess, whose acquaintance I had the pleasure of making during my stay in the East, to her compatriots and co-religionists. Originally written in Turkish, she translated it into French for my benefit, and the examination of the chief lines of argument will be the best way to convey to Englishwomen a sense of the necessity that exists for them to stretch forth a hand in sympathy to these cultured ladies who are striving to regain their former position of dignity and social usefulness. The fact that the pleas for the removal of the restrictions that now lie heavy upon them are not based on any example that may have come to them across the seas from England or America, but are founded on the very principles and laws of their own religion, proves that the movement is sincere, and that it is one sprung from the hearts of those who dwell within the harems, and is not an extraneous growth of artificially grafted Western sentiment. On the contrary, the Princess throughout lays stress on the necessity of avoiding any servile copying of Occidental customs. Here her opinion tallies completely with that of a great English authority, the Earl of Cromer, whose experience has taught him the danger of introducing a European education unreservedly among Eastern people. 'A Europeanised Egyptian man usually becomes an Agnostic, and often assimilates many of the least worthy portions of European civilisation. Is there any reason why European education should not produce the same effect on the Europeanised Egyptian woman? I know of none.'[1] But while thus uncertain of its results, he despairs entirely of a civilisation equal to the European standard making any progress in Mahometan countries unless the condition of their women is improved.

> It may be asked [he says] whether anyone can conceive of the existence of true European civilisation on the assumption that the position which women occupy in Europe is abstracted from the general plan? As well can a man blind from his birth be made to conceive the existence of colour. Change the position of women, and one of the main pillars, not only of European civilisation, but at all events of the moral code based on the Christian religion, if not of Christianity itself, falls to the ground. The position of women in Egypt, and in Mahometan countries generally, is therefore a fatal obstacle to the attainment of that elevation of thought and character which should accompany the introduction of European civilisation, if that civilisation is to produce its full measure of beneficial effect. The obvious remedy would appear to be to educate the women.[2]

He rejoices also that the new movement in favour of female education is commencing to take root among the masculine population of Egypt. 'The younger generation are beginning to demand that their wives should possess some qualifications other than those which can be secured in the exclusion of the harem.'[3]

---

1 *Modern Egypt*, by the Earl of Cromer, 2: 541.
2 Ibid., 538.
3 *Modern Egypt*, by the Earl of Cromer, 2: 540.

So, with this preliminary testimony from the Earl of Cromer as to the need for and the awakening interest in female education among Mahometans, I will pass on to an account of the present state of affairs among Mahometan ladies, as seen and experienced by one of themselves.

The first point emphasised by the Princess is the great difference in the present position of Moslem women compared with that formerly held by them in the early days of Islam. The change has been a retrograde, not a progressive, one. The student of history knows that long ago a Moslem lady was capable of fulfilling the natural avocations of her sex, and also enjoyed the necessary liberty to engage in social work suited to her rank. On many occasions she achieved notable heights of culture and even of political influence. Nor did her male compatriots object to her thus entering upon the field of active duties. In those bygone days women were held in the deepest respect. The ordinances of their religion upheld them in their rights, and especially during the second century of the Hegira, that brilliant era of Arab civilisation, they were free to render important service to their country and worked on an equal footing with men to further the cause of civilisation and progress. 'Reigning sovereigns, preachers, magistrates, directors of religious bodies, and professors of theology can be cited amongst the remarkable women of that time,' says the Princess. 'Some held the posts of governors of important towns, while some even commanded strongholds, and accompanied their husbands when charging the enemy. I could name a score of these celebrated women as examples, but it will suffice for my argument to mention a few of those who have stood out more prominently in history than the rest.' The Princess then quotes a number of Moslem ladies who reigned as sovereigns in their own right at different periods of Turkish and Arabian history – Padicha Hatoume, Turkane Hatoume, Seyida Chadjar Hamatsu, Garize Lale. As military commanders she mentions Bilome, wife of the Sultan Orkane, who was entrusted with the command of the important fortress of Ismik, and Taffi Hatoume, wife of the Emir Ala-el-dine, who held a similar position at Thaissere (formerly Cesarea of Cappadocia). There were, moreover, she asserts, brilliant exponents of law and theology among Moslem women – Oumon Issa, daughter of the Imaum, Ibrahim el Harbi, whose judgments have been acknowledged as valuable by erudite doctors of law, and Hamda, who lived in the fourth century of the Hegira, whose pupil was the famous Ibni Semani. Later, in the eighth century of the Hegira, there were Sittel Fenkala, who numbered many celebrated men among her audience, and Sendala Halba, a famous lady teacher of theology and jurisprudence at Aleppo. Fatma-bint-Abbas, born in Egypt in the eighth century of the Hegira, is also mentioned by the Princess as a doctor of the canonical law, mother-superior of a religious community, and so renowned for her learning, eloquence, and power of debate that she proved superior in controversy to the greatest savants of her day. Zeymildar-Waginha, whose husband was a magistrate in Andalusia, presided at the tribunal alongside of him, and her decisions were quite as much respected as those of her husband. In the reign of the Ottoman Sultan Bayazid I, Selma gave lessons in the mosques and public schools to students of both sexes, for at that period the co-education of boys and girls was an accepted system.

The enthusiasm and courage of the Moslem women in time of war is a matter of history. The Princess in support of this quotes the instance of the battle fought in the year 541 A.D. between the Khalif Omar and Heraclius, where the women, besides helping in the fight, also acted as guardian angels in tending the fallen, carrying water to the thirsty, binding up their wounds, and all the while exhorting the combatants to renewed efforts. Thus encouraged by their intrepid womenfolk, the soldiers dared not turn their backs on the enemy.

So we find Moslem women in early days preparing themselves for work in all domains of learning and administration, and occupying a position even more exalted than women hold in modern society. What, then, are the causes which led to their repression and which have closed every outlet to their energy and ambition?

The Princess gives the reason in a few words. 'The decadence of our women can be traced from the moment when the Mahometan world itself fell into degenerate habits, and began to imitate the nefarious customs of other nations, whilst it tried to stifle its conscience by giving false interpretations to the laws of the Koran.' Towards the end of the dynasty of the Abbasid Khalifs, the Moslem woman first found herself sinking from her high place of honour. Luxury and debauchery took possession of the Court; woman became a mere chattel, the instrument of her lord and master's vicious pleasure. The conquest of Constantinople gave the finishing stroke to the liberties of Moslem women, and from that day the sensuous, indulgent life of the harem, with its soft divans and silken cushions, its jewels and voluptuous pleasures, has gradually sapped the intellectual and moral strength of its denizens. The daughter of the famous Turkish historian Fatma Alija thus writes, says the Princess, of the fair sex at Byzantium:

> The Moslem women are accustomed to luxurious palaces full of soft divans, which seem to invite one to lead a life of inaction and repose. They breathe a poisonous atmosphere of sensual pleasure, and in so subtle a form of indulgence that by its prodigality the intellect becomes weakened, while the physical powers become equally relaxed. Like all Byzantine women, they acquire an inordinate love of jewellery and dress, and give heed only to the poetry of the senses, which appeals to passion rather than to true affection, and to an exaggerated adulation

of their mere personal charms. They seem bewitched by the melodious sounds of a lullaby, which soothes their higher nature into dangerous somnolence. Awaking from this lethargy they open their eyes day by day to a repetition of this idle luxury, and have no moral strength to withstand the fatal dead weight of ignorance, which little by little has reduced these incarcerated voluptuaries to a state of imbecility which renders them an easy prey to its deadening properties. These mere puppets of humanity, whose foreheads are encircled by precious stones, their necks laden with heavy pendants, and wrists weighed down with bracelets, do not care any longer to preserve their greater gifts, the treasures of the mind, which lie unused behind the gewgaws which ornament their silken tresses.

Their arms, which at one time were able to withstand the onslaught of the foe, whose fingers could use the pen with such ability, now lie idle, whilst they listen to songs extolling the beauty of their slender forms, their carmine complexions, and arched eyebrows, sung by their fawning minstrels. Not one of these vacuous beings would care to listen to an ode to their courage, talents, or merit, which would appear far too dull a theme. They like to hear of thousands of lives sacrificed for the sake of a woman's glance from behind the window of a harem, or of fortunes wasted to obtain the smile of another. Confused, dazzled, and misled, these unfortunate women imagine themselves to be at the very apogee of happiness, whereas they are daily consenting to their own degradation by losing every scrap of individuality as well as the actual rights of their sex.

These are the women to whom the care of the next generation is entrusted! English readers may judge for themselves whether women brought up among the vice and idle luxury of the Turkish harems thus described are likely to exercise a purifying, uplifting influence upon their sons and daughters.

The Princess then proceeds to emphasise the fact, that her countrywomen, while desirous to combat this love of luxury, pleasure, and license, must avoid the danger of running into the opposite extreme and following the example of Western women who are struggling for liberties of a kind foreign to the Eastern woman's nature. 'It is in our best interest to seize on and make use of those liberties already granted to us Moslem women by our own religious laws.'

An erroneous impression still prevails among Western nations that the seclusion of the harem was part of Mahomet's rule of life for women. No statement could be more misleading, for neither in theory nor in practice did the Prophet enjoin strict seclusion upon the female sex. The Koran does not order it, and Mahomet's own womenfolk were permitted great freedom from restraint. Ayesha, daughter of Abu Bakr, whom he married after the death of his first wife Khadija, took an active and distinguished part in the celebrated 'Battle of the Camel.' Khadija, his first wife, was his devoted comrade during the twenty-five years of their wedded life. Fatima, his daughter, called by her ardent adherents 'the lady of Paradise' and 'Our Lady of Light,' was permitted to take public share in political debate. Zainab, his granddaughter, was a woman of noted intrepidity both in public and private life. The seclusion of the harem was, therefore, only intended as a salutary precaution in a lawless country, not as a rule which admitted of no relaxation.

Modern critics of Moslem custom are even now apt to confuse the feelings toward women which were prevalent before the sway of Islam, when such sayings as 'Women are the whips of Satan,' and 'What has a woman to do with the councils of a nation?' passed into proverbs in Arabia. But if further proof be required that this was not the attitude of the Moslem religious leader, I may quote a few passages from the Koran which emphatically teach that believers of both sexes are equal before God. One is found in the Chapter of the Confederates, Surah xxxiii.35:

Verily men resigned and women resigned,
And believing men and believing women,
And devout men and devout women,
And truthful men and truthful women,
And patient men and patient women,
And humble men and humble women,
And almsgiving men and almsgiving women,
And fasting men and fasting women,
And chaste men and chaste women,
And men who remember God much, and women who remember Him, –
God has prepared for them forgiveness and mighty hire.[4]

Again, in the Chapter of Women, Surah iv.I, the Koran enjoins respect for women:

O ye folk, fear your Lord, who created you from one soul, and created therefrom its mate, and diffused from them twain many men and women. And fear God, in whose name ye beg of one another, and the wombs (mothers); verily God over you doth watch.[5]

Nor was knowledge intended to be to them 'a fountain sealed.' 'The search after knowledge,' says the Prophet, 'is a duty for every Moslem man or woman.'

Thus we find respect for women inculcated by Mahomet, and moreover the privilege was granted them of perfect equality with men in the exercise of legal

---

4 *Sacred Books of the East*, edited by F. Max Muller, 9: 143.
5 Ibid., 6: 71.

functions. The laws of divorce were re-modelled by him, the husband's power to divorce was restricted, women could obtain a separation, irrevocable divorce was rendered rarer by the enactment that a woman thus rejected could not return to her husband unless she were first married and divorced by another, and four eye-witnesses were required before a wife could be convicted of unfaithfulness. A woman had a legal right over her own fortune and could dispose of it as she pleased. She could introduce into the marriage contract certain conditions to protect her interests in case of divorce; she had the right to vote and take part in theological and legal debates. What is even more important is that these privileges were not merely nominal. They were freely used by Moslem women centuries ago.

At the present day under Mahometan law the women possess privileges which compare very favourably with those enjoyed by their sex in other countries. An unmarried woman until she is of age is under parental control. After that, she is entitled to similar property rights with men. She shares with her brothers in the inheritance of her parents' property, in different but relative proportions; she cannot be married without her consent; a marriage settlement by the husband upon the wife is demanded and enforced by law; the husband is compelled to support his wife; he has no right to her goods and property, nor may he appropriate her earnings, or ill-treat her. If the legal condition of Turkish women be considered in conjunction with that of their sex in several European lands, it will readily be seen that technically it need not fear scrutiny. In France, for example, a woman is a minor in the eyes of the law. A married woman there cannot undertake any employment or appear before a court of justice unless her husband has first granted his consent. It is only since 1907 that she has been legally entitled to dispose of her own earnings. In Germany a husband can, if he wish, forbid his wife to engage in any business. In Italy a married woman cannot sign or draw a cheque on her own account for her own money; her testimony alone is not accepted in a court of law; she cannot engage in trade or dispose of her own property without her husband's consent; he has full power over her earnings, and she cannot plead in a court of law without his permission.

The Turkish woman, then, has the letter of the law on her own side. But with these apparent provisions in her favour, why have her old rights of social and civic freedom been pushed aside? Why does the practice differ so totally from the theory? Why has she been forced into an inferior position for so long that, except to the more enlightened, the idea of entering upon a useful social career presents but few attractions?

The reasons why her privileges so sadly fell into abeyance sprang from the change in her surroundings, which necessitated the privacy of women; the misinterpretations of the law by the Fathers of the Church, Sultans, and Khalifs, who for their own pleasure or profit opposed the emancipation of women; and the general lack of culture among the rank and file of the Mahometan people to-day.

What is the remedy? Here, again, we revert once more to the Turkish Princess's appeal to her countrywomen.

> Unfortunately [she says] the vast majority of Moslem women are in total ignorance of the history and laws of Islam, and it is just this very ignorance that has been the great stumbling-block which prevents them from climbing up again into the position of our celebrated ancestresses. Our former rights having fallen into desuetude renders our position impotent at the present time, but it rests entirely in the hands of all Moslem women who have sufficient self-respect to readjust the position they have lost and show plainly that they have at heart a really honest desire to fulfil all their duties in life. They must aid both by intellectual ability and by material support, and prove that they intend to regain possession of their civic and moral rights. These means are all clearly pointed out, and within the reach of all who are earnestly determined to succeed. The study of the Sheriah (the Moslem religious code) will give us the most solid support ... will arm us with the most cogent arguments in our favour, and will also guide our first steps in the struggle to regain our legal rights and lost liberty of action.

This Moslem lady is fully aware of the necessity for caution in such schemes of reform. She is resolved to value her privileges, once regained, so highly as to make the same good use of them as did her talented forebears, who seldom abused their liberties but kept within the bounds of freedom granted them by their civil and religious codes. Unless her country women are prepared to use their privileges by filling their lives with useful work and social service, she sees nothing but a source of danger in opening fresh callings to them. She feels the need to advance cautiously at this critical period in their history, lest exaggerated action might do more harm than good to their cause.

It is remarkable how this lady, speaking on behalf of her fellow-countrywomen in their seclusion, reflects the opinion of the moderate party in England at the present moment, those who feel glad that women's scope for action in the world is widening, but sometimes fear the result of over-enthusiasm. Scientists hold the same view. Sir Oliver Lodge declares that 'to rush blindly on without regard to past history and racial experience, and heedless of dangers ahead, is fanatical rather than heroic; it is to imitate the activity of the runaway horse which brings itself and all connected with it to destruction.'[6]

With regard to the adjustment of relations between men and women, the

---

6 *The Position of Woman, Actual and Ideal*, vol. 70, no. 416.

Princess gives a wise admonition to Mahometan mothers to train their children from their earliest days in mutual help, mutual surrender, mutual consideration, according to their respective natures which God has given them. The division of duties between the sexes should begin almost from the cradle. 'Accustom them,' she says, 'to look upon each other as comrades who in a reciprocal spirit of justice recognise the rights due to each.' In this the Princess sees the mother's great importance to the future welfare of her country, and she urges her to realise fully her responsibilities for the education of the next generation, emphasising the paramount *rôle* which the Mahometan religion assigns to maternal influence by quoting the saying of the Prophet, that 'One finds Paradise at the feet of his mother,' and also, 'If all your relations call upon you at the same moment, your first answer must be to your mother.'

Her recognition of the fundamental differences between the sexes suggests that the Princess as leader of her countrywomen's evolution would proceed along the lines laid down by modern scientists. The constitutional disparities between the normal man and woman are considered by biologists to be so clearly marked and so deeply rooted in nature, that any attempt to interfere with them would surely prove unsuccessful. What women should aim at is to seek out an education and an occupation which will make the most of the natural differences in her physical and mental constitution. This is the rule which prudent men observe in fitting themselves for a useful career. A man who is fond of manual occupation does not deliberately immure himself in a city office. If he does, it is a coercive measure, and the result to the State is a less efficient citizen. In the same way, a woman in trying to accomplish what a man can do better than herself is running contrary to nature and wasting her own peculiar talents. What she requires is not an identical occupation but equal opportunity with men. Her best interest will be served not by rivalling man in his own fields and becoming, most likely, at best but a poor imitation of man, but by making the most of her own innate differences to advance her along paths in which there is no question of biological inefficiency. The world requires the peculiar excellences of both man and woman to help it onward towards 'that one far-off Divine event to which the whole creation moves.' The work of the one is as indispensable as that of the other.

So the Eastern woman on her entry into the world of public life finds herself at once confronted with one of the greatest modern problems of the West, the apparent difficulty of reconciling the domestic life with a professional career for women. In both extremes, an exclusively domestic, maternal education, or an exclusively professional training, there would seem to be danger ahead alike for East and West. 'We cannot countenance a theory,' says Professor J. Arthur Thomson, 'which deliberately leaves maternity to the less intellectual

... The idea of leaving maternity to a docile and domesticated type of cow-like placidity, while the intellectuals run the world, is curiously non-biological.'[7] With this view the Princess is in perfect harmony, for she shows that she would decisively taboo any profession or calling having as its tendency the weakening of the maternal instinct. Her theories are in cordial agreement with Dr T.S. Clouston's dictum that 'psychologically, physiologically, and racially this [the maternal instinct] is the most unique, the most wonderful, and the most important thing in the world.'[8] Therefore the Eastern woman must be taught from the outset that the domestic life is fully on a par with the economically independent life outside the home.

Yet another most useful and essential piece of advice does the Princess bestow upon her countrywomen – that they should endeavour to train themselves and others in an practical ways, which will enable them to meet the vicissitudes of life and the caprice of fortune with undaunted mien. This practical training, she hopes, will be a preparation for life, to help her sisters to face troubles or difficulties with courage and resourcefulness. Here again the Princess puts forward what is a psychological fact attested by modern scientists – viz., the control of the emotions which the modern standard of practical education confers upon woman. There is no doubt that such mastery of the feelings and their expression will give woman an immense advantage which she has hitherto lacked in her contact with the world. A woman prepared by a sound, practical education is less liable to sudden impulse and unreasoning action, less prone to the dangerous play of emotions. So self-control, that great virtue of the East, is added also to the list of her qualities. Here also we see signs that the Princess would be the last to foster an unpractical, over-literary education, which, though exercising a refining, uplifting effect, is often by no means the best adapted to fit a woman to buffet with the world. An education, to be successful, must prepare its students for the life which they will be called upon to follow. If it does not achieve this end, it must be dubbed a failure.

The Princess describes the attitude of her countrymen and women towards the movement which she has at heart, and again the reader is struck by the similarity between East and West.

Among the ardent leaders of this reform [she writes] there is an *élite* who work calmly within the limits of the possible, and without making any remarkable manifestations in aid of our cause, are smoothing the way towards the eventual recovery of our rights. These leaders have to struggle in two opposite directions.

---

7 Ibid., 23.
8 Ibid., 107.

On the one hand, they must try to subdue the tactless enthusiasm of the majority of those who are co-operating with them, while on the other side they must fight against the nervous dread of some who fear the result of any great change, and who throw cold water on the aspirations of the ardent supporters of reform ... The effect of this nervousness is trying, and rather paralyses the efforts made by those who are thoroughly cognizant of the true meaning of liberty, and wish to realize its application, in the first instance, by raising the condition of their women-kind. The leading spirits of the movement are fully aware that the best wisdom is to be found in going by degrees. *Festina lente.* To get rid of customs and ideas long-rooted amongst us, we must prove by deeds, not words, that we believe these changes to be absolutely necessary, and therefore that they ought to be granted to us.

This holding back on the part of a section of the Turkish women is not surprising. Students of history will recall how some of the American slaves when granted emancipation did not care for the boon so long withheld. When Stein's legislation abolished serfdom after 1807, the Prussian peasants petitioned that they might be allowed to remain as they were, 'for who should care for them when they were sick and old?'[9]

In conclusion, the Princess once more points out the need to guard against a slavish imitation of Western ideas. The Oriental woman must show that she can pick out from Western customs those which are most suitable to Eastern environment, but she must borrow nothing that would tend in any way to lead her away from the laws of her own religion or to efface her own racial personality. By becoming a mere reflection of the Occidental woman she would lose more than she would gain.

That wide, free charity which is the greatest of all the virtues is present in every page of the Princess's appeal.

Those amongst us [she says] who are placed by birth or fortune in more advantageous circumstances in life should make the best use of our good, and instead of spending them on selfish pleasures, extend by their means a helping hand to those less well endowed, for, in the saying of the Prophet, 'that man who is most considerate to his kind is that favourite of God.' Not by material aid alone can we aid others, but by attempting from our more varied knowledge and experience to imbue to women who have not had these educational advantages with loftier ideals, and to create in them a desire to advance along the same road of learning by dint of

---

9 Bebel, *Woman, Past, Present, Future*, trans. P. Walther, 35.

patient and assiduous study. All of us, of course, ought to give from our purse, but there are many ways besides that of charity in which we women can aid the nation.

That they may prove the best possible mothers of their children, the Princess urges her country women to acquire knowledge. In this

there is no time to lose. Every moment spent in gaining instruction is a step in advance, and is therefore a stride in the direction of progress. Let us all study the history of Islam, and particularly that portion of its laws which refers to women. The laws of our country will be the greatest help to us in attaining even a superficial grasp of what ought to regulate and influence every act of our lives.

Nowadays, when respect for religion and authority seems to be weakening in so many quarters, this firm resolve of the Princess to keep within the bounds of what is permitted her by Divine and human ordinance must surely awaken admiration. None the less striking is her display of public spirit, and of that *camaraderie* with her sex which the latter has so often been accused of lacking.

The Princess, therefore, would thoroughly sympathise with a free educational policy for Turkish ladies, provided it does not offend against the rules of her religion, which she shows to be actually most favourable to her countrywomen, though centuries of misinterpretation have made her Eastern sisters forget the broad, noble sphere which the founder of their faith fully intended them to enjoy. She encourages her compatriots by mentioning the names of two Moslem ladies who have so far leapt 'the rotten pale of prejudice' as to study medicine and take their doctor's degree at St Petersburg. These two enterprising contemporaries are Gulsome Hanem and Abramanona Hanem, whose energy and perseverance, it is hoped, will spur their more apathetic countrywomen to shake off dull sloth, lay aside cramping conceptions, and fit themselves to undertake honourable careers. Such labour, on the part of women students will, she maintains, both procure them a life of self-respecting independence, and also enable them to be of some assistance to their fellow-beings.

One grieves to reflect upon the talents that have hitherto been wasted, the good brains stultified through lack of cultivation, and the progress arrested for centuries through ignorance, want of opportunity, and the dead weight of a hopeless inertia. And to think of all this continuing in the twentieth century, when other people are beginning to fly upward into space, while our women scarcely know how to place their feet on *terra firma*!

Thus this brave lady adjures her more lethargic sisters to abandon their inactive *dolce far niente* and come forth from their Commerian darkness into the light of day. But she would not have them as feeble moths, dazzled by the bright beams of an alluring dangerous light. Rather they are to keep that light as a beacon before them, to illumine the rough places of the unknown pathway which many will, if but a little help and sympathy be granted them, so gladly and fearlessly follow.

Throughout this article I have endeavoured to make no general statements of my own, but have purposely confined myself to giving the views and arguments of authorities upon several aspects of the evolution that is quietly taking place amid the harems of the Turkish ladies. I have supported the Princess's points by quotations from the Mahometan religious code, and from contemporary men of note in science and administration. I must now leave the women of England to judge whether the cause be worthy of their friendly aid, and whether they are willing to stretch forth a hand in loving sympathy and friendly interest to their veiled sisters in the East.

[Source: *The Nineteenth Century* no. 416 (October 1911): 762–94.]

Carrie Chapman Catt (1859–1947) became involved with the cause of women's suffrage in Iowa during the late 1880s. She joined the Women's Christian Temperance Union, and later became a member of the National American Woman Suffrage Association (NAWSA) and was twice elected its president (1900–4 and 1915–20). She helped to found the International Woman Suffrage Alliance (IWSA) in 1902, serving as its president from 1904 until 1923.

Carrie Chapman Catt
Egypt (1912)

If the veil is the outward and visible sign of the degree of seclusion of Mohammedan women, one must conclude that the position of Egyptian women is being liberalized. In Palestine and Syria the entire face is covered around the head, holding the veil securely in place. The veil itself is black, thick and unusually heavily figured. Not a hand or arm is displayed and no passer by could possibly detect whether a veiled woman was old or young. In Egypt arms and hands are not concealed and the veil is white, very thin and fastened over the top of the ears so that it falls just below the eyes. The head-covering is loosely worn, often revealing the ears and side face, as well as eyes and forehead. The veil is often dropped to the tip of the nose and faces are not infrequently uncovered in public places. Indeed, one gets the impression that among the upper classes the veil is no longer an emblem of seclusion, but a fashion which is not a bit more ridiculous than many of those which come from Paris. If a woman is good-looking the white veil enhances her beauty, and if she is not, effectively conceals her ugliness – facts which the young women undoubtedly fully appreciate.

To the newcomer the unveiling of the Moslem woman seems the obvious first step towards an improvement of their position, but further acquaintance leads me to think that the veil is only an unimportant symptom of a condition. The seclusion of women and the wearing of the veil is not in response to commands of the Koran, but are customs which are supposed to have grown out of the long religious wars when no woman's life of virtue was held sacred. Christian women were as carefully secluded and throughout this Eastern country wore the veil. A young Syrian lady told me she remembered her grandmother who never failed to wear her veil upon the street and in church, although the custom had so far disappeared, that her mother was unveiled. (The Copts are the direct descendants of the old Egyptians who have been Christians since the days of St Mark.) Even yet the Copt women of Egypt wear the veil. It is evident that the veil will soon take its departure, but it is not so easy a thing to unveil as it appears to the outsider. For centuries women have been rigidly secluded within the home, and there they have lived their entire existence. Now, in Egypt as elsewhere, the home loom and spinning wheel have given way to bazaars full of factory-woven goods of endless variety. The women follow naturally and groups of them may be seen in any of the native bazaars, chatting and bargaining with lively tongues. All this seems very inconsequential to us, but so new is it to this Eastern world, that such women are subjected to annoying remarks by men sitting on the street, such as: 'O, what a beautiful figure,' 'I wish I could peep under the veil,' 'You better go home and mind the children,' 'Does your husband know where you are going?' etc. Women who can afford a carriage will not walk on the streets on account of the insults certain to be aimed at them. The better educated women do not approve of the veil and are much dissatisfied with the conditions which compel them to wear it. For the present, however, it is a protection which will doubtless continue, until the men of the land have been taught to respect women more than they do now.

[Source: *Jus Suffragii: International Women Suffrage News* 6, no. 8 (1912): 76. Available through the Gerritsen Collection.]

Margaret Cousins (1878–1954), together with Hannah Sheehy-Skeffington, founded the Irish Women's Franchise League in 1908; her participation in women's suffrage demonstrations in London in 1910 led to a month's imprisonment in Holloway prison, and in 1913 she was jailed again in Tullamore for suffrage activism in Ireland; she went on a hunger strike to secure her release. In 1915 Cousins moved with her husband James to India, where in 1917 she co-founded the Women's Indian Association with Annie Besant and Dorothy Jinarajadasa. Cousins was appointed the first woman magistrate in India in 1922, and in 1927 she co-founded the All-India Women's Conference.

Margaret E. Cousins
From *The Awakening of Asian Womanhood* (1922)

Notwithstanding the immense extent of the continent of Asia, and the great number and variety of the races inhabiting it, it is very remarkable how, from time to time, it responds as one entity to a single well-defined current of thought. History shows us how a wave of religious revival has swept over it from end to end at one time, a wave of artistic expression at another time, of political weakness at still another; and at the present time there is rising in the hearts of Asian womanhood a mighty wave of desire for freedom.

From Palestine to Japan it displays itself. It whispers its presence amongst the Moslem women; it shouts of itself along the streets of Canton; and it wins its victory in South India. Everywhere there is a shaking off of shackles – and everywhere it is from within that the effort comes to get rid of them. It is not Westerners who are coming along and, from outside, striking off fetters. No! the women of Asia are, of their own initiative, and through their own growing surge of desire for self-expression, pressing against their barriers and breaking them down. People hardly realise how much activity is going on in these directions. The feeling shows itself in different ways in different countries. In one place women rebel against veils; in another country, or part of a country, they begin to make use of umbrellas and sandals; in another they rebel against the binding of the feet; in others they ask for educational facilities or for political recognition.

Intercommunication between the various countries of Asia is comparatively small. The Indian woman, as a rule, knows much more about the women of Britain or America, thousands of miles away from her, than of the Chinese women who are her next-door neighbours. Yet a fair amount of information has been gleaned from various sources by the Women's Indian Association about the details of the growing feminist movement in Asia, and progressive men and women everywhere will no doubt be glad to have it brought to their notice in a collected form.

Reviewing broadly the peoples which comprise Asian womanhood, the chief are – the Muhammadan, the Jewish, the Indian, the Burmese, the Chinese, and the Japanese. Amongst the Muhammadan women, whether of Asia Minor, Arabia, Persia, Turkistan, or India, the stirrings of a new life are discernible, the movement for removing veils being so strong in Teheran among the Persian women that a deputation of well-known women waited some time ago on their Prime Minister to request him to help them in their attempts at emancipation. The Armenian women have volunteered to fill administrative posts in order to release their men for active military service in an army which the Armenians have mobilised to oppress the Turks. The Republic of Armenia has been the first to appoint a woman as a Consul, having constituted an Armenian widow its Consul to the Empire of Japan. So advanced is education for women and girls in Afghanistan that a Women's University for the study of medicine has been built in Kabul, and has five hundred women students in attendance. The Turkish women have been forced out of their very strict *purdah* by the rigours and hardships of war, and the poor things are now in a very deplorable state, preliminary doubtless to a freer life in the future.

Twenty-five women representatives of different countries in the Near and Middle East attended a World Conference of Communist Women at Moscow in 1921. The presence of these Asian women, who had surmounted almost incredible difficulties in journeying thither, created a very profound impression. One of them, Tursum Baya, a member of the Executive Committee of the Soviet Republic of Turkistan, replied to greetings on their behalf as follows: 'I greet the International Women's Conference from the women of Turkistan. The struggle of the Russian proletariat has opened the doors to the women of the East. We who have been slaves of slaves are now entering a life of freedom. We join hands with you in a common cause.' The Conference made a great impression in Europe.

The women in Palestine have started a Jewish Women's Equal Rights Association to combat the possibility of women being subjected to the authority of the Rabbinical Courts – courts which apparently scarcely recognise that a woman has a separate existence at all. According to the orthodox Jewish teaching, a woman cannot be a witness, or the guardian of her children, nor can she inherit, or own her own earnings. She remains all her life under the tutelage of her father, husband or brother. The Jewish women have sent forward a memorandum to the Government praying that they may not have to come under the jurisdiction of these courts as they cannot submit to such a degradation.

Turning then to India, one finds that, though the percentage of education is appallingly low, the tradition of Indian law leaves women very free to take any position for which they show themselves capable. No Indian political organisations were at any time closed to women. Women have at every stage of Indian history taken high positions in their country's public service. Springing from their religious philosophy there is fundamentally a belief in sex equality, and this shows itself when critical periods demand it. This has been clearly shown during the movement of the past ten years for self-government. Women have had their share in all the local Conferences and in the National Congress. No one who was present can easily forget the sight of the platform at the Calcutta Congress of 1917 when three women leaders, Mrs Annie Besant, President of the Congress, Mrs Sarojini Naidu, representative of the Hindu women, and Bibi Amman, mother of the Ali brothers and representative of the Muslim women, sat side by side, peeresses of such men-leaders (also present) as Tilak, Gandhi and Tagore, and receiving equal honour with them. [...]

The grant of the suffrage to Indian women will undoubtedly be a driving force in enabling them to secure greater educational facilities for themselves, and when education becomes compulsory and has extended its period of years, the future of India will be rosy, indeed. An incident will illustrate the spirit of the new life in women. When a group of Muhammadan women went recently to vote at a South Indian Municipal election, though a special polling booth had been arranged for women with a woman registrar of votes, these women would not be content until the male superintendent of the polling station came and personally guaranteed that their votes were legitimate and would be effective for their candidate!

The Non-co-operation movement is playing a large part in the awakening of Indian women. The wives of imprisoned leaders become themselves leaders and public speakers, Presidents of Conferences, organisers of meetings, etc. Large numbers of women are collectors for the funds of the movement, and everywhere women encourage in all ways its policy of *swadeshi* (home manufacture).

It is quite probable that one day the women of India will lead the women of the East in all public movements, as they are the first to get their hands on the helm of government. [...]

In order to measure adequately the significance of the various attempts at revolt that are taking place throughout the womanhood of Asia, one must remember how different has been and still is the point of view in the East regarding womanhood from that in the West. Throughout hundreds of centuries the Eastern woman has fitted into the Eastern scheme of things, not as the companion, chum, partner, co-equal of man; not as the self-chosen, to be wooed and won by the lover; not as the independent soul working out her own salvation, but as the passive, secondary, remote, dependent, usually ignorant but necessary female, whose purpose in life was fulfilled only through her ability to produce sons – and daughters as a concession. The Eastern view gives little or no value to a woman as an individual soul; therefore it is that the young widow is considered such a waste product and is so despised. But to the woman *as mother*, unlimited honour is accorded in theory, and often, though not always, in practice. As marriage is the gateway to freedom for French women, and economic independence for American, so is motherhood for all Eastern women. The roots of this honour of the mother-woman are deeply imbedded in the religions of Asia, all of which preach a doctrine of spiritual entail (through a son) more stringent and binding than any merely material entail of land or title. [...]

All over Asia there is a natural shrinking in women from publicity; there is intense shyness; there is a great deal of self-consciousness and sex-consciousness, out of which education alone will lift the women. Although the *purdah* has been drawn in many cases, or but a thin one still exists, its memory and its shadow hang over the actions of all Eastern women. For instance, the courage needed by an Indian woman to walk through a street, carrying her baby and her book, to an afternoon class for continuing the lessons which were cut off from her at twelve years old, is as great as that needed by Englishwomen to go and serve on the battlefield. The Eastern woman is, moreover, unaccustomed to any form of individual initiative. All her life she is accustomed to having a number of women around her. No action is private. The joint family system sees to that. It takes a remarkably strong-willed individual to hew out her own way when every detail of it has to pass in review before a score of interested relatives, all having little to talk about except family gossip.

These factors, and many others of a similar nature, have to be borne in mind as the background to every effort for progress that is being made by women right across Asia. That the same movement for emancipation is displaying itself from end to end of the continent without much impact from the West, is a proof that Asia is one by links of religion, fundamental custom, temperament, attitude to life, and, above all, by its ideal of women.

[Source: *The Awakening of Asian Womanhood* (Madras: Ganesh, 1922), 1–6, 7–8, 13–14, 15–16.]

Adelaide Casely Hayford (1868–1960) was born of mixed Fante and English descent, in Sierra Leone, which was at that point still a British colony. She moved to England when she was still quite young. Twenty-five years after leaving Sierra Leone, Casely Hayford made a journey back to her homeland with her sisters, after which she met and married Joseph Ephraim Casely Hayford, a staunch Pan-Africanist. Along with her niece, she would spend the rest of her life travelling, attempting to correct mistaken American beliefs about Africa, and raising funds for a Girls' Vocational School. Although Casely Hayford was strongly and outspokenly opposed to colonialism, the British authorities awarded her the King's Silver Jubilee Medal in 1935, and the Order of the British Empire in 1950.

Adelaide Casely Hayford
A Girls' School in West Africa (1926)

The World War left much misery and desolation in its wake. But in spite of its destructive force it created one glorious, outstanding feature – the worldwide desire for expansion and development on better educational lines. In West Africa this influence was felt in a marked degree, and in the spring of 1920 my niece, the late Kathleen Easmon Simango, and I became obsessed with the idea that the education of our girls especially was not all that could be desired. While the mission schools were doing splendid work on academic lines, the practical, useful arts of life were being neglected. Very little was being done to qualify the girls for the responsibilities of motherhood, the care of children, the comfort of the husband, and the duties of the home.

At the back of my mind, too, was a remark of one of my own countrymen who had quite recently visited our home, and who, I felt, was voicing the opinion of thousands of others. Upon observing some draperies and curtains of native art work decorating the room, he had exclaimed, 'Well! I never thought much of those things, but they look quite beautiful in this room.'

'But of course they are beautiful,' I responded. 'Whatever did you think?'

'I never thought anything at all about them in that way. I did not think that anything made by black people was beautiful. I thought all beauty came from Europe.'

Instantly my eyes were opened to the fact that the education meted out to us had, either consciously or unconsciously, taught us to despise ourselves, and that our immediate need was an education which would instil into us a love of country, a pride of race, an enthusiasm for a black man's capabilities, and a genuine admiration for Africa's wonderful art work. We needed an education more adapted to our requirements, which, while assimilating all that was good in European education, would help us to maintain our natural heritage of African individuality, and to become the best type of African we could be.

In my mind's eye I could see a school in which girls, instead of blindly copying European fashions, would be dressed in attractive native garments which would enhance their personal charms. I could see them sitting in homes which combined European order, method, and cleanliness with the beauty of native basket furniture, artwork, and drapes. I could see the young mothers teaching the little children on their knees that to be black was not a curse nor a disgrace; that the color scheme of the races was part of God's divine plan, and that just as it was impossible to make a rainbow without the primary colors, so it was impossible to make a world without the Negro. I could hear the young mothers teaching their sons the glory of black citizenship, rather than encouraging them to bewail the fact that they were not white. I could hear the native musical instruments, developed on scientific European lines discoursing sweet music in the place of wheezy harmoniums. I could image the artistic youth of the hereafter painting pictures depicting black faces rather than white ones. I could visualize the listless, lethargic, educated town girl of today, through the medium of equipped gymnasiums and trained physical-culture teachers, enjoying the energy and vitality of her grandmother who thought nothing of spending days hoeing fields or of carrying loads as weighty as any man's. I could picture the sons and daughters of Africa's race 'looking the whole world in the face,' without any apology whatsoever for the color of their skin, and with such self-respect as to command the respect of all other nations.

With the imagination so vividly stirred, my niece and I decided to go to America for the purpose of visiting the schools and, if possible, to raise enough funds to return home and start a vocational school along these lines. Backed up by a few conscientious well-wishers, with a very strong faith and a very diminutive purse, we arrived in New York in August 1920. America, both black and white, opened her arms and took us in, and whatever the future may hold in store, nothing can ever obliterate the memory of that visit. The right hand of fellowship, the kindly spirit, the desire to co-operate, the spontaneous generosity, the courtesy and friendliness that surrounded us wherever we went, have made an impression on my mind which time can never efface.

After nearly two years in the United States my niece left me to be married. But this did not incapacitate her for a life of usefulness. It simply meant transferring her field of labor from West to East Africa by the side of her missionary husband, Kamba Simango.

I returned home alone with only $1000 to the good but with a fixed determination to open a school at all costs. A large, fairly commodious house was placed at the disposal of the executive committee for a year, rent free. Opposition was rife, and a prophet was without honor in his own country. Sierra Leone, the smallest as well as the most conservative of the British West African colonies, wanted no innovations which would disturb the even tenor of her literary curriculum. The adverse criticism was enough to daunt the stoutest heart, but we forged steadily ahead.

Our original intention was to take girls who had received their literary training elsewhere for a practical course in home economics, but local conditions had to be considered, and it was found advisable to combine the training of the head with the training of the hand. On October 1, 1923, our little school opened with fourteen small children ranging in age from five to nine years. My heart sank as I saw my pet project vanish into thin air, but after the morning session I retired for a private communication with the Great Heart of the Eternal who pointed out that He was doing the very best He could for us by giving us children to train from the very beginning, so as to guide their little footsteps in the way they should go. I immediately set out to qualify myself for kindergarten and junior-grade work, assisted by two young teachers.

The pictures of the school's growth speak for themselves. Unfortunately we have not been able to carry out our plans as we would wish. Even the idea of wearing native apparel has met with such stern disapproval that for the present it has had to be abandoned. From the very first we have been fearfully handicapped by lack of funds. Although His Excellency, the Governor of the Colony, has recognized our work by nominating me a member of his educational board, financial help could not be obtained from the Government until a school had been established for two years – so that door was closed. Then as the people are desperately poor, and the few who have amassed a little money by trading have not yet fully recognized the importance of an education more suited to their needs, the fees are so small that they pay only one month's expenses out of every three. Hence the financial burden has been stupendous, and I should like to take this opportunity of thanking those American friends who have held up our hands so generously ever since we started.

In August 1924 our exchequer was so low that we had no funds to meet the salaries for the month. It was holiday time and as I sat drinking a cup of tea in the quiet solitude I heard the postman's knock. I opened the door and received a fat letter with the New York postmark. In it was a check for $1000 from an American lady whose heart is as large as her purse, and whose sympathies seem to stretch to the very ends of the earth. In this way God has helped us all the time so that we have been enabled to keep our heads above water.

We call ourselves a 'Vocational School,' but hitherto we have hardly been able to live up to our calling for lack of proper accommodations, proper equipment, and properly trained teachers, and unless we are to demonstrate this type of training on really methodical, well-organized lines, it will be very difficult to impress the public with the advantages to be derived from it.

Of course, vocational work in civilized countries has a far greater significance and scope than anything we can do in Africa at present. It is a rule rather than an exception that a girl should be so trained as to be capable of earning her own living. But it will serve our purpose if we can only train the African girl of today for the highest vocation of all – the vocation of motherhood tomorrow. Home life is the bedrock foundation upon which all rational life is built. Hence we need mothers whose duties to their husbands and the training of their children will form the main objective of their existence; mothers whose brains are sufficiently developed to take an intelligent interest in the doings of the whole world and Africa in particular; mothers who are so imbued with the spirit of Christ – the spirit of integrity, honesty, sincerity, service, and patriotism – that their children must leave their mark on the Africa of the future; mothers who are so qualified for their duties as to make the home the most sacred spot on earth. We feel that if we can do nothing more than to improve the home life of our country our labor will not have been in vain.

There is one phase of our work which has found very little favor in the eyes of the Sierra Leone public, possibly because we as a people do not fully realize its significance – the development of native arts and crafts. At present this work is entirely in the hands of illiterates. Hitherto it has received very little encouragement in the town schools; hence the hands of the educated populace have lost their cunning. Our aboriginal women who do beautiful basketry cannot be relied upon for systematic labor. Consequently I sent one of my teachers into the Protectorate to get a first-hand knowledge of this craft, with the result that at the Government Educational Exhibit held in December 1924 our school came off with third prize. My sister, Mrs Farrell Easmon, mother of the late Mrs Simango, who has undergone a thorough training in weaving, has recently returned home and is most anxious to give her services to the school for the development of the native cloth industry, but here again we have been handicapped by lack of equipment.

The school has had somewhat of a set-back during the last year owing to the fact that a good many parents were desirous that their children work for public examinations which meant devoting the whole of the time to literary work, leaving none whatsoever for domestic science. We felt, however, that we should be filling a far greater need by adhering to our original plan of combining a trained hand with a trained head, especially as there are mission schools already doing admirable work along literary lines. This decision has meant a decline in the number of pupils but I am quite confident time will show we have adopted a wise course.

In a country where there are no normal schools for the training of women teachers the personnel of the staff becomes a mighty problem. It was my intention, in spite of indifferent health, to visit America this spring with a view not only of laying our cause before its generous-hearted public, but also to try to get two thoroughly trained Negro teachers who would be willing to give us three years' service while two of our own girls were being trained in America to take their places. But with my plans practically mature for action the doctors absolutely forbid my undertaking any such strenuous work for the present. My dear niece, Kathleen Simango, passed away on July 27, 1924. However she 'being dead yet speaketh,' and her call to higher service has been a great stimulus and incentive, in spite of advanced years, for renewed energy, further effort, and deeper consecration on my part, in the work for the uplift of the women of my beloved home-land.

[Source: *The Southern Workman* (October 1926): 449–56.]

Katherine Mayo (1867–1940) was a US journalist and social historian known for the muckraking style that informs this, her most famous work, *Mother India* (1927), which Gandhi pronounced 'the report of a drain inspector.' Many of Mayo's books aimed at social reform and were marked by her anti-immigrant, anti-black, and anti-Catholic politics. Mayo was a supporter of the Asian Exclusion Acts, US laws dating from the late nineteenth century which sharply restricted immigration from Asia and Africa.

Katherine Mayo
From *Mother India*: 'Behind the Veil' (1927)

The chapters preceding have chiefly dealt with the Hindu, who forms, roughly, three-quarters of the population of India. The remaining quarter, the Muhammadans, differ considerably as between the northern element, whose blood contains a substantial strain of the old conquering Persian and Afghan stock, and the southern contingent, who are, for the larger part, descendants of Hindu converts retaining, in greater or less degree, many of the qualities of Hindu character.

   In some respects, Muhammadan women enjoy great advantages over their Hindu sisters. Conspicuous among such advantages is their freedom from infant marriage and from enforced widowhood, with the train of miseries evoked by each. Their consequent better inheritance, supported by a diet greatly superior to that of the Hindu, brings them to the threshold of a maturity sturdier than that of the Hindu type. Upon crossing that threshold the advantage of Muhammadan women of the better class is, however, forfeit. For they pass into practical life-imprisonment within the four walls of the home.

   Purdah, as this system of women's seclusion is called, having been introduced by the Muslim conquerors and by them observed, soon came to be regarded by higher caste Hindus as a hall-mark of social prestige. These, there-fore, adopted it as a matter of mode. And today, as a consequence of the grow-ing prosperity of the country, this medieval custom, like the interdiction of re-marriage of virgin widows among the Hindus, seems to be actually on the increase. For every woman at the top of the scale whom western influence sets free, several humbler but prospering sisters, socially ambitious, deliberately assume the bonds.

That view of women which makes them the proper loot of war was probably the origin of the custom of *purdah*. When a man has his women shut up within his own four walls, he can guard the door. Taking Indian evidence on the ques-tion, it appears that in some degree the same necessity exists today. In a part of India where *purdah* but little obtains, I observed the united request of several Hindu ladies of high position that the Amusement Club for English and Indian ladies to which they belong reduce the minimum age required for membership to twelve, or, better, to eleven years. This, they frankly said, was because they were afraid to leave their daughters of that age at home, even for one afternoon, without a mother's eye and accessible to the men of the family.

Far down the social scale the same anxiety is found. The Hindu peasant villager's wife will not leave her girl child at home alone for the space of an hour, being practically sure that, if she does so, the child will be ruined. I dare not affirm that this condition everywhere obtains. But I can affirm that it was brought to my attention by Indians and by Occidentals, as regulating daily life in widely separated sections of the country.

No typical Muhammadan will trust another man in his *zenana*, simply because he knows that such liberty would be regarded as opportunity. If there be a handful of Hindus of another persuasion, it is almost or quite invariably because they are reflecting some part of the western attitude toward women; and this they do without abatement of their distrust of their fellow-men. Inter-course between men and women which is both free and innocent is a thing well-nigh incredible to the Indian mind.

In many parts of India the precincts of the *zenana*, among better-class Hin-dus, are therefore closed and the women cloistered within. And the cloistered Muhammadan women, if they emerge from their seclusion, do so under con-cealing veils, or in concealing vehicles. The Rolls-Royce of a Hindu reigning prince's wife may sometimes possess dark window-glasses, through which the lady looks out at ease, herself unseen. But the wife of a prosperous Muham-madan cook, if she go out on an errand, will cover herself from the crown of the head downward in a thick cotton shroud, through whose scant three inches of mesh-covered eye-space she peers half-blinded.

I happened to be present at a '*purdah* party' – a party for veiled ladies attended by ladies only – in a private house in Delhi when tragedy hovered nigh. The Indian ladies had all arrived, stepping heavily swathed from their close-curtained motor-cars. Their hostess, wife of a high English official, herself had met them on her threshold; for, out of deference to the custom of the *purdah*, all the men-servants had been banished from the house, leaving Lady — alone to conduct her guests to the drawing-room. There they had laid aside their swathings. And now, in all the grace of their native costumes, they were sitting about the room, gently conversing with the English ladies invited to meet them. The senior Indian lady easily dominated her party. She was far advanced in years, they said, and she wore long, light blue velvet trousers, tight from the knee down, golden slippers, a smart little jacket of silk brocade, and a beautifully embroidered Kashmir shawl draped over her head.

We went in to tea. And again Lady —, single-handed, except for the help of the English ladies, moved back and forth, from pantry to tea-table, serving her Indian guests.

Suddenly from the veranda without, arose a sound of incursion – a rushing – men's voices, women's voices, loud, louder, coming close. The hostess with a face of dismay dashed for the door. Within the room panic prevailed. Their great white mantles being out of reach, the Indian ladies ran into the corners, turning their backs, while the English, understanding their plight, stood before them to screen them as best might be.

Meantime, out on the veranda, more fracas had arisen – then a sudden silence and a whir of retreating wheels. Lady — returned, panting, all apologies and relief.

'I am *too* sorry! But it is all over now. Do forgive it! Nothing shall frighten you again,' she said to the trembling Indian ladies; and, to the rest of us: 'It was the young Roosevelts come to call. They didn't know!'

It was in the talk immediately following that one of the youngest of the Indian ladies exclaimed: 'You find it difficult to like our *purdah*. But we have known nothing else. We lead a quiet, peaceful, protected life within our own homes. And, with men as they are, we should be miserable, terrified, outside.'

But one of the ladies of middle age expressed another mind: 'I have been with my husband to England,' she said, speaking quietly to escape the others' ears. 'While we were there he let me leave off *purdah*, for women are respected in England. So I went about freely, in streets and shops and galleries and gardens and to the houses of friends, quite comfortable always. No one frightened or disturbed me and I had much interesting talk with gentlemen as well as ladies. Oh, it was wonderful – a paradise! But here – here there is nothing. I must stay within the *zenana*, keeping strict *purdah*, as becomes our rank, seeing no one but the women and my husband. We see nothing. We know nothing.

We have nothing to say to each other. We quarrel. It is *dull*. But they,' nodding surreptitiously toward the oldest woman, 'will have it so. It is only because of our hostess that such as she would come here today. More they would never consent to. And they know how to make life horrible for us in each household, if we offer to relax an atom of the *purdah* law.'

Then, looking from face to face, one saw the illustration of the talk – the pretty, blank features of the novices; the unutterable listlessness and fatigue of those of the speaker's age; the sharp-eyed, iron-lipped authority of the old.

The report of the Calcutta University Commission says:[1]

All orthodox Bengali women of the higher classes, whether Hindu or Muslim, pass at an early age behind the *purdah*, and spend the rest of their lives in the complete seclusion of their homes, and under the control of the eldest woman of the household. This seclusion is more strict among the Musalmans than among the Hindus ... A few westernized women have emancipated themselves, ... [but] they are regarded by most of their countrywomen as denationalized.

Bombay, however, practises but little *purdah*, largely, no doubt, because of the advanced status and liberalizing influence of the Parsi ladies; and in the Province of Madras it is as a rule peculiar only to the Muhammadans and the wealthy Hindus. From two Hindu gentlemen, both trained in England to a scientific profession, I heard that they themselves had insisted that their wives quit *purdah*, and that they were bringing up their little daughters in a European school. But their wives, they added, unhappy in what seemed to them too great exposure, would be only too glad to resume their former sheltered state. And, viewing things as they are, one can scarcely escape the conclusion that much is to be said on that side. One frequently hears, in India and out of it, of the beauty of the sayings of the Hindu masters on the exalted position of women. One finds often quoted such passages as the precept of Manu:

Where a woman is not honoured
Vain is sacrificial rite.

But, as Mr Gandhi tersely sums it up: 'What is the teaching worth, if their practice denies it?'[2]

One consequence of *purdah* seclusion is its incubation of tuberculosis. Dr

---

1 Vol. 2, part 1, pp. 4–5.
2 Statement to the author, Sabarmati, Ahmedabad, 17 March 1926.

Arthur Lankester[3] has shown that among the *purdah*-keeping classes the mortality of women from tuberculosis is terribly high. It is also shown that, among persons living in the same locality and of the same habits and means, the men of the *purdah*-keeping classes display a higher incidence of death from tuberculosis than do those whose women are less shut in.

The Health Officer for Calcutta declares in his report for 1917:

> In spite of the improvement in the general death-rate of the city, the death-rate amongst females is still more than 40 per cent higher than amongst males ... Until it is realized that the strict observance of the *purdah* system in a large city, except in the case of the very wealthy who can afford spacious homes standing in their own grounds, necessarily involves the premature death of a large number of women, this standing reproach to the city will never be removed.

Dr Andrew Balfour, Director of the London School of Hygiene and Tropical Medicine, in pointing out how perfectly the habits of the Indian peoples favour the spread of the disease, speaks of 'the system by which big families live together; the *purdah* custom relegating women to the dark and dingy parts of the house; the early marriages, sapping the vitality of thousands of the young; the pernicious habit of indiscriminate spitting.'[4] These, added to dirt, bad sanitation, confinement, lack of air and exercise, make a perfect breeding-place for the White Death. Between nine hundred thousand and one million persons, it is estimated, die annually of tuberculosis in India.[5]

It has been further estimated that forty million Indian women, Muhammadan and Hindu, are today in *purdah*.[6] In the opinion, however, of those experienced officers whom I could consult, this estimate, if it is intended to represent the number of women kept so strictly cloistered that they never leave their apartments nor see any male save husband and son, is probably three times too high. Those who never see the outer world, from their marriage day till the day of their death, number by careful estimate of minimum and maximum between 11,250,000 and 17,290,000 persons.

As to the mental effect of the *purdah* system upon those who live under it, one may leave its characterization to Indian authorities.

---

3 Arthur Lankester, *Tuberculosis in India* (London: M.D. Butterworth & Co., 1920), 140.
4 Dr Andrew Balfour and Dr H.H. Scott Collins, *Health Problems of the Empire* (London, 1924), 286.
5 Ibid., 285.
6 The Bishop of Dornakal, *India and Missions*.

Says Dr N. N. Parakh, the Indian physician:[7] 'Ignorance and the *purdah* system have brought the women of India to the level of animals. They are unable to look after themselves, nor have they any will of their own. They are slaves to their masculine owners.'[8]

Said that outstanding Swarajist leader, Lala Lajpat Rai, in his Presidential address to the Bindu Mahasabha Conference held in Bombay in December, 1925:

> The great feature of present-day Hindu life is passivity. 'Let it be so' sums up all their psychology, individual and social. They have got into the habit of taking things lying down. They have imbibed this tendency and this psychology and this habit from their mothers. It seems as if it was in their blood ... Our women labour under many handicaps. It is not only ignorance and superstition that corrode their intelligence, but even physically they are a poor race ... Women get very little open air and almost no exercise. How on earth is the race, then, to improve and become efficient? A large number of our women develop consumption and die at an early age. Such of them as are mothers, infect their children also. Segregation of cases affected by tuberculosis is almost impossible ... There is nothing so hateful as a quarrelsome, unnecessarily assertive, impudent, ill-mannered woman, but even if that were the only road which the Hindu woman must traverse in order to be an efficient, courageous, independent and physically fit mother, I would prefer it to the existing state of things.

At this point, the practical experience of a school-mistress, the English principal of a Calcutta girls' college, may be cited. Dated eight years later than the Report of the Calcutta Health Officer already quoted, it concerns the daughters of the most progressive and liberal of Bengal's families.[9]

> They dislike exercise and take it only under compulsion. They will not go into the fresh air if they can avoid doing so. The average student is very weak. She needs good food, exercise, and often remedial gymnastics. The chest is contracted, and the spine often curved. She has no desire for games ... We want the authority ... to compel the student to take those remedies which will help her to grow into a woman.

---

7 *Legislative Assebly Debates*, vol. 3, part 1, p. 881.

8 Cf., however, ibid., pp. 77, 80, 109, 116, and passim.

9 Sister Mary Victoria, principal of the Diocesan College for Girls, *Fifth Quinquennial Review of the Progress of Education in Bengal*, paragraphs 521–4.

But the introduction of physical training as a help to the bankrupt physiques of India's girls is thus far only a dream of the occidental intruder. Old India will not have it so.

> The Hindu father is prone to complain that he does not want his daughter turned into a *nautch* girl. She has to be married into one of a limited number of families; and there is always a chance of one of the old ladies exclaiming, 'This girl has been taught to kick her legs about in public. Surely such a shameless one is not to be brought into our house!'[10]

'It is, indeed, only among the orthodox,' says the authority quoting this testimony, 'that this kind of objection is taken. But the orthodox are the majority.'[11]

Under the heading, 'Thou Shalt Do NO Murder,' the Oxford Mission of Calcutta printed, in its weekly journal of February 20, 1926, an editorial beginning as follows:

> A few years ago we published an article with the above heading in which was vividly described by a woman writer the appalling destruction of life and health which was going on in Bengal behind the *purdah* and in *zenanas* amongst the women herded there. We thought that the revelations then made, based on the health officer's reports, would bring to us a stream of indignant letters demanding instant reform. The effect amongst menfolk was entirely *nil*. Apparently not a spark of interest was roused. An article condemning the silly credulity of the use of charms and talismans at once evokes criticism, and the absurdities of superstition are vigorously defended even by men who are graduates. But not a voice was raised in horror at the fact that for every male who dies of tuberculosis in Calcutta five females die.

Yet among young western-educated men a certain abstract uneasiness begins to appear concerning things as they are. After they have driven the Occident out of India, many of them say, they must surely take up this matter of women. Not often, however, does one find impatience such as that of Abani Mohan Das Gupta, of Calcutta, expressed in the journal just quoted.

> I shudder to think about the condition of our mothers and sisters in the 'harem' ... From early morn till late at night they are working out the same routine throughout the whole of their lives without a murmur, as if they are patience

---

10 The Inspectress for Eastern Bengal, *Calcutta University Commission Report*, vol. 2, part 1, p. 23.

11 Ibid., 24.

incarnate. There are many instances where a woman has entered the house of her husband at the time of the marriage and did not leave it until death had carried her away. They are always in harness as if they have no will or woe but only to suffer – suffer without any protest … I appeal to young Indians to unfurl their flag for the freedom of women. Allow them their right … Am I crying in the wilderness?

Bengal is the seat of bitterest political unrest – the producer of India's main crop of anarchists, bomb-throwers and assassins. Bengal is also among the most sexually exaggerated regions of India; and medical and police authorities in any country observe the link between that quality and 'queer' criminal minds – the exhaustion of normal avenues of excitement creating a thirst and a search in the abnormal for gratification. But Bengal is also the stronghold of strict *purdah*, and one cannot but speculate as to how many explosions of eccentric crime in which the young politicals of Bengal have indulged, were given the detonating touch by the unspeakable flatness of their *purdah*-deadened home lives, made the more irksome by their own half-digested dose of foreign doctrines.

Edith Emily Jones (1875–1952) was born in London, England. In 1904 she married Rev. John Jones and travelled with him to Australia, where he became head of the Church of England mission. The couple toured Australia promoting mission work with Aborigines. Edith's energetic approach to social and political reform soon led her to form the first branches of the women's auxiliary of the mission board, and she campaigned successfully for women's greater involvement through their direct appointment to the board. Jones served on the executive of the National Council of Women and as a member of its social hygiene committee. Joining the Victorian Women Citizens' Movement in the early 1920s, Jones became its second president. Her growing expertise on Aboriginal issues was recognized by the Australian government in 1929 when she gave evidence on Aboriginal status and conditions to a royal commission on the constitution. She advocated federal control of Aboriginal affairs and the rights of Aboriginal women.

Edith Emily Jones

The Case for the Australian Aboriginals in Central and Northern Australia (1930)

Mrs Jones said: In the Australian House of Representatives, where no woman has yet taken her place, the sorrowful sighing of the Aboriginal woman of Central and Northern Australia has found an echo for the first time in the Commonwealth Parliament when Mr Jackson, member for Bass (Tasmania), made his memorable speech on the 18th October, 1927, beginning: 'It is fitting that in this the first Session of the National Parliament in our own Capital and territory, attention should be directed to the obligation the nation owes to the Aboriginal races of Australia – probably the world will remember how we treated our Aboriginals. We assert the right to every man to live, yet we, the usurpers, deny the Aboriginals the right to live, or even to *die*, where they like in their native land. The position of the black women lodged at the compound in Darwin when I was there,' says Mr Jackson, 'was pitiful. Something must be done for these unfortunate people. Except the work of the Missions, nothing at all has been done, and our responsibility for their depravity lies in the condonation of offences against them, the stealing of their women and the supplying to them of intoxicants in order to facilitate these thefts. Those have been the causes of ninety per cent of the trouble with the blacks. Most of the diseases from which they suffer have been disseminated among them by members of the white race.'

Why are there so many half castes in Central Australia? Mrs Standley, formerly Matron at Alice Springs Compound, stated: 'I cannot keep these little children in the compound. They are enticed out by white men, and more half-castes are being born.'

After the citation of many other native disabilities, Mr Jackson proposed the appointment of a joint Select Parliamentary Committee to enquire and report. The Committee did not materialize, but instead Mr J. Bleakley, Chief Protector of Aboriginals in Queensland, was appointed a Royal Commissioner to the Federal Government, to enquire into the state of Aboriginals in North and Central Australia.

COMMONWEALTH TERRITORY. During 1928, Mr Bleakley carried out his enquiry, travelling throughout the areas inhabited by Aboriginals in Central and Northern Territory. His report to the Commonwealth Government was published early in 1929. The following are short extracts from the same: 'It is universally admitted that the pastoral industry in the Territories absolutely depended upon the blacks for labour, both domestic and field; white women were only enabled to live in Central Australia by the help of their Aboriginal sisters.' Of the [21,000] Aboriginals in Central and Northern Australia, about [400] are halfcastes; about 2,500 are in employment; about one in twelve is cared for in Government or Mission Institutions. Eighty per cent of those employed are on cattle stations; the owners may, on payment of 10s. per annum, employ an unlimited number of Aboriginals without payment, on condition of supplying them with clothes and food and shelter. While the first two conditions are generally complied with, the third is seldom honoured, the natives living in unsanitary kennels detrimental to their own health and the health of the whites on the stations. No evidence of serious ill-treatment was seen, but the standard of living conditions depended upon the generosity of the employer.

No attempt is made to elevate or educate the young Aboriginals who work on the cattle stations – they have therefore a *hopeless outlook*. Few employers display any sympathy or interest in the question though uneducated Aboriginal children are a menace to the white children on the stations.

Old women who have often been the pioneer workers on stations depend for sustenance on the gifts of working natives and on portions of 'offal' served out to them on 'killing days.'

The prostitution of women is often due to semi-starvation – conditions in the camps which mean the women become the easy prey to passing travelers – often they are paid on counterfeit coin. Station managers have no authority to suppress 'gin-sprees' – i.e., motor car loads of white men from railway construction camps and bush townships who 'hire' gins (i.e. Aboriginal women) from their fathers and husbands, generally in exchange for a stick of trade tobacco or a bottle of bad whiskey. *Women in indigent camps* in the vicinity of telegraph stations and police stations have periodical rations of good medicine and clothing material issued to them by the local 'Protectors' who are generally unmarried police officers, but some of these camps are large enough to provide whole time work for a 'missionary mother' to dispense good medicine and moral protection.

Mr Bleakley's report was followed up in April, 1929, by a Conference in Melbourne, convened by the Minister for Home Affairs of the Commonwealth of Australia.

Of the four women delegates to this Conference, three, including myself, represented the Australian Federation of Women Voters affiliated to the British Commonwealth League, and I had the honour to move the following recommendations to the Commonwealth Government – they were passed unanimously by the members of the Conference, numbering about eight representatives from various States of Australia: –

1 That the Commonwealth Government take steps to co-operate with the States Governments in the general scheme for better conditions for Aboriginals.
2 That in the future management of the Aboriginals in Central and Northern Australia qualified women be given a definite place on any advisory Council which may be formed by the Government.

3 That a protector be appointed, preferably a medical woman, to act as an assistant to the chief protector, one for the North and one for Central Australia.
4 That women with police powers be appointed to enforce the law in the neighbourhood of railway construction camps.

I made the following statement with Mr Abbott in the chair, and without any dissent being expressed by any members of the Conference: – 'If a woman, white or black, has not the control of her body she is a slave. Some of these black women are slaves, their bodies are not subject to their own discretion if they are traded by their black men for tobacco or whisky.'

In summing up the Conference Mr Abbot said he wished first to state that the women delegates to the Conference had made a most useful contribution, and that he should personally consider their opinions; the Government was, however, shortly after defeated, and nothing has been done to further the matters embodied in the Resolutions alluded to by Mr Abbot. However, the present Minister for Home Affairs has made a statement from which the following are extracts: –

1 The Government proposes erecting a new home for half castes in Central Australia.
2 I have prohibited the chaining of prisoners being brought into stations from the bush.
3 In North Australia an additional medical officer was appointed for whites and Aboriginals in the inland districts.
4 Until the beginning of this year there was no Government medical officer in Central Australia. A full time Government medical officer has now been appointed, and has been entrusted with the duties of chief Protector of Aboriginals in that territory; previously the chief Protector was the Sergeant of Police at Alice Springs.
5 So far as the Government is concerned a steady policy will be pursued of converting single quarters into married quarters, particularly for police officers; and of stationing married men in the interior, and by providing medical facilities to the extent of the funds available for the purpose.
6 I propose to recommend for the approval of the Government certain suggestions made by Mr Bleakley for the amendment of the law, particularly those relating to procuring and soliciting.

No doubt Mr Blakely (the Minister for Home Affairs) intends to honour these promises, but governments are here today and gone tomorrow, and such an important piece of work as the control and protection of Aboriginals should

be in the hands of a permanent department with an advisory Council of experienced and sympathetic men and women, including educated Aboriginals.
The question of better government for the Aboriginals is one needing the most
delicate and tactful approach from the outsider – it cannot be broached inside
the British Parliament, nor yet by direct approach between the two countries,
and it must be remembered that besides the difficulty of the government of the
Australian Aboriginals being a 'domestic question' it is further a 'domestic'
question as between the Commonwealth Government and the government of
the various States, who each govern their own Aboriginals.

Outside of course the moral power of the press there seems to be only one
avenue and that is the consideration of the subject by the League of Nations, of
which Australia was constituted an original member, and although she cannot
be asked for an annual report of the welfare of the Aboriginals as is demanded
of Australia for natives in her mandated territory of New Guinea – yet she can
be asked to honour the agreement made by her with all other national members
of the League in Article 28 of the Covenant Sections a, b and c, by which she
is bound to secure *fair* and *humane* conditions of labour and just treatment of
native inhabitants in territories under her control and to entrust the League to
deal with questions arising in regard to traffic in women and children.

However strongly it may be asserted that the lot of the Aboriginal has been
greatly improved, it should be remembered that he cannot own land; has no
vote and therefore no representative in Parliament; he has no claim to be educated; he is not legal guardian of his children; he cannot (in Federal Territory)
claim to be paid his wages in money; educated half and quarter castes are subjected to the same legal and economic disabilities.

[Source: *British Commonwealth League Conference, Thursday, June 19th,
1930, Morning Session*, 34–7.]

Alice Kandaleft (?–?) represented Syria at the meetings of the International
Congress of Women in Chicago in 1933.

Alice Kandaleft

The World as It Is and as It Could Be: Syria (1933)

I am very happy to have this opportunity to present to this highly esteemed audience, a picture, incomplete as it is, of what is going on in the other hemisphere
of our globe – a picture of human deprivation and suffering, of moral and social

suppression and annihilation. I am specially happy to have this opportunity, because the audience consists of some of the least prejudiced people in the world of the socially and internationally minded; above all, of those who have taken keen, warm, and active interest in the welfare of humanity, because the world has had enough of those whose interests in the vital problems of humanity, whether economic, social or political, national or international, does not go beyond the listening, contemplating and even discussing stage.

The world now, as never before, is at the parting of the ways. Issues have to be decided, steps to be taken; we can no more be satisfied in contemplation or mere discussion; we need action.

The economic dilemma of the last couple of years has turned the minds of thousands and millions of thinking people in the serious study of conditions and other courses. The point of attack and mode of presentation of the various studies made varied according to the background, experiences, and philosophies of the individual. But it is interesting to notice that all study and research has dealt almost mainly with the Western Hemisphere, neglecting the Eastern, which is the larger, the more wretched, and not the less important by any means, to say nothing about its relationship to the depression.

If we accept the fact that our present economic world is a network whose threads are tied up with every corner of the earth; if we have the picture of world interdependence and interrelationship clearly enough, we find that any study that ignores or neglects this other part of the world, the East, is complete in its treatment as well as in its effects and results. A congress like this, which has taken such a warm, active interest in the study of present civilization, would not want to miss this great problem of modern civilization, namely, Imperialism and Colonization, the exploitation of the weak by the strong.

That my subject is not new, I quite well realize, but, in spite of this I feel that what people know about imperialism, about the ways and manners in which it is carried on, about its aims and purposes, is usually limited, and most often a defective sort of knowledge. It is one of the subjects with which propaganda has played most and misrepresented a good deal in order to suit the imperialistic powers and some other purposes. Moreover, I feel my subject has the strongest relationship with the general subject of this conference – security and opportunity for all everywhere – the thing that imperialism is in direct opposition to.

Modern imperialism is only a new form and technique of the old historic activity of confiscation and exploitation of one people by another. But it did not begin with this manner or this purpose.

With the advent of the industrial revolution, of the machine power, production increased very highly and reflooded the European markets. This increase in production was not paralleled by an increase in consumption. This made men of industry and of trade look about and around for foreign markets, as well as for foreign raw material. This process began in England and was followed by other European countries, differing in time and strength, according to the development and growth of industry in the various countries. There and thus was born that huge monster, modern imperialism.

Imperialism, therefore, began after the advent of the machine for economic purposes and projects. Do you suppose the men of the eighteenth century could have ever foreseen or foretold what that mere exchange of goods in the form of raw material or finished products brought of keen suffering and misery to the three families of the globe, or that they could have ever foretold the series of wars to which humanity was driven as a result of their innocent desire to exchange?

Let us see now how that innocent exchange of goods brought about all these sufferings and human woes. It was said that as industry grew and developed steadily, a constant need was felt for more markets and more raw material. These were possible to get by means of three things: (1) an increase in the consuming capacity of local markets; (2) in finding new markets; (3) in organizing the old markets. The first means of increasing the consuming capacity of local markets soon reached its saturation point, and attention and effort were soon directed in the other two schemes – to the foreign markets and the organization of the old.

The search for new foreign markets created new rivalries between the European power and new relationship with the East. The effort to organize old markets caused an increased interference on the part of the business man in local affairs to the extent that he gradually controlled the political and administrative affairs of the country and gradually robbed completely the colonized countries of their independence. Thus, power was moved entirely into the hands of the colonizer and this brought imperialism to a new phase and created new relationship and new needs. Imperialism in India is, perhaps, the best illustration of these various phases and stages in imperialism.

But imperialistic countries learned through experience other and shorter ways of colonization and exploitation, and resorted more to the old methods of acquisition and domination, namely, by force of arms, as happened when France colonized the North African regions, and Italy, Tripoli.

Suppose it is asked what happens when the colonizer gets possession of a certain country? The story is quite complicated and the picture differs according to the colonizer and the colonized. But one thing all imperialistic powers have in common, and do, is, that they put their hands on the natural resources of the country, exploiting the labor and effort of the people. Some of the imperialistic powers, however, have been satisfied with limiting their interference to the administration of the country and to the extent that guarantees their economic interests and others haven't.

Some may happen to think that this kind of imperialism is mutually profitable and therefore it is accepted and quite lawful. But the peoples of the East, most of which have glorious histories and proud achievements, have begun in their turn to develop along lines similar to those along which the people of Europe began to develop during the last few centuries since the Renaissance; likewise, their old philosophies and methods of life have been greatly affected and changed for good or for bad. They have in their turn begun to realize the value of their natural resources and to desire to profit by them to live better and on higher standards.

This desire of the colonized certainly works against the interests of the colonizer. He, therefore, directs his effort to thwart the development of the colonized, so as to protect his own interests. This explains one of the great causes of the constant complaint and cry of the people under any form of imperialistic governments. In every land exploited and dominated by foreign power, there is a constant conflict between two nations – a conflict that is best illustrated by two fighting men, the one armed and in full control of all means of power, and the other, unarmed, having no power but the power of right. The weaker attempts to rise on his feet and to gain some strength; the strong man gives him a blow and throws him down helpless, motionless. Often, sometimes, the weak and unarmed regains strength and tries to rise again, but he gets another heavy blow, and thus the conflict continues. These attempts at rising and standing on one's feet take the form of revolutions, strikes, demonstrations, and the like, on the part of the weaker, and the blows take the form of machine guns, tanks, sometimes bombs and bombardments, other times prisons or exiles, on the part of the stronger.

Warfare in the colonies and countries under other types of foreign domination is not caused by this factor alone, namely, the desire of the weak to rise and stand on his feet, to have control of his natural resources. Business and domination brought wealth to the colonizer, and poverty to the colonized, to such an extent that you find in those countries, most wealthy in their natural resources, millions of people have but one meal a day. Modern methods of irrigation, railways, seaports, banks, etc., hardly benefit the people themselves; they are only a part of the well-organized system of exploitation of the colonies.

But there is another kind of imperialism which is even more cruel and most unhuman. It is the one that aims at the exploitation of human life, for the colonies are not looked upon only as a source of wealth, but they are considered as a reservoir of men to be made use of in time of war between the imperialistic powers themselves.

The colonizer, therefore, exploits the people as well as their land and fortunes. To achieve this exploitation of the people successfully, he tries to kill their national characteristics and cultural consciousness, to make them tools – laborers during peace, and soldiers during the war, as it is in Algeria, Tunis, Morocco, the French Colonies of North Africa, and it is being done in the Lebanons.

A third kind of imperialism which we should not fail to mention, for it is even more brutal, is the imperialism carried by those nations when population has overgrown in proportion to the land, and which seeks other lands for the relief of population.

At the surface, this seems very reasonable and lawful also, but when we consider that those lands they confiscate have their own proprietors and holders, we realize the various methods used by the colonizer to rob the colonized of his land. Among the things he schemes and plans for is the extermination of the colonized. When this is not accomplished soon enough by gradual means, it is done by wholesale massacres, as the Italians did in Tripoli last year.

It is concluded, therefore, that modern imperialism and colonization include all the forms that come under it, even the mildest. The mandate system from which suffers a great part of Asia and Africa, may be divided into three kinds: (1) which aims at exploration of material resources, under which the people of the land are reduced to slaves; (2) which aims at the exploration of human beings, by killing their national and cultural consciousness, and using them as machines of flesh and blood, to be used specially during war; (3) which aims at the full extermination of the people, in order to take their lands. What services for humanity or civilization can you find in either of them?

Allow me now to stop a minute and in a very brief manner say a word about this most modern form of exploitation called the 'Mandate System' specially as it was created and shaped to clothe the purposes of the Imperialistic Powers in Arab lands.

During the war, the Arabs helped the Allies by rebelling against the Turks, and forming an army that fought side by side with the Allies on those frontiers of the Turkish Empire which were most crucial. But this they did with the understanding and on the basis of an agreement with the Allies made by the famous British viceroy in Egypt – Sir Henry MacMahon.

The agreement promised several things to the Arabs, two of which shall be mentioned only because of their relation to our subject.

The first promise is that Great Britain, on behalf of the Allies, recognized the independence of all the Arab provinces in Asia except Aden and Mersin; the second, that the Allies would not sign any treaty of peace if it did not assure the independence of the Arabs. That was agreed upon in March, 1916. Two months later, in May, England and France signed a secret treaty in which they agreed to divide Arabia and definitely assigned the boundaries of the shares of each. Onez Hajoj and Gemen were to be left independent. Of this shift behind the scene, the Arabs were not aware, of course. On the contrary, Great Britain continued to stimulate the Arab nationalistic hopes and hinder their fighting zeal against the Turks.

But the end of the War brought this comic tragedy to an end, and the Arabs realized that they had been tricked. Had it not been for H. H. Emu Faisal, the son of King Hussain, now H. M. King of Iraq, the Arabs would have exploded at once.

King Faisal, realizing the great power of the Allies and still having faith in them and in the moral strength of the position of the Arab, besought his countrymen to let him plead their cause at the Peace Conference at Versailles. This he did, and with eloquence and dignity, but all in vain. The benevolent powers graciously conferred on some of the Arabs' provinces, in recognition of their valiant fighting, the Mandate System.

This shameful story of breach of promise is well recorded in certain books, such as Condé's *The Truth about Mesopotamia, Palestine and Syria*, and in Colonel Lawrence's writings, such as *A Revolt in the Desert*.

But even with the terms of the Mandate System, the great powers were not sincere enough to allude. One of its terms states that 'the wishes of the communities must be a principal consideration in the selection of the Mandatory.' France took the Mandate over Syria by force of arms and even fought an actual battle a few miles out of Damascus called the Battle of Maisalsun.

The Syrian revolution, the bombardment of Damascus in 1925, the parading of tanks and armed automobiles in the street of Damascus every now and then up to the present – in all their land, France is there by force, and against the wish of the people, because might is right.

If anyone in this audience is interested to know definitely, or know in general more about the kind of calamities that Syria has suffered at the hands of the French officials, I shall be glad to give him or her an authentic brief report written by a Syrian student of Political Science and Economy and presented to the Youth Conference held last summer, in Geneva.

May I mention only one instance of her monetary exploitation? The French Law established in Syria an institution called the Syrian Bank which is neither Syrian nor a bank. It issued 25,000,000 Syrian paper pounds on a reserve of 500,000 French pounds, through the tricky game of raising and depreciating the value of the Syrian paper pound. They robbed the country of more than 75 per cent of its monetary wealth. They played another game, which is no less mean. The French declared that the Syrian Bank was the inheritor of the Turkish Bank in which most of the wealth of the Syrians was deposited before the War in gold pounds. That declaration was followed by a law that all pre-war gold debts were to be paid in Syrian paper money, one for one. The £2,000,000 that the Syrians had deposited in the bank were paid back in depreciated paper money, and the bank gained £1,300,000 in gold, which was also shipped to France. If you realize how poor the Great War had left Syria, you would certainly appreciate the horror of such games and tricks.

Before leaving this topic of Mandates, it is necessary to point out two advantages that it has over the other forms of Imperialism: first, at times, the League of Nations does put a check to the misbehavior of the Mandatory power; second, under the Mandate, a door of escape is left open, a dim light of hope keeps shining that one day the Mandatory power somehow, in some way, will have to leave the country.

Yes, such things and worse take place in countries under imperialistic forms of government, even under the most modern and benevolent among them. Some atrocities take place of which you could not even form a mental picture, but very few people in the West know about these things. Why? Because they don't care to know and because the Imperialistic Powers would not let the truth be known. They realize that, once it is known, there is enough sense of right and wrong in their people to condemn this behavior and stand against them.

For example, the Syrians believe that the French people, well-known for their love of liberty and freedom, for their firmness of sentiments, their traditional standing for right, if they knew what their government is doing, would never support her. The government publishes, in papers and otherwise, stories of the great service they are rendering these backward nations; they speak of the handling of railroads, seaports, public gardens, of banks, etc., but they do not tell who own all these or profit by them. The natives of the country have the privilege of looking at them, of paying for building them, and the opportunity to be used as laborers in building them.

Another thing the Imperialistic Powers say, to justify their stay against the wish of the people, is that these people are very backward and there are so many different races and religions, that if they were left alone, there would be constant civil war. But they don't say how they attempt to keep them at this stage of backwardness, how they nurture religious prejudices, and emphasize racial differences, according to the maxim 'Divide a[nd] Rule.'

This is a rather sketchy picture of the results and effects of imperialism, and of the condition it creates in the exploited countries. But this is not all. There are other sides to the picture which I shall mention only in passing, and which are very important from the point of view of this Congress.

(1) The rivalries that develop between the European powers on account of

the various regions under exploitation or good for exploitation, and the world wars that result and will result always from these rivalries.

(2) The need of the various imperialistic powers for standing armies, to keep the people quiet and to put down any revolutions that may start against them, such as the revolt of Ahdulkar, of Morocco and the Syrian Revolution of 1925, which lasted almost two years. This need for more and more arms as the days go by certainly works against the idea of disarmament and the principles of all disarmament conferences which are earnestly desired by this Congress.

Having gone together over these few points about Imperialism, its consequences in East and West, having seen how it opposes in principle and practice the kind of civilization that this Congress would like to see, a civilization that gives security and opportunity for all, everywhere, I hardly need to make my plea to this audience that Imperialism in all its forms must be condemned by this Congress, causing such a constant, dangerous undercurrent to the peace of the world, and being such a great shame to present-day civilization.

[Source: *Our Common Cause: Civilization: Report of the National Council of Women of the United States. Including the Series of Round Tables, July 16–22, 1933, Chicago, Illinois* (New York: National Council of Women of the United States, 1973), 148–54.]

PART THREE
Suffrage

There is perhaps no more iconic struggle associated with first wave feminism than women's suffrage, yet as Caroline Daley and Melanie Nolan point out, very few nations granted suffrage to women before the 1940s.[1] Kuwaiti women were granted full political rights as recently as 2005 and participated in full legislative elections both as voters and candidates for the first time in 2006; women won seats in the Kuwaiti parliament for the first time in 2009. Suffrage, moreover, was not universally regarded as either necessary or desirable by those engaged in women's movements around the world. The Chilean feminist Amanda Labarca, for instance, was extremely critical of the unfeminine actions of the British suffragettes, and distanced herself from the international struggle for enfranchisement by declaring, in 1914, 'I am not a militant feminist, nor am I a suffragist, for above all I am Chilean, and in Chile today the vote for women is out of order.'[2] The position of Chilean feminists on the question of suffrage gradually changed, but this example and that of Kuwaiti women serve as reminders that however international the struggle for suffrage, the terms of the struggle and the time-frame in which it was conducted varied considerably from nation to nation.

Despite these important differences, women did seek to collaborate internationally, and gained mutual inspiration as well as more substantial kinds of support from one another's struggles. As Ellen Carol DuBois puts it, 'Women's international cooperation gave them resources to combat their marginalisation in the politics of their own nations.'[3] The letter from the French socialist women Jeanne Deroin and Pauline Roland to the US Women's Rights Convention of 1851 is a case in point. In the context of the failed revolution of 1848 in France, in which the provisional republican government had proclaimed universal suffrage only to have it overturned with Louis Napoleon's coup d'état in 1851, these French women wrote from their prison cells to champion the cause of women's suffrage and citizenship rights in the United States and elsewhere. Hubertine Auclert's call to French feminists to establish a national suffrage association cites the examples of English and American associations. The success of New Zealand feminists in 1893, who were the first in the world to win the right to vote for women, shaped debates about suffrage in other nations, and the international travels of women like Kate Sheppard enabled the sharing of strategies and arguments across national borders through public and private meetings and publication, as her piece from the *Woman's Signal* attests. Before the enfranchisement of New Zealand women, antipodean feminists had made use of international suffragist collaboration. One of the earliest suffrage organizations to work internationally was the World Women's Christian Temperance Union, whose arguments for women's suffrage were echoed by many women's organizations around the world. The emphasis on suffrage less as a goal in itself than as a means to moral and social reforms resonated with women as far away as Japan, which established its own branch of the WCTU.

In taking New Zealand as an exemplary case, women in Europe and the Americas tended to overlook the fact that Maori women were also enfranchised in 1893, although they were restricted to voting for Maori candidates and thus had less influence than white New Zealand women.[4] Women's suffrage was often more sharply divided by race than in the New Zealand case – and it is important to recognize that New Zealand was by no means race-blind. In Australia, for instance, Aborigine women were not granted the franchise when white women won the right to vote in piecemeal fashion between 1894 and 1902. And in the United States, as the contribution here of Elizabeth Cady Stanton demonstrates, the enfranchisement of black men in the wake of the US Civil War proved a sore point for many white feminists, whether or not they opposed slavery as Stanton did. Suffragists could extend support to one another across lines of race and empire, as the statement made by members of the International Women Suffrage Alliance in England on behalf of Indian women indicates; yet even this support did not come unaccompanied by patronizing sentiment.

Class was also a point of contention, particularly for socialist feminists. Clara Zetkin's address at the International Socialist Congress in Stuttgart in 1907 pointedly links women's suffrage to the broader struggle against capitalism, arguing that the political equality that comes with suffrage is important for enabling women to struggle for broader forms of social equality. While Zetkin claims that suffrage is, in contrast, the 'final goal' of bourgeois feminists, she nonetheless argues that proletarian women and bourgeois suffragists can 'march separately but fight together.' Emmeline Pankhurst's 1908 speech in the Portman Rooms in London presents evidence that not all bourgeois feminists took suffrage as their final goal – as, indeed, does Willard's article and many others. Pankhurst, despite her own class position, also justifies suffrage as a means of securing the right to work for working-class women, as well as outlining a number of other areas of citizenship to which women might and should contribute, were they to secure the franchise. Where socialist and bourgeois women did differ substantially was in the willingness of bourgeois women to accept limited women's suffrage based on age, class, and race qualifications.

The dominance of European and white-settler-colony feminists in the struggle for suffrage as in other areas of first wave feminist activity is evident in Millicent Garrett Fawcett's address to 'Women of All Nations' following the First World War. Yet non-European women were also either enfranchised or actively pursuing suffrage, as Mabel Dove's column in the *West African Times* and Kikue Ide's history of Japanese women's suffrage indicate. Dove encourages those women who had the right to vote, like men on a limited basis, to use that right and to participate actively in upcoming elections for the Gold Coast Legislative Council. Ide writes to provide source material in preparation for the Pan-Pacific Women's Association Conference in 1928 about the various stages of the struggle for women's suffrage in Japan.

NOTES

1 Caroline Daley and Melanie Nolan, introduction to *Suffrage and Beyond: International Feminist Perspectives*, ed. Caroline Daley and Melanie Nolan (New York: New York UP, 1994), 10.

2 Quoted in Corinne A. Pernet, 'Chilean Feminists, the International Women's Movement, and Suffrage, 1915–1950,' *Pacific Historical Review* 69, no. 4 (2000): 667. Labarca feared the influence of the Catholic church over women in Chile, and feared that granting women the vote would produce a very conservative electorate as a consequence of that influence. See Christine Ehrick, '*Madrinas* and Missionaries: Uruguay and the Pan-American Women's Movement,' in *Feminisms and Internationalism*, ed. Mralini Sinha, Donna Guy, and Angela Woollacott (Oxford: Blackwell, 1999): 62–80.

3 Carol Ellen DuBois, 'Woman Suffrage around the World: Three Phases of Suffragist Internationalism,' in Daley and Nolan, *Suffrage and Beyond*, 254.

4 Raewyn Dalziel, 'Presenting the Enfranchisement of New Zealand Women Abroad,' in Daley and Nolan, *Suffrage and Beyond*, 57.

The Woman's Protest   9

Sample of Suffragist Logic as Shown in Their Cartoons.

Over 25,000 Women Employed in St. Louis
Have no Voice in the Laws Governing Industry

WHICH IS MORE DIGNIFIED
THIS

At the Factory: Get Busy   OR THIS

At the Polls: Your Place is at Home

Which shall we use in immediate legislation
Dealing with
Board of Childrens Guardians
Increased powers of Public Recreation Commission
Smoke Abatement
Fire Prevention
Regulation of Water Supply

The Cartoons shown here are reproduced from those exhibited at the Child Welfare Exhibit at St. Louis recently. They give the usual deceptive impression of the suffragists, that votes are cast for measures, not men, but are valuable as showing their peculiar logic. The Child Welfare Exhibit probably did more to influence public opinion toward helping the conditions of women and children than the votes of all the women in Missouri could do in ten years.

The concession to women of the right to vote—with all that it involves—would promote the assimilation of the vocations, habits and interests of the sexes to a degree inconsistent with the full vitality of the race. Woman suffrage would be followed by racial decadence.—Heber Hart, LL.D.

We hear of the "Mission" and the "Rights" of Woman, as if these could ever be separate from the mission and rights of man. Each has what the other has not, each completes the other, and is completed by the other.—Ruskin.

How strangely some women deceive themselves in fancying that they can win in the battle of life by their own strength and yet not sacrifice the moral ascendency which centuries of civilization have secured to them. Blind and petty ambition! They cannot have it both ways.—Frederic Harrison.

The whole thing sums itself up in my belief that the man votes not as a man but as the head of the family, and that wifehood and motherhood more than balance in their importance to the commonwealth the man's function as the household voter.—Jacob A. Riis.

[Source: *The Woman's Protest against Woman Suffrage* 1.2 (1912), p. 9. Image published with permission of ProQuest. Further reproduction is prohibited without permission.]

Jeanne Deroin (1805–94) and Pauline Roland (1805–52) were two of fifty people arrested and imprisoned in Paris in May of 1850, after attempting to resuscitate the cooperative movement among workers. Both were writers, teachers, and vocal feminists, Deroin contributing to and founding feminist journals, and Roland entering into a 'free union' with Jean Aicard, demanding that her children bear her last name and declaring that marriage was structured in such a way as to perpetuate women's oppression. Throughout their many months in prison Deroin and Roland remained committed to the socialist and women's movements, penning the following letter in an effort to unite women everywhere.

Jeanne Deroin and Pauline Roland
Letter to the Convention of the Women of America (1851)

To the Convention of the Women of America:
DEAR SISTERS:– Your courageous declaration of Woman's Rights has resounded even to our prison, and has filled our souls with inexpressible joy.

In France the reaction has suppressed the cry of liberty of the women of the future. Deprived, like their brothers, of the Democracy, of the right to civil and political equality, and the fiscal laws which trammel the liberty of the press, hinder the propagation of those eternal truths which must regenerate humanity.

They wish the women of France to found a hospitable tribunal, which shall receive the cry of the oppressed and suffering, and vindicate in the name of humanity, solidarity, the social right for both sexes equally; and where woman, the mother of humanity, may claim in the name of her children, mutilated by tyranny, her right to true liberty, to the complete development and free exercise of all her faculties, and reveal that half of truth which is in her, and without which no social work can be complete.

The darkness of reaction has obscured the sun of 1848, which seemed to rise so radiantly. Why? Because the revolutionary tempest, in over-turning at the same time the throne and the scaffold, in breaking the chain of the black slave, forgot to break the chain of the most oppressed of all of the pariahs of humanity.

'There shall be no more slaves,' said our brethren. 'We proclaim universal suffrage. All shall have the right to elect the agents who shall carry out the Constitution which should be based on the principles of liberty, equality, and fraternity. Let each one come and deposit his vote; the barrier of privilege is overturned; before the electoral urn there are no more oppressed, no more masters and slaves.'

Woman, in listening to this appeal, rises and approaches the liberating urn to exercise her right of suffrage as a member of society. But the barrier of privilege rises also before her. 'You must wait,' they say. But by this claim alone woman affirms the right, not yet recognized, of the half of humanity – the right of woman to liberty, equality, and fraternity. She obliges man to verify the fatal attack which he makes on the integrity of his principles.

Soon, in fact during the wonderful days of June, 1848, liberty glides from her pedestal in the flood of the victims of the reaction; based on the 'right of the strongest,' she falls, overturned in the name of 'the right of the strongest.'

The Assembly kept silence in regard to the right of one-half of humanity, for which only one of its members raised his voice, but in vain. No mention was made of the right of woman in a Constitution framed in the name of Liberty, Equality, and Fraternity.

It is in the name of these principles that woman comes to claim her right to take part in the Legislative Assembly, and to help to form the laws which must govern society, of which she is a member.

She comes to demand of the electors the consecration of the principle of equality by the election of a woman, and by this act she obliges man to prove that the fundamental law which he has formed in the sole name of liberty, equality, and fraternity, is still based upon privilege, and soon privilege triumphs over this phantom of universal suffrage, which, being but half of itself, sinks on the 31st of May, 1850.

But while those selected by the half of the people – by men alone – evoke force to stifle liberty, and forge restrictive laws to establish order by compression, woman, guided by fraternity, foreseeing incessant struggles, and in the hope of putting an end to them, makes an appeal to the laborer to found liberty and equality on fraternal solidarity. The participation of woman gave to this work of enfranchisement an eminently pacific character, and the laborer recognizes the right of woman, his companion in labor.

The delegates of a hundred and four associations, united, without distinction of sex, elected two women, with several of their brethren, to participate equally with them in the administration of the interests of labor, and in the organization of the work of solidarity.

Fraternal associations were formed with the object of enfranchising the laborer from the yoke of spoilage and patronage, but, isolated in the midst of the Old World, their efforts could only produce a feeble amelioration for themselves.

The union of associations based on fraternal solidarity had for its end the organization of labor; that is to say, an equal division of labor, of instruments, and of the products of labor.

The means were, the union of labor, and of credit among the workers of all professions, in order to acquire the instruments of labor and the necessary materials, and to form a mutual guarantee for the education of their children, and to provide for the needs of the old, the sick; and the infirm.

In this organization all the workers, without distinction of sex or procession, having an equal right to election, and being eligible for all functions, and all having equally the initiative and the sovereign decision in the acts of common interests, they laid the foundation of a new society based on liberty, equality, and fraternity.

It is in the name of law framed by man only – by those elected by privilege – that the Old World, wishing to stifle in the germ the holy work of pacific enfranchisement, has shut up within the walls of a prison those who had founded it – those elected by the laborers.

But the impulse has been given, a grand act has been accomplished. The right of woman has been recognized by the laborers, and they have consecrated that right by the election of those who had claimed it in vain for both sexes, before the electoral urn and before the electoral committees. They have received the true civil baptism, were elected by the laborers to accomplish the mission of enfranchisement, and after having shared their rights and their duties, they share today their captivity.

It is from the depths of their prison that they address to you the relation of these facts, which contain in themselves high instruction. It is by labor, it is by entering resolutely into the ranks of the working people, that women will conquer the civil and political equality on which depends the happiness of the world. As to moral equality, has she not conquered it by the power of sentiment? It is, therefore, by the sentiment of the love of humanity that the mother of humanity will find power to accomplish her high mission. It is when she shall have well comprehended the holy law of solidarity – which is not an obscure and mysterious dogma, but a living providential fact – that the kingdom of God promised by Jesus, and which is no other than the kingdom of equality and justice, shall be realized on earth.

Sisters of America! your socialist sisters of France are united with you in the vindication of the right of woman to civil and political equality. We have, moreover, the profound conviction that only by the power of association based on solidarity – by the union of the working-classes of both sexes to organize labor – can be acquired, completely and pacifically, the civil and political equality of woman, and the social right for all.

It is in this confidence that, from the depths of the jail which still imprisons our bodies without reaching our hearts, we cry to you, Faith, Love, Hope, and send to you our sisterly salutations.

JEANNE DEROIN,
PAULINE ROLAND.

Paris, Prisons of St Lagare, June 15, 1851.

[Source: 'Letter to the Convention of the Women of America,' in vol. 1 of *History of Woman Suffrage*, ed. Elizabeth Cady Stanton, Susan B. Anthony, and Matilda Joslyn Gage (Rochester, NY: Charles Mann, 1889), 234–7.]

Elizabeth Cady Stanton (1815–1902) was a US social activist, an abolitionist, and a leader of the early women's rights movement. After the Civil War, Stanton's commitment to female suffrage caused a schism in the women's rights movement when she and Susan B. Anthony refused to support passage of the Fourteenth and Fifteenth Amendments to the United States Constitution. She opposed giving added legal protection and voting rights to African American men while women were denied the same rights.

Elizabeth Cady Stanton
Speech before the Woman Suffrage Convention, Washington, DC, 18 January 1869

A great idea of progress is near its consummation, when statesmen in the councils of the nation propose to frame it into statutes and constitutions; when Reverend Fathers recognize it by a new interpretation of their creeds and canons; when the Bar and Bench at its command set aside the legislation of centuries, and girls of twenty put their heels on the Cokes and Blackstones of the past.

Those who represent what is called 'the Woman's Rights Movement,' have argued their right to political equality from every standpoint of justice, religion, and logic, for the last twenty years. They have quoted the Constitution, the Declaration of Independence, the Bible, the opinions of great men and women in all ages; they have pled the theory of our government; suffrage a natural, inalienable right; shown from the lessons of history, that one class can not legislate for another; that disfranchised classes must ever be neglected and degraded; and that all privileges are but mockery to the citizen, until he has a voice in the making and administering of law. Such arguments have been made over and over in conventions and before the legislatures of the several States. Judges, lawyers, priests, and politicians have said again and again, that our logic was unanswerable, and although much nonsense has emanated from the male tongue and pen on this subject, no man has yet made a fair argument on the other side. Knowing that we hold the Gibraltar rock of reason on this question, they resort to ridicule and petty objections ... There are no new arguments to be made on human rights; our work today is to apply to ourselves those so familiar to all; to teach man that woman is not an anomalous being, outside all laws and constitutions, but one whose rights are to be established by the same process of reason as that by which he demands his own.

When our Fathers made out their famous bill of impeachment against England, they specified eighteen grievances. When the women of this country surveyed the situation in their first convention, they found they had precisely that number, and quite similar in character; and reading over the old revolutionary arguments of Jefferson, Patrick Henry, Otis, and Adams, they found they applied remarkably well to their case. The same arguments made in this country for extending suffrage from time to time, to white men, native born citizens, without property and education, and to foreigners; the same used by John Bright in England, to extend it to a million new voters, and the same used by the great Republican party to enfranchise a million black men in the South, all these arguments we have today to offer for woman, and one, in addition, stronger than all besides, the difference in man and woman. Because man and woman are the complement of one another, we need woman's thought in national affairs to make a safe and stable government.

The Republican party today congratulates itself on having carried the Fifteenth Amendment of the Constitution, thus securing 'manhood suffrage' and establishing an aristocracy of sex on this continent. As several bills to secure Woman's Suffrage in the District and the Territories have been already presented in both houses of Congress, and as by Mr Julian's bill, the question of so amending the Constitution as to extend suffrage to all the women of the country has been presented to the nation for consideration, it is not only the right but the duty of every thoughtful woman to express her opinion on a Sixteenth Amendment. While I hail the late discussions in Congress and the various bills presented as so many signs of progress, I am especially gratified with those of Messrs Julian and Pomeroy, which forbid any State to deny the right of suffrage to any of its citizens on account of sex or color.

This fundamental principle of our government – the equality of all the citizens of the republic – should be incorporated in the Federal Constitution, there to remain forever. To leave this question to the States and partial acts of Congress, is to defer indefinitely its settlement, for what is done by this Congress may be repealed by the next; and politics in the several States differ so widely, that no harmonious action on any question can ever be secured, except as a strict party measure. Hence, we appeal to the party now in power, everywhere, to end this protracted debate on suffrage, and declare it the inalienable right of every citizen who is amenable to the laws of the land, who pays taxes and the penalty of crime. We have a splendid theory of a genuine republic, why not realize it and make our government homogeneous, from Maine to California. The Republican party has the power to do this, and now is its only opportunity. Woman's Suffrage, in 1872, may be as good a card for the Republicans as Gen. Grant was in the last election. It is said that the Republican party made him President, not because they thought him the most desirable man in the nation for that office, but they were afraid the Democrats would take him if they did not. We would suggest, there may be the same danger of Democrats taking up Woman Suffrage if they do not. God, in his providence, may have purified that party in the furnace of affliction. They have had the opportunity, safe from the turmoil of political life and the temptations of office, to study and apply the divine principles of justice and equality to life; for minorities are always in a position to carry principles to their logical results, while majorities are governed only by votes. You see my faith in Democrats is based on sound philosophy. In the next Congress, the Democratic party will gain thirty-four new members, hence the Republicans have had their last chance to do justice to woman. It will be no enviable record for the Fortieth Congress that in the darkest days of the republic it placed our free institutions in the care and keeping of every type of manhood, ignoring womanhood, all the elevating and purifying influences of the most virtuous and humane half of the American people ...

I urge a speedy adoption of a Sixteenth Amendment for the following reasons:

1. A government, based on the principle of caste and class, can not stand. The aristocratic idea, in any form, is opposed to the genius of our free institutions, to our own declaration of rights, and to the civilization of the age. All artificial distinctions, whether of family, blood, wealth, color, or sex, are equally oppressive to the subject classes, and equally destructive to national life and prosperity. Governments based on every form of aristocracy, on every degree and variety of inequality, have been tried in despotisms, monarchies, and republics, and all alike have perished ... On all sides the cry is echoed, 'Republicanism is a failure,' though that great principle of a government 'by the people, of the people, for the people,' has never been tried. Thus far, all nations have been built on caste and failed. Why, in this hour of reconstruction, with the experience of generations before us, make another experiment in the same direction? If serfdom, peasantry, and slavery have shattered kingdoms, deluged continents with blood, scattered republics like dust before the wind, and rent our own Union asunder, what kind of a government, think you, American statesmen, you can build, with the mothers of the race crouching at your feet, while iron-heeled peasants, serfs, and slaves, exalted by your hands, tread

our inalienable rights into the dust? While all men, everywhere, are rejoicing in new-found liberties, shall woman alone be denied the rights, privileges, and immunities of citizenship? While in England men are coming up from the coal mines of Cornwall, from the factories of Birmingham and Manchester, demanding the suffrage; while in frigid Russia the 22,000,000 newly-emancipated serfs are already claiming a voice in the government; while here, in our own land, slaves, but just rejoicing in the proclamation of emancipation, ignorant alike of its power and significance, have the ballot unasked, unsought, already laid at their feet – think you the daughters of Adams, Jefferson, and Patrick Henry, in whose veins flows the blood of two Revolutions, will forever linger round the campfires of an old barbarism, with no longings to join this grand army of freedom in its onward march to roll back the golden gates of a higher and better civilization? Of all kinds of aristocracy, that of sex is the most odious and unnatural; invading, as it does, our homes, desecrating our family altars, dividing those whom God has joined together, exalting the son above the mother who bore him, and subjugating, everywhere, moral power to brute force. Such a government would not be worth the blood and treasure so freely poured out in its long struggles for freedom ...

2. I urge a Sixteenth Amendment, because 'manhood suffrage' or a man's government, is civil, religious, and social disorganization. The male element is a destructive force, stern, selfish, aggrandizing, loving war, violence, conquest, acquisition, breeding in the material and moral world alike discord, disorder, disease, and death. See what a record of blood and cruelty the pages of history reveal! Through what slavery, slaughter, and sacrifice, through what inquisitions and imprisonments, pains and persecutions, black codes and gloomy creeds, the soul of humanity has struggled for the centuries, while mercy has veiled her face and all hearts have been dead alike to love and hope! The male element has held high carnival thus far, it has fairly run riot from the beginning, overpowering the feminine element everywhere, crushing out all the diviner qualities in human nature, until we know but little of true manhood and womanhood, of the latter comparatively nothing, for it has scarce been recognized as a power until within the last century. Society is but the reflection of man himself, untempered by woman's thought, the hard iron rule we feel alike in the church, the state, and the home. No one need wonder at the disorganization, at the fragmentary condition of everything, when we remember that man, who represents but half a complete being, with but half an idea on every subject, has undertaken the absolute control of all sublunary matters.

People object to the demands of those whom they choose to call the strong-minded, because they say, 'the right of suffrage will make the women masculine.' That is just the difficulty in which we are involved today. Though disfranchised we have few women in the best sense; we have simply so many reflections, varieties, and dilutions of the masculine gender. The strong, natural characteristics of womanhood are repressed and ignored in dependence, for so long as man feeds woman she will try to please the giver and adapt herself to his condition. To keep a foothold in society woman must be as near like man as possible, reflect his ideas, opinions, virtues, motives, prejudices, and vices. She must respect his statutes, though they strip her of every inalienable right, and conflict with that higher law written by the finger of God on her own soul. She must believe his theology, though it pave the highways of hell with the skulls of new-born infants, and make God a monster of vengeance and hypocrisy. She must look at everything from its dollar and cent point of view, or she is a mere romancer. She must accept things as they are and make the best of them. To mourn over the miseries of others, the poverty of the poor, their hardships in jails, prisons, asylums, the horrors of war, cruelty, and brutality in every form, all this would be mere sentimentalizing. To protest against the intrigue, bribery, and corruption of public life, to desire that her sons might follow some business that did not involve lying, cheating, and a hard, grinding selfishness, would be arrant nonsense. In this way man has been moulding woman to his ideas by direct and positive influences, while she, if not a negation, has used indirect means to control him, and in most cases developed the very characteristics both in him and herself that needed repression. And now man himself stands appalled at the results of his own excesses, and mourns in bitterness that falsehood, selfishness, and violence are the law of life. The need of this hour is not territory, gold mines, railroads, or specie payments, but a new evangel of womanhood, to exalt purity, virtue, morality, true religion, to lift man up into the higher realms of thought and action.

We ask woman's enfranchisement, as the first step toward the recognition of that essential element in government that can only secure the health, strength, and prosperity of the nation. Whatever is done to lift woman to her true position will help to usher in a new day of peace and perfection for the race. In speaking of the masculine element, I do not wish to be understood to say that all men are hard, selfish, and brutal, for many of the most beautiful spirits the world has known have been clothed with manhood; but I refer to those characteristics, though often marked in woman, that distinguish what is called the stronger sex. For example, the love of acquisition and conquest, the very pioneers of civilization, when expended on the earth, the sea, the elements, the riches and forces of Nature, are powers of destruction when used to subjugate one man to another or to sacrifice nations to ambition. Here that great conservator of woman's love, if permitted to assert itself, as it naturally would in freedom against oppression, violence, and war, would hold all these destructive forces in check, for woman knows the cost of life better than man does, and not with her consent would one drop of blood ever be shed, one life sacrificed in vain. With violence and disturbance in the natural world, we see a constant effort to maintain an equilibrium of forces. Nature, like a loving mother, is ever trying to keep land and sea, mountain and valley each in its place, to hush the angry winds and waves, balance the extremes of heat and cold, of rain and drought, that peace, harmony, and beauty may reign supreme. There is a striking analogy between matter and mind, and the present disorganization of society warns us, that in the dethronement of woman we have let loose the elements of violence and ruin that she only has the power to curb. If the civilization of the age calls for an extension of the suffrage, surely a government of the most virtuous, educated men and women would better represent the whole, and protect the interests of all, than could the representation of either sex alone. But government gains no new element of strength in admitting all men to the ballot-box, for we have too much of the manpower there already. We see this in every department of legislation, and it is a common remark, that unless some new virtue is infused into our public life the nation is doomed to destruction. Will the foreign element, the dregs of China, Germany, England, Ireland, and Africa supply this needed force, or the nobler types of American womanhood who have taught our presidents, senators, and congressmen the rudiments of all they know?

3. I urge a Sixteenth Amendment because, when 'manhood suffrage' is established from Maine to California, woman has reached the lowest depths of political degradation. So long as there is a disfranchised class in this country, and that class [is] women, a man's government is worse than a white man's government with suffrage limited by property and educational qualifications, because in proportion as you multiply the rulers, the condition of the politically ostracised is more hopeless and degraded. John Stuart Mill, in his work on 'Liberty,' shows that the condition of one disfranchised man in a nation is worse than when the whole nation is under one man, because in the latter case, if the one man is despotic, the nation can easily throw him off, but what can one man do with a nation of tyrants over him? If American women find it hard to bear the oppressions of their own Saxon fathers, the best orders of manhood, what may they not be called to endure when all the lower orders of foreigners now crowding our shores legislate for them and their daughters. Think of Patrick and Sambo and Hans and Yung Tung, who do not know the difference between a monarchy and a republic, who can not read the Declaration of Independence or Webster's spelling-book, making laws for Lucretia Mott, Ernestine L. Rose, and Anna E. Dickinson. Think of jurors and jailors drawn from these ranks to watch and try young girls for the crime of infanticide, to decide the moral code by which the mothers of this Republic shall be governed? This

manhood suffrage is an appalling question, and it would be well for thinking women, who seem to consider it so magnanimous to hold their own claims in abeyance until all men are crowned with citizenship, to remember that the most ignorant men are ever the most hostile to the equality of women, as they have known them only in slavery and degradation.

Go to our courts of justice, our jails and prisons; go into the world of work; into the trades and professions; into the temples of science and learning, and see what is meted out everywhere to women – to those who have no advocates in our courts, no representatives in the councils of the nation. Shall we prolong and perpetuate such injustice, and by increasing this power risk worse oppressions for ourselves and daughters? It is an open, deliberate insult to American womanhood to be cast down under the iron-heeled peasantry of the Old World and the slaves of the New, as we shall be in the practical working of the Fifteenth Amendment, and the only atonement the Republican party can make is now to complete its work, by enfranchising the women of the nation. I have not forgotten their action four years ago, when Article XIV., Sec. 2, was amended[1] by invidiously introducing the word 'male' into the Federal Constitution, where it had never been before, thus counting out of the basis of representation all men not permitted to vote, thereby making it the interest of every State to enfranchise its male citizens, and virtually declaring it no crime to disfranchise its women. As political sagacity moved our rulers thus to guard the interests of the negro for party purposes, common justice might have compelled them to show like respect for their own mothers, by counting woman too out of the basis of representation, that she might no longer swell the numbers to legislate adversely to her interests. And this desecration of the last will and testament of the fathers, this retrogressive legislation for woman, was in the face of the earnest protests of thousands of the best educated, most refined and cultivated women of the North.

Now, when the attention of the whole world is turned to this question of suffrage, and women themselves are throwing off the lethargy of ages, and in England, France, Germany, Switzerland, and Russia are holding their conventions, and their rulers are everywhere giving them a respectful hearing, shall American statesmen, claiming to be liberal, so amend their constitutions as to make their wives and mothers the political inferiors of unlettered and unwashed

---

1 The amendment as proposed by the Hon. Thaddeus Stevens, of Pennsylvania, extended the right of suffrage to 'all citizens,' which included both white and black women. At the bare thought of such an impending calamity, the more timid Republicans were filled with alarm, and the word 'male' promptly inserted.

ditch-diggers, boot-blacks, butchers, and barbers, fresh from the slave planta-tions of the South, and the effete civilizations of the Old World? While poets and philosophers, statesmen and men of science are all alike pointing to wom-an as the new hope for the redemption of the race, shall the freest Government on the earth be the first to establish an aristocracy based on sex alone? to exalt ignorance above education, vice above virtue, brutality and barbarism above refinement and religion? Not since God first called light out of darkness and order out of chaos, was there ever made so base a proposition as 'manhood suffrage' in this American Republic, after all the discussions we have had on human rights in the last century. On all the blackest pages of history there is no record of an act like this, in any nation, where native born citizens, having the same religion, speaking the same language, equal to their rulers in wealth, fam-ily, and education, have been politically ostracised by their own countrymen, outlawed with savages, and subjected to the government of outside barbar-ians. Remember the Fifteenth Amendment takes in a larger population than the 2,000,000 black men on the Southern plantation. It takes in all the foreigners daily landing in our eastern cities, the Chinese crowding our western shores, the inhabitants of Alaska, and all those western isles that will soon be ours. American statesmen may flatter themselves that by superior intelligence and political sagacity the higher orders of men will always govern, but when the ignorant foreign vote already holds the balance of power in all the large cities by sheer force of numbers, it is simply a question of impulse or passion, brib-ery or fraud, how our elections will be carried. When the highest offices in the gift of the people are bought and sold in Wall Street, it is a mere chance who will be our rulers. Whither is a nation tending when brains count for less than bullion, and clowns make laws for queens?

[Source: Vol. 2 of *History of Woman Suffrage*, ed. Elizabeth Cady Stanton, Susan B. Anthony, and Matilda Joslyn Gage (Rochester, NY: Charles Mann, 1889), 348–55.]

Katherine Wilson Sheppard (1848–1934) was born to Scottish parents in Liv-erpool, England, but moved to New Zealand in 1869, where she would become deeply involved in the women's movement. She helped to found and run the New Zealand Women's Christian Temperance Union, the organization which would eventually present three petitions to the Parliament declaring women's right to the vote. In 1893, after the WCTU had submitted the last of these petitions, Parliament passed a women's suffrage bill, making the women of New Zealand the first to win full voting rights. Sheppard was the first president of New Zealand's National Council of Women and the widely acknowledged leader of the New Zealand feminist movement.

Kate W. Sheppard
Womanhood Suffrage (1894)

Now that Womanhood Suffrage is one of the leading political questions of the day, and the discussion of the amendment in the Registration Bill is looked forward to by many with the keenest interest, it may help some, who, either from want of time or inclination, have not given the subject the consideration it deserves, to publish a few facts connected with the extension of the Suffrage to the women of New Zealand, and the results on the recent elections in that country.

Although the question was first introduced into the New Zealand Parliament in 1878, it was not until the women themselves began to organize in 1885 that the subject was received with anything like seriousness either by the people or their representatives. The establishment of the Women's Christian Temperance Union with its various departments of work, embracing almost all questions of social and moral reform, was the means of gathering in a large number of thoughtful, earnest women.

Inform and Reform

So broad was the scope of the Union that the officers of each department had full liberty to procure assistance from, and work with, all who wished to do so, whether they were members of the Union or not. Thus, when the Franchise department circulated its petition for Womanhood Suffrage throughout the length and breadth of the land, at least one-third of the women who collected the signatures were not members of any Temperance body. The appeal embodied in the petition was made on the broad ground of citizenship irrespective of sex, so that every woman who realized to some degree the disabilities under which her sex laboured was enlisted as a helper in the Suffrage cause.

It should be noted, however, that the women were not thoroughly roused to a sense of their need for direct representation until they found that all their attempts at reform were practically futile without it.

Petitions, largely signed by women, were at various times presented to Parliament, pleading for enactments, which, if passed, would have been for the betterment and elevation of humanity. These were relegated to a 'Petitions Committee,' the members of which usually decided that they had 'a recommendation to make.' Then the women resolved to work for equal suffrage. Without it they were helpless, with it they would at least be fairly represented and their wishes respected. Candidates for Parliamentary honours were publicly questioned, and their replies noted; meetings were held, literature was distributed, and every device resorted to that could help in influencing public opinion on the question. Suffrage Leagues were established in 1890 and did good work.

A Suffrage Champion

Sir John Hall was the special champion of the measure in the House of Representatives introducing various Women's Franchise Bills from time to time, until the Balance Government in 1891 incorporated the suffrage clauses into the Electoral Bill, and passed the measure in 1893. After some violent opposition in the Legislative Council, that body also passed the measure. The Governor, Lord Glasgow, gave his assent to the bill on September 19th, and for the first time in the life of this 'Britain of the South' her people were free.

It had been said by the opponents of the measure, that women did not care for the Franchise, and would not use it even if they had the opportunity given them. Recent events have proved the fallacy of this assertion. The newly qualified electors were allowed very little time for registration, as the rolls were closed early in November and the general election was held on November 26th.

In spite of this disadvantage, 109,461 women were enrolled, and 90,290 recorded their votes at the election. There were at the same time 193,536 men on the electoral rolls, and out of that number 120,792 voted. It will be seen, therefore, that the proportion of women who voted was larger than that of men.

It was found that the presence of large numbers of women at the booths was a far more effectual restraint on ruffianism than the police force could have been.

Every male voter had a sister, wife, mother, daughter, or some one equally dear to him for whose sake all riotousness must be restrained. The daily papers were unanimous in their remarks as to the orderliness of the elections, and the freedom from drinking. One of the results of the election has been a crushing defeat of the old Conservative party, but many causes operated to produce this effect, which cannot be dwelt on here. Another result is that the present parliament is a cleansed and purified one. A number of M.H.R.s, whose reputation had been unsavoury, have been rejected, even though professing the popular creed in politics.

In all this it will be seen that the moral and social condition of the nation is, from a woman's standpoint, the first consideration, and most fair-minded people will admit that hitherto this side of human affairs has not been emphasised too much. We do not want a one-eyed government, but one with a perfect vision, which is able to focus and legislate for the wants of the whole nation.

There are other phases of the question that ought to be, and have been, considered, such as the many legal disabilities which affect women as wives and mothers, and also those which handicap them as units of the industrial army; but these have been entered into so often that there is no occasion to refer to them here.

The women of England have been working for their political freedom for many years. Why have they not got it today? Is it because of vested interests, which tend directly and indirectly to demoralization, and the promoters of which, therefore, dread the woman's vote? Is it because England is encrusted with a shell of conventionality so impenetrable and immovable as to retard anything like real growth and progress? Or is it because women have not had the courage of their convictions, and asked boldly for their rightful privileges, or know the reason why they have not got them? Let the Englishwomen answer.

[Source: *The Woman's Signal*, 21 June 1894, 432.]

Frances Willard (1839–98) was the president of the US Woman's Christian Temperance Union and founder of the World WCTU in 1883. Willard was the founder and editor of the magazine *The Union Signal*, and was also a writer of several books and many articles. Throughout her life, Willard toiled tirelessly for suffrage and prohibition, travelling across the United States speaking on these issues at an average of four hundred lectures per year during one ten-year period.

Frances E. Willard
Reasons for Woman's Enfranchisement (1898)

Doubtless the strongest points in favor of woman suffrage are:

1. That it is founded on the unchanging principles of justice. Every reasonable man knows that it is not right to tax a class without representing that class, to inflict penalties upon a class that had no hand in determining what those penalties should be, to govern one half of the human race by the other half. All injustice to one class works harm to every other.

2. The best government known to the race is found in a home where father and mother have equal power, as is the case in an enlightened modern Christian family. No other place is so free from temptation, and no other conserves so completely the best interest of all who dwell therein. Reasoning from analogy, the larger home of society, and that largest home of all called government, might be more like this typical home, and in proportion as they are made like unto it, society and government will more thoroughly conserve the interest of all, and shut out the pests of civilization.

3. The two most strongly marked instincts of woman are those for herself and little ones, and of love and loyalty to her husband and her son. On the other hand, the two strongest instincts that to-day defend the liquor traffic and drink habit are avarice in the dealer and appetite in the drinker. It has been said that civilization has nothing with which it can offset these two tremendous forces. But may it not be found that in the home, through the reserve power never yet called into government on a large scale, woman's instincts of self-protection and of love are a sufficient offset to appetite and avarice, and will out-vote both at the polls? For it must be remembered that, in a republic, all questions of morality sooner or later find their way to the ballot-box, and are voted up or down.

4. Women constitute more than two-thirds of our church members, and less than one-fifth of our criminals. As a class women hold the balance of power morally in the republic.

5. There is no enemy dreaded so much by liquor-dealers and saloon-keepers as a woman – with the ballot in her hand. Secret circulars sent out by them, and intercepted by our temperance leaders, state this explicitly. One of these is addressed to a legislator, and reads to this effect: 'Set your heel upon the woman suffrage movement every time, for the ballot in the hand of woman means the downfall of our trade.' When the bill by which the women of Washington Territory had the ballot and secured local opposition, was declared unconstitutional by the Supreme Court of the Territory, there were bonfires, bell-ringings, and beer on tap in the public square of many a town and village, where the saloon-keepers celebrated their jubilee because the women had lost their right to vote.

6. Whenever women have had the ballot, they have used it in the interest of the home and against the saloons, the gambling-houses, and the haunts of infamy.

In Wyoming, women obtained full suffrage in 1869. Rev. Dr B. F. Crary, presiding elder of the M. E. churches in that State, wrote years ago of the equal suffrage law, 'Liquor-sellers and gamblers are unanimous in cursing it.' Chief Justice Groesbeck, of Wyoming, wrote, in 1897: 'The influence of the women voters has always been on the side of temperance, morality and good government, and opposed to drunkenness, gambling and immorality.' Wyoming was the first State in the Union to raise the age of protection for girls to eighteen.

Colorado granted full suffrage to women in 1893. Equal suffrage has raised the age of protection to eighteen; has equalized the property laws between husband and wife; has secured a law making fathers and mothers equal guardians of their children; has greatly increased the number of women serving on educational boards; and has more than quadrupled the number of no-license towns in Colorado.

Kansas gave municipal suffrage to women in 1887. Several years ago the Chief Justice of Kansas and all the judges of the Supreme Court united in paying tribute to the good results. All concurred in substance with Judge W. A. Johnston, who wrote: 'In consequence, our elections are more orderly and fair, a higher class of officers are chosen, and we have cleaner and stronger city governments.'

After seven years' experience of municipal suffrage, Kansas submitted to the voters, for the second time, an amendment to extend full suffrage to women. A German-American Liquor League was organized from one end of the State to the other, to fight it – a sure proof that the women had used their municipal vote well. The amendment was defeated, but received an affirmative vote more than ten times as large as when a similar amendment was first submitted, some years before.

In 1880, Arkansas passed a law that the opening of a saloon within three miles of a church or schoolhouse might be prevented by a petition from a majority of the adult inhabitants, men and women. The liquor dealers contested the constitutionality of the law. Their attorney, in his argument before the Supreme Court, said:

> None but male persons of sound mind can vote; but their rights are destroyed, and the idiots, aliens and females step in and usurp their rights in popular government. Since females, idiots, and aliens cannot vote, they should not be permitted to accomplish the same purpose by signing a petition; for the signature of an adult to a petition is the substance of a ballot in taking the popular sense of the community. It merely changes the form, and is identical in effect.

The Supreme Court, however, upheld the constitutionality of the law. Under it, the saloons have been cleared out of three fourths of the counties in Arkansas.

In Idaho, full suffrage was granted to women in 1896. William Balderston, of Boise, editor of one of Idaho's principal dailies, writes:

> An interesting result of the new law was observed during the session of the Legislature last winter. In Idaho there had been a law legalizing gambling. Up to the time of the adoption of equal suffrage, it would have been impracticable to repeal it; but when a bill was introduced last winter for that purpose, it went through with

a large majority. The majority for it was universally credited to the addition of the woman element to the electorate.

Even at the antipodes, women stand for the home. Equal suffrage was given to the women of New Zealand in 1893. Now comes the news of a movement in New Zealand to put down gambling. 'Sweep-stakes' have been declared illegal, and a bill to legalize them has been defeated on the avowed ground that the large associations of women, whose votes would be needed at the next election, were against the bill.

The Woman's Christian Temperance Union, while fully convinced that the ballot is the right of every woman in the nation, just as much as it is the right of every man, does not base its line of argument upon this fact, but upon the practical value that woman's vote will have in helping the nation to put away the liquor traffic and its accompanying abominations. We do not ask it for ourselves alone; we are impartial friends of the whole human race in both its fractions, man and woman, and hence we are not more in earnest for this great advance because of the good it brings to the gentler, than because of the blessing that it promises to the stronger sex; it is for these practical reasons that we claim that woman's ballot should be one of the planks in the platform of every righteous party in America.

[Source: *The Woman's Journal* 18, no. 10 (1898): 73.]

Mary Church Terrell (1863–1954) was a writer and civil rights activist. Both her parents, Robert Reed Church and Louisa Ayers, were former slaves. Terrell majored in classics at Oberlin College, where she received her bachelor's degree in 1884, one of the first African American women awarded a college degree. Through her father, she met Frederick Douglass and Booker T. Washington. She was especially close to Douglass and worked with him on several civil rights campaigns. Terrell was an active member of the National American Woman Suffrage Association and was particularly concerned about ensuring the organization continued to fight for black woman suffrage.

Mary Church Terrell
The Progress of Colored Women (1898)
Address Delivered to the National American Woman Suffrage Association

Fifty years ago a meeting such as this, planned, conducted and addressed by women would have been an impossibility. Less than forty years ago, few sane men would have predicted that either a slave or one of his descendents would in this century at least, address such an audience in the Nation's Capital at the invitation of women representing the highest, broadest, best type of womanhood that can be found anywhere in the world. Thus to me this semi-centennial of the National American Woman Suffrage Association is a double jubilee, rejoicing as I do, not only in the prospective enfranchisement of my sex but in the emancipation of my race. When Ernestine Rose, Lucretia Mott, Elizabeth Cady Stanton, Lucy Stone and Susan B. Anthony began that agitation by which colleges were opened to women and the numerous reforms inaugurated for the amelioration of their condition along all lines, their sisters who groaned in bondage had little reason to hope that these blessings would ever brighten their crushed and blighted lives, for during those days of oppression and despair, colored women were not only refused admittance to institutions of learning, but the law of the States in which the majority lived made it a crime to teach them to read. Not only could they possess no property, but even their bodies were not their own. Nothing, in short, that could degrade or brutalize the womanhood of the race was lacking in that system from which colored women then had little hope of escape. So gloomy were their prospects, so fatal the laws, so pernicious the customs, only fifty years ago. But, from the day their fetters were broken and their minds released from the darkness of ignorance to which for more than two hundred years they had been doomed, from the day they could stand erect in the dignity of womanhood, no longer bond but free, till tonight, colored women have forged steadily ahead in the acquisition of knowledge and in the cultivation of those virtues which make for good. To use a thought of the illustrious Frederick Douglass, if judged by the depths from which they have come, rather than by the heights to which those blessed with centuries of opportunities have attained, colored women need not hang their heads in shame. Consider if you will, the almost insurmountable obstacles which have confronted colored women in their efforts to educate and cultivate themselves since their emancipation, and I dare assert, not boastfully, but with pardonable pride, I hope, that the progress they have made and the work they have accomplished, will bear a favorable comparison at least with that of their more fortunate sisters, from whom the opportunity of acquiring knowledge and the means of self-culture have never been entirely withheld. For, not only are colored women with ambition and aspiration handicapped on account of their sex, but they are everywhere baffled and mocked on account of their race. Desperately and continuously they are forced to fight that opposition, born of a cruel, unreasonable prejudice which neither their merit nor necessity seems able to subdue. Not only because they are women, but because they are colored women, are discouragement and disappointment meeting them at every turn. Avocations opened and opportunities offered to their more favored sisters have been and are tonight closed and barred against them. While those of the dominant race have a variety of trades and pursuits from which they may choose, the woman through whose veins one drop of African blood is known to flow is limited to a pitiful few. So overcrowded are the avocations in which colored women may engage and so poor is the pay in consequence, that only the barest livelihood can be eked out by the rank and file. And yet, in spite of the opposition encountered, and the obstacles opposed to their acquisition of knowledge and their accumulation of property, the progress made by colored women along these lines has never been surpassed by that of any people in the history of the world. Though the slaves were liberated less than forty years ago, penniless and ignorant, with neither shelter nor food, so great was their thirst for knowledge and so Herculean were their efforts to secure it, that there are today hundreds of negroes, many of them women, who are graduates, some of them having taken degrees from the best institutions of the land. From Oberlin, that friend of the oppressed, Oberlin, my dear alma mater, whose name will always be loved and whose praise will ever be sung as the first college in the country which was just, broad and benevolent enough to open its doors to negroes and to women on an equal footing with men; from Wellesley and Vassar, from Cornell and Ann Arbor, from the best high schools throughout the North, East and West, colored girls have been graduated with honors, and have thus forever settled the question of their capacity and worth. But a few years ago in an examination in which a large number of young women and men competed for a scholarship, entitling the successful competitor to an entire course through the Chicago University, the only colored girl among them stood first and captured this great prize. And so, wherever colored girls have studied, their instructors bear testimony to their intelligence, diligence and success.

With this increase of wisdom there has sprung up in the hearts of colored women an ardent desire to do good in the world. No sooner had the favored few availed themselves of such advantages as they could secure than they hastened to dispense these blessings to the less fortunate of their race. With tireless energy and eager zeal, colored women have, since their emancipation, been continuously prosecuting the work of educating and elevating their race, as though upon themselves alone devolved the accomplishment of this great task. Of the teachers engaged in instructing colored youth, it is perhaps no exaggeration to say that fully ninety per cent are women. In the back-woods, remote from the civilization, and comforts of the city and town, on the plantations, reeking with ignorance and vice, our colored women may be found battling with evils which such conditions always entail. Many a heroine, of whom the world will never hear, has thus sacrificed her life to her race, amid surroundings and in the face of privations, which only martyrs can tolerate and bear. Shirking responsibility has never been a fault with which colored women might be truthfully charged. Indefatigably and conscientiously, in public work of all kinds they engage, that they may benefit and elevate their race. The result of this labor has been prodigious indeed. By banding themselves together in the interest of education and morality, by adopting the most practical and useful means to this end, colored women have in thirty short years, become a great power for good. Through the National Association of Colored Women, which was formed by the union of two large organizations in July, 1896, and which is now the only national body among colored women, much good has been done in the past, and more will be accomplished in the future, we hope […]

Under the direction of the Tuskegee, Alabama branch of the National Association, the work of bringing the light of knowledge and the gospel of cleanliness to their benighted sisters on the plantations has been conducted with signal success. Their efforts have thus far been confined to four estates comprising thousands of acres of land, on which live hundreds of colored people, yet in the darkness of ignorance and the grip of sin, miles away from churches and schools. Under the evil influences of plantation owners and through no fault of their own the condition of the colored people is, in some sections today no better than it was at the close of the war. Feeling the great responsibility resting upon them, therefore, colored women, both in organizations under the National Association and as individuals are working with might and main to afford their unfortunate sisters opportunities of civilization and education, which without them, they would be unable to secure […]

In New York City a mission has been established and is entirely supported by colored women under supervision of the New York City Board. It has in operation a kindergarten, classes in cooking and sewing, mothers' meetings, men's meetings, a reading circle and a manual training school for boys. Much the same kind of work is done by the Colored Woman's League and the Ladies Auxiliary of this city, the   Kansas City League of Missouri, the Woman's Era Club of Boston, the Woman's Loyal Union of New York, and other organizations representing almost every State in the Union. The Phyllis Wheatley Club of New Orleans, another daughter of the National Association, has in two short years succeeded in establishing a Sanatorium and a Training School for nurses. The conditions which caused the colored women of New Orleans to choose this special field in which to operate are such as exist in many other sections of our land. From the city hospitals colored doctors are excluded altogether, not even being allowed to practice in the colored wards, and colored patients – no matter how wealthy they are – are not received at all unless they are willing to go into the charity wards. Thus the establishment of a Sanatorium answers a variety of purposes. It affords colored medical students an opportunity of gaining a practical knowledge of their profession, and it furnishes a well-equipped establishment for colored patients who do not care to go into the charity wards of the public hospitals [...]

Dotted all over the country are charitable organizations for the aged, orphaned and poor, which have been established by colored women; just how many, it is difficult to state. Since there is such an imperative need of statistics, bearing on the progress, possessions, and prowess of colored women, the National Association has undertaken to secure this data of such value and importance to the race. Among the charitable institutions, either founded, conducted or supported by colored women, may be mentioned the Hale Infirmary of Montgomery, Alabama; the Carrie Steel Orphanage of Atlanta; the Reed Orphan Home of Covington; the Haines Industrial School of Augusta in the State of Georgia; a Home for the Aged of both races at New Bedford and St Monica's Home of Boston in Massachusetts; Old Folks' Home of Memphis, Tenn.; Colored Orphan's Home, Lexington, Ky., together with others of which time forbids me to speak [...]

Questions affecting our legal status as a race are also constantly agitated by our women. In Louisiana and Tennessee, colored women have several times petitioned the legislatures of their respective States to appeal the obnoxious 'Jim Crow Car' Laws, nor will any stone be left unturned until this iniquitous and unjust enactment against respectable American citizens be forever wiped from the statutes of the South. Against the barbarous Convict Lease System of Georgia, of which negroes, especially the female prisoners, are the principal victims, colored women are waging a ceaseless war. By two lecturers, each of whom under the Woman's Christian Temperance Union have been National Superintendent of work among colored people, the cause of temperance has for many years been eloquently espoused.

In business, colored women have had signal success. There is in Alabama a large milling and cotton business belonging to and controlled entirely by a colored woman who has sometimes as many as seventy-five men in her employ. In Halifax, Nova Scotia, the principal ice plant of the city is owned and managed by one of our women. In the professions we have dentists and doctors, whose practice is lucrative and large. Ever since the publication, in 1773, of a book entitled 'Poems on Various Subjects, Religious and Moral,' by Phyllis [sic] Wheatley, negro servant of Mr John Wheatley of Boston, colored women have from time to time given abundant evidence of literary ability. In sculpture we are represented by a woman upon whose chisel Italy has set her seal of approval; in painting, by Bougereau's pupil, whose work was exhibited in the last Paris Salon; and in Music by young women holding diplomas from the first conservatory in the land.

And, finally, as an organization of women nothing lies nearer the heart of the National Association than the children, many of whose lives, sad and dark, we might brighten and bless. It is the kindergarten we need. Free kindergartens in every city and hamlet of this broad land we must have, if the children are to receive from us what it is our duty to give. Already during the past year kindergartens have been established and successfully maintained by several organizations, from which most encouraging reports have come [...] As an organization, the National Association of Colored Women feels that the establishment of kindergartens is the special mission which we are called to fulfill. So keenly alive are we to the necessity of rescuing our little ones, whose noble qualities are deadened and dwarfed by the very atmosphere which they breathe, that the officers of the Association are now trying to secure means by which to send out a kindergarten organizer, whose duty it shall be to arouse the consciousness of our women, and to establish kindergartens, wherever the means therefore can be secured.

And so, lifting as we climb, onward and upward we go, struggling and striving and hoping that the buds and blossoms of our desires will burst into glorious fruition ere long. With courage born of success achieved in the past, with a keen sense of the responsibility which we shall continue to assume, we look forward to a future large with promise and hope. Seeking no favors because of our color, nor patronage because of our needs, we knock at the bar of justice, asking an equal chance.

[Note: Among the speakers at the convention were Susan B. Anthony, Isabella Beecher Hooker, Rev. Anna H. Shaw, Lillie Deverux, May Wright Sewell, and Carrie Chapman Catt.

Source: *The Progress of Colored Women* (Washington, DC: Smith Brothers, 1898), 7–10, 10–11, 11–12, 12, 13–15. Available through the Gerritsen Collection.]

Hubertine Auclert (1848–1914) was a leading French feminist and a campaigner for women's suffrage. Inspired by the high-profile activities of Maria Deraismes and Léon Richer, Hubertine Auclert became involved with feminist work and eventually took a job as Richer's secretary. In 1878, the 'International Congress on Women's Rights' was held in Paris, but to Auclert's dismay it did not support women's suffrage, a cause which she took up with tremendous energy. In February of 1881 she launched *La Citoyenne*, a newspaper that argued vociferously for women's enfranchisement, and in 1883 she founded the National Women's Suffrage Society.

Hubertine Auclert
Woman Suffrage (1883)

French feminists, close ranks.

To be ready for any eventuality, we believe it indispensable to rally the support and sympathy we have acquired. Association has this benefit for the partisans of a given cause: it is that in bringing together the efforts of each one to increase the strength of all, the collective provides the means and the dedication, and sufficient energy, talent and money to extend and develop the idea that serves to bring people together.

The association we are organizing under the title of the 'National Women's Suffrage Society' (*Société nationale du suffrage des femmes*) is modelled on the powerful English and American associations that have already had fruitful results, such as winning for women in England the municipal vote; in the Isle of Man the municipal and political vote; in the isle of Islande in Denmark the municipal vote; and in the territories of Wyoming and Utah in the United States the municipal and political vote.

The French association, created in equally favourable circumstances, will have even greater success than these foreign associations; it will assure in short order the political rights of women.

How? By force?

No. By persuasion.

In placing itself above political and religious discussions, the National Women's Suffrage Society opens its doors to all loyal and rational French people; and in determining its goal of suffrage while enabling partisans of the complete emancipation of woman to know who they are and to be counted, it closes the door on inconsequential discussions.

At the present time, feminists in France are divided into two camps: the old school that wants a restricted suffrage, a partial vote that relies on the good graces of the representatives of the law; and the new school that, affirming the principle of equality, wants for women without restrictions the complete and immediate right, with all the prerogatives it entails, to vote and to stand for election; that is to say they want women to have the power to enfranchise themselves politically.

It is hardly necessary to explain that between the adherents of the two groups there is all the difference that exists between one who lays claim to her due and a beggar who extends her hand for alms. Women destitute of rights are not beggars; they lay claim to what for too long has already been accorded to men. They must assume as soon as possible their share of sovereignty, in both the public interest and their own.

We therefore call upon those who are pursuing a purely theoretical course toward civil rights to abandon their dreams to follow us on the firm ground of political rights, the keystone of all other rights for women.

One cannot demand of human nature more perfection than it is endowed with. As long as men are the only guardians of power, they will exercise it for their own profit; as long as men alone make the laws, they will make laws that serve their interests and not ours. A chamber of men, three quarters of whom are enriched by marriage, will never reform the law that enjoins men to pocket, like vulgar Alphonses, the dowry or the salary of their wives. A chamber of men will vote for divorce in its broadest compass, so that women remain defrauded given that man, at once judge and litigant, remains the only one who prosecutes divorce.

Women who desire civil rights, who want divorce on an egalitarian basis, reform of marriage laws, the admission of women into paid employment, should more than anyone else organize to win political power because this power will give them the right to fashion the laws they wish for.

Everyone who does not want to preserve the status quo should join the National Women's Suffrage Society. And it is not enough to join oneself; one must get one's parents and friends to join; one must by one's proselytising attract the hamlets, the boroughs, the cities.

This society, which counts Madam Edmond Adam, the eminent director of the *Nouvelle Revue*, among its honorary members, in whose salon liberal patriots have so often in grave times deliberated in the interest of France and the republic, and in whose brainstorming committee municipal counsellors from Paris and the provinces, by enlightening the masses on their rights and their duties, will spark a great movement of public opinion from which will come woman's liberation ...

[Source: *La Citoyenne*, 5 February to 4 March 1883. L'APRPP microfilm. Trans. M. Moynagh.]

Clara Zetkin (1857–1933) was an active German socialist, joining such organizations as the Socialist Workers' Party, the Social Democratic Party of Germany, the Independent Social Democratic Party of Germany, and the Spartacist League. As much a feminist as she was a pacifist and a socialist, Zetkin established a feminist program within the Socialist International, edited the newspaper *Die Gleichheit* (Equality), launched the first International Women's Day in 1911, and interviewed Lenin on women's issues in 1920.

Clara Zetkin
From 'Women's Right to Vote' (1907)

A Resolution Introduced at the International Socialist Congress

The International Socialist Congress welcomes joyfully the fact that for the first time an International Socialist Women's Conference has congregated at Stuttgart and it expresses solidarity with the demands made at that Conference. The Socialist parties of all countries are obligated to fight energetically for the introduction of the universal suffrage for women. Their battles waged on behalf of the proletariat's suffrage leading to the democratization of the legislative state and county governing bodies must be simultaneously waged as battles for women's suffrage, which is to be demanded energetically in the propaganda campaigns as well as in the parliaments. In countries where the democratization of men's suffrage has already progressed very far or has been accomplished, the Socialist parties must take up the battle for the introduction of universal women's suffrage. They must, of course, at the same time support all demands which are still made in the interests of full civil rights for the male proletariat. It is the duty of the Socialist women's movements of all countries to participate with all of their energy in all battles waged by the Socialist parties for the democratization of the suffrage, but also to employ the same amount of energy to take part in all battles in which the demand for universal women's suffrage is seriously raised on the basis of its fundamental importance and practical significance. The International Congress recognizes the inappropriateness for every country to announce a timetable for the commencement of the voting rights campaign but, at the same time, it declares that wherever a struggle is to be waged for the right to vote, it must be conducted only according to Socialist principles, i.e., with the demand for universal suffrage for both women and men.

In Support of the Resolution on Women's Right to Vote

I must report to you about the deliberations of the Commission on Women's

Suffrage and the resolution before you which was also adopted by the First International Socialist Conference by a vote of 47 to 11. The Socialist women do not consider the women's right to vote as the most significant question, whose solution will remove all social obstacles which exist in the path of the free and harmonious development and activity of the female sex. That is because it does not touch upon the deepest cause: Private property in which is rooted the exploitation and suppression of one human being by another. This is clearly illustrated by the situation of the politically emancipated, yet socially suppressed and exploited, male proletariat. The granting of suffrage to the female sex does not eliminate the class differences between the exploiters and the exploited from which are derived the most serious social obstacles to the free and harmonious development of the female proletarian. It also does not eliminate the conflicts which are created for women as members of their sex from the social contradictions that occur between men and women within the capitalist system. On the contrary: The complete political equality of the female sex prepares the ground on which the conflicts will be fought with the greatest intensity. These conflicts are varied, but the most serious and painful one is the conflict between professional work and motherhood. For us Socialists, therefore, women's suffrage cannot be the 'final goal' as it is for bourgeois women. However, we yearn most fervently for its acquisition as one phase of the battle towards our final goal. The obtainment of suffrage aids the bourgeois women to tear down the barriers in the form of male prerogatives which tend to limit their educative and professional opportunities. It arms the female proletarians in their battle against class exploitation and class rule, in their effort to acquire their full humanity. It enables them to participate to a higher degree than heretofore in the attainment of political power by the proletariat, for the purpose of erecting a Socialist order which alone will solve the women's question.

We Socialists do not demand women's suffrage as a natural right with which women are born. We demand it as a social right which is anchored in the revolutionized economic activity and in the revolutionized social state and personal consciousness of women. Capitalist production has sent the domestically employed housewife of the good old days to an old-age home. The professional woman, especially the salaried woman who stands right at the center of the economic life of society, has taken her place and become the typical form which female economic activity represents in its most essential social capacity. The professional and trade statistics of all capitalist countries reflect this change. That which women at an earlier time produced within their four walls served the consumption and the welfare of their family. Today, whatever streams out of her industrious hands, whatever her brain thinks of that is useful, acceptable and pleasant, appear as goods on the social market. Millions of women themselves appear as sellers of their labor, the most important social good on society's labor market. Thus a revolution is wrought in her position within the family and society. The woman is detached from the household as the source of her livelihood and she gains her independence from her family and her husband. In many cases, too, the family no longer offers her a satisfactory meaning of life. Just like the man under equally hard conditions (and at times under even more difficult ones), she has to take up the fight for the vital necessities against a hostile environment. She needs for this, just like the man, her full political rights because such rights are weapons with which she can and must defend her interests. Together with her social being, her world of perception and thought is being revolutionized. The political impotence which the female sex accepted as natural for so many centuries is [now] viewed by her as an outrageous injustice. By a slow, painful developmental process, women are emerging from the narrowness of family life to the forum of political activity. They are demanding their full political equality as it is symbolized by suffrage as a vital social necessity and a social emancipation. The obtainment of suffrage is the necessary corollary to the economic independence of women.

One would assume that in view of this situation, the entire politically disenfranchised female sex would form one phalanx to fight for universal women's suffrage. But that is not the case at all. The bourgeois women do not even stand united and determined behind the principle of the full political equality of the female sex. They are even more reluctant to fight energetically, as one united force, for universal women's suffrage. In the final analysis, this is not due to the ignorance and shortsighted tactics of the leaders of the suffragettes' camp, even though they can be correctly blamed for a number of deficiencies. It is the inevitable consequence of the diverse social strata to which women belong. The value of enfranchisement stands in a reverse relationship to the size of the estate. It is of least importance to the women of the Upper Ten Thousand and it means the most to the female proletarians. Thus the struggle for women's suffrage, too, is dominated by class contradictions and class struggle. There cannot be a unified struggle for the entire sex, particularly when this battle does not relate to a bloodless principle, but rather to the concrete and vital question of the women's right to vote. We cannot expect bourgeois women to proceed against their very nature. The female proletarians in their struggle for civil rights cannot, therefore, count on the support of the bourgeois women because the class contradictions preclude that female proletarians will join the bourgeois suffragette movement. All of this does not mean that they should reject the bourgeois suffragettes who want to march behind them or at their side in the battle for the women's right to vote. They may march separately but fight together. But the female proletarians must know that they cannot acquire the right to vote in a struggle of the female sex without class distinctions against the male sex. No, it must be a class struggle of all the exploited without differences of sex against all exploiters no matter what sex they belong to.

In their fight for the attainment of universal women's suffrage, the proletarian women find strong allies in the Socialist parties of all countries. The advocacy of universal women's suffrage by the Socialist parties is not based on ideological and ethical considerations. It is dictated by historical perception but, above all, by an understanding of the class situation as well as the practical battle needs of the proletariat. This proletariat cannot fight its economic and political battles without the participation of its women who, awakened to class consciousness, organized and trained, have been equipped with social rights. Due to the increased employment of women in industry, movements that fight for increased wages can be successful only if they include female workers who have become trained and organized class fighters. But political work, the political work of the proletariat, must also be shared by women. The intensification of the class struggle between the exploiters and the exploited increases the significance of the awakening of class consciousness in women and their participation in the proletarian movement of emancipation. Contrary to the expectations of bourgeois fools, the strengthening of trade union organizations has not resulted in social peace but in an era of gigantic lockouts and strikes. The resolute involvement of the proletariat in the political life has led to the sharpest intensification of the political battle, an intensification which has led to new methods and means of combat. In Belgium and Holland, the proletariat had to complement its parliamentary struggle by the political mass strike. In Russia it tried the same weapon during the revolution with the greatest success. In order to grasp the suffrage reform from its enemies, the Austrian proletariat had to keep the revolutionary weapon of the mass strike in readiness. Gigantic strikes and gigantic lockouts, especially, however, revolutionary mass strikes, call for the greatest sacrifices on the part of the proletariat. It cannot, like the possessing classes, devolve these sacrifices upon hirelings and it cannot pay for them out of a well-filled purse. These are sacrifices that every member of this class must personally bear. That is why these sacrifices can only be made if the proletarian women, too, are filled with historical insight into the necessity and the significance of them. Just how significant and indispensable it is that the female proletariat be imbued with Socialist convictions from which a willingness to sacrifice and heroism flow, has just been demonstrated by the brilliant Austrian suffrage battle. It would not have ended victoriously without the active participation of the proletarian women. It must be emphasized that the success of our Austrian brothers was to a considerable extent the result of the loyalty, hard work, willingness to sacrifice and courage displayed by our Austrian women comrades. (*Bravo!*)

This brief sketch shows that the proletariat has a vital stake in the political equality of the female sex and that it must fight for the full civil rights for women. This battle arouses the women masses and helps them to acquire a sense of class consciousness. The granting of women's suffrage is the prerequisite for the resolute participation of women proletarians in the proletarian class struggle. At the same time, it creates the strongest incentive to awaken, gather and train the female proletariat with the same fervor as the enlightenment and organization of the male proletariat is being pursued. As long as women are politically disenfranchised, they are frequently viewed as powerless and the influence which they exercise upon political life is underestimated. At the stock exchange of parliamentary life, only the ballot possesses an exchange value. The shortsighted individuals who view the political struggle only within the framework of ballots and mandates view the efforts to arouse the female proletariat to a class-conscious life merely as a kind of amusement and luxury which Social-Democracy should only indulge in if it possesses an excess of time, energy and money. They overlook the proletariat's compelling class interest in seeing to it that the class struggle also develops within the women's world so that the female proletarians will fight resolutely alongside their brothers. From the moment when women will be emancipated and capable of casting their votes, this interest will become clear to even the most shortsighted individual in our ranks. A race will begin by all parties to obtain the votes of the female proletarians since they constitute the majority of the female sex. The Socialist parties then must make sure that their enlightenment campaign will keep away all the bourgeois parties and their fight for the attainment of civil rights by women must work in that direction. This has been proven by the history of the suffrage battle in Finland and by the first suffrage campaign there which was conducted in a situation in which both men and women had the right to vote. Women's suffrage is an excellent means to push forward into the last, and perhaps the strongest, bulwark of the ignorant masses: The political indifference and backwardness of broad segments of the female proletariat. This fortress aggravates and hurts our current proletarian struggle and threatens the future of our class. That is why we have to do away with it. (*Bravo!*)

In these days of intensified class struggle, the question arises: For what kind of women's suffrage should the Socialist parties fight? Years ago, this question would hardly have mattered. One would have answered: For women's suffrage, period. Then too, limited women's suffrage was regarded as an imperfection and insufficient progress, but still it was viewed as the first phase of the political emancipation of the female sex. Today this naive concept is no longer justified. Today the Socialist parties must emphatically declare that they can only fight for universal women's suffrage and that they decisively reject limited women's suffrage as a falsification and mockery of the principle of the equality of women. What was previously done instinctively – by the introduction of limited women's rights in order to strengthen the position of property – is now done consciously. Two tendencies are at work within the bourgeois parties that will break the fundamental resistance against the women's suffrage: The rising external and internal difficulties of large circles of the bourgeois women's world that have to fight for their civil rights and the growing fear of the political advances of the fighting proletariat. In such a situation, the introduction of limited women's suffrage appears as a saving alternative. The proletariat is slated to pay for the costs of maintaining the peace between the men and women of the possessing classes. The possessing classes consider the introduction of limited women's suffrage because they view it as a protective wall against the increasing power of the fighting proletariat. This was first demonstrated by the events in Norway. When universal suffrage in respect to local elections could no longer be denied to the attacking proletariat which was fighting under the leadership of Social-Democracy, this reform was vitiated by the introduction of limited women's suffrage. Bourgeois politicians declared candidly that the limited suffrage for women is designed as a counterweight to the universal suffrage for men [...]

As far as the suffrage is concerned, the Socialist parties must fight for all demands that they raise on principle in the interest of the proletariat. They will carry home as loot as much as they are able to wrest from the enemy. What is important is that women's suffrage must be emphatically demanded in the course of agitation among the masses or in parliament, and the intensity of the demand must correspond to the importance of the subject. We are aware of the fact that in most countries the conquest of women's suffrage will not occur from one day to the next because of such action. On the other hand, we also know that it is just such an action which will make preparations for a future victory.

In the proletarian battle for the civil rights of the female sex, the Socialist women must be the driving force, not only by participating with all of their energy in the proletarian suffrage battles but also by persuading the mass of female proletarians to become their co-fighters. By incorporating the masses of female proletarians into the ranks of the fighting brothers, they prove two things, i.e., that the masses of women themselves desire the right to vote and that the female proletarians are mature enough to use the suffrage correctly. Let us step forward without hesitation to battle for women's suffrage. It serves to arouse the female proletariat to a class-conscious political life which is of the highest significance for the present and future of the proletariat and its war of liberation. Not the patient bearer of crosses, not the dull slave, but the resolute fighting woman will raise a generation of strong male and female fighters. With every reason, the woman can state that avengers will rise from her bones, children who were nourished by the bold thoughts of her brain and the passionate wishes of her heart, male and female fighters who will not only replace her one day, but even surpass her as far as their battle virtues are concerned.

[Original source: *The International Socialist Congress at Stuttgart, August 18, 1907* (Berlin 1907); repr. as 'Women's Right to Vote,' in *Clara Zetkin: Selected Writing*, ed. Philip S. Foner (New York: International Publishers, 1984), 98–104, 107.]

Emmeline Pankhurst (1879–1928) was born to abolitionist and feminist parents, married a supporter of the women's suffrage movement, raised two feminist daughters, and spent her life surrounded by activists. Often a controversial and confrontational woman, Pankhurst was imprisoned repeatedly because of her militant approach towards winning the vote. In 1903 she created the Women's Social and Political Union, whose newspaper, *The Suffragette*, included pro-war and pro-conscription articles, as well as those discussing women's rights. Pankhurst died in 1928, after seeing the women of the United Kingdom gain equal voting rights with men.

Emmeline Pankhurst

The Importance of the Vote (1908)
Speech in the Portman Rooms, London, 24 March 1908

It seems to me a very strange thing that large numbers of women should have met together tonight to consider whether the vote is of importance, while all day long, across the water, in the Peckham By-election, men, whether they realise the importance of the vote or not, have been exercising it, and in exercising it settling for women as well as for themselves great questions of public importance.

What, then, is this vote that we are hearing so much about just now, so much more than people have heard in discussion at least, for a great many years? I think we may give the vote a threefold description. We may describe the vote as, first of all, a symbol, secondly, a safeguard, and thirdly, an instrument. It is a symbol of freedom, a symbol of citizenship, a symbol of liberty. It is a safe-guard of all those liberties which it symbolises. And in these later days it has come to be regarded more than anything else as an instrument, something with which you can get a great many more things than our forefathers who fought for the vote ever realised as possible to get with it. It seems to me that such a thing is worth fighting for, and women today are fighting very strenuously in order to get it.

Wherever masses of people are gathered together there must be government. Government without the vote is more or less a form of tyranny. Government with the vote is more or less representative according to the extent to which the vote is given. In this country they tell us we have representative government. So far as women are concerned, while you have representative government for men, you have despotic government for women. So it is in order that the government of the country may be made really representative, may represent not only all classes of the community, but both sexes of the community, that this struggle for the vote is going on on the part of women.

Today, women are working very hard for it. And there is no doubt whatever that very, very soon the fight will be over, and victory will be won.

Part II: Breaking Silence

[...]

Men politicians are in the habit of talking to women as if there were no laws that affect women. 'The fact is,' they say, 'the home is the place for women. Their interests are the rearing and training of children. These are the things that interest women. Politics have nothing to do with these things, and therefore politics do not concern women.' Yet the laws decide how women are to live in marriage, how their children are to be trained and educated, and what the future of their children is to be. All that is decided by Act of Parliament. Let us take a few of these laws, and see what there is to say about them from the women's point of view.

First of all, let us take the marriage laws. They are made by men for women. Let us consider whether they are equal, whether they are just, whether they are wise. What security of maintenance has the married woman? Many a married woman having given up her economic independence in order to marry, how is she compensated for that loss? What security does she get in that marriage for which she gave up economic independence? Take the case of a woman who has been earning a good income. She is told that she ought to give up her employment when she becomes a wife and mother. What does she get in return? All that a married man is obliged by law to do for his wife is to provide for her shelter of some kind, food of some kind, and clothing of some kind. It is left to his good pleasure to decide what the shelter shall be, what the food shall be, what the clothing shall be. It is left to him to decide what money shall be spent on the home, and how it shall be spent; the wife has no voice legally in deciding any of these things. She has no legal claim upon any definite portion of his income. If he is a good man, a conscientious man, he does the right thing. If he is not, if he chooses almost to starve his wife, she has no remedy. What he thinks sufficient is what she has to be content with.

I quite agree, in all these illustrations, that the majority of men are considerably better than the law compels them to be, so the majority of women do not suffer as much as they might suffer if men were all as bad as they might be, but since there are some bad men, some unjust men, don't you agree with me that the law ought to be altered so that those men could be dealt with?

Take what happens to the woman if her husband dies and leaves her a widow, sometimes with little children. If a man is so insensible to his duties as a husband and father when he makes his will, as to leave all his property away from his wife and children, the law allows him to do it. That will is a valid one. So you see that the married woman's position is not a very secure one. It depends entirely on her getting a good ticket in the lottery. If she has a good husband, well and good: if she has a bad one, she has to suffer, and she has no remedy. That is her position as a wife, and it is far from satisfactory.

Now let us look at her position if she has been very unfortunate in marriage, so unfortunate as to get a bad husband, an immoral husband, a vicious husband, a husband unfit to be the father of little children. We turn to the Divorce Court. How is she to get rid of such a man? If a man has got married to a bad wife, and he wants to get rid of her, he has but to prove against her one act of infidelity. But if a woman who is married to a vicious husband wants to get rid of him, not one act nor a thousand acts of infidelity entitle her to a divorce; she must prove either bigamy, desertion, or gross cruelty, in addition to immorality before she can get rid of that man.

Let us consider her position as a mother. We have repeated this so often at our meetings that I think the echo of what we have said must have reached many. By English law no married woman exists as the mother of the child she brings into the world. In the eyes of the law she is not the parent of her child. The child, according to our marriage laws, has only one parent, who can decide the future of the child, who can decide where it shall live, how it shall live, how much shall be spent upon it, how it shall be educated, and what religion it shall profess. That parent is the father.

These are examples of some of the laws that men have made, laws that concern women. I ask you, if women had had the vote, should we have had such laws? If women had had the vote, as men have the vote, we should have had equal laws. We should have had equal laws for divorce, and the law should recognise that they have two parents.

I have spoken to you about the position of the married woman, who does not exist legally as a parent, the parent of her own child. In marriage, children have one parent. Out of marriage children have also one parent. That parent is the mother – the unfortunate mother. She alone is responsible for the future of her child: she alone is punished if her child is neglected and suffers from neglect. But let me give you one illustration. I was in Herefordshire during the by-election. While I was there, an unmarried mother was brought before the bench of magistrates charged with having neglected her illegitimate child. She was a domestic servant, and had put the child out to nurse. The magistrates – there were colonels and landowners on that bench – did not ask what wages the mother got; they did not ask who the father was or whether he contributed to the support of the child. They sent that woman to prison for three months for having neglected her child. I ask you women here tonight, if women had had some share in the making of laws, don't you think they would have found a way of making all fathers of such children equally responsible with the mothers for the welfare of those children? [...]

Now let us look a little to the future. If it ever was important for women to have the vote, it is ten times more important today, because you cannot take up a newspaper, you cannot go to a conference, you cannot even go to church, without hearing a great deal of talk about social reform and a demand for social legislation. Of course, it is obvious that that kind of legislation – and the Liberal Government tell us that if they remain in office long enough we are going to have a great deal of it – is of vital importance to women. If we have the right kind of social legislation it will be a very good thing for women and children. If we have the wrong kind of social legislation, we may have the worst kind of tyranny that women have ever known since the world began.

We are hearing about legislation to decide what kind of homes people are to live in. That surely is a question for women. Surely every woman, when she seriously thinks about it, will wonder how men by themselves can have the audacity to think that they can say what homes ought to be without consulting women. Then take education. Since 1870 men have been trying to find out how to educate children. I think that they have not yet realised that if they are ever to find out how to educate children, they will have to take women into their confidence, and try to learn from women some of those lessons that the long experience of ages has taught to them. One cannot wonder that whole sessions of Parliament should be wasted on Education Bills. For, you see, it is only just lately that men have begun to consider education, or to try to learn what the word means. So as we are going to have a great deal more time devoted to education, I think it will be a great economy of time if we get the vote, if only that we may have an opportunity of deciding how girls are to be trained, even in those domestic duties which gentlemen are so fond of reminding us we ought to attend to [...]

I know the cotton workers of Lancashire. Not long ago, we were in the Rosendale Valley, Mr Harcourt's constituency. In that constituency more women earn wages than men. You find daughters earning more money than their fathers. You find wives earning more money than their husbands. They do piece work, and they often earn better wages than the men. I was talking one day to one – a married woman worker whom I met in the train. She was going home from the mill. She had a child three or four years of age, well dressed, very blithe, and looking well fed. I asked her if she worked in the mill. She said, 'Yes.' I asked her what wages she earned. She said, 'Thirty shillings a week.' She told me she had other children. 'Who looks after the children while you are at work?' 'I have a housekeeper,' she answered. I said to her, 'You are not going to be allowed to work much longer. Mr John Burns is going to make you stay at home and look after the children.' And she said, 'I don't know what we shall do then. I suppose we shall have to clem.' I don't know whether you all know our Lancashire word 'clem.' When we say clem, we mean starve. In thousands of homes in Lancashire, if we get Mr John Burns' proposal carried into law, little children, now well clothed and well fed and well cared for, will have clemmed before many months are over. These women say a shilling that they earn themselves is worth two shillings of their husbands' money, for it is their own. They know far better than their husbands how much money is needed for food, how much is needed to be spent on the home. I do not think there is a woman in Lancashire who does not realise that it is better to earn an income of her own than to be dependent on her husband. They realise it better than women of the upper classes who provide nurses and governesses for their children. I put it to you whether the woman of the working class, so long as she sees that her children are well fed and are well enough cared for, has not as much right as her well-off sister to provide a nurse for her children. We should like to say this to Mr John Burns, that when women get the vote, they will take very much better care of babies than men have been able to do.

There may be many women in this room tonight who do not know much about the industrial women from practical experience. I want to say something about them. Here in London last year there was the Sweated Industries Exhibition. That Exhibition went to Manchester. It went to Birmingham. The papers were full of it. After it was held there were conferences in the Guildhall, conferences in the large centres of population, and resolutions were carried demanding legislation to deal with the sweating evil. Nothing has come of it all. If any of you women are doubtful about the value of the vote to women, that example ought to be enough. Look at the Government's proposals. What do you get in the forefront of their programme? You get an eight hours' day for miners. But you get nothing for the sweated women. Why is the miner being attended to rather than the sweated worker? The miner is being attended to because he, the miner, has got a vote. You see what the vote will do. You see what political power will do. If women had had the vote there would have been proposals to help the sweated woman worker in the Government programme of this session. I think that women, realising the horrible degradation of these workers, the degradation not only to themselves, but to all of us, caused by that evil of sweating, ought to be eager to get political freedom, in order that something may be done to get for the sweated woman labourer some kind of pay that would enable her to live at least a moral and a decent life.

[...] In all grades of education, certainly in elementary education, women are better qualified for the work than the men. You get a better type of woman. Yet for work equal to that of men, she cannot get equal pay. If women teachers had the Parliamentary vote, those men who go to the House of Commons to represent the interests of teachers would have to represent the interests of women teachers as well as the interests of the men. I think that the gentleman who made the teachers the stepping-stone to office, and who talks at by-elections about manhood suffrage would have taken up the interests of the women who have paid his wages if he felt that he was responsible to women voters [...]

Then there is the administrative side of public life. We want the vote not merely to get laws made. I think the possession of the Parliamentary vote is very important on the administrative side of politics. I have every reason to think that, because I have just come out of prison. We may congratulate ourselves that the Militant Suffragists, of whom I am one, have at least succeeded in forcing the Government to appoint the first woman inspector of prisons. Of course, it is a very small thing, but it means a very great deal. It means the beginning of prison reform, reform in prison discipline and prison treatment that have been needed for a very long time. Well, when we get the vote, it won't take many years talking about things to get one woman inspector appointed. The immediate result of our getting the vote will be the appointment of many more women inspectors of factories. When I last made inquiries there was only one woman inspector of factories in all Ireland. Yet in Belfast alone, more women and girls are working in factories than men and boys. The need there for inspection is enormous in those linen and jute factories. It is perfectly obvious that when you have women and girls working in factories, if they are to be properly inspected, you must have women inspectors. We shall get them as soon as we are able to get women's interests properly attended to, which we shall only be able to do when we are in possession of the vote [...]

I hope that there may be a few men and women here who will go away determined at least to give this question more consideration than they have in the past. They will see that we women who are doing so much to get the vote, want it because we realise how much good we can do with it when we have got it. We do not want it in order to boast of how much we have got. We do not want it because we want to imitate men or to be like men. We want it because without it we cannot do that work which it is necessary and right and proper that every man and woman should be ready and willing to undertake in the interests of the community of which they form a part.

[Source: *Speeches and Trials of the Militant Suffragettes*, ed. Cheryl R. Jorgensen-Earp (Madison: Fairleigh Dickinson UP, 1999), 31, 33–4, 36, 38–9, 39–40, 41.]

Dame Millicent Garrett Fawcett (1847–1929), Alys Russell (1867–1951), Ray Strachey (1887–1940), and Margaret Jones (?–?) all worked in Britain and abroad to unite women and to win the vote, collaborating through such organizations as the National Union of Women's Suffrage Societies, touring the globe giving lectures on women's issues, and writing articles in journals like the International Woman Suffrage Alliance's *Jus Suffragii*.

Millicent Garrett Fawcett, Alys Russell, Ray Strachey, and Margaret Jones
Suffragists of Great Britain Uphold the Claims of the Women of India (1918)

A letter was recently addressed to the Imperial War Conference (consisting of representative statesmen from all parts of the British Dominions) by the officers of the National Union of Women's Suffrage Societies, urging the adoption throughout the British Empire of the principle of woman suffrage. The latter, and greater, part of the letter is as follows: –
    We venture to urge that this principle – i.e., the share of women in national and political life and their special responsibility for certain aspects of it – should be recognized in India, whatever may be the form which the practical carrying out of the pledges given by H. M.'s Government on August 20, 1917, may take.
    It is unnecessary to dwell on the capacity of Indian women. From time immemorial the names of certain Indian Princesses stand out among the ablest and most sagacious rulers of their respective provinces. The changes of the

last fifty years have opened university education to women, and there are now considerable numbers of Indian ladies who have availed themselves of it, who practice medicine, lecture on law, and conduct schools with skill and success second to none in western countries. To leave such women out of 'the progressive realization of responsible government in India' to which H. M.'s Government are pledged, would be an omission which could only produce in an ever-increasing number of able women a sense of grievance leading to unrest and discontent. We have lately received communications from groups of such women in this sense.

Our convictions on this subject are strengthened by the fact that many of the practical problems which call for government action in India are concerned with education, marriage, and the family – subjects on which women in all countries have special knowledge and responsibility. Therefore, to leave them entirely out of the electorates which may probably be formed in fulfillment of the pledges of the Government would be a national disaster which would go far to nullify the benefits which might otherwise be expected from the projected reforms.

We are aware that the subject on which we write is surrounded by peculiar difficulties in India, but we are convinced that serious dangers will also arise from doing nothing, and we believe that the presence of His Highness the Maharajah of Patiala and Sir Satyendra Sinha gives an invaluable opportunity for utilizing their knowledge of India for introducing the principle of the representation of women in such a way as would commend itself to the most enlightened public opinion of their country. – We have the honour to remain,

Millicent Garrett Fawcett
Alys Russell
Ray Strachey
Margaret Jones

[Source: *Jus Suffragii: International Women Suffrage News* 12, no. 11 (1912): 173. Available through the Gerritsen Collection.]

Dame Millicent Garrett Fawcett (1847–1929) came under the influence of feminism early. Her sister Elizabeth became the first woman to qualify as a physician in Britain, and Elizabeth's friend Emily Davies campaigned long and hard on behalf of women in education. Fawcett became a tireless campaigner for suffrage, which led to her eventually becoming president of the National Union of Women's Suffrage Societies, a position she held from 1897–1919. Unlike Emmeline Pankhurt's militant suffragettes, who stopped all work on the suffrage movement to support the First World War, Fawcett campaigned endlessly before, during, and after the war. She resigned as president of the NUWSS a year after women won the vote, and devoted herself to writing about women and feminism.

Millicent Garrett Fawcett
To Women of All Nations (1918)

In every country throughout the world there is deep thankfulness that the war is over. The earnest prayer of men and women in every country is that a new international organisation may be created at the Peace Conference, a League of Nations which will make a repetition of 1914–18 for ever impossible. Looking back, we can see that in many countries the war has brought political enfranchisement to women. Women in Great Britain, Canada, and Denmark have been enfranchised since the war began. Great progress has been made in the U.S.A. The President has identified himself with the cause of woman suffrage in a way that would have been regarded as a miracle a few years ago. The Italian Prime Minister has declared himself a suffragist. Even in Germany and Austria the new organisation of society brought about by this war seems almost certain to give a great lift forward to the forces which make for freedom, and consequently to the emancipation of women. However wide our differences in other respects, here, therefore, is a subject on which women of all the countries in the I.W.S.A. can rejoice together.

[Source: *Jus Suffragii: International Women Suffrage News* 13, no. 3 (1918): 26. Available through the Gerritsen Collection.]

Kikue Ide (1896–?), a college professor, was one of the leaders of the woman suffrage movement in Japan. She was head of the Women's Problems Institute of Osaka, and was eager for women to study law as a means of reforming Japan's legal system and the place of women in it.

Kikue Ide
History and Problems of the Women's Suffrage Movement in Japan (1928)

Compared with the women's political emancipation movements of some other countries, which have a record of fifty or seventy years, the history of the women's suffrage movement of Japan may seem to have, externally speaking, little to boast of. Indeed, it is of such recent development that a noted suffragist has said that there is, as yet, no such thing as a history connected with it. This decade has seen the rise of the first important women's suffrage organizations, and the first enactments on the part of the Diet removing basic inequalities with regard to women. And yet, if history has to deal with causes and effects, we cannot deny the influences of the long period of self-awakening, growth, and struggle that have preceded the more recent developments. Four periods may be recognised in the story.

The first 33 years of the Era of Meiji – down to the year 1900 – may be called the Early Period. This closed with the promulgation of the Public Safety Police Regulations, wherein women were forbidden to take part in political meetings. It was followed by a period of struggle lasting for 22 years, till, in the eleventh year of the Taisho Era, one of the two fatal clauses of the Regulations was struck out. The third period extended down to the general election of February 1928, under the Manhood Suffrage Law of 1925. The fourth period, in which the movement now is, dates from the February election prior to the 55th session of the Kikai on 20 April 1928, in which, for the first time, members of the Proletarian Parties took their seats.

In order to understand the significance of the first or Early Period, it is important to know first the general conditions of the time, particularly from women's point of view. Dynamic changes at the time of the Restoration of 1867 produced profound effects upon the life of women in general. Destruction of old manners and customs freed the women of the ruling classes as well as the commoners. The breaking down of old caste systems, emancipating the four classes of the oppressed, also affected women and stimulated among them the idea of equality. The life of women in the home was exposed to a great economic revolution, and the old family system was gradually transformed into the family system of the present civil law. Simultaneously, a modern educational plan was introduced. Overwhelming tides of foreign thought played upon women as well as upon men. The thinking of Mill, Bentham, and Rousseau was absorbed by women. In a word, the old ideal of womanhood as portrayed in the sacred book of Great Precepts for Women, written under the combined influences of the old family system, Confucianism, and Buddhism, was waning before the dawn of the new womanhood.

Already two women were outstandingly active in the political world of this time. They were Toshiko Kishida and Eiko Fukuda. It seemed as if women of this period had more hope of favourable political development than had those of later days. Some men of prominence, and some public authorities were in favour of women's participation in political affairs. In the 13th year of Meiji, for example, a village community in the Nagano Prefecture submitted to the

Government of the Prefecture an official statement that they desired women householders to be given the right to vote upon the then prevailing property qualification. In the 21st year of the same era, municipal and communal regulations enacted that voting power might be given to taxpayers above a certain minimum, without qualification of sex. But the growth of this liberal attitude was checked by the adoption of the Imperial Constitution in Meiji 22, establishing the principle of constitution[al] government, but hedging it about with precaution, which meant injustice for more than one group. The 19th article of the constitution, together with the laws related thereto, disqualified women from taking up public duties as civil officers. The Gikai Election Law of the same year excluded women as well as a large proportion of the male population of the country. After the Sino-Japanese war, the question of the extension of the suffrage was freely discussed, and when a proposal was being brought forward to lower the tax qualification from fifteen to ten yen, efforts to have the right of suffrage admitted for women were also under way, when, in Meiji 33, there were passed the famous Public Safety Police Regulations by which women were forbidden to attend political meetings and to be their originators. Neither were they allowed to enter political parties. This, the hardest blow ever given to women's efforts to obtain recognition of their rights, marked the beginning of the Period of Struggle.

By the very nature of the legal prohibitions imposed upon them, it followed that the women's suffrage movement as such, in the narrow sense of the word, became politically dead. But, on the other hand, the general progress of women's emancipation was proceeding. By education, by literature both foreign and domestic, and, toward the close of the period, by the thinking of socialism, women were becoming vastly influenced. Under the influence of socialism, which advocated suffrage, women of the Commoners' Society, and those of a magazine called the 'Twentieth Century,' took the first momentous step in the history of the movement, and lodged written petitions in the Gikai. Women continued their campaigns and petitions until, in Meiji 40, their petition to have the second clause of article 5 of the Public Safety Police Regulations struck out was adopted, and a bill was introduced into the lower house. It was passed in this chamber, and though it did not then become law, it marked an epoch in the struggle.

Upon the eve of the Era of Taisho, a noted women's organization, the Seitosha, came into existence. It was primarily a literary society, organized with the object of fostering women's part in literature. But it provided a foothold for those minorities who were particularly interested in women's emancipation movements, and, in addition, influenced widely the life of women in general. In writing, translating, and thinking, in spite of harsh criticism and persecution, it lavished its services upon the women of the day. In the 9th year of Taisho came the celebrated New Women's Association, with an extensive program for the obtaining of women's just rights, and for their emancipation in general. They set up a department of politics and law, and held, in the first year of their existence, 1920, the first political meeting ever held under the auspices of women. A determined Kikai Campaign was inaugurated, and through successive sessions they carried on their work. Finally, in the eleventh year of Taisho, women obtained freedom to attend, and to originate, political meetings. In referring to the amendment, Mr Jiro Hoshijima, at a meeting to celebrate the occasion held under the auspices of the Association, said: 'The phrase "women and" may be considered insignificant, but I wonder what great changes it may bring upon us all in the near future, politically as well as socially.'

The following period was marked by three striking features. It was a period of organization, producing a number of women's suffrage groups, and demonstrating a marked development in administration. Second, it was the period in which women's suffrage came to the attention of the Gikai. Third, it was a time of awakening political consciousness on the part of women in general, and of much activity in their political education on the part of the organized groups.

The New Women's Association, once so active, was forced to dissolve, and was replaced in its suffrage activities by the Women's Suffrage Alliance. A second organization, the League to Secure Women's Suffrage, was organized in the 14th year of Taisho. Upon the return of Mrs Gauntlett from the Eighth Congress of the International Women's Suffrage Alliance, the Women's Suffrage Association of Japan was established and affiliated with the world organization. To this, existing suffrage organizations, including those of the proletarian parties, bear relation. The formation at about the same time of the Women's Federations of Tokyo and West Japan, the former containing more than 40 organizations, and including a section on women's suffrage, gives a much greater scope to the activities of the individual suffrage groups. Mention must also be made of the W.C.T.U. of Japan, which for many years had stood for the principle of women's suffrage.

Continuous activity on the part of these groups kept the question of Women's Citizenship Rights and Suffrage Rights before the Gikai. In 1925, in the Diet Session which passed the Manhood Suffrage Bill, a bill to further amend the Police Regulations, together with other propositional bills on citizenship, suffrage, and higher education of women, was introduced into the Business Committee. The session discussed the question, but took no action. The Minister of Home Affairs, in answer to a question, stated that the Government was of the opinion that it was not harmful to give the vote to a certain group of women, and that the time would surely come when it would be so. Opinion generally was, however, that the question should wait till the Manhood Suffrage Law had been put into effect.

Thus, when the General Election of February 1928 took place, the two large women's federations determined to propagate the spirit as well as the principles of universal suffrage, and by every means in their power, achieve success in the ideal execution of the existing law. Women's organizations and individual women all over the country took part in the election campaign. 'The most significant thing in the General Election of this time,' says the Osaka Mainichi and the Tokyo Nichinichi of this first occasion when all men in Japan had the right to vote, 'is that it took women out from their homes into the streets and obliged them to speak on politics with their own lips. Most of these women stood on the platforms either for their husbands, fathers, or men whom they respected and many of them were proletarian candidates ... In their activities there was something of the strength unique of womanhood. Women's speech-making is appropriate to the General Election, and has had much to do with the propagation of political ideas among the people. Women's Suffrage should come next.'

The fourth period, which came into being at the February election for the fifty-fifth session of the Gikai convening on 20 April 1928 – an extraordinary session, and significant in being the first in which members elected under manhood suffrage have taken their seats – has been significant for women's suffrage. Realizing that this would be so, seven organizations in Tokyo and one in West Japan appointed a Committee of Seventeen to carry out an effective campaign in the Gikai. But the political feuds which marked the session, and the uncertainty of the position of the government, led this committee to decide upon a policy of waiting. Some women, however, convinced that this session should not end without the challenge of the women's position, presented in the name of a single organization in Osaka petitions for the recognition of women's rights of citizenship, association, and suffrage. The Committee of Seventeen saw value only in obtaining bills upon these questions. Considerable support was evinced by members of the lower house when canvassed on the matter in question, and in the House of Peers, Count Matsuura was the introducer of the written petitions. At a late moment in the sessions all three were adopted, and thus there is a record, in this important first session, of the claims of women.

Of the present political parties, the Seiyukai, the present Government party, does not put forth women's suffrage upon its platform, but it has produced in the past many staunch supporters of the principle, and their numbers are increasing. At a meeting of the party executive on 7 April 1928, it is recorded that there was discussion of women's suffrage in local government. When the session convened, two members of this party drafted a bill in favour of women's suffrage, obtaining the names of 80 members of different parties in its support. The question has also been discussed in the councils of the Minseito, the Opposition party. Two other minority parties have taken a similar stand, while the Proletarian parties definitely declare their stand in favour of full citizenship and voting rights for Japanese women.

Thus, the history of the Movement. But problems of no mean order await those women who are in the forefront of the struggle. When and how should they next proceed? How, on securing their political rights, should they make full use of them? What are their aims in politics? Should they, to hasten the time of securing partial rights, propose first that they be given Municipal Suffrage, or should they try for suffrage on equal terms with men? They know that the struggle for the second will be longer.

To answer these questions, they are studying the opinion of members of local and national legislatures, and are considering the position of women in general. Opinion generally is that municipal rights should be first aimed at, but there is not wanting an expression in influential representative circles that citizenship rights should be conceded at once upon equal terms with men. It has to be realized that Japanese women have three stages through which they have to go – to become recognized as individual citizens before the law, to obtain the right of association, enabling them to become members of political parties, and, finally, to obtain the right to vote. In the second of these, the prohibition is already self-contradicted by facts, and positive legal recognition of the right of association cannot survive long.

Should they, to reach their goal, ally themselves with existing political parties, whose ugly feuds they decry? But how, keeping aloof, can they keep themselves always in sight of their political goals? And, within the ranks of women's organizations now aiming at a common suffrage goal, what should be their interrelationship if the time comes when any or all of them may join political parties of the right or left or centre?

Whatever the answer to these questions, significant indeed in the minds of the thoughtful leaders of the movement, there is no hesitation on their part as to the absolute necessity for obtaining full rights. Present inequalities in educational opportunity, in holding public office, in holding, say, administrative positions in the educational world, will not be removed without this fundamental right being acquired. The great numbers of women in Japan at present suffering economic pressure, and who are engaged in industrial life – 60 per cent of all industrial labourers in Japan are women – contributing as they do to the national life, need the vote for the obtaining of their full womanhood. Woman's social position in Japan has some unsatisfactory features, and these cannot be remedied without legal enactment. 'Law is the mirror of society, and social standards are reflected in law.' The present civil law, especially in its sections on family relations, which are considered the most unjust of all, must be changed, and it is only in women's suffrage that the way can be found to this.

The need is great, the task is great. For the solution of the one and the accomplishment of the other, Japanese women need conviction, and faith. They must be willing to sink personal differences and organizational differences. They must refuse to be the slaves of the movement, but by their spirit, create out of the movement a spiritual value for the nation and for its women.

[Source: *Mid-Pacific Magazine*, September 1928, 217–22.]

Mabel Dove (1905–84) was a Ghanaian journalist and fiction writer who for many years wrote a women's column for the *West African Times* under the pen name Marjorie Mensah. She used the column to address a wide range of feminist concerns, from social reform, to female education, to suffrage. In the 1950s, Dove ran for public office herself and won a seat in 1954 in Kwame Nkrumah's government, the first African woman to be elected to a national assembly.

Mabel Dove
[On Suffrage in West Africa] (July 1931)

Oh, what a thrilling time we are in for! How exceedingly restive is the whole town. What is there all in the atmosphere that seems to possess it like that awful pause that heralds a storm. And I suppose, a storm there will be. The coming election[1] is, indeed, the first talk of the country, and now that we are about to be called upon to return a suitable member of the community to represent the interest of the people in the Legislative Council we are naturally kept very busy examining our material on hand with an eye to business. Everywhere discussion is legion and tends to be very divided. But what about our side of the question? No one seems to have given it thought. Surely, the women of the country must have their particular side. There are many of us entitled to vote – or in other words qualified to vote: such as Mrs Hansen Sackey, Mrs Flora

---

1 Under the 1925 constitution three unofficial members on the Gold Coast Legislative Council were directly elected from the Accra, Cape Coast, and Sekondi municipalities to serve a five-year term. An election was held in 1927 and again in 1931.

Vanderpuye, Mrs Bampo[2] and quite a score of others too numerous to name here. They all come within the category of Ratepayers and property owners, and naturally their votes are of some weight and may materially assist to either equalise the balance or turn it entirely. And why should we not vote? ... The event must be made as popular as possible and as representative as possible. We cannot stand still and leave it all to the men. This is, indeed, a new age. Everyone seems to have realised the consciousness of her right. And we must have that right. Given the same opportunities the women of the world – and in this country – have proved that we are capable of drawing level with the men in practically every walk of life. We need more opportunity. We must utilise our votes, those of us who are entitled – in a measure we are nearly all qualified; and although we may not be considered ripe as yet to put up an independent candidate ourselves for the vacant seat, as I have already said, we can throw in our lot in a judicious manner.

But before we offer our precious votes to any particular candidate we must be convinced that that candidate can 'deliver the goods' – to use the popular phrase. Men are such fickle beings, they never fail to give you a surprise when you least expect it. What, I think, we really want is a man possessing sound common sense, who has foresight, grit and courage – yes courage, plenty of it; not the mamby-pamby reservist, the fellow who always has a lot to say and forgets it all when he gets up to speak in the Council or elsewhere, only to remember it most effectively when he is at a safe distance from the place. I think the community wants a man who can always compel the attention of Government, and at the same time, keep always within certain rational and reasonable bounds.

I am not a politician – very far from it. I just thought that the situation as it stands affects not only the masculine element – but all of us, and in this respect every woman ought to be interested.

It seems to me that men always have a passion to make too much of a thing and it would appear how things are going along, that it may be to some advantage if they were to leave the question of returning a member to Council entirely to us we would soon have an effective Committee at work examining the credentials of all the candidates most minutely; especially, those shadow candidates who are being kept in the background to spring upon us with surprise if certain things occur. We should examine all of them and declare our choice. In our task we will have to put aside sentiment; it is really a big job that we are about to tackle.

---

2 These were elite women who had married into prominent Ga families. Any male or female
   adult who occupied a house of a rateable value of £6 per annum was eligible to vote.

Personally I would wish that a woman was plucky enough to stand for the Council. But if we cannot have a woman we must look into the men and each make her personal choice. Personally I love Mr Quist[3] – he speaks so well of us women, and I remember some nice things he said of us when, on the occasion of the banquet in honour of Dr Nanka Bruce[4] a year or two ago, he proposed the toast of 'Our ladies' and did it with éclat and an encore. I shouldn't be surprised if Mr Quist in Council got the duty on silk reduced and enabled us to have our dresses and stockings cheaper. Anyway the right man must be in the right place.

[Original source: The newspaper *Times of West Africa* or *West African Times*, 10–11 July 1931; repr. in *Selected Writings of a Pioneer West African Feminist*, ed. Audrey Gadzekpo and Stephanie Newell (Nottingham: Trent Editions, 2004), 7–8.]

---

3 E.C. Quist was a barrister, town councillor, and member of the legislative council who contested and lost the 1931 legislative council elections to Dr Frederick V. Nanka Bruce (see n. 4).

4 Dr Frederick Victor Nanka Bruce was a member of the Gold Coast Legislative Council for Accra and one of the founders of the *Gold Coast Independent* in 1918. On the tenth anniversary of the paper in March 1930, his friends gave a dinner in his honour in appreciation of his services to the country.

PART FOUR
Nationalism / Internationalism

While feminist internationalism may be traced back to the Quakers and the activities of anti-slavery women in the early nineteenth century, as Millicent Garret Fawcett points out in her essay 'Women and Internationalism,'[1] it was not until the late nineteenth century that feminists set about creating organizations that were explicitly international. With the founding of the World Women's Christian Temperance Union in 1884, and the International Council of Women (ICW) in 1893, feminists began to develop organizational structures that formalized their transnational collaborations. In addition to the three largest organizations – the ICW, the International Women's Suffrage Alliance (IWSA), founded in 1904, and the Women's International League for Peace and Freedom (WILPF), founded in 1915 – there were many smaller regionally based organizations like the Inter-American Commission of Women (1928) and the Pan-Pacific Women's Association (1928), as well as organizations with a very specifically defined mandate, like Equal Rights International (1930).

Underpinning these structures, Leila Rupp has argued, was a discourse of internationalism notable for its vagueness, and frequently bearing more than a few traces of imperialist sentiment, as Ian Tyrell's study of the World WCTU demonstrates.[2] These sorts of definitional and ideological difficulties emerge nowhere more clearly than in the relationship of these international organizations to the nation and to nationalism. The clearest rationale for transnational collaboration and for the creation of international organizations to facilitate that collaboration had to do with providing international resources and support for national action. To be sure, many struggles, suffrage key among them, had to be waged nationally. Eventually, though, the creation of international political and legal structures led to the notion that some struggles were much better conducted at the supra-national level, as the efforts at establishing an equal rights treaty in the Americas attest. Because of the need to effect reform at the national level, most of the international organizations sought to maintain national autonomy, in large part by organizing on the basis of national sections. This organizational principle, however, led to difficulties over the defining of 'nation,' given that Eurocentric definitions such as the ICW notion that a parliament and a constitution were requisite features excluded many colonies and dependent nations, not to mention sub-national minorities.[3] Working across national boundaries, however they were defined, required considerable diplomacy and a readiness to avoid positions that put members in conflict with one another. One of the by-laws of the IWSA constitution, for instance, reads: 'The International Woman Suffrage Alliance, by mutual consent of its auxiliaries, stands pledged to preserve absolute neutrality on all questions that are strictly national.'[4] Such neutrality was not always maintained, and conflicts perhaps inevitably arose.

For many women in colonial contexts, particularly in India and the Middle East, nationalist struggle and feminist organizing went hand in hand.[5] Members of the All-India Women's Conference (AIWC), while they assiduously avoided 'political' questions so as to be able to work across ethnic, religious, and caste lines, eventually made explicit their support for India's nationalist movement, an alignment that made them reluctant to identify themselves as feminists or suffragettes.[6] Matiel Mogannam argues that it was a crisis in the Palestinian national movement that impelled Palestinian women to take up a public role in politics, thus affirming the link between feminist activism and the nationalist struggle in that context. The link between nationalism and anti-colonial resistance, especially coming from Egyptian and Palestinian women's organizations, often did not sit well with European feminists, as Marjorie Evans's essay on Egyptian women makes clear. Particularly glaring are her contention that the 'backward' population of Egypt is in need of British assistance and her resentment at Huda Shaarawi's refusal to recognize the validity of 'British interests' in Suez. For their part, women involved in nationalist movements did not necessarily regard participation in international women's organizations as a contradiction, as the active participation of Huda Shaarawi and Saiza Nabarawi in the International Alliance of Women (formerly the IWSA) attests, even if they and other Arab women found the organization's position on the future of Palestine increasingly untenable.[7] The AIWC endorsement of the IAW resolution on east–west cooperation attests to a similar internationalism on the part of Indian women activists, as does Dr Muthulakshmi Reddi's address at the ICW congress in 1933. Reddi insists that national self-determination is a prerequisite for the full citizenship of Indian women, even as she applauds the international character of the women's movement; for her, it is clear, 'world citizenship' entails detailed knowledge of each nation's specificity. Participation in international organizations could nonetheless be fraught. Egyptian feminists seeking to affiliate with the WILPF in 1937, for instance, were unable to accept the organization's position on disarmament in view of Egypt's status as a dependent nation subordinate to British imperial power.[8]

More complex still is the articulation of internationalism and nationalism in the essay by Martiniquan feminist Paulette Nardal, who contends that the 'awakening' of a black diasporan consciousness among francophone West Indians is owed to a group of women from the Antilles living in Paris. The specific combination of metropolitan experience with their status as black *women* meant they felt the need for racial solidarity in ways their male compatriots did not. Another tension around nation within international women's organizations had to do with a tendency on the part of the dominant members of those organizations to 'other' non-white or non-European women with sweeping gestures to 'women of the East' or 'Latin American women.' Lily Kelly's speech at the 1933 ICW meeting in Chicago pointedly resists the tendency of US and European feminists to homogenize Latin American women; called upon to represent the 'Woman Movement in Latin America,' Kelly claims only to be able to speak about women in her own country, Argentina. Yet Latin American feminists did collaborate in hemispheric organizations like the Inter-American Commission of Women, which contributed to the Lima Declaration in Favour of Women's Rights in 1938, as well as to the Resolution on the Problem of Indigenous Women in the Americas. Participation in international organizations also meant, in some cases, that white women learned to rethink their attitudes to questions of race and nation. Marilyn Lake argues that 'through membership, especially, of the British Commonwealth League and the Pan-Pacific Congresses ... and visits to the All India Women's Conference, Australian feminists came to reorient their national and gender identity in response to their links with Aboriginal, Asian and Pacific women.'[9]

Another conception of internationalism among feminists was that fostered by the Socialist and Communist Internationals, for whom class, as much as gender, functioned as a category of social location that transcended national boundaries. In addition to those women who belonged to these Internationals, there were significant numbers of women who, following the Russian Revolution in 1917, travelled to the Soviet Union to see first hand what the revolution was doing for women and to report on their findings. Finally, there were those, like Doris Stevens of the Inter-American Commission on Women, who regarded nations as often having deleterious effects on women's lives, and who sought therefore to legislate on behalf of women in international venues like the League of Nations. Similarly, Madeleine Doty articulates a feminist cosmopolitanism in her rationale for a world section of the WILPF. There is perhaps no more frequently cited example of the view that the nation was antithetical to women than Virginia Woolf's statement in *Three Guineas*.

NOTES

1 In *Time and Tide* 7, no. 10 (926): 227–8 and continued in 7, no. 11 (1926): 252.
2 Leila J. Rupp, *Worlds of Women: The Making of an International Women's Movement* (Princeton: Princeton UP, 1997), 108; Ian Tyrell, *Woman's World, Woman's Empire: The Women's Christian Temperance Union in International Perspective* (Chapel Hill: U of North Carolina P, 1991).
3 See Rupp, *Worlds of Women*, 112–13.
4 *Jus Suffragii* 14, no. 5 (1920): 66.
5 See Aparna Basu, *Women's Struggle: A History of the All India Women's Conference, 1927–1990* (New Delhi: Manohar, 1990); Geraldine Forbes, 'The Indian Women's Movement: A Struggle for Women's Rights or National Liberation?' in *The Extended Family: Women and Political Participation in India and Pakistan*, ed. Gail Minault (Delhi: Chanakya Publications, 1981), 49–82; Margot Badran, *Feminists, Islam, and Nation: Gender and the Making of Modern Egypt* (Princeton: Princeton UP, 1995); Charlotte Weber, 'Unveiling Sheherazade,' *Feminist Studies* 27, no. 1 (2001): 125–57.
6 Forbes, 'The Indian Women's Movement,' 56, 59, 61.
7 Weber, 'Unveiling Sheherazade,' 150.
8 Rupp, *Worlds of Women*, 122–3; see also the section on Peace.
9 Marilyn Lake, 'Between Old Worlds and New: Feminist Citizenship, Nation and Race, the Destabilisation of Identity,' in *Suffrage and Beyond: International Feminist Perspectives*, ed. Caroline Daley and Melanie Nolan (New York: New York UP, 1994), 290.

May Wright Sewall (1844–1920) helped found the Indianapolis Equal Suffrage Society in 1878, and in 1881–3 she led a campaign that narrowly failed to secure woman suffrage in Indiana. From 1882 to 1890 she was chairman of the executive committee of the National Woman Suffrage Association. From 1891 to 1892 she travelled extensively in Europe to build support for the World's Congress of Representative Women, which was to be held in conjunction with the World's Columbian Exposition in Chicago in 1893. Leading up to and during the First World War, Sewall devoted her energies to the cause of peace.

May Wright Sewall
The International Council of Women – Its Genesis (1899)

In proportion to the complexity of an organism, is its genesis interesting. On the eve of the opening of the second quinquennial session of the International Council, in which will be convened women of divers nationalities, tongues, convictions, and ideals, inquiries concerning it multiply. Where, when, how, under what circumstances, by whom was it conceived?

The International Council finely illustrates the evolutionary process. In 1882, Elizabeth Cady Stanton, having enjoyed in a partial tour of Europe the privilege of conference with distinguished publicists and reformers of different countries, suggested the organisation of an International Woman Suffrage Society; Miss Susan B. Anthony approving the suggestion, the two friends decided to call a conference for its formal consideration. However, this was rendered unnecessary, and an occasion for announcing their purpose was afforded by a suffrage meeting held at Liverpool, November 15, 1883, to pay them honour prior to their departure from England. To close that meeting, Mrs Margaret E. Parker, of Scotland, introduced the following resolution, which, supported by Mrs Priscilla Bright McLaren, was passed by the unanimous vote of those present:

> Recognising that union is strength, and that the time has come when women all over the world should unite in the just demand for their political enfranchisement, therefore
>
> Resolved: That we do here appoint a Committee of Correspondence, preparatory to forming an International Woman Suffrage Association.

The Committee immediately formed, comprised forty-one men and women, representing England, Ireland, Scotland, France, and the United States of America. The Committee thus named did not organize; indeed was never convened, and correspondence with its members has shown that many of them were never advised of the honour which had been bestowed.

The next public reference to Mrs Stanton's plan was made at Washington, D.C., in January, 1887, when Miss Anthony explained it before the nineteenth annual Convention of the National Woman Suffrage Association. At the close of a lengthy discussion, in which it was pointed out –

(1) That many organisations of women, still holding aloof from suffrage, owed their very existence to changes in public opinion, custom, and law, wrought by the suffragists; and

(2) That in many countries the ballot is not recognised as an instrument of legitimate power in the hands of either men or women:

Miss Anthony moved:

> That the National Woman Suffrage Association of the United States shall celebrate the approaching fortieth anniversary of the first meeting ever held in behalf of an extension of Women's Rights, by convening an International Council of Women, to which all associations of women in the trades, professions, and moral reforms, as well as those advocating the political emancipation of women, shall be invited.

This resolution was adopted with two others, the first of which placed the whole financial burden upon the National Woman Suffrage Association, while the second entrusted all preparations to its Executive Committee. The official statement published on the adjournment of the Council announced that in its session from March 25 to April 2, 1888, inclusive, fifty-three different organisations of women, most of them national in scope, and all national in value, had been represented on its platform by eighty speakers and forty-nine delegates from England, France, Germany, Denmark, Finland, India, Canada, and the United States.

Early in this session, viz., on March 24, at a special meeting of the Committee of Arrangements, to which all of the delegates were invited, the Acting Chairman of that Committee, who was also the Chairman of the Executive Committee of the National Woman Suffrage Association (the writer of this article) proposed that, as a fitting result of the labour involved in arranging for the first transient Council, two permanent organisations, viz., a National Council of Women of the United States and an International Council of Women of the World, should be formed, thus making possible meetings for conference at regular intervals. The Chairman concluded an ample exposition of her plan by moving: 'That a Committee be appointed to consider the question of such National and International Councils, and to report to the delegates a basis of organization.'

The motion was concurred in by a large majority of the delegates, and the

Committee appointed by Miss Anthony included fifteen women, with Frances
E. Willard as Chairman.

On March 27, this Committee submitted a report favourable to permanent
organization, including skeleton constitutions for the two councils, which were
referred to a Sub-committee[1] of three for completion. On March 31, 1888, the
Constitution for the International Council was adopted by the unanimous vote
of all the delegates present excepting Mrs Seatcherd, of England, who, having dissented from the proposition that an International Council was desirable,
withdrew from the meeting.

Character

The character of an organization, like that of an individual, must be sought in
its motive, its purpose, and its method. These are succinctly set forth in the
Constitution of the International, and although certain amendments pending
may affect, or rather perfect its method, they will leave motive and purpose
essentially untouched.

Motive and ultimate purpose may be inferred from the preamble, which runs
thus:

> We women of all nations, sincerely believing that the best good of humanity
> will be advanced by greater unity of thought, sympathy, and purpose, and that an
> organized movement of women will best conserve the highest good of the family
> and of the State, do hereby band ourselves together in a confederation of workers
> to further the application of the Golden Rule to Society, Custom, and Law.

The fundamental idea in its policy is thus expressed in Article II:

> The International Council is organised in the interest of no one propaganda, and
> has no power over its members beyond that of suggestion and sympathy. There-
> fore no National Council voting to enter the International shall thereby render
> itself liable to be interfered with in respect to its complete organic unity, independ-
> ence, or methods of work or shall be committed to any principle, or any method of
> any other Council, or to any act or utterance of this International Council beyond
> compliance with the terms of this Constitution.

Growth

The first officers of the International Council were: Mrs Fawcett (England),

---

1 Frances E. Willard, Mary F. Eastman, and May Wright Sewall.

President; Clara Barton (U.S.A.), Vice-President; Rachel Foster Avery (U.S.A.), Corresponding Secretary; Kirstine Frederiksen (Denmark), Recording Secretary; Isabelle Bogelot (France), Treasurer. During the first five years the International Council made no progress nor did the Council Idea flourish outside the United States.

The National Council of that country had attained a numerical strength and a public recognition which made it inevitable that the arrangements for the 'World's Congress of Representative Women,' convened by the World's Congress Auxiliary, should be entrusted to its general officers. The expiration of the first term of the International Council coming in 1893, coincident with the Columbian Exposition and its Auxiliary Congresses, it was likewise in the natural order that its first quinquennial session should be convened in Chicago, and become a department meeting of the great Congress.

As the National Council of the United States constituted the only working factor of the International Council, its Executive Committee united with the three officers of the International Council present in inviting all of the foreign delegates to the World's Congress to join in discussing the future of the International, and in selecting officers for its second term. Thirty-two nationalities were represented by seventy-eight delegates in that informal conference, which dated a new birth for the Council Idea.

Happily the President elected in 1893, the Countess of Aberdeen, discerned the possibilities of the organisation, and set about their development. Happily, too, the World's Congress of Representative Women had demonstrated the feasibility of the International movement. The delegates accredited to it returned home to form National Councils in their respective countries. The second term, for practical reasons, has extended one year beyond the constitutional limit.

Since 1893 National Councils have been formed in Canada, Germany, Sweden, Great Britain and Ireland, New Zealand, New South Wales, Denmark, Holland, Italy, and Tasmania. These (excepting only the Council of Italy), together with the Council of the United States, constitute the International Council, the aggregate membership of which will be augmented soon by the Councils of Switzerland, Belgium, Greece, Victoria, Austria, Persia, and Russia, where honorary Vice-Presidents are already doing the work preliminary to formal organisation.

To realise the constituency, present and possible, of the International Council, one must bear in mind that, excepting as patrons and as contributors, women come into Council membership *not as individuals, but as members of Associations.*

The Council Idea not only serves the world in its International application and each separate country in its national form, but brings corresponding blessings to the metropolis and to the hamlet. As any national organisation of women whose constitution is not inharmonious with the principles above stated is eligible to membership in the National Council of its country, so is any local organisation of women eligible to enter the Local Council of its own community.

The double purpose of every Council, Local, National, and International, is:

(a) To promote greater unity of thought, sympathy and purpose among women workers of all classes, parties, creeds and nationalities.

(b) To further the application of the Golden Rule to society, custom, and law.

The first purpose is sentimental; the second, Utopian; so say the critics. We reply: Sympathy is the only solution which will render intelligible to one class, one party, one creed, one nationality, members of another class, &c. Sympathy presupposes intelligence and just interpretation, both of which are conditioned upon a knowledge to be derived only through acquaintance – first-hand acquaintance with original sources of information. Hitherto organisation has united people of one mind who seek one end by the same route. The Council unites people of different, even of opposing, minds, whose only common aim is to find the general principles which must underlie their diverse objects, and to discover the path in which their different routes must converge.

Hitherto the Golden Rule has been recommended to individuals only. It is the function of the Council to apply this test to society in the aggregate, and to hold the State to a standard at least not lower than that prescribed for the individual citizen.

In short, the International Council is the harbinger of the New Civilisation; its leaders, to use the happy phrase of Lady Aberdeen, are International Women, who do not love their own countries the less for having learned to love humanity more. The International Council is the feminine counterpart and the forerunner of that permanent International Parliament suggested in that International Court of Arbitration, which the Conference now in progress at the Hague lifts into nearer view.

[Source: *The Fortnightly Review* 349 (1899): 156–9.]

A poet and political activist, Sarojini Naidu (1879–1949) was born into a prominent Bengali family. She studied at Hyderabad, and then in 1895 went to England on scholarship, where she studied at King's College, London, and Girton College, Cambridge. Upon returning to India, she became active in efforts to protect Hindu widows and to promote the education of women, eventually dividing her time between the nationalist and women's movements. She

led the 1919 Home Rule League deputation to England, and participated in
Gandhi's Satygraha Movement; in 1925 she was elected president of the Indian
National Congress.

Sarojini Naidu
Women in National Life (1915)

*Mrs Sarojini Naidu in proposing the Resolution on the above subject in the
Indian National Social Conference held at Bombay in December, 30, 1915,
said:*

President, Brother-Delegates, Ladies and Gentlemen, – This resolution that
I have to propose, although it came third on the list of resolutions, had to be
changed for my personal convenience; it is a happy thought to have put it first
because it embodies a resolution that deals with the most important problems
of our social progress, and that is the education of our women. As I was listening to that inspiring and stirring address by our revered President a little while
ago, it seemed to me that no woman could have pleaded the cause of women
with a greater conviction of her rights and her privileges and her destiny in the
future as an unbroken historic tradition from the past; and whatever I might
say speaking as a woman, and an Indian woman, for my sisters, cannot possibly carry the same weight with you, because it will not go from me with that
tradition of sacrifice, that living reality of daily service in the cause of women
which Prof. Karve has embodied in his life. But when I look around me today
and consider that 10 years ago in Calcutta from the platform of the Social
Conference I pleaded for the education of women, there was not a gathering
of women quite as much as the gathering present here today, and that itself
is sufficient to prove that within the last 10 years not only the men, but those
more intimately and essentially concerned, the women themselves, have begun
to realise the cause of a new spirit which is nothing but a renaissance of the
old spirit which gave to India those Gargis, Maitrayis, those Savitris and Sitas
of whom Mr Bhupendra Nath Basu spoke a little while ago. And if I speak to
you today in favour and in support of this educational policy for our women,
for a more liberal grant from the authorities, for more co-operation from our
men, I will demand from my sisters not merely that liberality of endowment
that we ask from Government, not merely the co-operation from our brothers,
but from them their pledge of individual and personal consecration to this great
cause; I will demand from every sister of mine her personal dedication to this
cause, because it is not from Government or even from the co-operation of the
manhood of the country that the solution of this question will come. It is not

from them that you will get the impetus to wipe off the stain from our national history, but rather from the womanhood of India which is suffering from a wrong. My reproach is to the women of India in India, and though I make it in their presence I do it as a woman speaking to women, and do it with the fullest realisation of what I am saying because I feel the voices of millions of my sons crying out from one end to another end. Let the womanhood of the country wake and work. Let us strengthen the hands of our men. Those prayers that we prayed, those thoughts that we uttered in the thousands gathered together year after year, passing resolutions, are but the sincerest desire of every member of the society that has the interest of the country. When I was in Europe a little more than a year ago, after 15 years of absence from the continent of progress, during my last visit to Europe, what struck me in that great continent of rapid changes, of evolution going on at a rate that one can hardly calculate by the hands of a clock, that it was the womanhood of Europe that had begun to realise the full measure of its strength, the full height of its responsibility, the full sanctity and seriousness of its duty in the nation building of Europe. Everywhere I found that women of all classes that had been considered luxury-loving had become transmuted into servers of the country's good. Women, whose chief assets 15 years ago might have been the jewels or the ornaments, had for their asset now that living sympathy, that personal service to the poor, that share of responsibility in solving the great problems of the generation, every nation is called upon to solve. And when I came back to India a year ago the first thing that struck me after nearly two years of absence was that the womanhood of India was beginning to wake in an unmistakable way. I have come in contact with thousands and thousands of women in every part of India and the same message comes forth that unity of Indian Womanhood, if it is desired to achieve it, is to be found in the national service. When I was in the Krishna-Godawari District it surprised me to find how in that country where there is a new movement to re-establish a national consciousness, how the women of that country stood side by side with their men in every detail, and not merely in the abstract ideals of achieving that regeneration, that renaissance of the Andhra country. Everywhere I found that wherever there was a school to be started or a mission for social service, wherever there was a movement to bring back to the Indian consciousness that sense of national dignity, that sense of national responsibility, the women of the Andhra country stood side by side with their men. In Bengal, I found in that sweet country, where the very educational ardour is transmuted in devotion for the country, there I found man and woman ready to bring his or her life like a lotus flower in consecration to the feet of *Bharat varsha*.

In this Presidency where every community is represented not in minorities but in equal proportions of strength and prosperity, where there is that whole-some stimulus for every good work, I find the spirit of the womanhood of this Presidency, the women of the Maharashtra, the women of the Zoroastrian community and the women who say *Yah Allah, Yah Allah* of Mahomedanism, though they are divided by race and creed and religion, they are yet indivisible, one by the realization of their common womanhood, and they are one by the consciousness of their common duty which is the duty of every woman whose destiny it is to create the generation of the citizens of to-morrow, and if this resolution comes into a Conference like this it comes with a whole-hearted support of this great gathering of women who, though great with their numbers are still only a fraction of that large majority who are thinking and desiring and hoping and struggling to bring back to India that dignity, that liberty, that deliv-erance from evil, that freedom of all social laws which comes of education.

They are trying here, as elsewhere, to realise that their share in co-operating with their men is the only condition of national regeneration. They are begin-ning to realise that it is not only by having large ideals that this service is to be achieved but rather by analysing those great ideals into their component practi-cal parts, and everyone taking up a little share of practical service, and all those ideals and all those visions of tomorrow are centred round this supreme question of the education of women. Other national questions come and go. They are the result of the changing time spirit, but the one question that has never changed since the beginning of time itself, and life itself, the duty of womanhood, the influence of womanhood, the sanctity of womanhood, the simple womanhood as the divinity of God upon earth, the responsibility of womanhood in shaping the divinity into daily life. Friends, two nights ago I was speaking in Poona at the All-India Mahomedan Educational Conference, and I was the one repre-sentative of my sect in the midst of hundreds of Mahomedan men, and I was asked to thank on behalf of those women who are separated from their men, not merely by virtue of sect, but rather divided from them by the tradition and custom. It was I who said, Oh Men, unless and until you give to your women all those equal privileges that form the highest and noblest teaching of your great nation-builder and Prophet, you will not attain that regeneration of your race, that renaissance of Islamic glory, and today in the presence of this great gathering chiefly of Hindus, I say, oh friends, oh brothers, oh sisters look back to the past and look forward to the future, and let your future draw its diffused inspiration, its highest vitality, just from those living traditions that are our greatest inheritance. We ask for nothing that is foreign to our ideals, rather we ask for restoration of those rights, the rights that are the immortal treasures. We ask only that we may be given that chance to develop our body and spirit and mind in that evolution that will re-establish for you ideal womanhood, not an impossible womanhood such as poets may dream of, but an ideal womanhood that will make noble wives who are helpmates, strong mothers, brave mothers, teaching the sons their first lesson of national service.

[Source: *Speeches and Writings of Sarojini Naidu* (Madras: G.A. Natesan, 1918), 96a–6h.]

Chrystal Macmillan (1882–1937) was one of the first female lawyers in England, and the first woman to plead before the House of Lords, declaring that women graduates should be granted the vote. She worked for policy change on matters such as women losing citizenship after marrying a foreigner. For seven years Macmillan was the secretary for the International Woman Suffrage Alliance, and she was also one of the organizers of the Women's Peace Conference at the Hague.

Chrystal Macmillan
The Future of the International Woman Suffrage Alliance (1920)

At the Congress of the Alliance, which is meeting after seven years of separation, the chief work will be to estimate how far the Alliance has attained its object: 'The enfranchisement of the women of all nations,' and how it can, under the changed conditions of this meeting, best further this object in the future. In the call to the Madrid meeting it is asked: 'Is our work together at an end? Or shall we go on till the women of every land are likewise emancipated? Is the emancipation of women complete, or is there other work to be done before that end is attained? Do the women of the world send a call to us for additional service which bids us march further on?'

Looking at these questions, and thinking how much there is yet to be done before the women of all nations have secured their enfranchisement – political, civil, economic, and moral – not only in countries where women have not yet gained the vote, but also in the Woman Suffrage countries, and in the more primitive communities where work for the emancipation of women has hardly begun, it is difficult to know where to begin. The Alliance will require to give a wider interpretation to 'the enfranchisement of women,' and to draw up a Woman's Charter defining the concrete reforms necessary to its attainment, and lay down a policy for its execution.

Unenfranchised Countries

There are still many countries without the vote. Not one of the four Latin countries of Europe, or the twenty Latin countries of South America, has enfranchised its women. Among other countries where some form of constitutional government exists, women are still without the suffrage in Greece, Turkey, Bulgaria, Roumania, Belgium (the present number of women voting is negligible), Serbia, Switzerland, Newfoundland, the Union of South Africa, British India, China, Japan, and the Philippines. In many of the newly enfranchised countries the governments are so recently established that watchfulness will be necessary to prevent the disfranchisement of women under any new regime that might arise. The constitution of the new countries being set up in Europe should be based on the equality of the sexes, and the same measure of justice should be given to women in the counties of the East which are rapidly demanding the adoption of government by an elective legislature.

The Enfranchised Countries

But in the countries where women already vote the work of full enfranchisement has only begun. At the first Congress of the Alliance in Berlin, in 1904, it was declared that men and women 'were equally entitled to the free exercise of their individual rights and liberties.' The vote is a weapon which may be used to make possible the free exercise of the individual rights and liberties of women.

In few countries, if any, is the full equality of husband and wife recognised. The wife may be subject to marital authority; she may be forbidden to use her own property or earnings; she may be denied the right to choose her own domicile or nationality; she may be ignored as the guardian of her children.

In no country has even a beginning been made in putting women economically on a level with men. The whole law and custom of every land are such that the bulk of the national income is under the control of the male portion of the population. The vast majority of married women, although they actually handle the family income, dispense it not as a right, but merely as the agents of their husbands. In almost every country the mother of young children has a lower economic status than any other member of the community.

If men's right to work is now almost universally recognised, the fact that a woman has any corresponding right is in practice constantly ignored; still more the woman's right to have equal pay for the work she does. The State and the municipalities deny her permission to compete for the higher positions; if qualified they deny her promotion; they dismiss her on marriage, and they refuse her equal pay for equal work. To-day, however, the power to admit the right to work in practice in many employments is not in the hands of the State, but in that of the trade unions. These bodies only too often forbid women to receive training, or to exercise their trades when trained, and use their powerful organisations otherwise to prevent the employment of women.

In most countries to-day law and custom conspire to punish inordinately the mother of the child born out of wedlock. They place on her the greater part of the burden which should be equally shared by both the responsible parties.

Can any country be named where an equal moral standard is operative, either legally or socially? The State regulation of vice, still in force in so many countries, definitely treats the woman as an outcast – a chattel to be kept clean for public use. In how many countries is solicitation for immoral purposes treated as the same offence in men as it is in women, or the buyer of the honour of a woman placed under the same disabilities as the seller? Even when the laws affecting moral offences are verbally equal between men and women, how often are they equally administered?

The Undeveloped Countries

Then, too, there is the emancipation of the women of the East. There are countries where to-day girls and women are bought and sold into marriage, or as servants, and it is fitting that the enfranchised women of the West should require the putting in force, for their protection, of the international laws against slavery. These women also require equal opportunities for education, and assistance towards the equal recognition of their political, social, and moral rights.

The League of Nations

There is also a new feature in our international political environment on which the Alliance will have to lay down a policy. When it last met national governments were the bodies to which women had to appeal to seek to have their reforms adopted. To-day many countries have their fate conditioned by their adherence to the League of Nations. The covenant of the League lays it down that 'all positions, under or in connection with the League, including the Secretariat, shall be open equally to men and women.' The Alliance will have to decide how it can best promote the appointment of women, really suitable women, under this Article. The International Labour Conference department of the League has already met and made recommendations with respect to women's right to work; the Alliance will have to prepare a plan of action to ensure that women are properly represented on that body, and that its policy on questions affecting the status of women shall be effectively brought before it. The League of Nations has taken powers to deal with such questions as the traffic in women, the setting up of an international health department, etc. The Alliance must lay its plans to bring the policy of its Women's Charter effectively before the League whenever the status of women is concerned. The League of Nations has made itself ultimately responsible for the administration of territory under mandates granted to different powers. The Alliance must demand that no mandates be granted without due guarantee of a satisfactory status for women.

Trade Unions – Syndicates – Soviets

Another new feature in our political environment not present at the last Alliance Congress is the rise into power, as rivals of the elected legislative assemblies, of the trade unions.

Governments, recently, in several countries have decided their policy not by consultation with the elected representatives in the legislature, but by a private bargain with the powerful trade unions, while in a few countries governments have been set up with the trade union instead of the territorial district as the political unit for election purposes. I am expressing no opinion on the justification or otherwise of such action, but call attention to it as one of the important factors in the politics of to-day. If we ask that women should have equal political power with men, and if the whole political power is no longer in the hands of the elected legislatures, even equal suffrage does not give to women equal political power. Is the Alliance to develop some policy on the question?

The Future of the Alliance

With these many reforms requiring attention in all countries, it is essential that there should be some international organisation of liberties, status, and opportunities in all spheres of life between men and women. There are other important women's organisations which are doing valuable work for women, but none which concentrate on this essential aim. There is the International Council of Women, of which the objects are 'to provide a means of communication between women's organisations in all countries, and to provide opportunities for women to meet together from all parts of the world to confer upon questions relating to the welfare of the commonwealth, the family, and the individual.' The work of the Council is correspondingly wide, and among its many departments it includes those which work for the equality of the sexes. The Women's International League for Peace and Freedom is also active, and supports movements to further 'Peace, Internationalism, and the Freedom of Women,' but is limited to those organisations which take a particular point of view on international questions. The World Women's Christian Temperance Union has also done wonderful work for the emancipation of women, but its membership is for those who are agreed on a particular line of action on the Drink question. There is the International Women's Socialist organization, which also urges many women's reforms, but whose membership is limited to one political party. Just as we required the Alliance to outline the policy of the political enfranchisement of women, and to act as the pioneer to convert the world to that reform, so we need still more the Alliance under the new conditions to outline the Feminist policy on the civil, moral, and economic enfranchisement of women, and to act as the pioneer to convert the world to these reforms. The meeting of the Alliance in Berlin in 1904 laid down the principles on which the demand for political enfranchisement was based, and these principles have been the foundation of the demand in all the affiliated countries, and will continue to be the bases in the still unenfranchised lands. I hope that at our meeting in Madrid we shall outline a Women's Charter, including the reforms necessary for the civil and economic enfranchisement of women, a statement of the principles on which that Charter is based, and a policy for its working out; and that this Charter and declaration of principles will become the text from which the women in each affiliated country will work to convert women's organisations, political parties, trade unions, national governments, the League of Nations, and the general public.

I would like to see our constitution altered to meet the changed circumstances. Why should we not admit any number of national Suffrage organisations from the unenfranchised countries? From the enfranchised countries I should like to see provision made to admit national associations working for any one or more reforms to establish equality between men and women, whether it is equal political, equal moral, equal economic, or equal civil status. In this way the Alliance would become the rallying ground for all the forces working to establish the full emancipation and enfranchisement of women, which is essential to the future welfare of the community.

[Source: *Jus Suffragii: International Women Suffrage News* 14, no.5 (1920): 65–7. Available through the Gerritsen Collection.]

Marjorie Evans (?–?) is not specifically identified.

Marjorie Evans
Women and the Egyptian Nationalist Movement (1925)

Egypt today is one of the troubled countries of the world, and I have attempted from general impressions and from conversations with Madame Charaoui Pasha and Madame Wissa Fahmy Bey, two of the Nationalist leaders, to see how far the women of Egypt are entering into her varied activities.

Egypt presents a strange problem of incongruity. In Cairo and Alexandria one sees everywhere the poorer classes of Moslems struggling in the filth of their daily life, from which they have neither the education nor the inclination to emerge; in the flat delta lands there are *fellahin*, the country people, illiterate and isolated in their white cluster of mud-brick huts. And yet everywhere, under a superficial quiet, one can realise how high and bitter political feeling runs, and how great is the force of resentment against the British. With this great mass of uneducated people, absorbed in their own struggle, whence does this political feeling arise and how far can it penetrate?

The Zaghlulist Nationalist Party has done its work of propaganda well; during its year of office, even though its influence has diminished, it has worked on the feelings of both the *fellahin* and the town people. In fact, the Nationalist Party has been so busy with its propaganda and its cry of 'Egypt for the Egyptian' that it has had no time to look to Egypt's welfare; and this seems the strangest of all the paradoxes here; so great is the political preoccupation and the desire to see Egypt rid of the British that all the crying needs of the country are either subordinated or unrealised.

Yet is this preoccupation so general as, at first, it seems? Five years ago, the *fellahin*, ninety per cent of the population, had their definite grievances arising from the deprivations and sufferings of the war period. Is it right to assume that apart from such specific, personal grievances they have an attachment to any abstract ideal of Egyptian nationalism? From all I can gather, and my impression was confirmed by that of officials who have worked among them, they feel the problem only as it touches them personally. In the past the problem of the *fellah* was the amount of his land-tax, the abolition of the *corvée*, the safety of his donkey or his camel. Today he cares above all for the safety of his Nile-water, upon which his very existence depends; if the British can appear to him as the masters of the water, and satisfy him that his lands will be properly irrigated, he will be prepared to let the political situation take care of itself.

The *fellah* woman, of whom about one per cent can read and write, is even further removed from the political problem. Women must always be inarticulate where politics remain in the region of force, not mind, and in Egypt they are doubly so. These *fellah* women are, of necessity, less secluded than those of the town; they work in the fields with the men, bring up their many children, and toil in the huts. Their immediate problem is food for themselves and their children, and rest at the end of the day. They may take up the parrot-cry of 'Egypt for the Egyptians' – in fact, women played a prominent part in the rioting of 1919 – but when they are aroused it is usually on personal issues, or, as in the case of women in the towns, some dimly-felt desire for freedom urges them to identify that with the political cause.

The ignorance and illiteracy of the Egyptian women opposes an almost insuperable barrier to social reform. They are hedged in by a mass of superstition and of religious tradition, which stifles progress. The rate of infantile mortality is nearly thirty per cent, which, even though largely accounted for by the almost unfailing death of babies born during the hot months, could be much reduced by sanitary conditions and hygienic methods. What can you expect where a woman will leave her baby in the sun while she works in the fields, and say 'It is the will of Allah!' when she returns to find it dead? Flies are allowed to settle in a black mass on the baby's face because to brush them away is to attract the Evil Eye: and a baby is, by religious ordinance, left unwashed for several weeks after birth. The flies bring disease and infect those people whose eyes have escaped the ravages of desert-sand or general neglect, so that ninety per cent of all the people have eye trouble in some form. The children die because only the strongest among them could possibly live. Yet this infantile mortality is nowhere considered seriously. Where women are of small account the children are of even less; and, more important still, Egypt's population is increasing in spite of it. Sooner or later Egypt will have to face the problem of a surplus population, and her high rate of infantile mortality conveniently averts the immediacy of this problem.

Social reform in Egypt must be accompanied by the breaking down of the barriers of national and religious custom: consequently the disruptive force must come from within. At present, therefore, the hope lies with the small group of educated Egyptian women who form the two feminist societies; the Women's Committee to the Egyptian Delegation, a political body, and the Feminist Party, concerned more directly with social questions. Of both of these groups Madame Charaoui Pasha is the President.

From conversations with Madame Charaoui Pasha I was impressed again with the supremacy which strictly political issues hold over social problems.

The women's political group is mainly Zaghlulist in outlook, although Madame Charaoui refuses to give her personal allegiance to Zaghlul Pasha. She is none the less an extreme Nationalist. She argued for the complete independence of Egypt and the Sudan, and even regarded the presence of British troops on the Suez Canal as an affront to the Egyptian nation. I urged upon her the necessity of British interests, particularly with regard to our passage to India. Madame Charaoui, however, refused to admit of any concessions whatsoever, and her general political attitude is so extreme that it cannot command sympathy in England. But I find the most hopeful aspect of the women's movements in Egypt in one remark which Madame Charaoui made. 'I am prepared,' she said, 'to unite with English women on feminist matters, even though I may disagree with those same women on political issues.' Turning from the activities of the political group to those of the Feminist Party, Madame Charaoui was able to point to but little that had been accomplished in definite reforms. Efforts have been made to adjust the age of marriage, which had in the past been as low as twelve or thirteen. The party has an ambitious social programme; but its efforts, like all efforts in this country, are concentrated on the political issue.

I gained the attitude of the more orthodox Zaghlulist element of the women's movement from Madame Wissa Fahmy Bey. She is herself a Copt – a Christian – a highly cultured and palpably sincere idealist. She believes in an Egypt of the future, regenerated by suffering and worthy of her ancient past. Her whole attitude is dominated by profound distrust of the British; she sincerely believes that if Egypt had her complete independence and yet England held the Sudan, England would not scruple to cut off the Nile waters from Egypt and starve the country. Such an opinion, honestly held, goes far to show how deeply distrust of the British has penetrated into certain sections of the Egyptian feminist party. Madame Wissa is so preoccupied with the political problem and the vision of fervent nationalism that I failed to arouse her interest in any of the social questions which I have discussed above. She believes that sooner or later women's emancipation must come from their very participation in politics, but this end is entirely subordinated to the Nationalist cause.

This, indeed, is the tragedy of Egypt today; her worthiest women are allied to her extreme political causes, and in the bitterness of the unequal struggle the general welfare of the country is forgotten. The struggle goes on, and meanwhile the people suffer.

[Source: *Time and Tide*, 30 January 1925, 107–8.]

Doris Stevens (1892–1963) was a co-founder of the Congressional Union for Woman Suffrage, later the National Woman's Party, which emulated the more militant methods used by Emmeline Pankhurst's Women's Social and Political Union in Britain. Over the years women of the CUWS were repeatedly arrested and imprisoned for blocking traffic with their huge demonstrations. Stevens published a book based on her experiences in jail. Her address at the Pan American Conference in Havana led to the establishment of the Inter-American Commission of Women, which she chaired for over twenty years.

Doris Stevens

Address in Behalf of the Equal Rights Treaty
Made before a Special Plenary Session of the Sixth Pan American Conference (1928)

February 7, 1928
Havana, Cuba

Honorable Delegates: we are met together on a great historic occasion. This is the first time in the history of the world that women are come before an international body to plead for treaty action on their rights.

We are met in this beautiful hall already consecrated to new ideals of Panamericanism. I ask you to look well at the moving tapestries which hang on these walls. Twenty-one medallions represent the 21 Republics assembled here today. What is the artist's conception of each republic? It is a very simple concept. The splendid figures of two human beings: Man and Woman. The artist is right. That, in the last analysis, is all there is to a State: Man and Woman!

Behind us is another moving concept of the artist. Where a crown once symbolised autocratic authority, you now have substituted a golden Western Hemisphere ablaze with light. The torch of Freedom lights the golden replica of this hemisphere.

We could not, if we had searched far and wide, have found more beautiful and appropriate symbols to the subject matter on which we address you today. These are the symbols of a new world, of a new hemisphere – with new ideals as to that most important of all human relationships: the relationship between man and woman. Humanly stated, our thesis today is Man and Woman; the ultimate power in the world.

You have it in your power to make these symbols come alive. You can, here and now, if you will, take decisive action toward making men and women equal before the law in this hemisphere. We are in the hands of a friendly body. You have already declared unanimously your belief that men and women should be equal before the law. Today we propose a method of obtaining that equality.

Great laws are born of deep convictions. They are not made by technicians. It is our deep convictions that we bring you today. But that is not all we bring you. We stand ready to work with you, as eminent jurists, through your appointed commission, to hasten the procedure of our proposal. For we do not come before you unprepared. We have studied carefully the merits of our proposal. And since with rare exception men cannot feel as we do, the sting of belonging to a group which is classed as inferior, we ask to be allowed authoritative power – not as auxiliaries but as colleagues – to consult between this Conference and the next with the sub-commission assigned to study the abolition of the present discriminations against women or until that legal subjection of women is abolished in the Americas. We shall not fold our standards until this subjection is removed. You might better act wisely and justly immediately on what you will only have eventually to do.

Since the beginning of time, men with the best of intentions no doubt, have been writing laws for our good. Since the beginning of time, brave and valiant women have been abolishing these same laws written for our good.

There is no limit to what man wishes to do for our good. Last week press despatches from the United States carried the news that a husband and father had killed his wife, the mother of his children, and the children. When questioned as to his motives, he replied that he did it for their good!

The Associated Press despatch reported from a seaport in Algeria last week also, another example of man's desire to protect woman for her good. For the Mahommedan Women's good, custom does not permit them to bathe at the same time as men. Five women were drowned when the bath-house collapsed, while men were getting up their courage to break the man-made custom and enter the building reserved that day for women-bathers.

This, in the realm of custom, is the logical if absurd outcome of the iniquity of one code of conduct for women and another for men.

Is it any wonder that enlightened women are in revolt today against acts done for their good? We want no more laws written for our good and without our consent. We must have the right to direct our own destiny jointly with you.

For, you see, no man, no group of men, no government, no nation, no group of nations – ever had the right to withhold from us the rights we ask today. We ask to have restored, rights which have been usurped. These are our human rights.

From the year 1846, when the code of Estevan de Ferrater of Barcelona was proposed, to the year 1928 – eminent men from all corners of the earth have drafted and proposed codes of international law embracing among many subjects, articles relating to the status of women. They have however been preeminently codes for men. A study of these codes shows at first a few articles concerning the status of women appearing. Each proposed article on the status of women reflects the then existing backward social position she held. More and more points on the status of women, it is true, have been included in these codes through the intervening years, although no code has been proposed giving women equality with men. Are we to permit to grow this vast network of one code for men with special articles inserted for women? If there were no free choice, it is conceivable that in two hundred years we might see our book-shelves staggering under the weight of a double stock of law books, heavy with special codes for women and special codes for men. It is even conceivable that in two hundred years a point would be reached where the codes for men and the codes for women might become identical. But we are not condemned to take any risk. We can exercise free choice. We can stop this method of codification and begin to write now international law for all human beings irrespective of sex.

Another danger which attends waiting upon evolution, lies in the fact that there is no marked tendency to take the most advanced law regarding women on each point. Though eminent jurists advocate and propose what they call 'progressive codification,' it is not found to be so for women. The most distinguished jurists agree that codification should be a rehabilitation of law, and even a creation of new laws when public opinion demands it.

Furthermore, when public opinion demands it, newer and speedier methods are taken to reach a goal.

We have chosen the road we propose to travel. That right at least cannot be denied us today.

It is fitting that the American Continent should be the first union of republics to be asked for an equal rights treaty. The demand for women's rights was born on this continent. Abigail Adams was, so far as we know, the first woman in modern history to write to her husband, John Adams, when the United States constitution was being formed after our war of independence: 'While you are writing this new constitution, I pray you, do not forget the ladies. If you do, we shall foment a hot rebellion.' Again, it was in 1848 in the United States of America that our great pioneers called a congress and wrote a stirring declaration of our rights. This agitation continued until our civil war in 1861. Again, the women demanded their rights at the same time that they demanded freedom for the black slaves. The slaves were freed. The women were not. It was not until 1919 that the political rights of women were written into our constitution.

It is not in our traditions to be content with what we have gained. It is not in our traditions to be laggards of liberty. The impulse to gather together our power and push on more rapidly is strong in us.

We have chosen the treaty method because it is the most dignified. It is the easiest. It is the most permanent. It will not only abolish existing national and international inequalities. It will prevent new ones from being written. And lastly it obviates a cruel waste of energy. For we ought never be compelled to appeal for our rights to the most backward opinion in any State. Our appeal to the most select, the most cultivated, the most imaginative men in the world, should be welcomed, approved and answered in this most dignified method.

Some will tell us that rights of women lie exclusively in the domain of domestic law. This is purely a matter of opinion.

The extension of what was formerly considered purely domestic law into the domain of international law has been the most distinctive feature of legal history in the last quarter of a century. There is every reason to believe that international action will expand to embrace more and more all the acts of humankind. Global action may come in the future. Our proposal lies in the current of our time. You may delay it. You cannot stop it. We want to accelerate it.

Timid souls may say this has never been done. That answer does not move us. All compelling history of the world has been made by those who dared to establish great precedents, who adventured in unknown paths, who led the way. The men who follow are never remembered – it is those who lead, who direct the current of civilization.

There will be those who say: 'Woman's rights are not a fit subject for treaty action.' To this we answer: 'Discriminations against women have already been made the subject of action by convention by certain of the Americas and amongst European nations through the League of Nations. If discriminations against us as women on the sole ground of sex can be made the subject of international conventions, so can our rights.

Let us examine the treaty-making power of my own country. The treaty-making power of the United States is granted in the constitution without any express limitation as to the subject matter of the treaty. Limitations on the subject matter are only implied. They are undefined and not judicially determined. Since no treaty has ever been held unconstitutional by any court in the United States – federal or state – it cannot be given as more than a matter of opinion (not law) that the subject matter of our treaty would be so held. Everything written on the point of what is and what is not fit subject for treaty action – and there has been a mass of opinion – is purely academic. It is *obiter dicta*. The best thought is that restraints on the treaty-making power ought to exist only in the concrete – not in the abstract.

Charles Henry Butler goes so far as to say that 'it is still an undecided question whether the judicial department of the court has the power either to declare void a treaty made and ratified according to constitutional method, or to declare that the executive and legislative departments of the government exceeded the power vested in them by the people.' (See Charles Henry Butler, 'The Treaty-Making Power of the United States,' vol. II, 351–63. Also Woolsey, 'International Law,' item 103, p. 160, 6 ed.; also *Ware v. Hylton* – U.S. 1796 – 3 Dall. 199.)

Regarding the supremacy of a treaty over a conflicting state law, eminent jurists disagree. Time permitting, we could cite you opinions on each side of this controversy with the balance of modern opinion, perhaps, on the side of the supremacy of the national government. 'The very words of our constitution imply that some treaties will be made in contravention of the laws of the State, whether the legislative authority under which they are passed is concurrent with that of Congress, or exclusive of that of Congress,' says that eminent jurist Elihu Root (address made by Elihu Root at first annual meeting of the American Society of International Law ... *American Journal International Law*, vol. I, 278–83, April 1907).

Finally, your distinguished member, His Excellency Orestes Ferrara, said in his report on 'Treaties' to the Commission on Public International Law last week – in reference to the code of Public International Law, drawn up by the Conference of Jurists at Rio de Janeiro, April 1927:

'In not a single clause has limitation as to the content of treaties been defined ... The will of contracting parties (to a treaty) has been left in complete and absolute liberty.'

We therefore offer you a treaty which we believe the United States Government and other governments of Panamerica are fully empowered to enter into. Legal interpretations may offer barriers. The U.S. constitution states none.

Men may differ as to their willingness to accept the rights of women as proper subject matter for treaty action. To persuade them to our point of view is the task we have undertaken.

We can only touch upon these points here.

We shall hope to discuss them exhaustively with the commission appointed to study equal rights for women.

Our proposed method of establishing equal rights is not as revolutionary as you might think – revolutionary in thought perhaps, but not in international procedure.

At the first conference of the International Labor Office of the League of Nations (Washington 1919), three out of seven conventions were written for women-workers on the ground of sex. The second conference (Genoa 1920) wrote conventions applying to both sexes (adults and children). At the Third Conference (Geneva 1921) more conventions were written for both sexes among adults and children. In 1927 (Geneva) the same office wrote conventions on sickness insurance for workers of both sexes.

These are but a few of many examples which prove two things. Jurists have written conventions making women unequal before international law. Jurists have written conventions making men and women equal before international law. There is no fixed policy – except as there is the general evasion of accepting the idea of laws for human beings. Some of the conventions are for women and children of one sex. Some are for women and children of both sexes. Some are for men and women. The result is not only an appalling hodge-podge. It is manifestly stupid and unfair to both adults and children.

How much simpler it would be to take our clear and decisive method! The result would be one body of conventions for adult men and women, and another for children of both sexes. There could then be a housecleaning of all the useless conventions based on the arbitrary factor of sex.

Conventions have been proposed and ratified regulating the hours of work of women, regulating the time of day when women shall work – as was done by the convention of the International Conference at Berne in 1906 – as was done by the Convention for the Unification of Protective Laws for Workmen and Laborers, signed February 7th, 1923, by Guatemala, El Salvador, Honduras, Nicaragua, Costa Rica. For example, Article I of this convention signed by the five central American countries, stipulates the time of day wherein women shall be permitted to work. Will you tell us this can be done and at the same time tell us that a treaty shall not be negotiated enabling adult women to choose their own times of work and their own occupations, which our treaty would enable them to do?

Again, will you tell us that the League of Nations (1921 Convention for Prevention of Traffic in Women and Children) can propose a convention for the suppression of the traffic in women, which convention is to date signed by more than thirty-five countries in the world – and in the same breath tell us that a treaty cannot be negotiated for other women? Must we become sex-slaves before we can be judged fit subjects for action by convention? International action was not taken on this shameful traffic primarily because women are sold and transported from one country to another. You know as well as we do that that international convention was written because the moral conscience of the world demanded it.

May I say in passing that it is our firm belief that if women were not held in contempt before the law, were not held socially inferior and cheap in the eyes of society, this traffic would never exist. Unconventionality yes, but not traffic in women. It is our firm belief that so swiftly as you make us your equals, so swiftly will your international conventions written on this subject fall into disuse because they will not be necessary.

We find, then, that international conventions are in operation affecting the following groups of women:

1 Women who work by day.
2 Women who work by night.
3 Women who are trafficked in.
4 Women before and after childbirth.
5 Women who are ill and proposed for.
6 Women who marry aliens.

Is it not folly to continue on this piecemeal path? Leave aside for a moment the justice of our claim. Leave aside all legal procedure, which is not always synonymous with common sense. Does not plain, homely common sense compel you to embrace by treaty action now, the rights of all women and scrap all this idiotic segregation of women in conventions? Does not wisdom call to you to save yourselves and ourselves from further bulky, cumbersome, unjust international action? We hope they do.

Some of the delegates have advised us not to propose an equal rights treaty at this time. 'This treaty will call up legal and juridical difficulties, and you will be defeated.' Our answer to this is, gentlemen, that if you find our proposal difficult, that is your misfortune. If statesmen avoid all questions because they are difficult, nothing vital will ever be accomplished. The first requisite is to agree on the broad, general principle of equality between men and women set forth in the proposed treaty, and if your heart is in that agreement, your intelligence will settle the technical difficulties. On the point of defeat, this must be said: a defeat of the treaty will be your defeat – not ours.

There is another point we would like to call to your attention. Since working with this Conference, we have heard the opinion expressed – I regret to say – by one of our compatriots, that equal rights may be all right for the women of North America, but that the women of Latin America are not yet ready for them. We women resent and disbelieve in any hint of sectional superiority. It may be that there is a hope implied that, although we women of North America may be out of hand, the women of Latin America may still be kept under legal subjection. We do not believe that the men of North America are called upon to be tender protectors of the women of Latin America.

We do not look with approval upon this attempt to divide women. Our subjection is world-wide. The abolition of our subjection will be accomplished by world-wide solidarity of women. Furthermore, we have not noticed that the men of the northern and the southern Americas are reluctant to unite in Panamericanism because there may exist different customs, differing attitudes of mind toward your mutual problems. The unwarranted presumption is again: one code of conduct for women, another for men.

We bear witness today before you to the growing solidarity among the women of the Americas.

This conference will long be remembered by what it does here for the women of the Americas. Nothing you gentlemen will do during this conference will be of such far-reaching importance as the action you will take toward the liberty of women. Nothing will so distinguish you for all time as to abandon at once all separate codes of law for men and women and to substitute in their place the great principle making women equal with men before the law.

We want to be your peers, your comrades, your helpmates, your partners in the great adventure of life. These we shall be in a properly civilized society. You can hasten that day.

So long as inequality before the law exists between men and women, less is expected of women by men. Less is expected by women of themselves. This in turn affects our whole body of opinion, our whole culture. Less courage, less balance in judgment, a lower standard of public spirit, an indifference in international cooperation. This is the reward of inequality. This is a menace to men as well as to women. To expect less is to receive less. We stand ready to give all of our abilities to society, not our limited, restricted abilities. Do you want less?

Will you welcome the opportunity, or will you hesitate? Will you condemn us further to the ignoble, unworthy, unlovely procedure of begging every laggard in our hemisphere to concur before action is taken, or will you men whom we choose to call our intellectual equals release us by your acts?

We ask for immediate recommendation by the Conference of the proposed Equal Rights treaty, a tentative draft of which we now present to you. This treaty – the Contracting States agree that upon the ratification of this treaty, men and women shall have equal rights throughout the territory subject to their respective jurisdictions – was drawn up by Alice Paul, of the United States, beloved feminist leader and distinguished scholar of international law.

We have told you what we want. The rest is up to you. Who will be the first country to dare to trust its women with that degree of equality which will come through the negotiation of the treaty? Which country among you will claim this honor?

Panamericanism will move at a swifter, lovelier, more rhythmic pace, if men and women run together.

Text of Resolution of the VI Conference
re Inter American Commission of Women[1]

The Sixth International Conference of American States resolves:

That an Inter American Commission of Women be constituted to take charge of the preparation of juridical information and data of any other kind which

---

1 Sixth International Conference of American States, La Habana, 1928. Final act, p. 123.

may be deemed advisable to enable the Seventh International Conference of American States to take up the consideration of the civil and political equality of women in the continent.

Said Commission shall be composed of seven women from various countries of America, appointed by the Pan American Union, this number to be increased by the Commission itself until every Republic in America has a representative on the Commission.

(Adopted 18 February 1928)

[Source: Equal Rights International Papers, Women's Library, London Metropolitan University.]

Eleanor Mary Hinder (1893–1963), born in New South Wales, Australia, began her professional life as a teacher, then a welfare officer, and was a member of such organizations as the Sydney University Women Graduates' Association and the Workers' Educational Association Club. Eventually Hinder's work became international, taking her to China to collaborate with Mary Dingman, international industrial secretary of the YWCA. Hinder would spend the rest of her life taking on welfare and labour issues, as well as women's rights issues, throughout the world. She participated in international gatherings like the International Labour Organization in Geneva, the International Federation of University Women's Congress at Oslo, and the Pan Pacific Women's Conference in Honolulu.

Eleanor M. Hinder

Pan-Pacific Women's Conference in Relation to World Conferences (1928) (reprinted from May issue of *Pan-Pacific Monthly* of Pan-Pacific Association of China)

The convening of the Pan-Pacific Women's Conference at Honolulu in 1928 is an event of immediate consequence, and of incalculable potentiality. It instantly throws into relief former international women's conferences held throughout the world. To visualize its significance and possibilities, an analysis of its relationship with other conferences and world organizations of women is necessary. Indeed an evaluation of the whole latter-day development of international conferences is equally vital to a realization of the place of the Pan-Pacific Women's Conference.

International organizations of an official and a voluntary nature have been one of the features of world-life in the twentieth century. In every department of human endeavor the need has been found for sharing the experience of national groups one with the other; to this end organizations have been formed and periodical international conferences been a frequent phase of their functioning. Historically one of the earliest such Conferences was called in Europe in the sixties of the last century, which concerned itself with internationalizing postal services for the better communication of country with country. Has it, for example, occurred to most of us that there had to be an international arrangement whereby a nation consented to waive the right to collect postage upon mail entering it, on the principle that there was a probable equalization of this loss of income, in that other countries did likewise?

To observe the list of international organizations which for the most part head up in Europe, is to know how widespread is this ramification of endeavor. International groups of employers lined up according to trade interest; similar international trade organizations of workers; multifarious professional groups; social polity groups; scientific groups; academic groups; educational groups and workers' educational groups; peace groups; women's groups ... These in addition to the official international lineup of nations, with its labor, economic, health, cultural, migration, and political phases.

At times the number is bewildering, and one is tempted to ask whether the tendency to organize has not run riot in this century, and whether international conferences are not expensive machinery to achieve a measure of common action. It may be good to share the experience of one nation with another, or one interest group within a nation to meet with similar groups from other countries; but in time and money, does it represent an outlay which can scarcely be justified? There are those who claim that with each international contact, international understanding is engendered. There are others who claim that national differences are sharpened by a clearer understanding of them and tolerance may be the last result obtained.

To trace out the ramifications of international organizations within any one sphere is to understand this new phase of human inter-relationship, and perhaps to help evaluate it. At the Third Pan-Pacific Science Congress held in Tokyo, Dr Joji Sakurai in his Presidential address analyzed existing international scientific organizations in the world. He showed them to be of four kinds – a first group such as the International Metric Commission, resting upon formal conventions between governments, which aims at establishing uniformity in standards of measurement. This is the oldest existing international scientific organization, dating back to 1869. A second type consists of those organizations where co-operation of observation is essential. As example he quotes the arrangement made between a number of astronomical observatories for the preparation of an astrographical chart. A third type consists of members whose interest is in one aspect of science, such as the Botanical Congress of the United States of America. A fourth is the International Research Council, which aims at coordinating the activities of other international scientific groups. It has been instrumental in correlating the activities of the International Unions of Astronomy, Chemistry, Geography, Biology, Mathematics, Physics, Radiotelegraphy, whose activities otherwise remain entirely in their respective spheres. It does not itself undertake any scientific work. Dr Sakurai then proceeds to examine the place of a Pacific Science Congress in relation to International Science groups.

After this general survey and analysis of various international scientific undertakings, past and present, it will be plain that the Pan-Pacific Science Congress differs in its organization and other respects from all others. It deals not with one but with several branches of science. And not with science in its absolute sense but with science as applied to certain problems. This is a necessary consequence of the primary object of the Congress.

Its primary object is to study the scientific problems of the Pacific by co-operative effort. It is not the direct advancement of knowledge in general, hence it is plainly evident that the activities of the Congress should be limited to sciences as applied to definite Pacific problems. A paper dealing for example with Atomic Disintegration in general would thus be out of place, while one dealing with the Chemistry and Physics of the sea water in different parts of the Pacific Ocean would not be only an appropriate but also a valuable contribution to the proceedings of the Congress.

In the sphere of women's activities there have arisen several large international voluntary organizations. Of these, the International Council of Women has the most universal interests. In addition there are the more special though strongly supported groups – the International Alliance for Suffrage and Equal Citizenship; the Women's International League for Peace and Freedom, and the World's Young Women's Christian Association. The headquarters of all these women's organizations center in Europe – three in London, one in Geneva. American women's organizations have a lively relationship to all of them. Those of the British Commonwealth of Nations, especially in its Anglo-Saxon portions, have equally close affiliations. In some cases the women of the Orient have touch with them, but the success of this international link is dependent upon the strength of the women's organizations within the country concerned as well as the vividness of contacts. Not

as yet in Asiatic countries, is there a degree of development of group formation approximating that in other countries – and it is possible that the peoples of the Orient will find other methods of expressing their interest than by
'organization.'

Of the four international groups mentioned, the only one with any reality to
touch in China, for example, is the Y.W.C.A., and this because of the wealth of
resident women from many countries who have come to work with the China
organization in the last twenty years. The Women's International League for
Peace and Freedom has seen the need for sending a delegation of a British and
a French woman to China in 1928. In their considered opinion, the available
woman power is not sufficient to proceed to the organization of a national
section of the League. Though there is a National Council of Women, it is
not national in scope, and its functioning is intermittent. There is a Women's
Suffrage Association, though its activities are also limited by the number of
women interested or available for the work.

The calling of a Pan-Pacific Women's Conference is then an effort of a
regional nature. What is the scope and value of a Pacific Women's Conference?
What is its place in relation to international women's organizations?

When the earliest forecasts of this Conference were made, the Joint Committee of Shanghai Women's Organizations wrote to ask what was its scope.
Would it concern itself with the discussion of the sections outlined by the
Conference, as 'life' issues, or as 'Pacific' issues? Wherein should the Pacific
emphasis come? In the educational section, for example, the discussion of the
importance of the pre-school age in children is not a 'Pacific' problem, it is a
'life' problem. Pacific peoples have different experience in their efforts to find
the solution to the problems of the pre-school age, but the world has made a
contribution to the outlining of the problem. Shall we say, as did Dr Sakurai
(changing the 'scientific' to 'educational' terms):

> The object of the Conference is not the direct advancement of knowledge in
> general, and it's plainly evident that the activities of the Congress should be lim-
> ited to 'education' (changing 'sciences') as applied to definite problems. A paper
> dealing for example with 'child psychology' in general (changed from 'Atomic
> Disintegration') would thus be out of place, while one dealing with experience in
> 'child thought' in different parts of the Pacific (changing 'dealing with the Chem-
> istry and Physics of the sea water in different parts of the Pacific') would not only
> be appropriate, but a valuable contribution to the proceedings of the Congress.

This problem is an important one. Until it is cleared, and a common basis
reached, the proceedings of the Women's Conference will lack point; the pro-

ceedings and the emphasis of the Conference will determine the outcome of the Conference. What is this to be?

Is there to be set up yet another 'Regional International Grouping of Women'? If the Pacific Women's Conference deliberates purely in terms of the Pacific, this will probably be the outcome, if not immediately, at any rate in a not-too-distant future. A Continuation Committee may be elected to provide for future Conferences which would ultimately form a Pacific Women's Organization. If, on the other hand, the problems under consideration are treated as 'world' or 'life' issues, the outcome will probably be vastly different. It must be admitted that the distance of many Pacific lands from European centers where International Women's Organizations head up, is such that touch with them is an unreal thing. Distance and money considerations make attendance at world conferences impossible, but for the very few. Has not the time come for the recognition of a Pacific Basin in women's international groupings, and for the creating of a Pacific focus for them? Regional conferences held, say, in Honolulu, within the spheres of interest of the larger women's organization, would result in immense stimulation of countries bordering the Pacific. Australia is six weeks' sail from Europe; so also is China. Each is two weeks' sail from Honolulu.

One of the logical results of the recognition of a Pacific focus is not only regional conferences, but the establishment of a clearing house for the material produced in agencies which center in Europe, and its dissemination to the Pacific countries. This is by no means a duplication of activity. It is a practical method of bringing Europe close to the Pacific. The establishment of a Pacific office where the results of effort of the suffrage groups, the peace groups, the International Council activities, could concentrate, would mean that bordering countries would be nearer the ideas which were purveyed to them from such a focus. The geographical position would mean possibility of visits to contiguous countries by an organizing secretary for the stimulating and maintaining of interest. Women's groups are recognized as enormously valuable agencies for adult education and can not be ignored in a developing Pacific consciousness. Can the vision of the continued education of Pacific women be enough to set this machinery in action?

It must not be imagined that the 'focus' would be merely a clearing house. Immediately constructive Pacific thinking would assert itself and become available to the European focus. That European women feel their links with the women of the Pacific to be poor, is evidenced by two experiences which have come to the attention of the Joint Committee of Shanghai Women's Organizations. Early in 1928, the Women's International League for Peace and Freedom sent delegates who frankly stated that they desired to discover what stage women's activities in China had reached. Not otherwise could they visualize any adequate world relationships for and with them. Again, both the International Council of Women and the International Women's Suffrage Alliance have written to the Joint Committee regretting the slenderness of connection with similar Chinese women's organizations and expressing the hope that vital relationships might be established.

What then should be done by Pacific women?

[Source: *Bulletin of the Pan-Pacific Union*, July 1928, 11–14.]

Madeleine Zabriskie Doty (1877–1963) was a US writer who addressed issues as varied as women's prison reform and peacekeeping. She became involved in an international group of pacifist women, attending the Women's Peace Congress, becoming the secretary for the Women's International League for Peace and Freedom, and eventually editing the League of Nations' *Pax International*. Doty would spend the rest of her life travelling as a pacifist and a feminist, attending conferences, working as a correspondent for newspapers, and lecturing.

Madeleine Z. Doty
The W.I.L. World Section (1930)

Tucked away in the constitution of the W.I.L. is a provision for a World Section, which shall be admitted to the W.I.L. and have the same rights and privileges as any other section. It has been there almost since the beginning of the W.I.L. Did the original founders of the Women's International League feel the time would come when such a section was needed? Has the time come?

Some of us got together after the Prague Congress to discuss this matter. It seemed to us the hour had struck for action. We found in our midst a woman born in one country, living in another and married to a man of a third nationality. Such a person could not and did not wish to claim any one nationality as her own.

We found others who having lived for years in many different lands had acquired a fondness for all of them, and preferred being a world citizen to belonging to any national group. We found others scattered about the face of the earth, who were so widely separated from their own national sections, that they wished to be part of a World Section.

JUS CARTOONS: No. VII.

THE ASSEMBLY OF THE LEAGUE OF NATIONS: 1930.

The International Chef (*weighing the ingredients presented to him*) : The proportions are better this year, but there is still not enough leaven for the lump.

[Source: *International Women's News: Jus Suffragii* 24, no. 12 (1930): 193. Image published with permission of ProQuest; further reproduction is prohibited without permission.]

Still others felt ethically that the time had come to do away with national boundaries. That as Mr de Madariaga said in his article in the December *Pax*: 'The world is one … everything which happens … influences everything else that happens.' Or as Mr Wells said in his article on the 'World State': 'Man has ceased to be part of a localized economic system and has become part of a vaguely developed but profoundly real world economic system.'

In short, there was a real demand for a World Section. We realize that for the majority the way to internationalism or world unity is through nationalism, that there cannot be a League of People without first having a League of Nations, that it is extremely important that the W.I.L. national sections continue their active and strong campaign among the people of their own lands to bring these people through nationalism to internationalism. But we felt it might aid the W.I.L. in its work for a united world to have a group in its midst who belonged to no nation and called themselves world citizens.

In the middle ages Joan of Arc rose to demand of the feudal lords that they unite and form a nation. That was the great ideal then. Today the demand is that the nations of the earth shall unite for the still greater ideal, a world union. A new world is dawning, a world based not on compromise but on 'new solutions born of our pooled intelligence.'

This sense of oneness and love for all should be the characteristic of the members of a world section otherwise the group will have no value.

To join such a group because you cannot get along personally with people in your own land is folly. If you cannot work with your neighbours how can you get along with Jew and Gentile, Christian and Buddist, French and German, English and Irish, Americans and Mexicans, for all these and many others are likely to form the World Section.

The constitution of the W.I.L. in this matter reads as follows: 'More than one hundred individuals living in at least five different countries agreeing with the aims of the League, without being members of any national section, may unite as a World Section, which shall then have the same rights and duties as any other section. Only one such section can be admitted.'

Note the important items. First you cannot be a member of a national section and join the world section. There must be a hundred people from five nations who want the section, and when formed the group is like any other section, it has the same duties and privileges. The members must believe in and support the principles of the W.I.L. and they may then, like any other section, elect and send to Congresses twenty delegates.

Those of us who discussed this matter and decided to try and form a world section drew up and signed the following statement:

We recognize that to a large extent the work of the League must be carried on by national groups in each country who unite to form an International League but we feel that in addition both in the league and in the world at large there is need for a body of women who shall call themselves world citizens and dedicate themselves solely to world affairs and to the service of humanity; who will act always for the benefit of all mankind even if at times such action may seem to clash with national welfare. We believe that the sovereign independence of states and peace is incompatible, that each step towards peace means a loss of separateness, that we must be bound together by a spiritual ideal which shall rise above both political and economic conflicts.

Such a group as this will provide a field of work for all those women who for geographical and other reasons are unable to identify themselves with their respective national sections.

It is therefore to reinforce the original purpose of the League that we the undersigned have decided to form a world section and while working as ardently as ever before in our own or other lands for peace, to relinquish our right to national membership in any national section of the W.I.L.P.F. and consecrate ourselves and our efforts to world peace through world citizenship and world action.

The original signers of this statement are: Marcelle Capy, France. Josephine Storey, England. Violet MacNaughton, Canada. Elin Waegner, Sweden. Madeleine Z. Doty, U.S.A. Juliette Rao, France. Elizabeth Watson, U.S.A. Madame Has-Menetrier, Switzerland. Madeleine Kuipers, Holland. Ida Rauh, U.S.A. Frauleins Huber and Ineichen, Switzerland.

Other names are now coming in. We have just received nine splendid names from Sweden.

Among the names are people representing five nationalities but we have not yet a hundred names. Are there others who believe in and wish to join a world section?

If enough people sign up within the next two or three months, then a petition can be presented to the International Executive Committee on April 23rd with a request for the admittance of the world section into the W.I.L.

The question will be asked what can such a group do if formed? At first nothing more than to throw our weight into any *international* action undertaken by the W.I.L. The first few months of existence will be needed to exchange ideas between the members as to our program.

I have agreed to act temporarily as secretary and circulate monthly the proposals.

Another question asked will be what relation does the world section bear to the International members? The same relation as any other Section. The

International members are those people belonging to national sections who have direct contact with Geneva Headquarters, and who by their 25 franc due support the Geneva office receiving in return all international literature. We should hope that a very large per cent of world section members would also be International members, for their interest would centre primarily in International Headquarters. We have fixed five francs, as due for world section members, half of this to go for a subscription to *Pax*, the rest to cover stationary and postage.

This whole project has been presented in *Pax* before realization in order that there may be comment and suggestion. The wish is to help W.I.L. activities and not hinder them. No one should consider joining the world section unless there is a strong urge to do so. If you have caught a vision of what a world section might be, a pioneer in a new world mentality, which sees the world as one, and which offers itself to the W.I.L. as a psychological laboratory for the development of that sense of oneness and world citizenship, then send in your name, care of Madeleine Z. Doty World Section, 11 rue Emile-Yung, Geneva.

[Source: *Pax* 5, no. 3 (1930).]

Paulette Nardal (1896–1985) was the eldest of seven black Martiniquan sisters. She was among the group of black students and scholars from French colonies living in Paris in the 1920s and 1930s, where she and her sister Jane hosted a salon. Paulette Nardal introduced French-speaking African and Caribbean writers to Harlem Renaissance writers through her articles in *La Revue du Monde Noir*. She also wrote for *La Dépêche Africaine*, the newspaper of a group of moderate anti-imperialist black intellectuals, and together with her sister Jane established ties between these black intellectuals and white French feminists who became allies in the struggle against imperialism and fascism.

Paulette Nardal
Awakening of Race Consciousness (1932)

I shall study this awakening more especially among the Antillian Negroes. Their attitude towards racial problems is certainly being modified. A few years ago, we might even say a few months ago, certain questions were simply tabooed in Martinica. Woe to those who dared to approach them! One could not speak about slavery or proclaim his pride of being of African descent without being considered as an over-excited or at least as an odd person. Such concerns roused no deep chord in the mature or in the young Antillians' thought. It is a fact that this almost disdainful indifference seems to be transforming itself into a wondering interest among the older generation and into a genuine enthusiasm among the younger.

However, certain Antillians had already been stirred to race consciousness, but it was the result of having left their small native islands. The uprooting and the ensuing estrangement they felt in the metropolis, where Negroes have not always been so favourably received as they seem to be since the Colonial Exhibition, had given them a real Negro soul, in spite of their Latin education. Yet they never made articulate this state of mind.

The general attitude of the Antillian Negroes towards race problems, which is so different from that of the Afro-Americans, can be obviously explained by the liberal spirit which characterizes the politics of France towards coloured peoples. Sieburg's book 'Is God French?' contains, among other things, a very sensible remark upon the power of assimilation of the French genius. According to him, the lack of colour prejudice among the French is due to the fact that they are certain to transform the mind of any coloured man into a truly French one in a relatively short time. Besides, it was natural that the Antillians who are generally half castes of Negro and white descent, imbued with their Latin culture and ignorant of the history of the black race should, in the end, return to the element that honoured them most.

Quite different was the situation among the American Negroes. Though they are not of pure African origin either, the deliberate scorn with which they have always been treated by white Americans, incited them to seek for reasons for social and cultural pride in their African past. Because they were obliged, immediately after the abolition of slavery, to try to solve their difficult race problem, the race question became the keynote of their concerns.

It would be interesting to find out how this situation has influenced the Afro-American literature. As it is the case with all vanquished peoples, three periods may be noted in the intellectual evolution of the American Negroes. First, an indispensable period of acquisition during which the Negroes imported from Africa had to master a strange language and adapt themselves to a hostile environment. It is a period of absorption of the white elements by the Negroes. From a purely literary point of view the American Negroes can only be the docile imitators of their white models. Only certain slave narratives retain all their original freshness and genuine emotion because they were written in dialect. The anti-slavery struggle saw the outburst of a literature of controversy and moral protest. Many orators of that time achieved real success. The poetry of that epoch was characterized by increasing appeals to pity. Of that period there remains a considerable number of documents and memoirs which from a historical point of view are undoubtedly valuable. Then from 1880 on, we witness the accession of the Negroes to real culture. Two opposing tend[e]ncies make themselves felt. On one side, Dunbar, poet and novelist who used both dialect and the English language, represents, if we may say so, the school of racial realism. On the other hand, Du Bois continued, as it were, the literature of racial protest by advocating equal civic and cultural rights for Negroes and whites. But it is owing to the influence exerted by Braithwaite that the modern writers, without discarding the racial themes and the emotional intensity due to their ancestral experiences, took them as the starting point of their inspiration and gave them a universal purport. It is important to note that they abandoned the Negro dialect in favour of the forms and symbols of traditional literature. The poems of Claude MacKay which were published in this Review have acquainted our readers with this new attitude, and more recently, those of Langston Hughes have shown how the young Negro writers, rejecting all inferiority complex, 'intend to express their individual dark-skinned selves without fear or shame.'

This interesting intellectual evolution of the American Negro leads us to ask our selves what stage of his own development his Antillian brother, who lived in a comparatively favourable environment, has reached. If Racial concern can hardly be found in the literary production which followed the abolition of slavery in the Antilles, it is because the 'great forefathers' were busily claiming equal liberty and political rights for the different categories of the black race living on the Antillian soil. Among the following generation of writers, we might cite the Martinicans Victor Duquesnay, Daniel Thaly, Salavina, the Guadelupean Oruno Lara, and many Haitian poets. They were at the phase of conscious imitation of the literature of the conquering race. But if the intellectual evolution of the Afro-Americans was rapid, that of the Antillians might be called prodigious. Romanticism was then reigning in European literature. The production of the Antillian writers were in no way inferior to those of the contemporary French writers, not to speak of such Antillian geniuses as the Dumas and Jose-Maria de Heredia.

If we examine the works of these precursors, we certainly meet with the glorification of their small far-away mother-lands, the 'Isles of Beauty' (Exoticism was already the fashion), but no race pride is to be found there. Indeed they speak lovingly of their native lands, but it happened that a stranger celebrated them a still more felicitous way and accorded to the racial types more appreciation and real attachment. Their successors will continue to derive their inspiration from Occidental or purely metropolitan themes.

However, between that period and the present one, may be classed a generation of men whose racial tend[e]ncies have literature, politics or humanitarian concerns as a starting point. Certain ideas are being launched. The theories of Marcus Garvey are commented upon. The first Pan-Negro Congress is organized. To literature, we owe 'Batouala' by René Maran to whom was awarded the Goncourt prize in 1920. Yet throughout this 'novel of objective observation' as the author himself stated in his preface, rings the most generous indignation. Then was published the first Negro journal of Paris: 'The Continents' which lasted only a few months. We must also cite an essay intitled 'Heimatlos' by a young man from Guiana who enjoyed a certain success in his time. The first Negro paper of long standing was 'La Dépêche Africaine,' whose director wrote a much appreciated History of Guadelupa under the Monarchy. In this journal, the movement which was to culminate in 'The Review of the Black World' was indicated. In the Antilles are to be found the remarkable works of M. Jules Monnerot published as 'A contribution to the history of Martinica' and more recently 'Galeries of Martiniquaises,' a valuable source of documents in which racial questions are treated with more frankness as usual by M. Césaire Philémon.

We can easily notice that in none of these works are the racial problems studied for themselves. These productions remain the tributaries of Latin culture. In none of them do we find the expression of a sincere faith in the future of the race and the necessity of creating a feeling of solidarity between the different groups of Negroes living throughout the globe.

However, parallel to the isolated efforts above mentioned, the aspirations which were to be crystallized around 'The Review of the Black World' asserted themselves among a group of Antillian women students in Paris. The coloured women living alone in the metropolis, until the Colonial Exhibition, have certainly been less favoured than coloured men who are content with a certain easy success. Long before the latter, they have felt the need of a racial solidarity which would [not be] merely material. They were thus aroused to race consciousness. The feeling of uprooting which they experienced which was so felicitously expressed by Roberte Horth, in 'A thing of no importance,' contributed to the 2nd number of 'The Review of the Black World,' was the starting point of their evolution. After a period of obedient imitation of their white models, they may have passed through their period of revolt, just as their American brothers. But, as they grew older, they became less strict, less ultra, since they have understood the relativity of all things. At present, their position is the middle ground.

In the course of their evolution, their intellectual curiosity applied itself to the history of their race and of their respective countries. They were thus led to regret the absence of such interesting matters in the educational programs ascribed to the Antillian schools. Instead of despising their retarded brothers or laying aside all hope [...] the possibility of the black race ever being on a par with the Aryans, they began to study. And as a matter of course, when the occasion came to select a subject for a memoir or a thesis, their choice went to the black race. For the first time, one of them took 'The life and work of Mrs Beecher Stowe (Uncle Tom's Cabin – Puritanism in New England)' as a subject for the Diplôme d'Études supérieures d'anglais. Later on, another student studied Lafcadio Hearn's work on the Antilles. A student of French selected the poems of John Antoine Nau, and the Works of R[everend] F[ather] Labat. We must say that at that time the Afro-American writers were still unknown in France. But the interest of the Antillian students in their own race had been aroused. We are informed that certain students are preparing memoirs on the American negro writers and poets who, in spite of their evident value, had hitherto been left aside in the different surveys of American literature published by French University professors.

Let us hope that the students coming up for degrees in History and Geography will avail themselves of the riches which the black race and the African continent offer to them. Let us hope also that they will give us the occasion of analysing in this Review some masterful theses of the doctorat. In this realm, they have had two distinguished precursors: M. Félix Eboué, administrateur en chef des Colonies, a contributor to the 'Review of the Black World,' who for long years has studied the Ethnology of certain African peoples; M. Grégoire-Micheli, member of the International Institute of Anthropology, who contributed remarkable articles to this Review, is an erudite specialist of the ancient religions of South America. Moreover, we know that René Maran's latest novel 'Le Livre de la Brousse,' whose translation is to be published in America, constitutes a real and splendid rehabilitation of the African civilisation. It may be announced as the masterpiece of the celebrated Negro writer.

It is worth noticing that some of our young friends seemed to have spontaneously arrived at the last phase observed by us in the intellectual evolution of the American Negroes. If, on one hand, they continue to treat purely Occidental subjects it is in an extremely modern form, on the other, they begin to bring into relief characteristic racial themes as our readers will soon verify in a series of poems we are going to publish.

Should one see in the tend[e]ncies here expressed a sort of implicit declaration of war upon Latin culture and the white world in general? It is our duty to eliminate such an error. We are fully conscious of our debts to the Latin culture and we have no intention of discarding it in order to promote I know not what return to ignorance. Without it, we would have never become conscious of our real selves. But we want to go beyond this culture, in order to give to our brethren, with the help of the white scientists and friends of the Negroes, the pride of being the members of a race which is perhaps the oldest in the world. Once informed of that civilization, they will no longer despair of the future of their own race, a part of which seems at the present time to be delayed in its evolution. They will tender to their retarded brothers a helping hand and endeavour to understand and love them better.

[Original source: *La Revue du Monde Noir / The Review of the Black World*, no. 6 (1932): 25–31; repr. in *La Revue du Monde Noir / The Review of the Black World 1931–1932 Collection complete no. 1 à 6* (Paris: Jean-Michel Place, 1992), 343–9.]

Muthulakshmi Reddi (1886–1968) was a medical practitioner and social reformer, and the first woman doctor in India. She was the founder-president of the Women's Indian Association (WIA), was nominated to the Madras legislature as a member of legislative council in 1926, and became the first woman to be a member of any legislature in India. Reddi also wrote one of the most important responses to Katherine Mayo's *Mother India*, presenting her critique to a gathering organized by the WIA. She was also an active member of the All-India Women's Conference.

Muthulakshmi Reddi
Creative Citizenship (1933)

Dr Muthulakshmi Reddi, Presiding Officer, All-Asia Conference of Women

Women of India are fully convinced that unless their men are free and responsible citizens, they – the women – never can hope to be free from the shackles of custom and convention. And we know from the examples of other countries, that women can secure full education, full freedom, and full rights. Therefore, if the British Government fails to grant fully responsible government for India, the women there will join the men in the struggle for political freedom.

I hardly can express to you the joy it gives me to find myself in the midst of an international gathering of women such as are here, all in the service of humanity. We women of India know how you have tried to help us, and we appreciate all the noble efforts you have made. We want you to know how much we desire to cooperate with you in fellowship, love, good will, and peace, and thus make the world civilized in the real sense of the word.

The woman movement is international; and we congratulate ourselves that we have developed an international outlook in our affairs, for I believe we are far ahead of the men in that respect. From its infancy, the women's movement was international in character, crossing all barriers of caste, color, creed, or race. Women often are referred to by men as mere imitators of fashion and dress, but I know we have proved to be as successful in our emulation of leaders in a good and noble cause. Woman's work and activities always have interested women of all countries, and the women who are free in one country have assisted their sisters of other creeds or races to secure their rights and privileges. That is how the woman movement has spread so rapidly from the West to the East and has aroused the women of the East to revolt and action.

India's woman movement has been of comparatively recent origin. It is the work of only two decades and we must confess that in India, the banner of women's freedom and emancipation was raised first, by men. Rajah Ram Mohan Roy was the first and foremost reformer in India, years ago. He championed the women's cause and tried to abolish the cruel suttee. Pundit Vidyasagar was responsible for the widow-remarriage act. As the world knows, for ages it has been the custom in India that if a woman's husband died, she never could re-marry. This, coupled with the custom of child-marriage, made many women widows before they ever had been wives, and condemned thousands and thousands of girls to loveless lives.

Now, in India, a widow can re-marry. Sir Hari Singh Gour was responsible for raising the age of consent for girls, another humanitarian act. Sir Haribalas Sarda worked for the act which restrains child marriage. So we have much for which we must thank our men. It is not strange that now, when they want political freedom, we women are willing to stand beside them in their efforts to attain it.

In the education of women in India, the Western missionary was the pioneer. He was followed by private, volunteer agencies. For many years, Governmental educational efforts among women had been tentative and hesitating. For long there was no money put aside to educate girls.

It is only during the last thirty years that the women of India have begun to interest themselves directly in their own affairs. There have been a few outstanding women here and there in the time elapsing from then until now. But the mass woman movement through organized women's associations really began only about fifteen years ago.

There are three women's organizations in India in which all the members are women of India, but in addition to these there are numerous local associations all engaged in education work, social health work and rescue work, in preventing child marriages and in combating 'untouchability.'

The Government has said, 'The beginning of a movement among certain India women is a most encouraging sign of India's progress, and we believe that this movement will be strengthened by increasing the influence of women at elections. The woman movement holds the key of progress and the results it may achieve are incalculably great.'

In every province of India, women are fully enfranchised citizens. While their Western sisters had to go through much agitation and struggle and even imprisonment, to get their citizen rights, the women of India received their rights by merely asking for them.

A woman has been a member of the public health body in the native state of Pravancore, and a woman has been Deputy Speaker in the Madras Legislature. Within the space of a decade, women have become honorary magistrates, members of the municipalities, district boards, and the Senate in Bombay, Calcutta, and Lucknow. Recently, in an election, women were returned to office in their municipalities, defeating men who ran for the same offices.

All trades and professions are open to women in India. We have one custom in contrast to the West – married women are preferred as workers to single women. And we never have any sex antagonism or sex hostility.

The most intelligent women in India have joined in this great movement of education for their sex. The women in India love and respect Gandhi and join his party in large numbers, because he is a strong advocate of women's freedom and of all progressive reforms in society.

The thinking women of India are against communal representation and are anxious to get a fully responsible government, feeling that, unless India gets her own government, no real progress in the field of education, social reform, and the industrial development of the country is possible. That is why they wish so much for their men to be politically free.

I know you are interested in the work we, in India, are doing toward creating citizenship. Until lately, our conception of a citizen was confined to the narrow idea of a home and family of one country and nation. But, assembled as we are here as world citizens, to survey a world problem, we must know each other, know the real state of things in our respective countries, and above all, be frank in our speech.

[Source: *Our Common Cause: Civilization: Report of the National Council of Women of the United States. Including the Series of Round Tables, July 16–22, 1933, Chicago, Illinois* (New York: National Council of Women of the United States, 1973), 178–80.]

Lily Kelly (?–?) is not specifically identified.

Lily Kelly
The Woman Movement in Latin America (1933)

Miss Lily Kelly, President, the Peace Circle, Argentina

I see that I am on the program to speak about the women of Latin America, and this, I must confess, is too big an order for me for it outmeasures my knowledge of the other Latin American countries besides my own. So what I have to say about the woman movement comprises specifically my own country.

It is quite usual to hear Latin America quoted as a unit; and this is one of the fallacies of everyday life. We have, no doubt, a common tongue, a common Spanish inheritance, and many common problems, but these factors have set into different backgrounds, and, therefore, we cannot be spoken of as a unit.

We studied this problem of Latin America in a student conference I was at a year ago in my country, and we came to the conclusion, out of our findings, that the unity of Latin America is specifically sentimental. To make this clear I will use a domestic comparison. We are as children who left home very young and have not seen much of each other since then, but foster a brotherly feeling because we know we all belong to the one family.

That is more or less the unity that exists in Latin America. There is very little interchange. I would not say very little, but there is not so much interchange between Latin American countries as there is between Latin America and European countries. This is due to the fact that water, which seems to be a dividing element, is nevertheless more binding than land.

On land you have to build railways and pierce through mountains and break through jungles. Water is easier to get across. Therefore, we are nearer to Europe than to Peru or to Ecuador. I have said that just to make clear that I am speaking only of the woman movement in my own country.

With the time I have allotted to speak, I will be able only to more or less enumerate the fields of action, the trends, I might say, of action of the women's movement in my country, and I realize this would be a very superficial survey. But I am willing to give further information to anybody who desires it.

I am sorry I cannot bring you an exotic, unique, colorful picture from my country. In this standardized era we are very much like the rest of the world. I gather from what I hear that you have the belief that the women in my country live under duress, in submission to men, and, of course, in comparison with the freedom of American women, there is certainly some truth in this view, provided it is not overemphasized.

We are not as free as the American women, but, since the necessities of life have taken Argentine women and pushed them into jobs and professions, things have changed greatly.

There is, of course, a certain social restraint that still weighs upon women, but by leaps and bounds we are getting free of this burden. Only seven years ago women were given the same legal status as men, and this is due particularly to the struggle for the daily bread which has opened up this channel. About seven years ago, a law was passed called the civil emancipation of women, and that gave women the right to decide for themselves and manage their own affairs – that is to say, to devise, sell, go into business, and take up any kind of profession – so legally we have the same status as men.

We are of the few countries that have not yet got the vote for women. The suffrage movement in my country dates back about thirty years, and the pioneers of this movement have had the same fate as their sisters elsewhere. They have had to put up with misunderstanding and ridicule, but they have certainly done their work. A few liberal-minded men have sponsored the cause of women in Congress and the subject has been brought up repeatedly and, although it has been repeatedly rejected, last year, in September, the suffrage law went through the House of Representatives and is now awaiting the decision of the Senate. So I do not think it will be long before the women in my country have the right to vote.

On the whole, I must say that there is not much interest in politics in the women of my country. Before election they get an enthusiasm for certain candidates, but this is more in a spirit of gamble than a real insight into the issues that are involved in elections. They do not study the programs that are at the back of these men, nor do they grasp the fundamental issues of the different parties.

Few women have really awakened to social problems in our country. Madame Lombroso, who wrote a book not long ago about women of the present age, claims that this is so in every country. It is certainly so in my country. I attended several courses in a free college for higher studies in Buenos Aires. It is a kind of unofficial university where you get the most modern trend of thought, and in the courses on social problems – democracy, cooperation, political delinquency – there were very few women.

On the other hand, art and literature and philosophy seem to be the main interest of the women of my country.

Due to the imminence of suffrage, we have been trying to awaken the women to the importance of these different problems and we have struggled lately to start schools of citizenship for women where we would like to give the most fundamental, although elementary, knowledge of community interests and the importance of the vote. This we were doing just when I came away.

In social work, women are greatly involved in my country, but the majority of them are just a kind of charitable institution. We have all kinds of societies for the protection and welfare of children, for mothers, for widows, the aged, and the diseased, and all such important issues, but in these fields of action women do not have much technical knowledge or efficiency. They do not make a study of the roots of these social evils, and, therefore, their methods are more curative than preventive.

The main field of action and influence of the women of my country lies in the educational field. They have the junior schools practically entirely in their hands. They have a great control over the high schools, and they are now working their way into the universities. A friend of mine had the privilege of being the first woman to secure a chair in the university.

Due to this scope in the educational field, women's sphere of influence is very great because they sow the seed in the minds of the future generations and they have a big hand in the shaping of the future.

Have they made the most of this opportunity? Have they made the most of other channels of influence such as home life and friendship and love? Frankly speaking, I do not think they have. If they had, the world would not be where it is today. I listened with great attention and pleasure to the lecture that Mrs Blair gave us this morning, and she emphasizes the point that women have always used men's technique. That is really what the women are doing in my country also, using the technique of men.

This brings me to the definite question on this program, whether the woman movement is won or lost. The woman movement as a mass movement has certainly made tremendous strides, but has it added a new quality to the social education? Women, on the whole, have fallen too easily into the same mistakes as men have made. They have gone the same way. They have used the same technique. I do not say this to belittle the woman movement of my country, nor by any means do I invite the women, as Madame Lombroso does, to return to their homes.

I think it is necessary for our women to get out of their petty domestic family affairs and get into the larger issues of life, but I do hope that women will try to scrutinize their methods and analyze their responsibilities, and strive to be really and effectively a new force in the social order.

I don't think that this can be achieved except by profound spiritual development.

[Source: *Our Common Cause: Civilization: Report of the National Council of Women of the United States. Including the Series of Round Tables, July 16–22, 1933, Chicago, Illinois* (New York: National Council of Women of the United States, 1973), 81–3.]

The All-India Women's Conference was founded in 1927 by Margaret Cousins and it became one of the most important women's organizations in India. Initially concerned with education, it expanded its mandate to address purdah, child marriage, widow's rights, women's property rights, suffrage and other issues of concern to Indian women. Several of the most prominent feminists were members of the AIWC, including Sarojini Naidu, Rameshwari Nehru, Vijaya Laxmi Pandit, Kamaladevi Chattopadhyaya, Rajkumari Amrit Kaur, Muthulakshmi Reddi, Lakshmi Menon, and Masuma Begum, each of whom served as its president. The AIWC remains an active organization with over a million members.

All-India Women's Conference
Resolution on East–West Co-operation (1936)

Endorsement of the resolution passed at the Istanbul meeting of the International Alliance for Suffrage and Equal Citizenship:

Whereas this Conference believes in the interest of true progress, the women of every country must advance on the lines of equality and justice, it pledges its hearty support to all the women of the West as well as of the East whether they struggle for the eradication of their special legal, social and economic disabilities and for the recognition of their rights to equal citizenship in their respective national units or whether they are in danger of losing these legal, political, and economic rights which they have achieved.

Welcoming the co-operation of the women of all parts of the world, the value of which has been strongly emphasised by this Congress, it expresses the wish that the women of the East and of the West be linked by ties which will grow and consequently serve the interest of Universal peace.

[Source: *All-India Women's Conference: Tenth Session* (Trivandrum: Government Press, 1936), 122.]

Matiel Mogannam (also Mughannam) (c. 1900–92) was born in Lebanon, and raised in the United States. Mogannam moved to Jerusalem with her husband Mogannam Mogannam in 1921, where both became active in the nationalist movement. Matiel Mogannam participated in the Palestine Arab Women's Conference in Jerusalem in 1929, was on the executive of Arab Women's Executive Committee, and participated in important regional women's conferences like the Arab Women's conference in Beirut in 1930. Mogannam's book *The Arab Woman and the Palestine Problem* is the only one on the Palestinian Women's Movement written in the Mandate period.

Matiel E.T. Mogannam
The Struggle for National Rights (1937)

No human being conscious of his duties as a citizen of any country can endure a continual molestation of his rights and a permanent trespass on his national prerogatives. The difference between an active opponent to an undesirable form of government and a peaceful worker for securing a change in such a form rests upon the view which each one takes in asserting his rights as a citizen. There appears to be no line of distinction between the two except in the manner in which each endeavours to attain his objective.

For twelve years or more the Arab women of Palestine, especially in the urban districts, took a passive attitude towards the peculiar situation in which the country was placed. For obvious reasons an Arab woman, especially a Moslem, could not until then take a direct and open action in the National Movement.

Although fully aware, as she was, of the position of the future of her children in their own country, threatened by an alien race, and of the destiny of the future generation, she did not consider that the time was ripe, as yet, for her to step in. She preferred – perhaps under pressure of uncontrollable circumstances – to rely upon the endeavours of the man in the national field and to restrict her activities to what may be called the social side of the problem. Palestine, it will be remembered, was, and is still, a Moslem country in population, in religion and in traditions. The Moslem section forms the overwhelming majority of the population, and the traditional social order of such a majority must always be given due consideration.

The Christian Arab woman, though not under the same handicap, has kept herself within the limits beyond which her Moslem sister could not well go. They both worked hand in hand in societies of social, charitable or educational character, and their humane touch has been a relief to many a bleeding heart and broken soul.

It should be remembered that even until now Moslem women in the East, and in Palestine in particular, have no free social association with men. Western influence and education have failed to alter the social customs which have been transmitted from generation to generation. Arab women have not as yet been granted political suffrage, although they have taken a keen interest in politics. It is true that there are now many highly educated Arab women, yet no Arab Moslem woman could until now speak publicly before a mixed gathering.

These as well as many other reasons prevented the Arab women, Moslem and Christian, from taking an active part in the political movement of the Arab national bodies. But in the history of every nation there are deciding moments which leave their permanent mark in the formation of its future. By force of circumstances a nation is compelled to follow without any previous determination a course in which it had no choice.

In August, 1929, Palestine suddenly emerged into a state of disorder. The deplorable disturbances which marked the history of that year will not be easily eradicated from the memory of the present generation, not only for their destructive consequences and losses in life and property, but for the bold step which was taken by the Arab women in organizing their ranks.

The Arab women could no more keep aloof; they found themselves unable to shirk the responsibility which was thrust upon their shoulders. Hundreds of men were sent to prison, hundreds of homes unmercifully destroyed, hundreds of children became orphans, without parents to whom they could turn for care and affection. Be it as it may, the responsibility lies somewhere. Someone must be held responsible to answer before God and man for all these consequences. Someone must remove the stain that has been added to the history of the Arab people, who were described in a proclamation issued by the British High Commissioner soon after his return from leave on September 1st, 1929, as 'ruthless and bloodthirsty.' Someone will have to pay the blood money for all the innocent blood that was shed on the altar of 'Imperialism.' Someone must be held responsible, at least in the annals of history, for all such atrocities of the twentieth century.

The defence by any person of the cause of his country, though perhaps it may be unintentionally accompanied by acts of violence, is considered under many laws a criminal act, although it may appear to the perpetrator as the highest degree of duty as a citizen. It was not strange, therefore, that such distressing circumstances as those in which Palestine was found in 1929 should have resulted in the greatest change in the life of the Arab women in Palestine and in the concentration of their forces.

The First Women's Congress

These factors, amongst other things, moved the Arab woman to the front, and to seek a remedy for the situation. It was thought that to consolidate the endeavours of all forces, individual or collective, the first step would be to convene a general women's congress. It was a bold step to take in view of the traditional restrictions which, until then, prevented the Arab woman in Palestine from taking part in any movement which might expose her to the public eye. But the endeavours which were exerted by the organizing ladies, strengthened by the support of the leaders of political parties, were sufficient to overcome such difficulties.

Eventually, on October 26th, 1929, the Arab Women's Congress of Palestine was held. It was the first of its kind to be held in the Holy Land, and was attended by over 200 delegates, both Moslem and Christian, from the various cities, towns and the larger villages. Madame Kazem Pasha Husseini, wife of the late President of the Arab Executive, was elected to the chair. During the sittings of the Congress the deplorable situation was the main topic of discussion. Many speakers considered the Mandatory Power, as represented by the Palestine Administration, to be solely responsible for all that took place, and a national movement for consolidated action on the part of all women's organizations was earnestly urged. At last the heated discussions resulted in the adoption of the following resolutions, which, taken alone, will indicate the depressed atmosphere under which the Congress was held. These memorable resolutions were in the following terms [...]

At first it was considered desirable to see Lady Chancellor, as Moslem members of the delegation could not properly appear before the High Commissioner. But in answer to a request made to Government it was stated that 'Lady Chancellor will not be able to receive ladies proposing to submit resolutions of political character, but that His Excellency is prepared to receive the Executive Committee of ten members for that purpose.'

Eventually the deputation had no other alternative but to wait upon the High Commissioner at Government House, and to ignore all traditional restrictions.

The deputation explained to the High Commissioner the reasons which moved the Arab women of Palestine to hold this Congress, and handed him the following Memorandum for transmission to His Majesty's Government on behalf of the Congress:

October 26th, 1929

We, the Arab women of Palestine, having been faced with great economic and political difficulties and seeing that our cause has not so far received the sympathy and assistance of which it is worthy, have finally decided to support our men in this cause, leaving aside all other duties and tasks in which we have hitherto engaged ourselves.

This deputation of all the Arab women in Palestine has now come to lay before Your Excellency their protests and resolutions passed in their first Congress and to ask, as of right, that our demands be granted.

The following is a brief summary of the resolutions of the Congress:

i. To protest against the Balfour Declaration, which has been the sole cause of all the troubles that took place in the country, and which may arise in future. We consider that this country will never enjoy peace and tranquillity so long as this Declaration is in force.

ii. To protest against Zionist immigration in view of the political and economic situation of the country.

iii. To protest against the enforcement of the Collective Punishment Ordinance.

iv. To protest against the maltreatment by the police of Arab prisoners.

In view of the above, the Congress unanimously decided:

1 To submit the above Memorandum to Your Excellency for submission to His Majesty's Government, praying that a more reasonable and equitable policy be adopted in the country towards the Arabs.

2 To thank Lord Rothermere for his distinguished and honourable activities for our cause.

3 To support all resolutions, decisions and demands of the Arab Executive.

In conclusion the Arab Women's Congress sincerely hopes that Your Excellency will be sympathetic to our cause and will assist us in the realization of our just and legitimate demands.

Sir John Chancellor received the deputation very cordially and assured them of his good intentions.

When the deputation returned to the Congress, which was still in session, and conveyed the proceedings of its interview with the High Commissioner, it was decided that all the members of the Congress should hold a demonstration, which should proceed through all the leading streets of Jerusalem, stopping at the Consulates of the various foreign Powers, where a Memorandum embodying the resolutions would be handed to the Consul.

[Source: 'The Struggle for National Rights,' in *The Arab Woman and the Palestine Problem* (London: Herbert Joseph, 1937), 67–70, 73–5.]

The Eighth International Conference of American States
The Lima Declaration in Favor of Women's Rights (1938)

Whereas:

Women, representing more than half of the population of America, demand full rights as an act of the most elementary human justice;

Women have participated effectively, with a high sense of responsibility, in the historical development of all the countries of America;

In the economic order women are a factor of primary importance, not only as producers but also as controllers and directors of the basic economy of the home;

They have amply demonstrated their ability in every phase of culture and human activity;

Their high sense of responsibility as mothers entitles them to the enjoyment of all of their rights; and

The women of America, before demanding their rights have assumed all of their responsibilities in the social order, thus setting the greatest example of conscientious patriotism,

The Eighth International Conference of American States
Agrees:
1 To declare that women have the right:
   a. To political treatment on the basis of equality with men;
   b. To the enjoyment of equality as to civil status;
   c. To full protection in and opportunity for work;
   d. To the most ample protection as mothers.
2 To urge the governments of the American Republics, which have not already done so, to adopt as soon as possible the necessary legislation to carry out fully the principles contained in this declaration, which shall be known as 'The Lima Declaration in Favor of Women's Rights.'

[Source: *The International Conferences of American States: First Supplement, 1933–1940* (Washington: Carnegie Endowment for International Peace, 1940), 250–1.]

Resolution on the Problem of the Indigenous Woman (1938)

Considering:
That the situation of the indigenous woman is of major importance as constituting one of the fundamental factors in the complete integration of the national life of the American Republics,
The Eighth International Conference of American States
RESOLVES:
That at the Conference of Experts on Indian Life in the Americas, provided for by the Seventh International Conference of American States:
(1) Special attention be given to the problems of the indigenous woman; and

(2) That the delegations appointed to the Conference of Experts on Indian Life in the Americas include women qualified to discuss the problems which directly affect the indigenous woman.
(Approved 21 December 1938)

[Source: *The International Conferences of American States: First Supplement, 1933–1940* (Washington: Carnegie Endowment for International Peace, 1940), 241–2.]

Virginia Woolf (1882–1941) was an acclaimed British novelist and essayist. Woolf at times tackled politically sensitive topics subtly and playfully, as in her novel *Orlando*, in which the protagonist's transformations from man to woman and woman to man serve to explore the issues of gender identity and same-sex desire. Elsewhere, Woolf was more direct in her attack, as in the famous *A Room of One's Own*, which examines the difficulties women face as writers and intellectuals, or in *Three Guineas*, a book-length essay in which Woolf addressed three questions: how to prevent war, why the government did not support women's higher education, and why women were excluded from professional work. In *Three Guineas* Woolf was able to tie together feminism and pacifism at a critical time in history, publishing the book shortly before the beginning of the Second World War.

Virginia Woolf
From *Three Guineas* (1938)

[…] Thus, Sir, while we respect you as a private person and prove it by giving you a guinea to spend as you choose, we believe that we can help you most effectively by refusing to join your society; by working for our common ends – justice and equality and liberty for all men and women – outside your society, not within.

But this, you will say, if it means anything, can only mean that you, the daughters of educated men, who have promised us your positive help, refuse to join our society in order that you may make another of your own. And what sort of society do you propose to found outside ours, but in co-operation with it, so that we may both work together for our common ends? That is a question which you have every right to ask, and which we must try to answer in order to justify our refusal to sign the form you send. Let us then draw rapidly in outline the kind of society which the daughters of educated men found and join outside your society but in co-operation with its ends. In the first place, this new society, you will be relieved to learn, would have no honorary treasurer, for it would need no funds. It would have no office, no committee, no secretary; it would call no meetings; it would hold no conferences. If name it must have, it could be called the Outsiders' Society. That is not a resonant name, but it has the advantage that it squares with facts – the facts of history, of law, of biography; even, it may be, with the still hidden facts of our still unknown psychology. It would consist of educated men's daughters working in their own class – how indeed can they work in any other?[1] – and by their own methods for liberty, equality and peace. Their first duty, to which they would bind themselves not by oath, for oaths and ceremonies have no part in a society which must be anonymous and elastic before everything, would be not to fight with arms. This is easy for them to observe, for in fact, as the papers inform us, 'the Army Council have no intention of opening recruiting for any women's corps.'[2] The country ensures it. Next they would refuse in the event of war to make munitions or nurse the wounded. Since in the last war both these activities were mainly discharged by the daughters of working men, the pressure upon them here too would be slight, though probably

---

1 In the nineteenth century much valuable work was done for the working class by educated men's daughters in the only way that was open to them. But now that some of them at least have received an expansive education, it is arguable that they can work much more effectively by remaining in their own class and using the methods of that class to improve a class which stands much in need of improvement. If on the other hand the educated (as so often happens) renounce the very qualities which education should have brought – reason, tolerance, knowledge – and play at belonging to the working class and adopting its cause, they merely expose that cause to the ridicule of the educated class, and do nothing to improve their own. But the number of books written by the educated about the working class would seem to show that the glamour of the working class and the emotional relief afforded by adopting its cause, are today as irresistible to the middle class as the glamour of the aristocracy was twenty years ago (see *A la Recherche du Temps Perdu*). Meanwhile it would be interesting to know what the true-born working man or woman thinks of the playboys and playgirls of the educated class who adopt the working-class cause without sacrificing middle-class capital, or sharing working-class experience. 'The average housewife,' according to Mrs Murphy, Home Service Director of the British Commercial Gas Association, 'washed an acre of dirty dishes, a mile of glass and three miles of clothes and scrubbed five miles of floor yearly' (*Daily Telegraph*, 29 September 1937). For a more detailed account of working-class life, see *Life as We Have Known It*, by Co-operative working women, edited by Margaret Llewelyn Davies. The *Life of Joseph Wright* also gives a remarkable account of working-class life at first hand and not through pro-proletarian spectacles.

2 'It was stated yesterday at the War Office that the Army Council have no intention of opening recruiting for any women's corps' (*The Times*, 22 October 1937). This marks a prime distinction between sexes. Pacifism is enforced upon women. Men are still allowed liberty of choice.

disagreeable. On the other hand the next duty to which they would pledge themselves is one of considerable difficulty, and calls not only for courage and initiative, but for the special knowledge of the educated man's daughter. It is, briefly, not to incite their brothers to fight, or to dissuade them, but to maintain an attitude of complete indifference. But the attitude expressed by the word 'indifference' is so complex and of such importance that it needs even here further definition. Indifference in the first place must be given a firm footing upon fact. As it is a fact that she cannot understand what instinct compels him, what glory, what interest, what manly satisfaction fighting provides for him – 'without war there would be no outlet for the manly qualities which fighting develops' – as fighting thus is a sex characteristic which she cannot share, the counterpart some claim of the maternal instinct which he cannot share, so is it an instinct which she cannot judge. The outsider therefore must leave him free to deal with this instinct by himself, because liberty of opinion must be respected, especially when it is based upon an instinct which is as foreign to her as centuries of tradition and education can make it.[3] This is a fundamental and instinctive distinction upon which indifference may be based. But the outsider will make it her duty not merely to base her indifference upon instinct, but upon reason. When he says, as history proves that he has said, and may say again, 'I am fighting to protect our country' and thus seeks to rouse her patriotic emotion, she will ask herself, 'What does "our country" mean to me an outsider?' To decide this she will analyse the meaning of patriotism in her own case. She will inform herself of the position of her sex and her class in the past. She will inform herself of the amount of land, wealth and property in the

---

3 The following quotation shows, however, that if sanctioned the fighting instinct easily develops. 'The eyes deeply sunk into the sockets, the features acute, the amazon keeps herself very straight on the stirrups at the head of her squadron ... Five English parliamentaries look at this woman with the respectful and a bit restless admiration one feels for a "fauve" of an unknown species ...

– Come nearer Amalia – orders the commandant. She pushes her horse towards us and salutes her chief with the sword.

– Sergeant Amalia Bonilla – continues the chief of the squadron – how old are you? – Thirty-six. – Where were you born? – In Granada. – Why have you joined the army? – My two daughters were militia-women. The younger has been killed in the Alto de Leon. I thought I had to supersede her and to avenge her. – And how many enemies have you killed to avenge her? – You know it, commandant, five. The sixth is not sure. – No, but you have taken his horse. The amazon Amalia rides in fact a magnificent dapple-grey horse, with glossy hair, which flatters like a parade horse ... This woman who has killed five men – but who feels not sure about the sixth – was for the envoys of the House of Commons an excellent introducer to the Spanish War' (*The Martyrdom of Madrid, Inedited Witnesses*, by Louis Delaprée, pp. 34, 5, 6. Madrid, 1937).

possession of her own sex and class in the present – how much of 'England' in fact belongs to her. From the same sources she will inform herself of the legal protection which the law has given her in the past and now gives her. And if he adds that he is fighting to protect her body, she will reflect upon the degree of physical protection that she now enjoys when the words 'Air Raid Precaution' are written on blank walls. And if he says that he is fighting to protect England from foreign rule, she will reflect that for her there are no 'foreigners,' since by law she becomes a foreigner if she marries a foreigner. And she will do her best to make this a fact, not by forced fraternity, but by human sympathy. All these facts will convince her reason (to put it in a nutshell) that her sex and class has very little to thank England for in the past; not much to thank England for in the present; while the security of her person in the future is highly dubious. But probably she will have imbibed, even from the governess, some romantic notion that Englishmen, those fathers and grandfathers whom she sees marching in the pictures of history, are 'superior' to the men of other countries. This she will consider it her duty to check by comparing French historians with English; German with French; the testimony of the ruled – the Indians or the Irish, say – with the claims made by their rulers. Still some 'patriotic' emotion, some ingrained belief in the intellectual superiority of her own country over other countries may remain. Then she will compare English painting with French painting; English music with German music; English literature with Greek literature, for translations abound. When all these comparisons have been faithfully made by the use of reason, the outsider will find herself in possession of very good reasons for her indifference. She will find that she has no good reason to ask her brother to fight on her behalf to protect 'our' country. 'Our country,' she will say, 'throughout the greater part of its history has treated me as a slave; it has denied me education or any share in its possessions. "Our" country denies me the means of protecting myself, forces me to pay others a very large sum annually to protect me, and is so little able, even so, to protect me that Air Raid precautions are written on the wall. Therefore if you insist upon fighting to protect me, or "our" country, let it be understood, soberly and rationally between us, that you are fighting to gratify a sex instinct which I cannot share; to procure benefits which I have not shared and probably will not share; but not to gratify my instincts, or to protect myself or my country. For,' the outsider will say, 'in fact, as a woman, I have no country. As a woman I want no country. As a woman my country is the whole world.' And if, when reason has said its say, still some obstinate emotion remains, some love of England dropped into a child's ears by the cawing of rooks in an elm tree, by the splash of waves on a beach, or by English voices murmuring nursery rhymes, this drop of pure, if irrational, emotion she will make serve her to give to England first what she desires of peace and freedom for the whole world.

Such then will be the nature of her 'indifference' and from this indifference certain actions must follow. She will bind herself to take no share in patriotic demonstrations; to assent to no form of national self-praise; to make no part of any claque or audience that encourages war; to absent herself from military displays, tournaments, tattoos, prize-givings and all such ceremonies as encourage the desire to impose 'our' civilization or 'our' dominion upon other people. The psychology of private life, more-over, warrants the belief that this use of indifference by the daughters of educated men would help materially to prevent war. For psychology would seem to show that it is far harder for human beings to take action when other people are indifferent and allow them complete freedom of action, than when their actions are made the centre of excited emotion. The small boy struts and trumpets outside the window: implore him to stop; he goes on; say nothing; he stops. That the daughters of educated men then should give their brothers neither the white feather of cowardice nor the red feather of courage, but no feather at all; that they should shut the bright eyes that rain influence, or let those eyes look elsewhere when war is discussed – that is the duty to which outsiders will train themselves in peace before the threat of death inevitably makes reason powerless.

Such then are some of the methods by which society, the anonymous and secret Society of Outsiders would help you, Sir, to prevent war and to ensure freedom.

PART FIVE
Citizenship

In an essay that set out to define the scope of activity undertaken by the International Alliance of Women as it moved beyond its early and foundational focus on suffrage, Margery Corbett Ashby wrote: 'It is a fact which cannot be ignored that women are not only feminists in a perpetual state of protest against restrictions and disabilities, they are also to an increasing extent, keen citizens, peace workers, reformers and educators. The greatest freedom won by women is surely precisely this equal right with men to effective interest in the whole of life.'[1] The 'whole of life' is, to be sure, a notably vague and broad descriptor of the scope of feminist activity, but for that very reason it is not a bad way to approach the question of citizenship. While subsequent sections will focus on more specifically defined areas of citizenship, such as moral reform, work, and peace activism, the documents assembled in this section provide a kind of cross-section of the concerns addressed by women internationally, having to do with their status as women, their legal rights, and their relationship to the states in which they lived and did or did not hold citizenship rights.

If the denial of citizenship rights based on gender is the unifying force that bound women together in their various struggles internationally, race not infrequently combined with gender in the legally constituted exclusions practised in many states. Often race articulated with gender in ways that divided groups of women within a given state. Marilyn Lake points out that in Australia, 'The federal legislation that enfranchised white Australian women had simultaneously disqualified Aborigines (but not Maoris) from Australian citizenship: the identity of the "enfranchised women of Australia" was constituted explicitly in terms of racial difference in a nation state founded on racial imperialism.'[2] One of the paradoxes of this situation was that some Australian women would subsequently exercise their citizenship in the service of 'protecting' Aboriginal women from the state policies that jeopardized them. In the United States, most citizenship rights were denied blacks, slave or free, women and men, in the period in which Frances Ellen Harper wrote 'The Colored People in America.' Yet, Harper contends, the struggle of African Americans to improve their lot through industry and education, through church communities and black publications attests to their fitness for citizenship as well as their just claim to it. Tsianina Redfeather Blackstone, a Creek-Cherokee and a member of the Society of American Indians (SAI), addressed the effects on Native Americans of colonization, the reservation system, and other legal strictures in her address at the ICW congress in Chicago. Blackstone lays claim to 'equal opportunity' on behalf of Native Americans by pointing both to the native peoples' prior claim to the land occupied by the United States and to their service in the First World War in defence of the United States, an argument that at once implicitly questions the right of a colonial state to legislate for native peoples and attests to the willing service of Native Americans, *as citizens*, to their country.

The petition written by the Native and Coloured Women's Association of the Orange Free State addresses another instance in which a state – in this case a sub-national state within the Union of South Africa – devised a legal exclusion that yoked gender with race. In 1893 legislation was created that applied influx controls to black women for the first time; the Orange Free State was the only one within the Union of South Africa to do so. This pass law meant that women who wanted to live in urban areas were compelled to find work as domestic servants, and it also meant that they risked police harassment, including rape, as they went about their business. The petition requesting the repeal of the pass law appeals to the British government in an effort to trump the power of the Orange Free State over black women. It was signed by 5000 women.[3] Ruth Yap takes yet another approach in her comparison of the legal status of Chinese women in China and in the diaspora, principally in Hawaii and the US mainland. In China she considers the changes in women's control over property within marriage, and the introduction of equal rights between men and women in the franchise and in education with the new Code of Laws introduced by the Guomindang in 1926. On the other hand, a woman of Chinese ancestry born in the United States had all the rights of a US citizen, but forfeited those rights upon marriage to anyone who was not also a US citizen. Immigrant women faced innumerable obstacles. In this comparative study, then, Yap implicitly addresses another central concern of first wave feminists: the rights of married women.

As Yap's account of what happened to the Chinese-American woman who married a non-US citizen suggests, one of the key citizenship issues for women was their loss of citizenship upon marriage to a foreigner. This was a question first taken up by the ICW in 1905, but it took on a broader urgency in the wake of the First World War.[4] The International Alliance circulated a questionnaire concerning the laws governing the relationship between marriage and citizenship in countries around the world. Marie Stritt outlines some of the results of that questionnaire while advocating that women be able to decide their nationality independently of their husbands. Vera Brittain addresses another issue for married women, their right to retain their own name in marriage. As she points out, for British women at least, this option was not *legally* denied women so much as it was *conventionally* denied women, so that officials of all sorts had to be persuaded that visas and passports and other official documents could be made out in the married woman's own name. The Six Point Group election manifesto of 1922 addresses a broad range of issues that concerned women, including the rights of widows and single mothers. The six points of the manifesto correspond to 'six points' the group resolved to pursue when it was founded in 1921. The rights of married women were central to its agenda. Together with the Open Door International, for instance, the Six Point Group campaigned for the right of married women to work. Efwa Kato adopts a seemingly more conservative position in urging Ghanaian women to serve their country by being good wives and mothers who foster a spirit of national pride and self-sacrifice in their children and husbands, but she also urges them to champion social justice in the face of imperialism and racial prejudice. She claims for those women who are not wives and mothers the right to pursue professional careers, including careers in science and politics.

Attia Habibullah explores the tensions between a conservative social and religious tradition and modern political rights in India, arguing that *purdah* gets in the way of women exercizing the rights of citizenship that they have under the law. For her, the notion of citizenship does not admit of the kind of differentiation between the sexes *purdah* entails. For Mary Austin, by contrast, citizenship clearly does entail different roles for men and women, but she argues that women have not, except during the First World War, been allowed to contribute to society to the full potential of their sex because men have, as she puts it, 'invented the State in the key of maleness.' For Kamaladevi Chattopadhyaya, the vast majority of women in India had more to gain by seeking the economic independence and equality that socialism promised than by pursuing bourgeois goals like the right to vote or the right to own property. Taking the Soviet Union as her model, Chattopadhyaya recommends communal kitchens, child care, clinics, and free schools as means of achieving equality for women within a socialist state.

Speaking at the Arab Feminist Conference in Cairo in 1944, Huda Shaarawi authorizes her claims for equal citizenship for Arab women by an appeal to Islam, which, she argues, recognizes the equality of women and men – unlike the men who have deprived Muslim women of their rights. In her closing speech at the conference, she appeals to men to recognize that Arab nations will benefit from the equal contributions of both sexes.

NOTES

1 M.I. Corbett Ashby, 'What Is the Alliance?' *Jus Suffragii* 22, no. 5 (1928): 69.
2 Marilyn Lake, 'Between Old Worlds and New: Feminist Citizenship, Nation and Race, the Destabilization of Identity,' in *Suffrage and Beyond: International Feminist Perspectives*, ed. Caroline Davey and Melanie Nolan (New York: New York UP, 1994), 281.
3 Rirhandzu Mageza, 'Petition of the Native and Coloured Women of the Province of the Orange Free State,' in *Women Writing Africa: The Southern Region*, ed. M.J. Daymond et al. (New York: Feminist Press, 2003), 159.
4 See Leila Rupp, *Worlds of Women: The Making of an International Women's Movement* (Princeton: Princeton UP, 1997), 146–50.

Frances Ellen Watkins Harper (1825–1911) was born to free parents in Baltimore, educated at a school run by her uncle, and allowed to pursue her literary ambitions when she went to work at the age of fourteen as a maid in a
Quaker household and was given access to their library. At the age of twenty
a collection of her poems was published and became very popular, running
through twenty editions over the next several years. After the 1850 Fugitive
Slave Act, which made life difficult even for free-born blacks, Harper moved
north, becoming active in helping escaped slaves on the Underground Railroad. She was a member of both the American Woman Suffrage Association
and the American Anti-Slavery Society, and continued to publish very well-
received poetry and fiction that addressed slavery, racism, and women's issues.

Frances Ellen W. Harper
The Colored People in America (1857)

Having been placed by a dominant race in circumstances over which we have
had no control, we have been the butt of ridicule and the mark of oppression.
Identified with a people over whom weary ages of degradation have passed,
whatever concerns them, as a race, concerns me. I have noticed among our
people a disposition to censure and upbraid each other, a disposition which has
its foundation rather, perhaps, in a want of common sympathy and consideration, than mutual hatred, or other unholy passions. Born to an inheritance of
misery, nurtured in degradation, and cradled in oppression, with the scorn of
the white man upon their souls, his fetters upon their limbs, his scourge upon
their flesh, what can be expected from their offspring, but a mournful reaction of that cursed system which spreads its baneful influence over body and
soul; which dwarfs the intellect, stunts its development, debases the spirit, and
degrades the soul? Place any nation in the same condition which has been our
hapless lot, fetter their limbs and degrade their souls, debase their sons and
corrupt their daughters, and when the restless yearnings for liberty shall burn
through heart and brain – when, tortured by wrong and goaded by oppression, the hearts that would madden with misery, or break in despair, resolve
to break their thrall, and escape from bondage, then let the bay of the bloodhound and the scent of the human tiger be upon their track; – let them feel
that, from the ceaseless murmur of the Atlantic to the sullen roar of the Pacific,
from the thunders of the rainbow-crowned Niagara to the swollen waters of
the Mexican gulf, they have no shelter for their bleeding feet, or resting-place
for their defenceless heads; let them, when nominally free, feel that they have
only exchanged the iron yoke of oppression for the galling fetters of a vitiated

public opinion; – let prejudice assign them the lowest places and the humblest positions, and make them 'hewers of wood and drawers of water'; – let their income be so small that they must from necessity bequeath to their children an inheritance of poverty and a limited education, – and tell me, reviler of our race! censurer of our people! if there is a nation in whose veins runs the purest Caucasian blood, upon whom the same causes would not produce the same effects; whose social condition, intellectual and moral character, would present a more favorable aspect than ours? But there is hope; yes, blessed be God! for our down-trodden and despised race. Public and private schools accommodate our children; and in my own southern home, I see women, whose lot is unremitted labor, saving a pittance from their scanty wages to defray the expense of learning to read. We have papers edited by colored editors, which we may consider it an honor to possess, and a credit to sustain. We have a church that is extending itself from east to west, from north to south, through poverty and reproach, persecution and pain. We have our faults, our want of union and concentration of purpose; but are there not extenuating circumstances around our darkest faults – palliating excuses for our most egregious errors? and shall we not hope, that the mental and moral aspect which we present is but the first step of a mighty advancement, the faintest coruscations of the day that will dawn with unclouded splendor upon our downtrodden and benighted race, and that ere long we may present to the admiring gaze of those who wish us well, a people to whom knowledge has given power, and righteousness exaltation?

[Source: *American Feminism: Key Source Documents 1848–1920*, ed. Janet Beer, Anne-Marie Ford, and Katherine Joslin (New York: Routledge, 2002), 77–8.]

Native and Coloured Women of the Province of the Orange Free State

Petition of the Native and Coloured Women of the Province of the Orange Free State (1912)

11th March 1912

To the Right Honourable General Louis Botha, P.C., M.L.A., Prime Minister of the Union of South Africa, CAPE TOWN.

Sir,
The petition of the undersigned humbly showeth: –

1. That your petitioners are residents of the various towns and villages in the Province of the Orange Free State, and are subjects of His Gracious Majesty King George V.
2. That your petitioners, as inhabitants of the said Province, are under a burden of having to carry Residential Passes in terms of Section 2 of Law 8 of 1893 (Orange Free State Statutes).
3. That this law is a source of grievance to your petitioners in that: –
    (a) It renders them liable to interference by any policeman at any time, and in that way deprives them of that liberty enjoyed by their women-folk in other Provinces.
    (b) It does not afford them that protection which may, peradventure, have been contemplated by the legislators, but on the other hand it subjects them to taxation, notwithstanding the sex to which they belong – a policy which was unknown in the late South African Republic, and is unknown in the history of British Rule.
    (c) It has a barbarous tendency of ignoring the consequences of marriage in respect of natives, especially the right of parents to control their children, a right which parents ought to exercise without interference from outside; and the effect of its operation upon the minds of our children is that it inculcates upon them the idea that as soon as they become liable to comply with the requirements of this law, their age of majority also commences, and can, therefore, act independently of their parents.
    (d) It is an effective means of enforcing labour, and as such, cannot have any justification whatever on the ground of necessity or expediency.
    (e) It lowers the dignity of women and throws to pieces every element of respect to which they are entitled; and for this reason it has no claim to recognition as a just, progressive and protective law, necessary for their elevation in the scale of civilisation; moreover it does not improve their social status.
    (f) It can only have one ground for its existence in that Statute Book – namely, that it is a most effective weapon the governing powers could resort to to make the natives and coloured women in the Province of the Orange Free State ever feel their inferiority, which is only another way of perpetuating oppression regardless of the feelings of those who are governed; whereas the essence of justice is 'Do unto others as you would be done by.'
4. That your petitioners are the only women in the whole of the Union who are subjected to such an oppressive law; the women in the other provinces are not subjected to any Pass Laws.
5. That representations were made to the Imperial Government about this matter by the Congress of the Orange Free State Native Association, and the Imperial Government replied that the matter was a local one in which they

could not interfere, but expressed a hope that the local authorities would find their way to grant your petitioners relief, and further that your petitioners would be better off under the Union Government of South Africa.

6. That further representations were made to the late Government of the Orange River Colony, the Conference of the Municipal Associations of the Orange River Colony, and to the Town Council of Bloemfontein, and all these bodies have referred the said Congress of the Orange Free State Native Association to the Union Parliament.

Wherefore your petitioners humbly pray that the Right Honourable the Prime Minister may be pleased: –

1. To grant them immediate relief from this burdensome law by introducing a Bill in Parliament repealing it.

or 2. If it be not within the province of the Right Honourable the Prime Minister to do so, then, the Minister responsible be charged with the introduction of this Bill by the Right Honourable the Prime Minister.

or 3. To grant your petitioners immediate relief from the operation of this law by suspending it, in so far as they are concerned, pending the introduction of this Bill into Parliament by the Minister responsible.

And your petitioners as in duty bound will ever pray.

[Source: *Women Writing Africa: The Southern Region*, ed. M.J. Daymond et al. (New York: Feminist Press at the City University of New York, 2003), 159–61.]

Marie Stritt (1855–1928) was the chairwoman of the Bund Deutscher Frauenvereine (Union of German Women's Associations) from 1899 to 1910 and one of the first German pacifists. She also founded the first legal protection union for German women in 1894, and was active internationally with the International Woman Suffrage Association. From 1900 to 1913, Stritt published the newsletter for the Union of German Women's Associations, the *Centralblatt des Bundes Deutscher Frauenvereine*.

Marie Stritt
The Nationality of Married Women (1917)

In all civilized countries there have been severe struggles to gain recognition by the civil law of the married woman's independence, and, in spite of undeniable progress, this right is nowhere fully acknowledged. The German Civil Code of 1900 abolished previous restrictions on women as a sex, but has still not done justice to the married woman. Looked upon by the legislator as a minor in relation to her husband, she is bound legally to submit to him in regard to her person, her property, and her children. Some protection, albeit inadequate, is afforded her against the possible misuse of marital authority, especially with regard to property, and a certain recognition is given of the personality of the married woman. In another sphere, that of nationality, no protection is afforded, and the standpoint adopted is the naively brutal one of the extinction of woman's individuality in marriage. Nowhere does the principle that a married woman is the property of her husband appear more clearly than in the law obtaining in almost all countries that a woman who marries a foreigner loses her nationality from that moment, even if she retains her domicile in her native land. The States in which that is not the case, or only to a limited extent, are Spain, Venezuela, New Zealand, and Australia. The two former possibly because women were altogether forgotten, as they so often are; the two latter because women had a voice in legislation.

That even the organized women's movement has paid so little attention to the subject is explicable by the fact that in normal times the women adversely affected are comparatively few. Nevertheless, the International Council of Women took up the question at the Berlin meeting in 1904, and urged the affiliated national societies to work for legislation to meet the case.

A questionnaire carried out by the President of the International Committee on Legislation, Baroness Olga von Beschwitz, was to serve as basis for a unified action in an international matter of the first importance. The result, which was published in the annual report for 1905–6 of the International Council of Women, does not include all the affiliated countries, but gives in brief form a picture of the circumstances in the various countries, which, with slight exception, is true to-day. To the question, *Does a foreigner gain the nationality of a given country by marrying one of its nationals?* 13 out of 14 countries answered simply 'Yes,' while the Australian Society replied: 'She can, but she is not bound to adopt her husband's nationality.' Similarly, the answer to the question, *Does a woman who marries a foreigner lose her nationality?* Was in the affirmative from all the countries except Australia, which replied: 'No, a British (i.e., Australian) born woman retains all her national rights quite independent of her husband's nationality.' France showed the possibility of exceptions. A Frenchwoman marrying a foreigner retains her French nationality if her husband has renounced his nationality.

The answers to the question *Under what conditions* (separation or husband's death) *can a married woman reacquire her former nationality?* showed a certain variety of conditions. Two usually progressive countries, the United States and Denmark, reported that no change of nationality was permissible for a married woman even after her marriage had come to an end, and Sweden reported that a woman can resume her own nationality after divorce, but not on widowhood. Other States provide for the reassumption of her original nationality by the divorced wife or widow; but, whereas Germany, Great Britain, and Canada permit it at the request of the widow, and on observance of certain formalities, the Netherlands and Switzerland make it a condition that the demand should be made within a year of divorce or within 10 years of the husband's death. In France, Austria, Hungary, and Norway, a widow or divorced woman can only reacquire her original nationality if she binds herself to reside permanently in her own country. Australia replied: 'Every woman is free to reacquire her former nationality when she desires.'

The question *Can a woman during her husband's lifetime claim another nationality?* was answered with a plain negative by the United States, Canada, Germany, Great Britain, the Netherlands, Switzerland, Italy, France, Norway, Austria, and Hungary. In Sweden and Denmark the wife can, under certain conditions, if she and her husband are both foreigners, be naturalized independently.

The answer from Australia on this question of principle was again 'Yes, on her own demand,' and the Secretary, Miss Rose Scott, added: 'I was accidentally in Melbourne when the naturalization law was being debated in the Commonwealth Parliament. I went to the Parliament with Miss Vida Goldstein, and we interviewed as many members as we could and protested against a woman's nationality being dependent on her husband's, and we found support everywhere. The law is better than that of any other State, and in this respect we may say we are really a free people. The fact that *every adult* man or woman has a vote in the Commonwealth as well as in the separate States gives a natural weight to our demands – we are a power to be reckoned with.'

Since this inquiry various changes have taken place in the different countries, but on the old lines, and show no progress, but rather the contrary, where women are concerned. This is, e.g., the case in England, where Parliament passed a new nationality law which applied the law of the United Kingdom of 1870 to the British Dominions, some of which had previously better laws. The representatives of the women's movement only heard of the threatened danger at the last moment, but they succeeded by dint of energetic protest in gaining valuable concessions; besides a facilitation of the reacquisition of British nationality by divorced women and widows, the most important in principle, because recognizing a different nationality for the husband, was the permission to a married woman to retain her own nationality if her husband changes his after marriage. British women also hope that, although Canada and Newfoundland have adopted this law without alteration, the women voters of Australia and New Zealand will oppose its adoption unless amended to suit them.

In the United States a retrograde tendency is still more evident. In the first nationality law of 1855 the principle (which holds good in New Zealand) was preserved that a foreign woman who marries an American becomes an American citizen, but that an American woman marrying a foreigner did not lose her American rights, even any political rights she might have, according to the Supreme Court. But by degrees another conception has entered legislation. At first a woman married to a foreigner was considered to have voluntarily forfeited her American rights if she took up residence abroad. Then in 1907 Congress passed a law that every American woman marrying a foreigner is to be counted a foreigner. It is curious that the Anglo-Saxon countries, otherwise the most progressive where the women's movement is concerned, show themselves reactionary in this particular question, and it would not be uninteresting to investigate the psychological explanation.

Conditions in Germany are no better. In 1912–13 the Reichstag considered a new nationality law, and the German National Council of Women and some other women's societies made certain demands – e.g., that the wife should share her husband's nationality, but should also retain her own, or that she herself should be free to decide whether she should retain her own or adopt that of her husband. The German Woman Suffrage Society supported the latter alternative, and added (as in certain circumstances the mother might be in a painful dilemma) that the minor children should share their mother's German nationality if they are living with the mother who is separated from the father. The German women's movement even then was fully aware of the extraordinary importance and bearing of the law, and studied carefully and thoroughly the difficult material and the problems arising out of it, as is shown by the argument in the petitions (mostly drawn up by Frau Camilla Jellinek).

But in spite of the irrefutable logic and unquestionable justice of the women's demands, they met with not the slightest consideration, and were not even mentioned in the discussions in the Reichstag. The Committee which threw the petitions in the waste-paper basket did so on the pretext of the 'unity of the family,' for which, always and everywhere, the wife and mother has to pay the reckoning.

As Frau Jellinek truly said:

> Women's demands may in themselves have not been entirely unacceptable to some of the gentlemen. In particular, the consequences of the unavoidable loss of nationality for a German woman on marriage with a foreigner may have appeared utterly unjust. And if in spite of that they could not make up their minds to abolish that ordinance, the reason was – although perhaps unconsciously in some cases – the feeling that no breach must be made in the sacred edifice of man's supremacy in marriage. And this

was what was involved – not 'the unity of the family.' Where this is threatened even the national question sinks into insignificance besides the international question of men's rights. It is more important that the foreign man should have the satisfaction that his German wife must give up her nationality for him, even when living in her own country, and can thus be banished from her own country, than that a German woman should not be deprived of her nationality against her will, which public opinion would otherwise insist upon. The pretexts of 'unity of the family' and 'sacredness of marriage' were used against giving a married woman control of her own property, and that the children she bore were only subject to her husband's control.

The war should open men's eyes to the suffering inflicted on women by the present laws of nationality. After the experiences of these terrible years their eyes should be opened to the cruel contradiction of appealing to women's patriotism as women's most sacred duty and banishing women abroad who are bound to their home by birth and the deepest ties.

[Source: *Jus Suffragii: International Women Suffrage News* 12, no.1 (1917): 2–3.]

The Six Point Group was founded in 1921 by Lady Rhondda (Margaret Haig Mackworth) with six objectives: (1) Legislation on child assault; (2) Legislation for the widowed mother; (3) Legislation for the unmarried mother and her child; (4) Equal rights of guardianship for married parents; (5) Equal pay for teachers; and (6) Equal opportunities for men and women in the civil service. The Six Point Group rejected protectionist labour laws for women, campaigned on strictly equality-based principles, and supported efforts to have the League of Nations pass an Equal Rights Treaty. From 1933, along with the Open Door Council, it campaigned for the right of married women to work.

Six Point Group

General Election Manifesto

The Six Point Group stands for:
(1) Satisfactory legislation on Child Assault.
(2) Satisfactory legislation for the Widowed Mother.
(3) Satisfactory legislation for the Unmarried Mother and her Child.
(4) Equal rights of Guardianship for Married Parents.
(5) Equal Pay for Teachers.
(6) Equal opportunities for Men and Women in the Civil Service.

As a necessary preliminary to gaining these Six Points, it demands the immediate rectification of the Sex Disqualification (Removal) Act, by the complete failure of which the position of all Six Points has been either directly or indirectly affected.

In the forthcoming General Election, the Six Point Group will not support any Political Party as such. It will aim only at returning to Westminster a Parliament which will carry out its Programme.

In pursuance of this Policy the Six Point Group, while questioning candidates as to their views upon its programme, will, in the case of those members of the last Parliament who are standing for re-election, place reliance rather upon their past record as shown by their speeches and votes in the Parliament of 1918–1922 than upon their statements in regard to their future intentions.

It will give its active support to those candidates only whose past record – whether in or out of Parliament – proves that their pledges of support are likely to be valuable.

It will actively oppose the return of those candidates whose record as members of the last House of Commons shows them to be opposed to its Programme. In this connection it will pay especial attention to the record of men of ministerial rank to whichever Party they may now belong.

Issued by the Six Point Group at 92 Victoria Street, London, S.W. 1

[Source: *Time and Tide*, 27 October 1922, 1042.]

Mary Austin (1868–1934) was a novelist, poet, critic, and playwright, as well as an early feminist and defender of Native American and Spanish-American rights. She moved to New York City's Greenwich Village in 1893, and lived for a time in London, but she eventually settled in New Mexico to write about her favourite landscape. Austin supported herself by writing sketches and stories for *The Overland Monthly*, *The Atlantic Monthly*, *Harper's Magazine*, and *Century Magazine*.

Mary Austin
Sex Emancipation through War (1918)

The Day the Most American writer came home from the front, I asked him what he thought it would all come to.

'Well,' he hesitated, 'I don't know that I can tell you until I have been home and talked it over with my wife.'

'If you have to do that,' I insisted, 'talk it over with your wife, I mean, then I know what you think.'

'I guess you do,' he soberly agreed, and when we had talked it over between us, that proved to be the case.

What this war will come to is the thing the world has needed more than anything else, more than Religion, though it will help to bring religion back; more than Democracy, though it is in its way a democratic phase; more than Civilization, though there can be no civilization without it. It will come to sex emancipation. It is so certain to come to this that it is probably perfectly safe to say that the war will not end until we are emancipated from sex, and anything we can accomplish toward that emancipation will have its share in bringing the war to an end.

Notice I say WE. We are in the habit of thinking that it is women only who are in need of sex emancipation. As a matter of fact, it is only women who are clever enough to know that they need it. Men are so wrapped and swaddled and tied into their sex that most of them don't know yet that this is not the natural order of things. They think that the political world is a male place into which women have broken by a not wholly fortunate accident, within which they can only stay by becoming in some fantastic way *un*womanly, *un*sexed. They – the men – are so gorged and saturated with sex, as sex may be expressed in social conditions, that they think of this war as cataclysmic, made in Germany or in Hell, or anywhere except where it actually is, in the very center of male con- sciousness, and made there only by virtue of our not being able to see it as an exhibition of masculinity run amuck.

Get it out of your mind for a moment that sex is a function. Sex is the organ- izing centre of personality. It is probably the chief difference between a man and a ghost. It is the whole round of the personal complex, with the machinery for perpetuation attached. For man it involves self-expression, combativeness, paternity, protectiveness; for woman, self-immolation, maternity, fostering.

Not to have all of these in some degree is to be undersexed; to have any one of them in excess is to be in need of sex emancipation. Judge for yourself what nations of the earth are at this moment most in need of it.

The world is really a very feminine place, a mother's place, conceptive, brooding, nourishing; a place of infinite patience and infinite elusiveness. It needs to be lived in more or less femininely, and the chief reason why we have never succeeded in being quite at home in it is that our method has been almost exclusively masculine. We have assaulted the earth, ripped out the treasure of its mines, cut down its forests, deflowered its fields and left them sterile for a thousand years. We have lived precisely on the same terms with our fellows, combatively, competitively, geocentrically. Nations have not struggled to make the world a better place, but only to make a more advantageous place in it for themselves. Man invented the State in the key of maleness, with combat for its major occupation, profit the spur and power the prize. This is the pattern of our politics, our economic and our international life, a pattern built not on common *human* traits of human kind, but on dominant sex traits of the male half of society. It is even marked, in certain quarters of the earth, with intrinsic male weaknesses, the strut, the flourish, the chip-on-its-shoulder, the greed of exclusive possessions, the mastery of the seas, the control of world finance.

Three Pet Sex Superstitions

There is no particular reason why the world should be lived in this fashion; no reason in intelligence, I mean, no logical compulsion. Other and more comfortable patterns have often been devised, but the things that tie us to the present are the things that clearly prove the first proposition; – that this war is war for sex emancipation. For we are tied to this androcentric pattern by three pet sex superstitions:

First, the superstition that the work a human being may do in the world is determined by sex.

Second, that the social value of a woman is established by what some man thinks of her.

Finally, that the man alone must 'support' the family.

A superstition is a belief persisted in after it has lost all foundation in experience. Even before the war we were beginning to suspect the footlessness of the old idea that Divine Providence had marked out women from the beginning for not more than two or three occupations. The war has come in time to save us endless agonies of doubt and discussion as to whether women have strength enough, or brains enough, for the four hundred and fifty-seven callings which war has added to those already open to women.

We have had so many other tremendous things to think of that many of us have missed the significance of this wholesale, bloodless overthrow of a five-thousand-year-old superstition. When you think what it cost to rid a small portion of the world of the superstition of idol worship, or of hearsay, what tortures and burnings and riving of families, this sudden reversal of ideas about work and women is one of the wonders of civilization.

The basic prejudice against women in the world's work has not been so much against their working as against the conditions of credit and wages. Wherever they could work in the obscurity of their own homes or social unimportance, dull and heavy labors requiring little more than brute strength for their accomplishment actually are performed by women in Europe, and to some extent in

America. Cooking for sixteen hay hands in a Mississippi Valley in August is not any more a ladylike occupation than harvesting the hay in Belgium.

Camouflage about Woman's Intellectual Achievement

And there has always been a great deal of camouflage about woman's intellectual achievement. When I was last in England I became very well acquainted with a woman whose business it was to furnish speeches for M.P.'s. She collected statistics and historical instances, suggested illustrative anecdotes, figures and apt comparisons. But she used to turn them over typewritten in such a way that, with a good conscience, the M.P. could call them 'notes,' in deference to the British superstition of male superiority, without which she could never have kept her job. I was also told in France that M. Curie's was not the only laboratory in which the scientific research was done by women, though it was the only one in which the woman scientist had acknowledgment. Things of this kind must have been true to a much greater extent than is generally imagined. Otherwise it would not have been possible for France and England to keep up their advance step on substitute labor, of a kind that was believed, and had believed itself, intrinsically impossible.

The truth is that we have never had any idea how sex-ridden industry is. The first great emancipator was the man who invented the press-the-button method. With the introduction of electrical and other labor-saving devices, human brawn as an element of factory production has been made to take a place second to woman's native faculty for concentrating her attention in seven different directions at once.

The most significant thing that F. R. Still found to report of British labor since the war, was that 'in no place was there the lugging, tugging, lifting, pushing, pounding or mauling' which he had formerly seen. For a great majority of operations required in munition factories, physical strength, though indispensable so long as the factories were run by men for men, had been superceded by cranes, levers, trolleys and the like contrivances for utilizing woman's nimbleness and rapidity. The same sort of statement is made by a Chicago manager with five hundred women employees. He says: 'Female labor, properly conditioned, is a benefit to the entire shop,' and goes on to explain that the necessity of fitting the work to the more delicate female mechanism has led to many improvements in processes and routing and turnovers. In other words, under modern conditions it turns out that the superstition of man's superior strength has clogged the wheels of industry. Men have put more physical force into industry than was necessary, simply because they had it to spend. Labor has used itself up in the interest of a sex distinction for which there is very little call or occasion.

Doubtless, the moment the end of the war is in sight there will be all sorts of hospitals set up for the rehabilitation of disabled social prejudices, but it is impossible to think that there will ever be a return to the 'lugging and tugging.'

Industry Keyed to Man's Rhythm

One of the most interesting examples of the emancipation of industry from the waste of sex prejudice comes from Ohio, where it was discovered that woman's instinctive fear of machinery could be turned to account. In an emergency women were put to the management of overhead cranes, these vast and clanking mechanisms which turn the beholder dizzy with their impersonal implacability. Very shortly it was found that the number of accidents was lessened, fewer risks were taken. Just how many lives annually are sacrificed to the male fetish of risk-taking it would be difficult to say. It is quite enough for our purpose to know that the woman operator is sufficiently afraid of the mechanism she handles not to be afraid to stop the machinery when there is a question of risk.

Most interesting of all the revelations made by studies in industrial efficiency of women is the one which relates to the periodic interruption of woman's energy. This has always been a stumbling block for the most enthusiastic advocate of women in industry.

Nobody is so stupid nowadays as not to know that the nation will eventually be the loser in any attempt to disregard and override the potential motherhood of its women. But all our efforts to deal with this factor have been very stupidly based on the notion that man is the norm, and any variation which woman exhibits is a disability. Even in factories where efficiency in production is attained by alternate periods of rest and activity, the whole business has been keyed to man's rhythm. Nobody knows just who first discovered that woman's rhythm was not less effectual, but simply different. I first saw it exemplified in a factory where women were testing steel balls for ball-bearing.

The test was the sense of touch, of the *back* of the hand, if you please, as being more sensitive than the inner surface.

The efficient manager had discovered that better results were attained if the alternation of touch and rest, touch and rest, went to a kind of tune; one two *rest*, one, two, three, *rest*.

That is the germ of the discovery that the chief reason why women fag earlier than men in many kinds of factory work, is that all our factories are speeded and set for men, who seem to get along perfectly on a steady, work, *rest*, work, *rest*, alternation. Change the rhythm of the work to one better suited to the age and sex of the operative, and the output will rise directly.

Man More Timid at the Untried than Woman

Similar discoveries are being made as to the intellectual fitness of women for work that has always been supposed to belong to men. There are probably ineradicable differences between the aptitudes of men and women, but the war has done much to demonstrate that they are not the traditional distinctions of superior and inferior. There is no difference in the *kind* of aptitude required for handling a telephone switchboard, which is universally conceded to women, and train dispatching, or the work of the 'tower women,' which railroads are finding it possible to employ.

The difference is one of *quality*, of being able to produce a steady quality of attention for given periods. In other words, it is not so much brains as nervous stability that is required.

Women themselves have always known that 'nervousness' in women is not a sex trait. As much of it as is not deliberately produced 'for the trade,' – since men thinking about women have liked to think of them as timorous – has been the result of woman's forced living in a world which she is permitted to know very little about. Man himself was 'nervous' when the world was comparatively an unknown place, likely to see ghosts, hear voices or be frightened into fits by the unexplainable. He is to this day more timid of the untried than woman. That nervous instability in women is part of our camouflage of sex, is shown by the report of the British Health Department, which demonstrates that with all their sorrow and strain, and in spite of their unaccustomed labors – perhaps because of them – the health of the English women has improved during the war. That means that their capacity for work involving nervous tension and responsibility has increased with the demand upon it.

But the nature of many employments thrust into women's hands by the war, has revealed still more the waste of our sex obsession. We move now in the neighborhood of subtle forces, X-rays, Hertzian waves, radioactivity, chemical reaction, – a region in which woman's finer sensibility becomes something more than a substitute instrument. For many such delicate adjustments women are indispensable. It begins to appear that by the exclusive use of maleness we have been trying to dissect our way to the secret of the universe with a spade instead of a scalpel. And right here we are afoul of the oldest, least reasonable of our sex superstitions.

There is no history of the development of the idea that a woman has no value to society except that which man gives her, as the object of his desire and the mother of his children. Like Topsy, it simply 'growed' out of man's nature. Men sacrifice themselves to womanhood, its racial function; they sacrifice themselves and the world to their love for a particular woman. But whoever heard of a man putting himself aside because the world needed some woman's gift for architecture, or biology, or sociology, more than it needed *his* contribution. Men have never hesitated to take a woman out of society and insist that every gift, every possible contribution of hers to general human welfare shall be excised, aborted, done with. That is probably why we have to have wars occasionally, and a desperate need of those woman gifts to teach us the crime of such social waste.

The Effect of the Uniform on Girls

The obsession of the personal in men's customary ways of thinking about women shows in ways little suspected by the men themselves. A Chicago manager of five hundred young women says that he has found uniforming the girls has proved a help in 'securing their modesty,' and the increased respect of the men workers 'not in a moral way,' he explains, 'but in the mental attitude.' What he means is that the uniform enables the men to think of girls not as 'the girls,' but as workers. A member of the National Council of Defense expressed something of the same thing to me recently. We were talking of women's part in the war, which I thought inadequate.

'But,' said he, puzzled, 'what work *can* women do in the war?'

'Well, there are eight million or so in the industries – ' I reminded him.

'Oh! you mean labor!'

What *he* meant was that those eight or ten million women had, for him, escaped the category of sex. They had been emancipated into labor. When he thought of them as women they were unimportant to the war, but as labor they were indispensable. I should say that three years of this war have set that type of sex emancipation at least a hundred years forward.

At one of these informal conferences of women which nobody ever hears about, but have much to do with determining our place among the nations, we were told of the efforts being made to overcome the industrial prejudice against mature age in women workers.

Women's Period of Industrial Efficiency

It seems that women wage workers go into the discard at thirty-five, ten years younger than men workers, twenty or thirty years younger than professional women. The speaker told how the women begin to break at thirty, after years of speeding up and inadequate feeding and, with the fear of dismissal hanging over them, succumb in a few years. She told what was being done to restore the working capacity of those women, their confidence in themselves and hope for the future. 'But that,' she said, 'is only half the story.'

'And the other half,' we insisted.

Well, the other half proved to be the half-conscious sex prejudice of managers and foremen; the desire to surround themselves with the freshness of youth and youth's flattering docility, unwillingness to pay to older women the deference of experience, undue valuation of the quality of 'pep,' vague resentment toward wage earning married women, and the dullness of perception exhibited by men generally toward women who make no sex appeal. And naturally the employment of girls leads to the work all being routed and speeded to young rhythm, to the consequent disadvantage of the mature worker.

Some of the freedom gained by this war will have to be surrendered at the end of it, but I think in calculating the returns of peace we underestimate two of the psychological factors. We underestimate the dramatizing effect of war work and the power of the drama to raise the plain of performance. The failure of chivalry between the sexes has been one of the terrors waved by the anti-feminists over every advance of sex emancipation, the fear that women doing work formerly done by men can not claim the feminine exemption. This has always been rather a stupid fear, because it assumes that the attention of chivalry is paid to an attitude, a posture of femininity rather than to a fact. But even where this is the case, the glamour of war adds a touch of heroism to the woman taking a man's place which seems to penetrate even the dullest maleness.

Deference to Girls in Industry

Nothing less favorable to fitness could be thought of than the subway rush-hour crowd. If such a crowd chose to demand of a young woman guard the physical capacity of a man, the young woman would be down and out in the first round.

But a finer democracy waking in the American spirit makes no such demand upon her; chivalry forbears to require her to fight with a weapon which she has not. To see a home-coming crowd defer to a girl conductor because they know that she can't do anything to them is the nicest thing that has happened in America since the war. It would be, if any Prussian could see and understand it, the best guarantee that America knows exactly what she means when she talks about keeping the world safe for Democracy. It means that Americans do not take advantage just because they think they are strong enough to get away with it.

The other force which we underestimate is the effect of the war on men, who through its adventures are released to fundamental male activities.

There seem to be at least three things that men universally and in the nature of things do better than women: exploration of the physical world, invention and poetry. Man is the perpetual adventurer, who by a long process of stupidity has been made over into a kind of social hermaphrodite, a male-mother, whose sole duty and occupation it is to trot back and forth between his job and his offspring with the expected morsel.

Vast numbers of men have been unsexed in this fashion to such a degree that only a war will pry them loose from it. They dare not adventure, do not know how to invent, and are ashamed to sing. If they have moments of rebellion against their fate they cloak it with the duty of 'supporting the family' and salve the hurt with the vanity of being the Distributor of Benefits.

Being in this unsexed and inferior state, they require continually to be kept up to their work by large doses of flattery, 'inspired,' they call it. But no man who is leading a full masculine life needs to be chucked up for it.

Now, there never was any reason in nature or logic why the man should be the sole support of his wife and children; it is just one of those things which has grown up out of the strange human impulse to associate habit with propriety. The natural duty of the individual is to contribute all that is in him to society, and to see that society gives back enough to provide for his offspring. It is utterly unimportant how or through which parent the provision comes. A lot of men are only going to learn this through the adventure of war releasing the mainspring of masculinity. Thousands of desk men and counter men are going to be raised by this war to something like their original male aptitude and capacity. And that is one of the things which is going to make it possible for many of them to accept the idea of their wives in their old jobs. The men aren't going to need a lot of those jobs back; never again. They are going to want something more their size, something more male than ribbon selling or bookkeeping.

You hear the awakened adventurousness of men discussed as one of the hazards of war. It is one of war's advantages. The periods of invention and enterprise which follow on war are due to the new alignment of sex normalities, more women released to conserving, nourishing labors; more men freed to break new ground.

Sex Mastery, Not Mystery, Needed

Of course these gains in the emancipation of industry from sex will have to be consolidated with mastery over some other phases of the relation of men and women. The stability of woman's hold on the work of the world depends on her control of the liability to child-bearing. Maternity must be voluntary; it must not lie forever a hideous uncertainty, to leap out upon her from her most sacred moments. Love must no more threaten with disease and disaster. There must be no more mystery about sex if there is to be mastery.

Toward this the war has helped prodigiously by lifting the taboo on sex intelligence. For the first time Europe has faced the cost in man-power of the Social Evil, it has faced the iniquity of the reproach of illegitimacy. At the end of the war the whole world will have to face the normal demand of women for marriage and children in a world depleted of marriageable men. It is too early to say how that demand will be met.

But it is not too early to say that if that problem forces us at last to look squarely and without superstition at the problem of marriage, it will be worth the cost in husband and children. Governments of the world must prepare themselves, not necessarily to have their women demanding marriage of some sort, but certainly demanding a rational basis for whatever decision is finally reached. If we can never be wholly emancipated from the facts of sex, we can at least emancipate our way of dealing with it.

[Original source: *Forum* 49 (May 1918): 611; repr. in *American Feminism: Key Source Documents 1848–1920, Volume IV, Women's Clubs and Settlements*, ed. Janet Beer, Anne-Marie Ford, and Katherine Joslin (London and New York: Routledge, 2003), 453–63.]

Vera Brittain (1893–1970) was a British writer, feminist, and pacifist. She was a Voluntary Aid Detachment nurse for most of the First World War, and worked as a fire warden during the Second World War, but, while helping the war effort, she also wrote in support of peace and pacifism. As a member of the Bombing Restriction Committee, Brittain protested the saturation bombing of German cities, which earned her public wrath. She worked to feed the starving victims of war in European countries occupied by Germany, which was similarly seen as a controversial move, as it was believed that this food would help 'the enemy.' Her pacifist work continued after the war, when she was one of the first to speak out against punishing the whole of Germany for Nazism. Brittain went on to support the Campaign for Nuclear Disarmament, Gandhi's nonviolent protests, anti-apartheid work in South Africa, and independence for colonized countries.

Vera Brittain
Married Women and Surnames (1926)

In certain ways the modern world has accommodated itself more readily than the Middle Ages to the social theory underlying the Tenth Commandment, which recognises a man's wife as his property, less valuable indeed than his house, but more important than his servant, his maid, his ox, or his ass, or any of his other worldly possessions. Even as late as the time of the Reformation, the wives of so relentless an autocrat as Henry VIII were generally known by the names to which they were born. Later generations, however, discovered that this practice implied a degree of individuality which was unbecoming in a married woman; they therefore labelled her with her husband's name on the same defensive principle as that which led them to inscribe 'Trespassers will be Prosecuted' or 'All Rights Reserved' on various other kinds of property.

Many years ago in America a League was started by Lucy Stone, the wife of Henry Blackwell, whose members insist upon the right to retain their maiden names after marriage. At present, no such movement exists in England, largely because, as [Elizabeth Robins,] the writer of 'Ancilla's Share' pointed out in her 'Indictment of Sex Antagonism,' the feminist movement suffers less from its opponents than from the large mass of women who are still unconscious of the sex-inferiority implied in a number of generally accepted customs. Among such customs is the convention that a woman, respected before marriage for her creative or practical work, should after marriage, as a matter of course and without being presented with any choice, so far merge her personality into that of her husband as to be known by his name instead of her own, and be regarded primarily as a married woman, rather than as a doctor, a sculptor, a writer, or a political worker.

A custom which undermines the reputation of the distinguished woman is of course not even challenged in those still too frequent cases where a woman's only title to achievement is her acquisition of a husband. There is, indeed, a subtle danger in the claim to the continued use of a maiden name so long as it is advanced only by writers, artists, and actresses, or by women whose names are identified with some conspicuous movement. It can be alleged that such a claim is not a common right, but merely the privilege of certain professions, or the reward of some particular achievement. Feminists have long been awake to the side-tracking of movements by the imputation of unworthy motives, and a further danger is that the claim to retain a name will often be greeted, not as a general demand on behalf of all women, but as an offensive manifestation of personal vanity.

Individual experience confirms the first of these impressions. The manager of my London Bank recently consoled himself for my determination to keep my account in my own name after my marriage by the reflection that it was, of course, my literary name. My protest that it was my name in any case, and only my writing name incidentally, he dismissed as an irrelevant consideration, being unwilling to suppose that any young woman of harmless appearance should harbour dark devices for striking at the solidarity of family life. Hence the need arises for women who belong to professions – such as that of teaching – which their harshest critics cannot label 'exhibitionist,' to insist upon their right to retain their surnames after marriage.

The need is further illustrated by the difficulties which a married woman who uses her maiden name at present encounters; difficulties whose strength lies in their very absurdity and triviality, and which can only be banished when an insistence now criticised or ridiculed becomes the recognised habit of at least all feminists. Vehement opposition is always easier to combat than those well-meant assumptions which are as unassailable as a silken cushion.

According to English law, a surname can be kept or acquired by reputation, but unfortunately this reputation depends partly upon society as well as upon the individual user of the name. The use of a maiden name may, in a conservative community, easily involve a battle royal between the wife herself, and the still large number of women who pursue a policy of militant inferiority for which they imagine the loftiest moral sanction. The more, in such circumstances, the wife describes herself by her own name; the oftener her opponents persist in addressing her by that of her husband.

Social opposition of this type, being insidious and perpetual, is far more difficult to encounter than legal convention, which presents a cut-and-dried issue capable of being settled once and for all. One exhibition of firm determination is sufficient to maintain the right to sign a will with a maiden name, or to keep a banking account or to hold shares in the name previously used. Similar resolution is now sufficient – at least in London – to obtain a passport issued in a maiden name. Minor clerks at the Passport Office will announce that this cannot be done, but the importunate applicant who insists upon seeing a higher official will meet with little difficulty. My own passport is made out in my full name, with the words 'British Subject by birth, wife of a British Subject' inserted below. My husband's name is noted only on the page reserved for 'observations,' and is inoffensively sandwiched between permission to enter the German Occupied Territory, and information concerning the acquisition of an American visa.

As soon, however, as travelling begins, the social difficulties recur. *Wagon-lit* attendants betray an undue interest in an apparently married couple who occupy one compartment but whose passports are made out in different names. Hotels accustomed to British habits are apt to be puzzled, inquisitive, or disapproving. The porter in a hotel in Budapest where I had stayed before my marriage endeavoured to solve the difficulty by addressing my husband as 'Mr Brittain.' My husband has always nobly shared in the campaign for the retention of my name, but after this incident he admitted that the sudden relegation of himself to mere husbandhood made him realise for the first time the full significance of the women's fight for individuality.

It is surprising that the news of the long-established Lucy Stone League does not yet appear to have penetrated into the American Consulate in London. The passport which the British Foreign Office had issued to me was visé in the name in which it was made out only after protest. The official with whom I dealt informed me that my 'case' was the first of this kind that had come to his notice, and grimly prophesied 'trouble' at the other end. His clerk eventually made out my papers as I wished, but in order to show me that women of advanced views are not encouraged in the land of liberty, she included, without asking me, a statement to the effect that my sole purpose in going to the United States was to accompany my husband, and that he had paid for my passage, which was untrue. Fortunately the Consulate was unduly pessimistic, and the anticipated 'trouble' failed to materialise.

The retention of a maiden name may seem a trivial matter to some who have not yet learnt the lesson of 'Ancilla's Share,' but it is by no means unconnected with the present urgent problem, of the marriage of professional women, which is driving many of the best and most vital women into the path of deliberate celibacy. A State which has officially pronounced that a woman shall no longer be debarred either by sex or by marriage from making her contribution to the intellectual life of her generation, is concerned with her private affairs only in so far as they affect the efficiency of her service and the welfare of future humanity. And even if we admit that in certain cases a minimum of interference is justifiable on the latter ground, there can be no possible argument for labelling a woman as married which does not apply with at least equal force in the case of a man.

[Source: *Time and Tide*, 15 January 1926, 52–3.]

Ruth L.T. Yap (?–?) was a resident of Hawaii who held the position of assistant professor of mathematics at the University of Hawaii–Manoa.

Ruth L.T. Yap
The Legal Status of Chinese Women in China and in Hawaii (1930)

From time immemorial, woman's place has been in the home, but Chinese women have antedated women of any modern country in government participation. In ancient Chinese history, we find the Empress Dowager aided in court matters during the absence of the Emperor as early as the Chow Dynasty (11th c. B.C.), then Empress Lu of the Ban Dynasty (206 B.C.–25 A.D.), Empress Dowager Wu of the Tang Dynasty (7th c. A.D.), and the famous and renowned Empress Dowager of the Ching Dynasty. Besides these, we find in greater numbers talented women elected to high offices – among the most recent being Dr Soomay Tcheng, educated in France and the holder of the degree doctor of laws.

In order to understand the position held by women in olden days, we must know something of the Chinese family system – how customs and ancestral worships have more or less hindered the progress of women. The individual family is the social unit, consisting of the father, mother, son and his wife and their offspring, and unmarried daughters, all living in one domestic establishment. Married daughters belong to their husband's family. Of course, the father is the nominal head, being responsible for the maintenance of the family, but it is usually the mother-in-law who is responsible for the harmony and clock-like workings of her household. She settles all disputes which sometimes occur among the various sisters-in-law. When she retires, the wife of the eldest son takes her place as a sort of regent in the household. On all occasions of sacrifice and of receiving guests, she has to ask for directions from her mother-in-law, while all the other sisters-in-law have to seek guidance and direction from her.

Should the father die, then his wife's position would be that of her husband's in the family organization, providing that she remains unmarried. Supposing, then, that the sons all want to divide the property. They cannot do so unless the mother gives her sanction.

The most recent Code of Laws, which is still in the process of being revised, was started under the Kuomintang in 1926 and advocates equal rights in inheriting property for men and women, equal rights in political franchise, equal rights in education and social intercourse.

In the old Provisional Code, with regard to succession to the family (section 78), the first point to be noted is that females, and all persons claiming through females, are entirely excluded. The origin of the distinction is apparent when we consider that a woman marrying leaves her father's family once and for all, and becomes part of her husband's family. Her children of course take their father's name and belong to the 'kindred' or 'tsung' (i.e., all those descended from a common ancestor who bear the same family name, and who can trace their descent continuously through males). To this alone, they are capable of succeeding.

Next as to the mode in which family property is divided. As we learned in the family system, the father maintains the family through the combined earnings of all his sons and everything is held in common. The family property then consists of all ancestral inherited property, the accumulations made by the head of the family, and also all property acquired by the sons. The division of property is an important event and no one had a right to compel a partition or to withdraw from society until it is dissolved by mutual consent or by the head of the family.

All persons entitled to the family property are as follows: All sons and their male descendants, whether born of the principal wife or of a concubine. These divide the whole estate equally between themselves, grandsons getting a father's share. Daughters are not entitled to any share. If they are already married, they have left the family for good and, of course, have no further claim, but a certain sum, called the marriage portion, as agreed upon in each particular case, is set apart before the division for the marriage of the unmarried daughters. Lately daughters in educated classes also have a right to the family property.

No provision is made for the widow, for she is usually cared for by the eldest son. If she has a family she can refuse to consent to division of property, in which case she has the practical control of the whole inheritance. If she is a widow of a son dying before division, she is entitled to the customary management of her husband's share in trust for her sons or the adopted successor. This prominent position of the mother is no doubt due to the custom of ancestral worship. Division of property also occurs before the death of the father.

As an example, let us say that the family property is $25,000 and that the family consisted of: father A, mother B, and 5 sons, C, D, E, F, G. At the death of the father the property is divided equally among the five sons, providing the mother sanctions the division. That means $5,000 each.

Suppose D is dead, but leaves two sons and one illegitimate son. The two sons would get $2,000 each and the illegitimate son would get $1,000.

Suppose E is dead, but leaves an adopted son and an illegitimate. Each would receive $2,500.

Suppose F is dead but leaves a wife, one son, and one daughter; $5,000 goes to the wife if she does not marry. The unmarried daughter may claim a certain sum of marriage expenses from the family property before it is divided among brothers. When the family has dissolved she takes the marriage portion and goes to live with her eldest brother.

Under the old system, the position of the wife was as follows:
1 She had no right to possess property.
2 She could not leave the family without her husband's consent.
3 If deserted by husband, she could not marry again before the expiration of three years, without first obtaining the sanction of a local magistrate, under the penalty of 100 blows.

4 If not doing so, the law considered her as an adulteress.
5 If at the death of her husband she remains unmarried, her position is that of her husband's in the family.

Under the new code the wife cannot do anything outside of domestic routine without first having the permission of her husband. However, she has the right to act without her husband's consent under the following conditions:
1 When husband's interest is in conflict with that of wife or vice versa.
2 When husband deserts wife.
3 When husband is interdicted or is subject to.
4 When husband is undergoing penal servitude of more than one year.
5 When wife wishes to request court to order an interdict upon the husband.

Further privileges of women under the new code:
1 Right to possess separate property.
2 Right to annul any contract made by her husband detrimental to general welfare of family, provided such annulment is not an injustice to the third party.

Divorce:
If husband and wife can't live together harmoniously and happily because of incompatibility of temperament, and if both parties agree to separate, marriage may be annulled. Court action is only necessary when husband and wife cannot reach agreement.

The new law holds the same principle. Under the new code, either husband or wife may obtain divorce by the following reasons:
1 Bigamy (by either party).
2 Adultery.
3 Because one party intends to kill the other.
4 Because one of the parties is ill-treated or highly insulted by the other.
5 Because wife ill-treats or insults relations of husband's parents.
6 Because husband is ill-treated or insulted by parents or relatives of his wife.
7 Because either party maliciously deserts the other.
8 Because either party has not known the whereabouts of the other for over three years.
9 If husband is under 30 and wife under 25, consent of parents of both parties is necessary for valid divorce.
10 Agreement for divorce must be registered at the office of the local magistrate before it is valid.

Each has equal rights in instituting of divorce proceedings, in custody of children, in property, and if wife is successful in divorce suit instituted on proper grounds, she has the right of alimony (amount according to the husband's social and financial positions).

In other words, we can say that the status of Chinese women as it stands now shows great improvement, and we are looking forward to see the prosperity of China through the raised standards of women. Legally, whereas women had no share in property division excepting her marriage portion, now, through the second national convention of the Kuomintang party in 1926, laws were passed giving equal rights to men and women on legal, educational, and economic aspects. In Article 12 of the resolutions passed by the Kuomintang in 1926 women have the right to inherit family property; married daughters, before this law was passed, could claim rights. Since the civil code was adopted divorce was easier to arrange. Whereas submission of women to men (i.e., daughter to father, wife to husband, mother to son), in case the husband is dead, is abolished, and men and women are equal, as given in the National Constitution and the Provincial Constitutions of some provinces.

I have shown you, I hope without many legal terms, the new status of Chinese women. I would like to say something of the woman-movement, showing how the Chinese women fought for their rights.

During the reign of Kuang-Hsu (1869–1905) a woman by the name of Yu Tseng-sih wrote an essay championing the rights of a widow to re-marry. This initiated the Woman's Rights Movement in China. This movement may be divided into two periods –the first period from 1894 to 1915; the second from 1916 to the present.

During the first period the movement against foot-binding in 1897 by Liang Chi-Chao, who organized the Anti-Foot-Binding Society in Shanghai, with girls of natural feet as members of the society, was very successful. The campaign of releasing the bound-feet of girls above eight years, to grow into natural form again, and the campaign against binding the feet of girls under eight years, were the important projects.

Along with this movement came the movement for education. The education of Chinese girls in Christian schools occurred in early times. About 1900, Liang Chi-Chao organized a girls' school in Shanghai, the first of its kind opened through Chinese initiative. No need to say that there was slow progress because of customs – antiquated customs – but the women showed their seriousness and earnestness by bobbing their hair, by turning into revolutionaries, joining the army and fighting for equal rights.

In 1910 a provisional government was established, with Dr Sun Yat Sen as president. Due to many impressive government matters, Dr Sun Yat Sen could not do much with the demands of the women for equality of educational opportunities, woman suffrage, and equality of rights with men in marriage. At any rate, he was in sympathy with the women's demands. When the Provisional Government was set up at Canton, several women were elected as members of the Provincial Assembly.

The student movement which followed was a great help to the woman-movement. Here women showed their strength by protesting against Japan for taking over German rights in Shantung. They paraded the streets, lectured to the people, and refused to attend classes unless the pro-Japanese and corrupt officials were ousted. Then, too, the aims of the student movement were in sympathy with the woman movement – such as thought revolution, social intercourse, emancipation of women, educational equality of sexes.

In the summer of 1922 women students of Peking University Law School and the Peking Girls' Higher Normal School started the Advancement of Woman's Suffrage Association and the Woman's Rights League.

The objects of the former were:

1 Abolishing of all laws made for the sole protection of men, in order to protect the rights of women.
2 Changing of inheritance laws whereby women may inherit, as the basis for economic independence.

The object of the Women's Rights Association were:

1 Educational opportunities.
2 Equal constitutional rights with men.
3 Protection of women in family relationships.
4 Prohibition of prostitution, girl slavery, and foot-binding.

This movement has been very successful because educated Chinese, who have been abroad, have profited and have seen the good women can accomplish. Naturally, women who qualified were placed as judge, mayor, and, lately, a foreign minister, and in other minor offices. With the backing of the Nationalist Government, Chinese women have a bright future, and under the able leadership of such women as Madam Sun Yat Sen, Mrs Liao Chung-Hai, Mrs Tang Ying-Chao, Mrs Chiang Kai-Shek, and others to follow, we are sure China will come forward to her place in the Pacific area.

Socially the women of China have done much in the past twenty years. Women- and child-labor welfare, liberty for slave-girls, abolition of singsong houses, anti-opium movement, employment for beggars, mass education, vocational training for women and girls, free hospitals, – these are some of the projects accomplished.

Economically they are abreast of their sisters across the Pacific. At present they are engaged in clerical and stenographic work, in teaching, in nursing, and other professions.

With the progress of women in social, legal, and economic affairs, China will soon become a world-power.

In Hawaii

The Chinese women born in Hawaii and the United States are American citizens, and as such they have all the rights of the American women. They have the right to vote; they have equal opportunities in education, business, and other fields. They have the right to own property, to inherit property, and are at liberty to marry anyone they choose. In the case of marrying an American citizen, she does not lose her citizenship, and can travel freely from country to country. Whereas, should she marry an alien, she loses her citizenship and she endures hardship while traveling in American territory, for she would be treated as an alien.

By the Immigration Act of 1924, wives of American citizens ineligible to citizenship are excluded from the United States. This was the meaning of Section 13 (c) of the said act as later interpreted by the United States Supreme Court in the famous case, Chin Bow vs. United States. The Supreme Court held that the law was constitutional and that the only remedy lies with Congress. Since then the Chinese-American citizens' organizations here and in San Francisco have tried to secure an amendment to the law. Congressman Dyer of Missouri introduced a bill in the 69th Congress to that effect. After three hearings (the last one took place March this year), nothing has been done about it by the Congress. These hearings were before the Sub-Committee of the House on Immigration and Naturalization. Both Senators King of Utah and Bingham of Connecticut have introduced similar bills, but they have not got any farther than the door of the Sub-Committee on Immigration of the Senate.

In the last hearing Delegate Houston from Hawaii appeared before the committee on behalf of the Chinese-American. By treaty provision the Chinese merchant, even though he be an alien, can bring into the United States his wife and minor children and make his residence here as long as he maintains the status of a merchant. Yet a Chinese who is a citizen is deprived of that right. It is so unjust!

We are glad that word has been received just recently that this bill introduced by Delegate Houston in regard to Chinese wives has passed the House. We hope that the Senate, too, will see the injustice, and vote favorably.

(Since this article was written the bill in question has been signed by President Hoover.)

[Source: *Mid-Pacific Magazine*, August 1930, 121–6.]

Tsianina Redfeather Blackstone (1882–1985) was a Creek-Cherokee mezzo-soprano who toured with Charles Wakefield Cadman, the US composer and pianist who collected and recorded Omaha and Winnebago music, from 1906–16. Although she is listed on Creek tribal rolls as Florence Evans, she went by the Cherokee name of Tsianina, and used that name in her career as a singer. Blackstone retired from singing in 1930. She was a founder of the Foundation for American Indian Education and she served on the board of the School of American Research from 1933 to 1963. She was also connected to the Society of American Indians and performed at several of their functions.

'Princess Tsianina' [Redfeather Blackstone]
Minority Needs – The Indian (1933)

It will be necessary for me to present a few pictures to give you perhaps a different attitude toward the Indian question.

In Isaiah 1:18, we read: 'Come now and let us reason together, saith the Lord.' And so we have come today to reason together, and our topic for discussion is 'Equal Opportunity.'

I should like first to take you back to the earliest primitive days when this country really belonged to us. I am sure you must realize how we loved it, how we thrilled over the beauty of it as we roamed about visiting our loved ones. Then an invasion threatened to come in and destroy everything that we held nearest and dearest to our hearts, and we rose to the occasion as best we could, but we lost, and in the losing there were many tragedies and massacres laid at our door that we were not responsible for. At that time we were taught that it was wrong to fight, that we should be peaceful, loving and kind.

Some of us understood that call to higher understanding, realizing that progress is born of experience, and obeyed the call, but some of us refused to accept such a call as consolation for the sorrows and tragedies that burned deep in our hearts.

So we find in every walk of life those who struggle and strive to build for higher ideals and those who constantly stand on the sidelines, creating turmoil and tearing down in general, who are a detriment to any community.

Many years after that first invasion the country was threatened again with another intrusion, and of course this was a different story. You sent out your call to arms for the late World War, and the American Indian was among the first to respond to that call. We didn't stop to think to whom the country belonged, but we gave from every possible angle, and went over there and fought by your sides as one of you.

I was in the midst of building a career for myself and was the first girl west of Chicago to respond to General Pershing's call for volunteer entertainers. I wanted to prove to the world that where patriotism is concerned the American Indian is never found lacking.

I am purposely touching the high spots, as our time is limited today, and I am anxious to give you a different impression of the American Indian question.

Let me offer a few illustrations.

Some years ago great agitation was started to eliminate ceremonial Indian dances because the Commissioner at that time said they were savage, immoral, and obscene. The one particular ceremony the Commissioner wanted to eliminate at once was one in which the Indians danced three days in succession without stopping. The Commissioner thought they inflicted great injury upon themselves in so doing. The purpose of the dance was to build up physical strength, physical endurance, as only the runners took part in it. There was a lot of nation-wide discussion pro and con about old poor Lo and his last bit of freedom being taken away from him, when along came the marathon dancers, and certainly if there has ever been anything that was a discredit to our intelligence it was the marathon dances. The command was withdrawn at once and nothing has been heard of it since.

Soon after this experience, I was in Los Angeles on a concert tour with Charles Wakefield Cadman, when upon hearing this story a friend said to me: 'You come with me to the downtown section of Los Angeles and I will show you something that will offset your Indian dance.' I went with her, and there in the downtown section of Los Angeles sat a man on a pole. He had been sitting there eighteen days to break a world's record. As I looked at him, the thought came to me: 'Here, I am supposedly the savage, wild Indian some say, and there you sit representing a race of people that I am supposed to copy, supposed to emulate, and yet in all my primitiveness and savagery I would have known better than to do something like that.'

So you see, friends, there are always two sides to every picture.

Let us present another picture. Just suppose that today millions of Chinese came across Lake Michigan and conquered Chicago, drove you out of your homes, destroyed your loved ones right before your very eyes, and then selected a piece of property nearby and said: 'Now you live there as long as I tell you to live, and I shall do your thinking for you.'

What would you do? You would fight to the last drop of your blood to prevent such an invasion that would take away your freedom, self-respect, and initiative. Some of you would follow the line of least resistance and accept the system with a shrug of your shoulders and say, 'What's the use?' But some of you would constantly rebel against such restrictions, fight for your right of self-expression and equal opportunity, and you would come forward regardless of any man-made laws. And so it is with the Indian.

Those who have accomplished things have done so in spite of our government or any of the injustices of civilization.

We often hear the words 'primitive' and 'savage' in speaking of the Indian. I want to ask a fair question. Who is the savage? Out of the heart of our civilization, so-called, supported and shielded by our Stars and Stripes, protected by our American Government, there stalks in the quiet of the night a fiend in human dress to commit a crime on an innocent child. You know, of course, that I refer to the Lindbergh tragedy. First, I know an Indian did not commit the crime, and secondly, I know that if it had been committed in the days of the so-called savage, the murderer would have been found and punished long before this.

A summary. What to do about it? The first and most important thing to do is to correct the pages of our American history that is so unfair and unjust to the American Indian. It would seem to me that we have come to the parting of the ways of truth and lies, and now is the time to tell the truth. I think it is time to rewrite those pages of American history that have called the conflict between the Indian and the whites a massacre if the Indian won and a battle if the white man won.

More than a hundred years ago an Indian girl, Sacajawea, blazed the trail to the Northwest for the Lewis and Clark Expedition, a hazardous journey that took two years to complete. A monument stands in Portland, Oregon, as mute evidence to the Indian's contribution to civilization. What do we hear of her? Practically nothing. I remember hearing a lady say once that she thought this was a remarkable thing for an Indian girl to do, and that she intended writing a book on outstanding Indian women of history. I am perfectly sure that, if any other woman had accomplished such a feat, our histories would be full of it and there would be monuments all over the country.

When we lose our false sense of race prejudice and lay aside our small, petty thoughts of big 'I,' self-egotism, then we can truly thrill over the achievements of other races and give the full credit for their contribution to progress.

The Indian is a victim of race prejudice, and, because of our governmental system, has had a severe case of inferiority complex forced upon him. America has denied the Indian race the right to self-expression, the equal opportunities, and then is prone to criticize the Indian for not advancing more rapidly. No race of people could give proper contribution to civilization, that is shut away from the rest of the world and has the doors closed on equal rights.

The Indian child is sent away to school many miles, in most cases, at a very tender age, which is in itself a handicap, because the mother-tie in Indian life is our strongest force, and many children get so homesick they fall ill.

While the child is away in school, the village is not prepared to meet the new thought upon its return, and the result is a wide breach. In the Indian race our fathers will not tolerate an expression of superiority; their code is equality. We need to do away with the system of years standing that has been such a failure. But the sad part of it is that there is too much money involved in the Indian question.

Free the Indian and let him take his proper place in civilization. He could not be in a worse plight than he is today. The Indian race has too long and too consistently had to follow other people's wishes instead of its own. For generations America has been bent upon trying to do something to them, not with them. Reluctant to admit her lack of success she says that the Indians are hopelessly primitive.

Eliminate all matters from schoolbooks tending to race prejudice. Write a new textbook that will give the Indian as fair a picture as you give yourselves. The Indians are too human to make good marionettes.

However, in all his sufferings, injustices, and handicaps, you never hear the Indian complain. He is a silent sufferer, and because of that he has been an easy victim. Perhaps his inherent dependence on the Great Spirit is his comfort and his solace. The average person's concept of the Indian religious thought is that the Indian is a worshiper of many gods. This is not true. The Indian worships one God, but he sees him reflected in all living things. He has never hoarded because he had faith that the Great Spirit would always provide for him if he kept himself purified.

Friends, our Heavenly Father left a law for you and me almost two thousand years ago when he said, 'Love one another, and love thy neighbor as thyself.' He didn't say the man next door was your neighbor, nor did He say if the man living next door to you happened to be an Indian, don't love him so much. No, friends, he meant that we should love our fellowman and give no thought to race, color, or creed.

We should remember that the world is wide, that there are a thousand million different human wills, opinions, ambitions, tastes, and loves, that each person has a different history, constitution, culture, character from all the rest. Then we should go forth into life with the smallest expectations, but with the largest patience, with a charity broad enough to cover the whole world's evil, and sweet enough to neutralize what is bitter in it.

Friends, it does not matter to whom the country belongs. None of us can take it with us when we leave this earth. So let us share it in a spirit of true brotherly love; let us be friends, and as we go down the trail of life, let us go as brothers and true fellowmen; and when we come to the end of that long trail and step into the Happy Hunting Grounds from which no hunter returns, let us go unafraid, with trust and faith in God and each other, so that we may receive the final benediction: Well done, thou good and faithful servant.

[Source: *Our Common Cause: Civilization: Report of the National Council of Women of the United States. Including the Series of Round Tables, July 16–22, 1933, Chicago, Illinois* (New York: National Council of Women of the United States, 1973), 794–6.]

Efwa Kato was a Fante woman from Ghana who studied in Great Britain in the 1930s. She published 'What We Women Can Do' in the journal of the West African Students Union of Great Britain and Ireland. She was thus among the African and Caribbean students and intellectuals gathering in metropolitan centres like London in this period who formed networks of solidarity and frequently became engaged in Pan-Africanist politics.

Efwa Kato
What We Women Can Do (1934)

The influence of woman for good or evil, particularly the latter, has been recognised throughout the ages. In the role of a tempter or seducer of man her reputation is world wide. Was it not Eve who was first seduced and through her man fell from primeval innocence? I think, however, that the world owes a lot to Eve for tempting Adam to eat of 'the tree of knowledge of good and evil'; for it is in the eating thereof that man owes his subsequent development. I admit that it is idyllic to pass one's life in keeping a garden and making pets of the animals. But who will deny that, in spite of its evils and sufferings, the world is far more interesting and exciting than it would otherwise have been but for Eve? And man loves to have it so. He finds in such a topsy-turvy world an opportunity for his initiative and of moulding it to his heart's desire. But we live in a thankless world. Instead of being grateful to Eve and her daughters, man has held woman in servitude for her alleged natural depravity. However, there has not been wanting, here and there, an acknowledgment of her greatness and nobility of character. Many a man has had to confess that but for his mother, sister, wife or – shall I say it? – lover, he would not have become the great man he became. And now the influence of woman for good has become an axiom.

It is on the influence of woman for good that I wish to direct the attention of my readers. Looking at the sufferings which our race has had to endure and is enduring, I have often asked myself the question which I daresay every other thinking woman of the race has asked herself, namely, What can we women do? The answer to the question depends on so many factors which need not detain us here. Assuming, however, a woman endowed with health, and education of some sort and a modicum of intelligence – all of which I am fortunate to be blessed with – I venture to suggest that the answer is to be found along the following lines: –

In order of importance, I would mention what we women can do as mothers. It has been truly said that the hand that rocks the cradle rules the world. It is those lessons which a child learns in the cradle, or, to put it graphically, on its mother's knees that invariably lead it in the direction it should go. It is therefore important that we women should be aware of our influence as mothers. At the threshold of life the child is dependent on its mother, not only for its physical needs but also for its moral training. I am assuming that every woman who is capable of understanding this article will take the trouble of acquiring, at least, an elementary knowledge of child rearing. I am here concerned with the moral as opposed to the physical welfare of the child. As soon as the child can understand, I suggest that the history of the race be unfolded to him. Our history is an epic in itself, capable of stirring even the dullest imagination. Such passive virtues, for examples, humility and patience, should be relegated to the background, if at all taught. Such virtues are gratuitous in a subject-race. What have we to be humble for? Are not our circumstances humiliating enough? Such positive virtues as courage, manliness, and, above all, that divine restlessness, the impetus of adventure and achievement, should be paramount in the child's moral training.

The mother's interest should not flag even when the child begins to attend school. There is the tendency, all too prevalent, I am afraid, of leaving the moral training of the child to the professional teacher. Admittedly, the teacher helps to mould the child's character, but he cannot take the place of the mother. After all, it is only a small percentage of the child's waking hours, about six, that are spent in school. The periods before and after school are the mother's. Through the child's lessons the mother can find the opportunity of inculcating the precepts enumerated above. As I write an instance comes up in my mind. It is most appropriate as illustrating the advantages a mother has over the teachers. During Empire Day celebrations, I wonder how many teachers have the hardihood to impart to their pupils the facts concerning the rise and development of the Empire. They are more concerned with drilling the children to make a good march past and in preparing their mind for the balderdash which is often given the children than in presenting the facts of the case as they really are. It would be asking too much to prevent a child from taking part in such celebrations; but after the function is over, the mother should ascertain what the 'lesson' was and seek to correct the false impression by giving a true account of the case. She must tell the child of the benefits which we derive from being members of the Commonwealth; but, at the same time, she should not forget to remind him of the injustice under which we labour for no other reason than that of the colour of our skin. The recent and most glaring example of injustice is the treatment of the natives of Kenya on the discovery of gold in their reserve. With tact the mother can fire the child with a passion for justice without inculcating race hatred.

With regard to the influence of woman as wife, much depends on the type of man the woman is fortunate or unfortunate to have as a husband. I am not one of those who prefer to reform a man after marriage. If he proves intractable during courtship, the odds are that he will remain so ever after. Perhaps it is well to begin with a discussion on the type of man most desirable or on the influence of woman during courtship. Of course tastes differ, but speaking for the average of which I am one, a woman should prefer a man who is first and foremost a patriot. I am afraid we women will have to change our standard of values in this respect. The majority are still influenced by 'the gold standard.' But surely, the time has come when we should 'go off gold' and appraise a man for his sterling character. Instead of having an eye on their bank accounts, we should demand of our prospective husbands an account of services of self-sacrifice to the race, failing which, we must make them understand that unless they are willing to participate in the fight for race upliftment, we shall have nothing more to do with them. During the war many a man had to join the colours just to please his sweetheart. If women can influence their men to commit murder (for war is murder, despite the euphemism by which it is called), why can't we influence our men for good? I know from experience that our men are not lacking in chivalry. The truth is that we women have not been demanding much of them. A few honeyed words from them and lo, and behold, the trick is done. But if they realise what type of woman they are up against, I am sure they will respond and show what a fine lot they are. I have heard many of them orating in the drawing rooms in England and America what great things they will do for Africa on their return home, and provided they could count on the support of the women, I have no doubt that they will endeavour to practise their ideals.

After the excitement of courtship comes the humdrum of married life. Here, again, the influence of woman is undisputable. Apart from running the home, which I hope every intelligent woman contemplating marriage should know how to do, there is the no less important task of being a help-mate to her husband. With the best will in the world, it is at this stage that many marriages are wrecked. Some wives treat their husbands as if they were still boys, and naturally, a man who is worthy of the name, resents such treatment. The right type of man welcomes criticism and advice from his wife. It all depends on the way in which they are proffered. The main task of the wife is to be a bulwark of moral support to the husband. However patriotic he might be, the rough and tumble of the work-a-day world, the scramble for places at the top tends to a depreciation of ideals. The plums of office are for 'safe' men, and a patriot is never considered 'safe' by the powers that be. Naturally, there will be the tendency on the part of the patriot to compromise and play for safety. Here is the wife's opportunity. Here she can exert her influence. Her duty is to keep the flag flying and to remind her spouse of the dreams of his youth. What is more, she should be prepared to forego the amenities which a 'successful career' brings – wealth and social prestige – remembering that it is not how much a man gets out of life but how much he puts into it that matters. Situated as our race is, not one of our ideals can be realised without self-sacrifice. And who but the wife can give the necessary encouragement in times of disappointment to provide the impetus to succeed?

But it is not the lot of every woman to be a mother or a wife. What then? Are there not other spheres in which woman can wield her influence? Assuredly, there are. Apart from the usual avenues of teaching, nursing, etc., the intelligent woman who is desirous of helping her race will find an outlet for her ambition. She need not believe in the hocus-pocus which passes muster as religion before undertaking the task of enlightening her less favoured sisters. A simple faith in the moral order of the universe is enough to create in her a 'passion for souls.' If she is a woman of means, she might become the Mary Kingsley of Africa to interpret the motherland to the world. Hitherto, such interpretation, rather misinterpretation, has been undertaken by foreigners, some of them knowing not even the language of the people they seek to interpret! Or is she interested in politics? In that case, she may become our Emmeline Pankhurst, the leading spirit of the Suffragette Movement in Africa. In any case, the woman who wishes to help her race can find out what she is capable of doing. My aim is to create in my sisters the desire to help. That done, then where there is a will, there is always a way. It is the women who have to set the pace; for no nation or race can rise above its womanhood.

[Source: *Women Writing Africa: West Africa and the Sahel*, ed. Esi Sutherland-Addy and Aminata Diaw (New York: Feminist Press at the City University of New York, 2005), 179–82.]

Attia Habibullah (1913–98) was a writer and a journalist who was born into a prominent family in Lucknow, India. Habibullah grew up surrounded by some of the great thinkers and politicians of the day, and was educated at Isabella Thoburn College, a prestigious college for women. During her thirties she began writing in newspapers and joined the Progressive Writers Movement, and eventually published short stories and novels that dealt with poverty, power, and Westernization. Habibullah moved to England in 1947, where she worked at the BBC in broadcast journalism, dealing with such issues as literature, history, and culture.

Attia Habibullah
Seclusion of Women (1936)

Among the major issues which have to be faced during India's transition from medieval to modern conditions is the problem of *purdah*, which has always been the subject of bitter controversy, sanctified as it is by religion and hallowed by custom. Though *purdah* has always been treated as a social problem, it cannot be considered apart from the political and economic problems with which it is inter-connected. No political institutions can prosper which are foreign in nature to the general structure of a country's social institutions, which in turn are given their general shape by economic conditions.

Among hunters and warriors or amongst a nomadic people who led a precarious existence, women became important only as a means of production of more males and as providers of their comforts. They became goods to be jealously guarded from robbers. Later, feudal society in the East with its despotic rulers and recognition of polygamy and even concubinage called for a safeguarding of women by some form or another of seclusion. In India constant invasions made this seclusion eventually take the rigid form of *purdah* as we know it today.

Even today men remain strongholds of medievalism where no woman can consider herself safe from the fancies of the despot. In a state of society where the rule of law is recognised the need does not arise for such artificial means of safeguarding them. The will of the people developed by the spirit of the time in relation to social development forms the best moral defence.

The socio-religious tenets of Islam, by which *purdah* is religiously justified, were based on problems of medieval society. However, as moral rules are always interpreted according to the spirit of the times, numerous and contradictory are the interpretations by various people of the same injunction from the same book. In its most extreme form *purdah* is taken to mean an absolute segregation of the sexes and the complete seclusion of women from all men except those whom religious law makes it impossible for them to marry. Some interpreters allow women, if completely covered, to move out of the *zenana*; others allow the exposure of the face, hand and feet. The interpretations in fact vary in proportion to the capability of men to resist temptation; they are a measure of men's moral strength!

That ultimately economics determined the extent and even the existence of *purdah* is proved by the fact that wherever economic necessity made women as economically productive as men they could not be secluded. *Purdah*, however, developed in spite of such women; the working classes did not form an influential enough community.

The recognition of *purdah* in a feudal state can be understood. Women were not considered part of the body politic – neither were the masses of the people given any importance. But in a state which professes democracy *purdah* is an anachronism. It implies the denial of rights and liberty to a large section of the people. The modern state is composed of citizens, not two sexes with divergent interests.

Purdah has been the greatest hindrance to the political development of Indian women. Under the new constitution they have been given a greater degree of political rights than they enjoy at present. Those rights can be of no value while conditions exist which have divorced women from politics and left them with little knowledge of their rights and duties as citizens. Moreover merely having the right to vote does not constitute the sum and substance of political rights. The value of the vote lies in the power to use it as an unhindered expression of free and independent thought. Democracy demands a political education which *purdah* women are denied. It is chiefly *purdah* which has prevented all but a few pioneers among women from representing their interests and taking their place in legislatures and other political organisations.

The administrative problems raised in relation to the exercising of the vote by *purdah* women and in identifying them, involve a waste of time and money. Attention being diverted to all these relatively minor problems aggravates the tendencies already present towards narrowing political vision and making politics merely local and personal. Nothing could be more unwelcome in the world as it is today; modern inventions and means of communication have so linked it together that apparently minor issues often assume world-wide significance. Political creeds of today therefore have an international outlook and seek to remould the whole structure of society.

The recent political awakening among women has done much to weaken the forces of *purdah*. The salient feature of the non-co-operation movement was that a large number of women left the seclusion of their homes to fight side by side with their men. They showed the force that women can be in modern political movements.

Economically, *purdah* has been responsible to a large extent for the low standard of living in India, for it has made a large section of the people unproductive and a burden on the productive section. Apart from the very poor working class women who do not observe *purdah*, women cannot earn their own living except as domestic servants, sempstresses and teachers. These fields of activity not being limitless the unemployed remain as economic drags on their families. The upper class women, too well born to work, have no choice but to be such economic drags until conveniently disposed of in marriage.

Those who oppose free economic competition among men and women point to the reaction to it in some countries of the West. Apart from the fact that in India for some time to come the problem cannot become so acute because the spheres of employment of men and women generally do not conflict, even in the West competition lost its free nature because of the difference in the scale of wages which encouraged antagonism between men and women workers. This economic antagonism has been expressed by age old sentimental platitudes about women's place being in the home. Fascist Italy and Nazi Germany actually started the drive of women 'back to their homes.' But the problem of unemployment still remains unsolved; it makes little difference whether women are unemployed or men. Moreover Italy and Germany cannot be taken as examples of nations facing modern problems rationally. Their need is the same as the primary need of the early hunters – for more and more 'war material' to be provided by women.

The influence of economic conditions on the practice of *purdah* has exposed its worst features. The rich can afford the luxury of light and fresh air while comfortably preserving their modesty. But what of the masses of the poor who live in their miserable hovels? What of those poor wretches who live in the congested rabbit warrens that constitute the Indian cities? It is on them that the burden falls of trying to preserve their honour by copying the rich in secluding themselves. Life is not the same for all classes and economic conditions temper even morality.

Purdah having deprived women of any significance in political and economic spheres left them with form of importance only in the home. Even here, however, woman's economic dependence on man and the Oriental ideology which makes man superior to woman, make it impossible for women to realise themselves as individuals. Brought up from childhood to believe that they are important only in relation to men as daughters, wives and mothers, they have to fashion themselves on a pattern most likely to please men and give them the greatest value in the marriage market. And marriage cannot be a matter of choice but a necessary evil. Believers in *purdah* must necessarily believe that sex is evil and relationships arising out of it are shameful. Therefore no respectable man or woman may voluntarily express a wish to marry nor after marriage talk of it and of the children born of its sin.

Illogically enough this shameful, sinful alliance is praised in platitudes about love for one's mate and family!

Human instincts cannot be denied. Forcible repression for women has meant mental and physical disease, lack of discipline and rational care in the upbringing of children, lack of harmony and beauty in the home, which has become the stronghold of convention and orthodoxy.

Men, with their economic power, found a means of escape. They divided women into two categories. Their wives, mothers, daughters, they forced to be guardians of morality at the expense of another class of women who exist only for men's pleasure. It is a strange comment on *purdah* society that the cultural standards of its men should be gauged from the culture of its prostitutes.

To justify this denial of all ethics, morality and justice a dual code of morality has been evolved which regards as something 'honourable or at worst a slight blemish to be easily tolerated' in a man what in a woman is a deadly crime involving legal punishment and social ostracism. After all men have no 'consequences' to fear and the world considers a sin is a sin only when it is found out.

It is in this false system of morality, conveniently upheld by men that *purdah* finds its greatest support and herein lies its weakness. Morality cannot exist by falsehoods and through negative beliefs. It must be born of positive convictions. The only external safeguards should be material so that the existence may be made possible of 'a generation of men who never in their life chanced to buy a woman's surrender for money or any other social instrument of power; and a generation of women who have never happened to give themselves to a man for any consideration other than love.'

Whatever the reasons for the existence of *purdah*, however strengthened by religion and custom it may be, the question arises whether it can continue to exist in any form whatsoever. It has not justified its existence by solving moral problems; and it has retarded all material progress. It is true that where it does not exist individuals have touched the depths of low morality, but freedom has made it possible for others to reach heights not possible but for the exceptional few under a system of repression.

The civilized world has condemned *purdah* and tendencies within the country are against it. In the present world no country can isolate itself and its ideas.

The minds of Indian men have been more open to the influence of world movements than those of women, and they are the indirect cause of the liberation of women. As long as women are dependent on men whether in the West or in the East they must continue to live up to men's standards. Modern men are not satisfied with wives who are only acquiescent slaves of their desire and mechanical producers of their 'legitimate' children. Women are therefore being given a more liberal education to make them better wives, combining attraction with docility, and incidentally better mothers. Some brave spirits have dared to imbibe the true spirit of education, to develop individual worth, to organise and to preach true equality.

Weakened by these external attacks, *purdah* finds even its moral force weakening. Sometimes love of position in the new society being formed on Western lines draws away its staunchest supporters. Others, not loving its virtues but fearing its upholders observe it only in places and among people where criticism can be bitter.

Between the two stages in social development from *purdah* to freedom lies the stage of inconsistency. Here all problems are intensified because to the initial ethical struggle is added the struggle of adjustment between the old and the new. Men and women, products of the old conditions find themselves thrown into new conditions. Untrained to the duties and prerogatives of their new freedom they face it with a background of entirely opposite ideas, with no preparation for the changes in standards of value. Such conflicts end too often in tragedies of frustration, broken homes, of husbands alienated mentally from wives, and wives from husbands.

In the general relationship of the sexes these problems are aggravated. Men whose womenfolk are in *purdah*, who are brought up to believe that women's virtue can exist only under artificial control, who have no 'positive' standards of self-control, can mix with women who have realised their freedom. Their beliefs, if sincere, are an aspersion on the virtue of such women, and stand in the way of real respect for them. Women have to face the criticism and slander of people ignorant of their new standards. That is the price of freedom.

[Source: *Our Cause: A Symposium of Indian Women*, ed. Shyam Kumari Nehru (Allahabad: Kitabistan, 1936), 205–11.]

A child widow, Kamaladevi Chattopadhyaya (1903–88) atypically both pursued her education and remarried after the death of her first husband. Her second husband, Harindranath Chattopadhyaya, was active in Indian nationalist politics, as were his sister, Sarojini Naidu, and his brother Virendranath

Chattopaydhyaya, who led one of the Indian Communist movements in exile. Kamaladevi was active in many women's associations, both nationally and internationally, and she was the first woman to run for elected office in the legislative assembly in Madras in 1926. She also joined the Congress Socialist Party in 1934, and spent time in prison for her participation in civil disobedience.

Kamaladevi Chattopadhyaya
From 'Future of the Indian Women's Movement' (1936)

The feminist movement in the accepted sense is a symptom of capitalist society and has no place or reality in a mass class struggle such as one visualises India to be heading for. And that is why it has never assumed the significance it did in the countries of Europe. Social customs and the position of women are conditioned not merely by the prevailing economic frame work of society, but by the whole economic history of the race. This then gives us the key-note to the future of the women's movement in India.

Before we proceed, let us first glance cursorily at the demands the feminist movement in India puts forward and see how far it touches the deeper problem and what relation it has to reality. Equal citizenship rights is already a recognised principle. Next come economic independence for women and property rights. Let us examine these. The right to work is essential to human happiness, but the need of the mass of Indian women today is not the 'right to work' but the 'right to the legitimate fruit of their labour.' To the millions today, economic independence only means the right to slave and starve, while their uncared for, underfed children drag through an existence which is nothing short of a living death. Thus, those who clamour for the right to work think only in terms of the few who are bound by the chain of idle respectability. As for property rights, India is essentially an agricultural country and 75% of her population is engaged in rural occupation. Over 53% of these are landless labourers and are unaffected by the property rights. Of the total cultivable land, nearly 1/3 is under semi-feudalistic condition, being under Maharajas and Zamindars, a confirmed parasitical class under whose régime the cultivators fare little better than slaves. Then for those who own land – their plight is no better. The average holding per family is 2 to 4 acres, which makes it more of a burden under the prevailing burden of high taxation. The lot of the women in industries is no better.

Therefore to demand property rights and economic freedom by the few bourgeois women within the present economic frame work is not only misleading, but distinctly dangerous for it means trying to secure privileges to one class at the expense of another and condemning the latter to perpetual exploitation. Economic freedom in its truest sense can become a reality only when there is a more scientific and rational system of production and distribution and the forces of economic progress which they set into motion are consciously guided.

On the social side the demand is for more rational and equitable laws relating to social relationship such as marriage, custody of children, etc. Now history proves that in a society where woman is an economic factor and she produces wealth side by side with man, she enjoys fuller freedom and suffers far less from restraints and taboos. Social disabilities are more a feature of bourgeois society than the working class who even today give more rights to the women such as divorce. Hence any advantageous economic adjustment for women is bound to secure for them social freedom as well, just as loss of economic freedom necessarily means the loss of social rights as well. The condition of women in Russia and the contrasting conditions in Germany and Italy proved this as an unchallenged fact.

Now we come to the question of general culture, physical well-being and social purity – education, health and social morals – they are inextricably bound up. Education and health are just as much governed by economic factors. Making education compulsory or promulgating sanitary codes cannot touch even the fringe of this immense problem. It is nothing short of cruelty to compel starving and half-fed children to study; nor can poverty make for cleanliness much less to fit women up to become mothers. 'The fact that a woman has no work and no one to care for her is the fundamental social cause of prostitution,' declared Ssyemashka, people's commissary for public health in Russia. The cause and spread of prostitution has already been explained. The feminist movement tends to deal with it more from the ethical point of view and is more ready to offer merciless police vigilance and a cold religion than food to those hungry mouths. None of the half-measures tried in capitalist countries will ever succeed for they do not reach the heart of the problem which is primarily rooted in economic necessity. Statistics prove that 90% of the prostitutes seek that profession from economic pressure and 4/5 are drawn from classes in extreme poverty. The only country which has so far successfully tackled this problem is Russia, for there alone the very root of this evil is sought to be eradicated not only through legislation, but by providing work, homes and more human conditions for these sad victims. When economic want and the social degradation which goes hand in hand with it is removed and woman along with man becomes a conscious living factor, she will resist against her being made to serve merely man's physical and social needs and live the helpless characterless life of a 'Female' to be a house-keeper and breeder of children. She will become an economic as well as a social unit, equal wages for equal work being recognised, and she will discard her position of inferiority. In such a society child-marriage and *purdah* have no place, for these vicious customs only prevail where women need protection and exist only as appendages to man, with no individual life of their own. Human life is one indivisible unit. No one aspect of it can be separated from another; the solution of one has a vital bearing on the solution of the others.

Then we finally come to their political demands. They ask for adult franchise and equal rights with men to enter legislatures, to share the right to legislate. In a country where the majority is denied franchise, the vote has a glamour beyond its rightful proportion. So long as a government is run within a capitalist frame work as in India – that is, finance, big business and private property control the administration, the vote counts for little. The sad plight of millions of peasants and workers in all capitalist countries where adult franchise has been in vogue for years, proves its impotency. The right to exercise the vote or enter legislatures counts for little so long as power is entrenched safely in the hands of vested interest which draws its wealth out of the sweated labour of the masses. Even the few concessions the manual workers had been able to win through years of struggle count for little today in a world lost in catastrophic economic chaos. The sad disillusioned workers today look with hope not to adult franchise, but direct action for their salvation.

Women easily show fervour for the political cause once the message is carried to them. In the political struggle of every country women have played a noble part. 'It is impossible to win the masses for politics unless we include the women,' said a great revolutionary. But the politics of the future are not the bourgeois politics of the past, where women along with men are exploited and used to win the cause of the bourgeoisie and tighten stronger the coils of oppression round them. Revolution after revolution has come in every country, millions have heroically shed their blood in the proud hope of inheriting a freer world and a brighter life, but have emerged out of the columns of smoke and risen from the rivers of blood to sink yet lower. It is only in the new State built on the solid foundation of mass will and mass power that politics in terms of the larger human life will have any meaning. In the old capitalist countries women's share in politics has been very negligible even in the most advanced areas, for politics has never had the same reality for her as her home, and social drudgery has denied the full opportunity to those who did feel the call. Political rights even when won have remained an impotent and dead factor. In England where the feminists fought and won a bitter battle for political rights, the lot of the poor, the working class women and their millions of children, is in no way better than the lot of their poor sisters and their children in France, where women enjoy no political rights. Hence we aim at a State in which the hand of woman is felt, where her influence makes for beauty and sunshine in life. That is only possible when power is wrested from the hands of vested interests and passes into the hands of the creators of wealth. As Lenin says: 'It is our task to make politics accessible to every working woman ... From the moment private property and private ownership of land and factories is abolished and the power of the land-owners and capitalists broken, political duties will become perfectly simple to the working masses and within the reach of all.' They will cease to be a hobby of the leisured few as now and become a dynamic weapon for the good of all.

The fundamental problem which faces India today is the human problem – the problem of creating a free, healthy, clean race. It is not this or that aspect of it which is at stake but the national life as a whole. The solution lies in radically reconstructing society, bringing about a fundamental change in its economic basis and its social character. Then alone can women hope to gain the freedom they thirst for and hand it on as a proud legacy to their progeny [...]

There is one other very vital factor that one sees revolutionising the position of the woman of tomorrow – the right to motherhood. Indivisibly linked up with her economic independence is her sexual independence. One without the other would be innocuous and it alone will make sex equality a true reality for her. Man's fight against woman's struggle to free herself from the penalty of undesired motherhood is one of the bitterest wars waged by him, for he knows that her victory will deal a death blow to his vested interest and devastate for ever that atrocious structure of a 'female character.' In savage life as well as in civilized, woman's irrepressible urge to freedom and desire for a larger life has ever led her to seek escape from the sentence nature decreed upon her, and man has ever sought by law, religious canons, public opinion and penalties to thwart her. The highest form of blessing bestowed on a married woman in India is that she may be blest with eight sons, a usage which no doubt has its origins in the old days of Imperialistic wars, for the more the ambition for Imperial glory, the keener the encouragement given to breeding and greater the consequent enslavement of women. No woman can call herself free who cannot own and control her body and who can be subdued and enslaved through that very quality of fertility which once raised her to the altar as a deity in the dawn of early civilization.

The first argument against birth control is that it will lead to abuse and immorality. But let us look at morality as it prevails today. 'Woman is today condemned to a system under which the lawful rapes exceed the unlawful ones, a million to one,' says Margaret Sanger. 'Fear and shame have stood as grim guardians against the gate of knowledge and constructive idealism. The sex life of women has been clouded in darkness, restrictive, repressive and morbid. Women have not had the opportunity to know themselves or to give play to their inner natures, that they might create a morality, practical, idealistic and high for their own needs ... She must not only know her own body, its care and needs but she must know the power of the sex force, its use, its abuse as well as how to direct it for the benefit of the race. Thus she can transmit to her children an equipment that will enable them to break the bonds that have held humanity enslaved for ages ... Abused soil brings forth stunted growths. An abused motherhood has brought forth a low order of humanity.' A free nation cannot be born out of slave mothers. Few have stressed the immorality of the 'Property Rights' of man over the body of woman, though religious and social codes and legal laws have been loud over the preservation of the chastity and purity of the unmarried. The crusaders in the cause of freedom must destroy that dead hand of the past which seeks to reach out to the present in its attempt to extinguish the flame of new idealism and crush the fingers who would carve out the new woman, new society and a new world.

Motherhood is one of the most sacred and unique functions of womanhood and should not be left to the mercy of exigencies of accidental circumstances or allowed to be determined by ignorance. It must be a conscious task undertaken with joy and a full sense of its responsibilities, controlled and regulated according to the emotional urge and physical capacity of the woman. For this reason sound knowledge on sex, birth control and use of contraceptives will have to be made easily accessible to every woman. From the point of national benefit birth control is necessary for reasons of health, eugenics, social and economic considerations. To put forth the plea that a useful and necessary weapon should not be brought into public use simply because it may be abused is utterly absurd and meaningless. One may as well advocate the stopping of manufacture of matches simply because we can set anything on fire with a match-stick.

The other argument against it is that it will lead to a drastic fall in population. This is a most misleading statement. Mere breeding adds neither to the quality nor the greatness of a nation, it merely lowers vitality, spreads diseases and brings unsound citizens into the world. Those who would have a healthy and clean nation must submit to scientific regulation and stop indiscriminate reproductions. The deadly scourge of venereal disease today is eating into the vitals of 47% of our people and if we would prevent its spreading, birth control is indispensable. That birth control does not necessarily cut down the population too drastically is proved by Russia, a country where birth control is legalised, but where the annual increase of population is something like 3 millions.

The future of women in India lies with those 90% who toil and labour in green fields and dark factories and the amount of consciousness that can be roused in them to the rights of their class, for it is with them that the rights of their sex are bound up and the measure of the power and influence they wield will be determined by the strength of the class they belong to. They who would win freedom for women, vindicate their rights and give them perfect equality, must work for the larger freedom of the exploited and the oppressed and wipe out the society which keeps the few in luxury at the expense of the many. The women's problem is the human problem and not merely the sex problem. It is not literacy or franchise which will fundamentally change their position to their advantage and satisfaction but the root-basis and entire construction of society. We have the two striking examples of Russia on the one hand and Italy and Germany on the other. Whereas in the former the women are establishing complete equality in the physical, material and human relationship, in the latter they are fast losing even their hard-won concessions and rights, for while in Russia vested interest has been overthrown, in Germany and Italy it is making its last desperate bid for an existence which is threatened. India must therefore look to a revolutionised future, when class shall have become a memory of the past, poverty shall have been wiped out and man and woman will have obtained not only their sex rights but their human rights as well and live as noble dignified human individuals and build the new race of equality.

[Source: *Our Cause: A Symposium of Indian Women*, ed. Shyam Kumari Nehru (Allahabad: Kitabistan, 1936), 390–402.]

Huda Shaarawi (1879–1947) was a passionate activist, leading demonstrations, publishing feminist magazines, and attending international feminist conferences. A feminist leader and an Egyptian nationalist who founded the Egyptian Feminist Union, she became its first president (a position she would hold until her death) and went to Rome on its behalf for the Ninth Congress of the International Women's Suffrage Alliance. On returning to Cairo she removed her face veil in public for the first time, a significant moment in Egyptian feminist history. Shaarawi was an essential part of the organization of the first Arab Feminist Conference in Cairo in 1944 and helped to establish the Arab Feminist Union in 1945. The speeches below were given at the first Arab Feminist Conference.

Huda Shaarawi
Pan-Arab Feminism (1944)

The Opening Speech

Ladies and Gentlemen, the Arab woman who is equal to the man in duties and obligations will not accept, in the twentieth century, the distinctions between the sexes that the advanced countries have done away with. The Arab woman will not agree to be chained in slavery and to pay for the consequences of men's mistakes with respect to her country's rights and the future of her children. The woman also demands with her loudest voice to be restored her political rights, rights granted to her by the *Sharia* and dictated to her by the demands of the present. The advanced nations have recognised that the man and the woman are to each other like the brain and heart are to the body; if the balance between these two organs is upset the system of the whole body will be upset. Likewise, if the balance between the two sexes in the nation is upset it will disintegrate and collapse. The advanced nations, after careful examination into the matter, have come to believe in the equality of sexes in all rights even though their religious and secular laws have not reached the level Islam has reached in terms of justice towards the woman. Islam has given her the right to vote for the ruler and has allowed her to give opinions on questions of jurisprudence and religion. The woman, given by the Creator the right to vote for the successor of the Prophet, is deprived of the right to vote for a deputy in a circuit or district election by a (male) being created by God. At the same time, this right is enjoyed by a man who might have less education and experience than the woman. And she is the mother who has given birth to the man and has raised him and guided him. The *Sharia* gave her the right to education, to take part in the *hijra* (referring to the time of the Prophet Muhammad and his flight from Mecca to Medina), and to fight in the ranks of warriors and has made her equal to the man in all rights and responsibilities, even in the crimes that either sex can commit. However, the man who alone distributes rights, has kept for himself the right to legislate and rule, generously turning over to his partner his own share of responsibilities and sanctions without seeking her opinion about the division. The woman today demands to regain her share of rights that have been taken from her and gives back to the man the responsibilities and sanctions he has given to her. Gentlemen, this is justice and I do not believe that the Arab man who demands that the others give him back his usurped rights would be avaricious and not give the woman back her own lawful rights, all the more so since he himself has tasted the bitterness of deprivation and usurped rights.

Whenever the woman has demanded her rights in legislation and ruling to participate with the man in all things that bring good and benefit to her nation and her children, he claims he wants to spare the woman the perils of election battles, forgetting that she is more zealous about the election of deputies than men and that she already participates in election battles, quite often influencing the results. It is strange that in these cases she becomes the subject of his respect and kindness, but when the election battle subsides he denies her what she has brought about.

If the man is sincere in what he says let him prove this by first giving the woman her political rights without her having to go through cruel political battles. In our parliamentary life there is wide opportunity for that in the elections of the governorates and municipality councils, and family affairs councils and in being appointed a member of the senate. Gentlemen, I leave room for the conferees to defend the rights of the woman in all areas.

The Closing Speech

In this final session of the conference please allow me, on behalf of myself and the conference organisers, to thank you for honouring us with your sustained presence during the four days of this conference despite the length of the sessions dealing with issues men are often ill at ease with. I thank you for the concern you have expressed on these matters and for the attention you have given to our objectives, a successful step on the road towards realising our demands. We are proud of this step which signals, thanks be to God, that we have gained the confidence of male intellectuals and reformers in the demonstrated abilities of women in effectively carrying out different kinds of work in the service of country and nation. There are some who still hesitate to give us this confidence and do not understand the benefits that accrue to the nation when women enjoy their political rights. Others fear that the women will compete with them in work. Let me assure you all that if depriving women of the political and civil rights they demand, and that men oppose, would benefit the country, or would increase men's rights, we would relinquish them with pleasure, but, unfortunately, they would be lost rights that men could not use for themselves or for the country. These rights, buried alive, are of no benefit to society.

Every woman who does not stand up for her legitimate rights would be considered as not standing up for the rights of her country and the future of her children and society. Every man who is pushed by his selfishness to trespass on the legitimate rights of women is robbing the rights of others and bringing harm to his country. He is an obstacle preventing the country from benefiting from the abilities and efforts of half the nation or more. He is impeding the advancement of his country and preventing it from being placed in the position it deserves – among the advanced nations whose civilisation was built on the shoulders of women and men together, just as Arab civilisation at the beginning of Islam was built on the co-operation and equality of the two sexes. Now after this feminist conference and the presentation of the cause of women to the public and the placing of its documents in a historical archive, it is incumbent upon man to record on his own page in the historical record that which will honour him and justify his stand before God, the nation, and future generations.

[Source: *Opening the Gates: A Century of Arab Feminist Writing*, trans. Ali Badran and Margot Badran, ed. Margot Badran and Miriam Cooke (Bloomington and Indianapolis: Indiana UP, 1990), 338–40.]

PART SIX
Moral Reform, Sexuality, and Birth Control

While moral reform and related issues like sexuality had been addressed by feminists internationally at least since the founding of the WCTU, for some feminists, these issues dangerously divided women who were striving to work across national boundaries. Karen Offen points out that the IAW, for instance, ruled out any consideration of 'free love, birth control, and 'marriage slavery' ... on the grounds that they had religious, national and cultural implications.'[1] Offen quotes Carrie Chapman Catt, who suggested that the organization 'must advise and aid very gently, but wait for the women themselves of each nation to move effectively.'[2] Leila Rupp notes that there were even tensions between European and North American feminists over sexual expressiveness and relationships with men or with women.[3] Whatever the difficulties and disagreements, women nonetheless worked transnationally to promote reforms of various kinds.

Concern over the double moral standard, operative in different forms in different nations, united feminists internationally and informed their activism quite as much as their essay writing. Madeleine Pelletier devotes a chapter to the subject in her book *L'Émancipation sexuelle de la femme* (1911), arguing that women's dependence on men is the reason such a double standard exists, and that the political emancipation of women will benefit both sexes by overturning this double standard whereby women must be virgins or faithful wives, while men are praised for promiscuity. The essay by the Lebanese scholar Nazira Zain al-Din, one of the lectures included in her book-length treatise *Unveiling and Veiling: Lectures and Views on the Liberation of the Woman and Social Renewal in the Arab World* (1928), presents the veil as an instrument of a sexual double standard. Like Pelletier, al-Din claims that men as well as women stand to gain by a repudiation of the moral and religious hypocrisy that, for her, veiling represented.

As Lucy Bland points out, in Victorian England 'moral and social reform converged,'[4] and this was no less true in Canada or the United States, or many countries around the world. Prostitution was, for many social reformers, 'a key site of intervention,'[5] and one directly linked to the question of a double moral standard as the contributions by Josephine Butler and Dr Paulina Luisi in this section make clear. The traffic in women was often referred to as the white slave trade, a reflection of liberal feminists' conviction in 'personal' rights and an unthinking racialism on the part of Euro-American women activists. As Marilyn Lake puts it, 'Feminists promoted ... the right to the sanctity of the woman's person, to woman's property in her body and in her labour. This theorisation of freedom and citizenship produced the figure of the "white slave" as central to their discourse. The white slave was the slave as woman, the sex slave.'[6] That this was ultimately an imperial discourse is clear: it implies an exclusive concern with white women where trafficking is concerned.

The regulation of prostitution was attacked as a means of maintaining a moral double standard. Josephine Butler's letter to the editor of *The Shield* addresses the link between the trafficking of young English girls on the Continent, specifically in Belgium, and the regulation of prostitution, governed in Britain by the Contagious Diseases Acts, which feminists held to enable promiscuity and prostitution, as well as the spread of disease. The Contagious Diseases Acts, dating from 1868, were developed in the wake of the Crimean War, and were designed to protect British soldiers from venereal disease. They allowed for registering and examining prostitutes and confining them to hospital for treatment. Elizabeth Van Heyningen points out that these acts 'were preeminently imperial legislation, designed to ensure the security of the British Empire.'[7] Legislation was introduced in Cape Colony, in Malta, in Australia, and especially in India, the focus of much of Josephine Butler's campaigning as, throughout the 1870s, she sought the abolition of these acts. While Butler's work on behalf of her Indian 'sisters' also has undeniable imperial elements, she does at least move beyond the discourse of the 'white' slave trade in recognizing the impact of legislation on non-white women.

The letter from the women of Keetmanshoop in Namibia offers another take on the colonial regulation of women's sexuality. In 1939 the colonial administration in South Africa, which ruled Namibia as a protectorate, instituted compulsory medical examinations of unmarried black women in order to check for venereal disease. Margie Orford points out that this measure also lent itself to economic control over black women in Namibia as it allowed for the registration of the women being examined; also since colonial officials did not recognize traditional marriages, most black women were open to the medical exams.[8] This letter written in Afrikaans and signed by several women representing the women of their respective 'locations,' or designated urban areas for blacks, exhibits alarm at the prospect of forced and unwelcome genital examinations and calls for a repeal of the legislation.

Venereal disease was of concern to feminists in the post–First World War era as well. If the military establishment was inclined to represent women as a threat to soldiers by virtue of the venereal disease risk they were meant to pose, for feminists concerned with the increase in venereal disease during the war, it was women who were at risk. The ICW commissioned a report by two French doctors, Thuillier-Landry and Montreuil-Strauss, based on the responses to a questionnaire distributed by the standing committees on Public Health and the Equal Moral Standard to the National Councils of Women affiliated with the ICW. While carefully acknowledging that approaches to addressing venereal disease will vary, since 'every nation has its own mentality,' the doctors discussed the most effective of the methods employed to curb the spread of VD.[9] The ICW resolution proposing the study indicates that as much as venereal disease itself, feminists were concerned about the re-introduction of regulations like the British Contagious Diseases Act. Thus, the committees on Public Health and the Equal Moral Standard were to collaborate in order to 'warn women all over the world to oppose the re-introduction of regulations which, under the guise of health measures against venereal disease, give power for the compulsory examination and detention of women.'[10] That this concern was shared by the IWSA is clear from the report Paulina Luisi prepared as chair of that organization's Committee on an Equal Moral Standard and Against the Traffic in Women. While the subject of Luisi's report is chiefly prostitution, venereal disease is a closely related theme, and with respect to both Luisi indicates the opposition of the national auxiliaries to regulation for fear that it (re) introduce a double moral standard.

More controversial for the international organizations were matters like birth control and abortion. Yet among birth control advocates in the early twentieth century, Margaret Sanger travelled extensively, lecturing and promoting access to information about birth control. Not only was she tremendously influential in Canada, the United Kingdom, and Europe, she also addressed the All-India Women's Conference in 1936. In England, Stella Browne campaigned for women's control over their reproductive health, including reform of the laws governing abortion. For Browne, having access to birth control and abortion gave women the means to explore their sexuality fully, something she regarded as central to mental and physical health. In 'Studies in Feminine Inversion' she argues that lesbian and transgendered women should have the same right, and joined fellow sexologists Edward Carpenter and Havelock Ellis in refusing to regard homosexuality as an abnormality or an illness. Ironically, according to Leila Rupp, 'Before the categorization of the "female invert" or "lesbian" at the end of the nineteenth century, women in the women's movement could more easily form intense and passionate relationships as "romantic friends" or choose to live out their lives as single women without a diagnosis of abnormality.'[11]

NOTES

1 Karen Offen, 'Women's Rights or Human Rights? International Feminism between the Wars,' in *Women's Rights and Human Rights: International Historical Perspectives* (Houndmills, Basingstoke: Palgrave, 2001), 245.

2 Carrie Chapman Catt, 'What Is the Alliance?' *Jus Suffragi* 22, no. 8 (1928): 117–18.

3 Leila Rupp, *Worlds of Women: The Making of an International Women's Movement* (Princeton: Princeton UP, 1997), 98–101.

4 Lucy Bland, *Banishing the Beast: Feminism, Sex and Morality, 1885–1914* (London: Penguin, 1995), 97.

5 Ibid., 98.

6 Marilyn Lake, 'Between Old Worlds and New: Feminist Citizenship, Nation and Race, the Destabilization of Identity,' in *Suffrage and Beyond: International Feminist Perspectives*, ed. Caroline Davey and Melanie Nolan (New York: New York UP, 1994), 281.

7 Elizabeth Van Heyningen, 'The Social Evil in the Cape Colony 1868–1902: Prostitution and the Contagious Diseases Acts,' *Journal of Southern African Studies* 10, no. 2 (1984): 173.

8 Margie Orford, 'Letter from Keetmanshoop,' in *Women Writing Africa: The Southern Region*, ed. M.J. Daymond et al. (New York: Feminist Press at the City University of New York, 2003), 219.

9 *The Crusade against Venereal Diseases: Being a Report based on the replies received to the Questionnaire sent out by the I.C.W. Standing Committees on Public Health and the Equal Moral Standard and Traffic in Women to the Affiliated National Councils of Women* (Executive Committee of the International Council of Women at their meeting at the Hague, 1922), 5.

10 National Council of Women of Canada website, ICW Resolutions, http://www .ncwc.ca/pdf/ICW-CIF_Resolutions.pdf.

11 Leila Rupp, 'Sexuality and Politics in the Early Twentieth Century: The Case of the International Women's Movement,' *Feminist Studies* 23, no. 3 (1997): 578.

Josephine Butler (1828–1906) was an English feminist who became involved in the campaign for higher education for women in the 1860s. She is best known, however, for leading the long campaign for the repeal of the Contagious Diseases Acts from 1869 to 1886. She was also involved in a related campaign to raise the age of consent in the United Kingdom of Great Britain and Ireland from thirteen to sixteen. She travelled widely to extend these struggles internationally, and as a result of her efforts, several international organizations, including the International Abolitionist Federation, were set up to campaign against state regulation of prostitution and the traffic in women and children.

Josephine E. Butler

The Modern Slave Trade, Letter to the Editor of *The Shield* (1880)

Sir –

I have just returned from France, and have recently met friends from Belgium with whom I have conferred on the subject of the measures to be taken against the slavery and slave traffic engendered by the system of regulated prostitution.

The progress of public opinion in France on our question is very encouraging to note. It is not however of this that I ask leave to address to you a few words just now, but on the more mournful side of the picture. Each visit we pay to the Continent implies a deeper insight into this '*Enfer*,' whose utmost depths seem truly unfathomable. We are sometimes entreated not to speak of these things, and even the ears of some of our best friends and fellow workers are too sensitive to endure the bitter cry of these outraged ones when brought very near to them. But, Sir, I can no longer refrain from echoing that cry, as it has recently sounded to me. I consider it to be a duty, even at the risk of scandalizing some of your readers, to tell them of some of the results of this illegal and cruel system; results and facts important for us English people, on account of the heavy responsibility in which they involve us as a nation.

The results I am about to speak of will, no doubt, be questioned by the unimaginative or illogical English reader, who is little capable of perceiving that certain given principles must inevitably produce practical results 'after their kind.' But mournful facts will be, before long, confirmed by witnesses whom it will be difficult for the most skeptical to discredit.

Your readers know something of the traffic in English girls between England and the Continent. M. Alexis Splingard, advocate of Brussels, does well to call our attention to the fact that the official houses of prostitution in Brussels are crowded with English minor girls, that there are far more of these than of any other country, and that their care affords a great opportunity for the English to strike a blow at the whole wicked system of regulation. Girls of other nationalities are as worthy to be fought for as our English girl, and ought to be, and shall be equally cared for by us. But the Penal Codes of other countries forbid the admission of any girl under twenty-one years of age into a *Maison Tolerée*, while the English law has no provision for the prevention of the registration of minors as official prostitutes. It is true that the keepers of these houses abroad do receive French, German, Swiss, and Belgian minors, but they do it at some risk. If an inquiry or search is made from any country, they may incur a heavy penalty. In receiving English minor girls, they offend it is true against the Belgian Penal Code, but they run no risk of having *English Law* brought to bear against them. God grant that they may, however, ere long, feel the strength of English justice and English manhood in this matter, not on behalf of the English minors only, but of all women and of womanhood! There being less risk connected with the trade in English girls, the traders and their clients take full advantage of the fact. Besides the English minor girls of about seventeen or eighteen years of age, whose histories we know, and whom our friends are labouring to save from this slavery, there are others! Let me take you, in imagination, to a house in Brussels, to one in Antwerp, and to another in Paris. A friend of mine enters with the noblest motive, but concealing his purpose from the keeper. It is a magnificent place – a palace; there are gorgeous rooms, and many of them, but there are only six inmates, only six registered at the Bureau des Moeurs as inhabiting the house. My friend knows very well that the householders are too greedy of gain to leave half their rooms unoccupied; he suspects; he goes to the butcher, the baker and other tradesmen who supply this house, and he finds that food, etc., is supplied for double the number of inmates. He goes further in his volunteer detective crusade and this is what he discovers – that in that house there are immured little children, English girls of from twelve to fifteen years of age, lovely creatures (for they do not care to pay for any who are not beautiful), innocent creatures too, stolen, kidnapped, betrayed, got from English country villages by every artifice and sold to these human shambles. The little creatures never leave these rooms. M. Alexis Splingard, in speaking of them, said, '*they never see the sun.*' He was about to add more, but emotion silenced him. Think of this, English fathers and mothers, these children *never see the sun*, and scarcely the daylight for their existence must be concealed from all but their buyers. The presence of these children is unknown to the ordinary visitors of the house. The secret is known to none except to the wealthy debauches who can pay large sums of money for the sacrifice of these innocents to their fastidious and shameful lusts. Hear also this other fact: – These Infants never live more than *two years* after their capture, seldom so much. Their keepers dare not send them when ill to the hospitals. Doctors are to be found who will not betray the secret, but will visit them in the house, but when worn out (at the age of thirteen or sixteen) they are buried (death having often been purposely hastened), without inquest, in the public cemetery. Quick murder with dagger or revolver would be mercy and gentleness compared with the slow and agonising two years' dying to which these beings are doomed. A malediction rests on those hands, on those cities where such crimes are (I will not say permitted) *but are known and not avenged*; and a malediction will rest on us English, if we – knowing these things – do not avenge our own flesh and blood. 'It were better that a millstone were hanged about that man's neck' who aids the destruction of one of these little ones. Yet the men who carry on this wholesale destruction and organised murder or who take advantage of it, are in our midst. The agents for the traffic are living in London, walking freely in the metropolis. Colonel Vincent and his metropolitan detectives know them all familiarly by name, and are aware each month in what city they are plying. We also know them; but our law does not enable us to touch them. This whole subject must be brought before the new Parliament; and meanwhile we are – or rather Providence is – preparing the proofs and the witnesses of these facts, in order that the scepticism of the English mind may be overcome. The London Press will continue its dogged and stupid silence, but there will one day be a terrible reaction, probably a bitter struggle, and blood will be shed before the end; for this organization of rape, torture, and murder cannot go unavenged. Belgian witnesses will tell us, however much refined ears may wince at hearing it, of the padded rooms in these houses (as in lunatic asylums), mattressed floors and walls, to prevent the cries of the tortured girls from being heard outside. They will tell us of the ex-convicts, the 'bullies' who inhabit these houses, and who, on any sign of disaffection in the slaves or of a wish to rescue on the part of a visitor, crawl out from beneath a sofa or table and present a revolver at the head of the recalcitrant or the suspected visitor. They will tell us these things, and more, from their own personal experience, and the warning which has sounded in our ears, *ad nauseam*, for eleven years past – 'you must be *very careful not to exaggerate*,' will be changed for silence, pale faces, and inward self-rebuke. Sir, it is *impossible* to exaggerate the horrors which are being practiced and endured daily. I knew all these things many years ago, but I knew that if I spoke then I should not be believed, and I waited, calling upon God to draw aside the veil, and show this reality of hell on earth which good men refuse to believe. 'Though one rose from the dead,' I often said to myself, 'they will not believe.' The victims *are* now rising from the dead to tell what they have endured, and I trust that these pale spectres will trouble the peace of every honest man until he has put forth his hand to do what he can in the work of holy vengeance.

Mdlle Appia (8, Rue Piepus, Paris), whom I saw last week, told me that she and her colleague at the Refuge which they superintend, have had to make up their minds that one whole year is required to bring back a girl who has been in a *maison tolérée* from a state of mental alienation to one of moderate intelligence, and that then, after that, the *moral* training may begin. For one year they are like 'aliences,' they do not know the right hand from the left, they have forgotten their real name, their parentage, &c. And this is what the partizans of 'necessary vice' are led to, the necessity of vice is followed logically by its organised institution, and this again necessitates the creation of beings to minister to the necessity, who are slaves, and in whom not only feeling, but intelligence, memory and will are extinguished.

When I speak of vengeance let it not be supposed that we on our part, would ever resort to physical force, or make use of any but just, lawful, and moral means in carrying on our great conflict. If force or violence are resorted to it will be by the slave dealers not by us. The only vengeance we desire is the utter demolition of the whole system of Regulation, with its horrible accompaniments and accessories, and the indignant repudiation by society of the doctrines and principles which gave it birth. At the same time, let us not forget that when liberty is not proclaimed to the captive by those who ought to proclaim it, the day of deliverance will nevertheless come, but it will come amidst disorders, and strife, and vengeances which will appal the most stout-hearted among us.

One word more of warning to our English people. Picture to yourselves, fathers and mothers, what that state of degradation must be to which the *men* of a country have sunk who can require and take a vile advantage of the *forcible* subjection by money grasping traders of terrified little girls – of the brutal lusts of male animals, men sunk in vice, diseased, cynical, worn out, old enough often to be these children's fathers or grandfathers. To what a state of hideous carnality devoid of all human sensibility or generosity, must these men have arrived who can devour the flesh of these tender lambs, slain at the shambles for this end – who desire merely a *thing* to debauch – no longer a human being but a *thing* in the shape of a woman, out of which all feeling, all hope, all intelligence, have been stamped by cruelty and violence! These children sometimes cry and weep and call upon their mothers, and it is only when stupefied or maddened by successive glasses of champagne that they cease to struggle. Terrible and heart-breaking as it would be, I had rather, however, have a daughter sacrificed thus, than a son, so lost, so brutalized, as to be capable of feeding his lusts upon a struggling, or slaughtered innocent; and yet this is the level to which our English-men will descend, if they endure the influence on English soil of the laws which regulate vice. Sexual vice is always ugly, but when you add to sexual vice, organised cruelty, rape, and murder, you double and treble its enormity, and you invite a curse upon your nation.

I remain, Sir, in sorrow and anger, and yet in hope.

Yours, &c.,

JOSEPHINE E. BUTLER

[Original source: *The Shield*, 1 May 1880, 63–5; repr. in *Josephine Butler and the Prostitution Campaigns, Volume IV*, ed. Jane Jordan and Ingrid Sharp (London and New York: Routledge Curzon, 2003), 20–4.]

Margaret Sanger (1879–1966) was a US birth control activist, an advocate of negative eugenics, as is evident in the pamphlet reprinted below, and the founder of the American Birth Control League. Her ideas met with fierce opposition in the early twentieth century, but Sanger also won support among feminists and social reformers nationally and internationally. She was instrumental in opening the way to universal access to birth control.

Margaret H. Sanger
Family Limitation (1914)

Introduction

There is no need for any one to explain to the working men and women in America what this pamphlet is written for or why it is necessary that they should have this information. They know better than I could tell them, so I shall not try.

I have tried to give the knowledge of the best French and Dutch physicians translated into the simplest English, that all may easily understand.

There are various and numerous mechanical means of prevention which I have not mentioned here, mainly because I have not come into personal contact with those who have used them or could recommend them as entirely satisfactory.

I feel there is sufficient information given here, which, if followed, will prevent a woman from becoming pregnant unless she desires to do so.

If a woman is too indolent to wash and cleanse herself, and the man too selfish to consider the consequences of the act, then it will be difficult to find a preventive to keep the woman from becoming pregnant.

Of course, it is troublesome to get up to douche, it is also a nuisance to have to trouble about the date of the menstrual period. It seems inartistic and sordid to insert a pessary or a suppository in anticipation of the sexual act. But it is far more sordid to find yourself several years later burdened down with half a dozen unwanted children, helpless, starved, shoddily clothed, dragging at your skirt, yourself a dragged out shadow of the woman you once were.

Don't be over sentimental in this important phase of hygiene. The inevitable fact is that unless you prevent the male sperm from entering the womb, you are going to become pregnant. Women of the working class, especially wage workers, should not have more than two children at most. The average working man can support no more and the average working woman can take care of no more in decent fashion. It has been my experience that more children are not really wanted, but that the women are compelled to have them either from lack of foresight or through ignorance of the hygiene of preventing conception.

It is only the workers who are ignorant of the knowledge of how to prevent bringing children in the world to fill jails and hospitals, factories and mills, insane asylums and premature graves.

The working women can use direct action by refusing to supply the market with children to be exploited, by refusing to populate the earth with slaves.

It is also the one most direct method for you working women to help yourself *today*.

Pass on this information to your neighbor and comrade workers. Write out any of the following information which you are sure will help her, and pass it along where it is needed. Spread this important knowledge!

The Small Family System: Is It Injurious or Immoral? By Dr C.V. Drysdale. B.W. Huebsch, New York City.

The Problem of Race Regeneration, by Havelock Ellis. Moffat, Yard & Co., New York City.

The Task of Social Hygiene, by Havelock Ellis. Houghton Mifflin & Co. Boston, Mass.

Christianity and Sex Problems, by Hugh Northcote. M.A.F.A. Davis Co., Philadelphia, Pa.

The Limitation of Offspring by the Prevention of Conception, by Dr Wm. J. Robinson. Critic & Guide Co., N.Y.C.

Husband and Wife, by Dr Lyman B. Sperry. Fleming H. Revell Co.

Jezebel, by Dr Charles Hiram Chapman. Portland, Ore.

War Brides, by Marion Craig Wentworth.

A Nurse's Advice to Women

Every woman who is desirous of preventing conception will follow this advice:

Don't wait to see if you do *not* menstruate (monthly sickness) but make it your duty to see that you *do*.

If you are due to be 'sick' on the eight of August, do not wait until the eighth to see, but begin as early as the fourth to take a good laxative for the bowels, and continue this each night until the eighth.

If there is the slightest possibility that the male fluid has entered the vagina, take on these same nights before retiring, five or ten grains of quinine, with a hot drink. The quinine in capsule form is considered fresher, but if this is taken do not use alcoholic drinks directly after, as it hardens to capsules, thus delaying the action of the quinine.

By taking the above precautions you will prevent the ovum from making its nest in the lining of the womb.

Women of intelligence who refuse to have children until they are ready for them, keep definite track of the date of their menstrual periods. A calendar should be kept, on which can be marked the date of the last menstruation, as well as the date when the next period should occur.

Women must learn to know their own bodies, and watch and know definitely how regular or irregular they are: if the period comes regularly every twenty-eight days (normal) or every thirty days as is in the case of many young girls.

Mark it accordingly on your private calendar; do not leave it to memory or guess work.

Only ignorance and indifference will cause one to be careless in this most important matter.

A very good laxative (though it is a patent medicine) is Beechams Pills. Two of these taken night and morning, four days before menstruation, will give a good cleansing of the bowels, and assist with the menstrual flow. Castor oil is also a good laxative.

The American physicians may object to this advice because Beechams Pills are a patent medicine. But until they are willing to give open advice on this subject, we must resort to such as the least harmful, until such time as they do.

If a woman will give herself attention BEFORE the menstrual period arrives, she will almost never have any trouble, but if she neglects herself and waits to see if she 'comes around,' she is likely to have difficulty.

If the action of quinine has not expelled the semen from the uterus, and a week has elapsed with no signs of the menstrual flow, then it is safe to assume conception has taken place.

Any attempt to interfere with the development of the fertilized ovum is called an abortion.

No one can doubt that there are times where an abortion is justifiable but they will become *unnecessary when care is taken to prevent conception.*

This is the *only* cure for abortions.

There is current among people an idea that conception can take place only at certain times of the month. For instance: ten days after the menstrual period, and four or five days before the next period. This is not to be relied upon at all, for it has been proven again and again that a woman can conceive at any time in the month. Do not depend upon this belief, for there is no reliable foundation for it. There is also the knowledge that nursing after childbirth prevents the return of the menstrual flow for several months and conception does not take place. It is well not to depend upon this too much, especially after the fifth or sixth month, for often a woman becomes pregnant again without having 'seen anything' or without her realizing that she has become pregnant. She thus finds herself with one at the breast and another in the womb. Use some preventive.

Again, it is believed that conception cannot take place if the woman lies upon her left side at the time of the act. It makes no difference which side she lies upon; she can become pregnant if the semen is not prevented from entering the womb.

Perhaps the commonest preventive excepting the use of the condom is 'coitus interruptus,' or withdrawal of the penis from the vagina shortly before the action of the semen. No one can doubt that this is a perfectly safe method; and it is not considered so dangerous to the man as some authorities have formerly viewed it, but it requires a man of the strongest will-power to be certain that he has withdrawn before any of the semen has been deposited in the vagina. It is very difficult to determine exactly whether this has been done. The greatest objection to this is the evil effect upon the woman's nervous condition. If she has not completed her desire, she is under a highly nervous tension, her whole being is perhaps on the verge of satisfaction. She is then left in this dissatisfied state. This does her injury. A mutual and satisfied sexual act is of great benefit to the average woman, the magnetism of it is healthy giving. When it is not desired on the part of the woman and she has no response, *it should not take place.* This is an act of prostitution and is degrading to the woman's finer sensibility, all the marriage certificates on earth to the contrary notwithstanding. Withdrawal on the part of the man should be substituted by some other means that does not injure the woman.

Douches and Their Importance

The most important part which every woman should learn in the methods of preventing conception is to cleanse herself thoroughly by means of the vaginal douche.

After the sexual act go as quickly as possible to the bath room and prepare a douche. Lie down upon the back in the bath tub. Hang the filled douche bag high over the tub, and let the water flow freely into the vagina, to wash out the male sperm which was deposited during the act.

Do not be afraid to assist the cleansing by introducing the first finger with the tube and washing out the semen from the folds of the membrane. One can soon learn to tell by the feeling when it is sufficiently clean. It is said, the French women are the most thorough douchers in the world, which helps greatly in keeping the organs in a clean and healthy condition, as well as preventing the male sperm from reaching the womb to mate with the ovum.

Following are some of the solutions to be used for the douche, which, when carefully used, will kill the male sperm or prevent its entering the womb:

Lysol – is a brown oily liquid which added to water forms a clear soapy solution. One teaspoonful of Lysol to 2 quarts of water (warm) makes a good solution for douching. Mix into a pitcher or vessel before placing it in the bag.

Bi-chloride – Get the tablets blue or white from the druggist; the blue are less dangerous to have about because of the color. Always mix this solution thoroughly in a glass or pitcher before turning it into the bag. Never drop the tablet directly into the bag. One tablet to two quarts of water makes a splendid solution for preventive purposes.

Potassium Permanganate – This also makes a good solution, especially where there is a vaginal discharge. The special objection to this is that it stains the skin and clothing. This can be purchased in crystal form, and one teaspoonful dissolved in two quarts of water is the proper strength.

Chinosol is highly recommended as a vaginal douche, as being less injurious to the membranes than bichloride.

Salt solution – Mix four tablespoons of table salt in one quart of warm or cold water and dissolve thoroughly. This is good and cheap.

Vinegar solution – Many peasants in Europe use vinegar as an antiseptic almost exclusively. One glassful to two quarts of water is the strength usually desired. Cider vinegar is preferred. Douche afterward with clear water.

Cold water douche – This will sometimes remove the semen quite effectively without the aid of an anti-septic. But as the semen can hide itself away in the wrinkled lining of the vaginal cavity, the cold water will only impede its progress for a time. As soon as the warmth of the body revives its activity, the semen continues on its journey to meet the ovum.

Every woman should possess a good quart rubber douche bag called fountain syringe. Hang it high enough to insure a steady direct flow.

Bulb syringes, such as the whirling spray syringes, have been found satisfactory by many women for the purpose of injecting antiseptic solutions. Directions with syringe.

Some women use the douche before the sexual act as a preventive. If this is done, any astringent such as boric acid, alum, citric acid, hydrochlorate of quinine used in the solution will do. Only a pint of solution is needed for this purpose, following the act a larger douche is used as a cleanser. This can also be allowed with the regular antiseptic douche.

The Use of the Condom or 'Cots'

There is little doubt that a thorough douching of the genital passage with an antiseptic solution performed by skilled hands immediately after the sexual act would destroy the male sperm, and nothing else would be necessary. But there is always the possibility that the sperm has entered the womb before the solution can reach it.

It is safer therefore to prevent the possibility of the contact of the semen and the ovum, by the interposition of a wall between them. One of the best is the condom or rubber 'cot.'

These are made of soft tissues which envelope the male organ (penis) completely and serve to catch the semen at the time of the act. In this way the sperm does not enter the vagina.

The condoms are obtainable at all drug stores at various prices. From two dollars a dozen for the skin gut tissues to one fifty a dozen for the rubber tissue. These are seamless, thin and elastic and yet tough; if properly adjusted will not break. Fear of breaking is the main objection to their use. If space has not been allowed for expansion of the penis, at the time the semen is expelled, the tissue is likely to split and the sperm finds its way into the uterus. The woman becomes pregnant without being conscious of it. If on the other hand care is given to the adjustment of the condom, not fitting it too close, it will act as one of the best protectors against both conception and venereal disease. Care must be exercised in withdrawing the penis after the act, not to allow the condom to peel off, thereby allowing the semen to pass into the vagina.

It is desirable to discard the condom after it has been used once. But as this is not always done, care must be taken to wash the condom in an antiseptic solution before drying it and placing it away for further use.

The condom is one of the most commonly known preventives in the United States. It has another value quite apart from prevention in decreasing the tendency in the male to arrive at the climax in the sexual act before the female.

There are few men and women so perfectly mated that the climax of the act is reached together. It is usual for the male to arrive at this stage earlier than the female, with the consequence that he is further incapacitated to satisfy her desire for some time after. During this time the woman is in a highly nervous condition, and it is the opinion of the best medical authorities that a continuous condition of this unsatisfied state brings on or causes disease of her generative organs, besides giving her a perfect horror and repulsion for the sexual act.

Thousands of well meaning men ask the advice of physicians as to the case of the sexual coldness and indifference of their wives. Nine times out of ten it is the fault of the man, who through ignorance and selfishness and inconsiderateness, has satisfied his own desire and promptly gone off to sleep. The woman in self defense has learned to protect herself from the long hours of sleepless nights and nervous tension by refusing to become interested.

The condom will often help in this difficulty. There are many girls who have had no education on this subject, no idea of the physiology of the act, who upon any contact of the semen have a disgust and repulsion, from which it takes some time to recover. Much depends upon the education of the girl, but more depends upon the attitude of the man toward the relation.

The Pessary and the Sponge

Another form of prevention is the pessary. This is one of the most common preventive articles used in France as well as among the women of the middle and upper class in America. At one time the cost of these ranged up to seven dollars, as they were imported into this country from France. Today they are manufactured in this country, and may be had from fifty cents up to two dollars. The Mizpath is the name of one of the best and costs one dollar and a half at any reliable drug store.

They come in three sizes – large, medium and small. It is well to get the medium size, as the small ones are only for very small boned women and easily get out of place.

In my estimation a well fitted pessary is the surest method of absolutely preventing conception. I have known hundreds of women who have used it for years with the most satisfactory results. The trouble is women are afraid of their own bodies, and are of course ignorant of their physical construction.

They are silly in thinking the pessary can go up too far, or that it could get lost, etc., etc., and therefore discard it. It can not get into the womb, neither can it get lost. The only thing it can do is to come out. And even that will give warning by the discomfort of the bulky feeling it causes, when it is out of place.

Follow the directions given with each box, and learn to adjust it correctly; one can soon feel that it is on right. After the pessary has been placed into the vagina deeply, it can be fitted well over the neck of the womb. One can feel it is fitted by pressing the finger around the soft part of the pessary, which should completely cover the mouth of the womb. If it is properly adjusted there will be no discomfort, the man will be unconscious that anything is used, and no germ or semen can enter the womb.

If the woman should fall asleep directly after no harm can happen, and it is not necessary to take a douche until the following morning. Take part of about a quart of an antiseptic douche BEFORE the pessary is removed; after removing it continue the douche and cleanse thoroughly.

Wash the pessary in clear cold water, dry well and place away in the box. One should last two years, if cared for.

I recommend the use of the pessary as the most convenient, the cheapest and the safest. Any nurse or doctor will teach one how to adjust it; then women can teach each other.

It is not advisable to wear the pessary all the time. Take it out after using, and wear it only when needed. A little experience will teach one that to place it is a simple matter.

Sponges

Sponges can also be had at the drug store. They have a tape attached to them to be conveniently removed. They should be soaked in an antiseptic solution for a few minutes before coitus and then introduced into the vagina far up as they can be placed. Some physicians have recommended the use of the cotton plug, instead of the sponge, to be soaked in a solution of three per cent carbolic and glycerine, before the act. The male sperm is destroyed by the weakest solution of carbolic acid. Some of the peasants in Europe use the cotton plug soaked in vinegar for the same purpose and find it satisfactory. In this country a boric acid solution had been used for the same purpose and with satisfactory results. Of course this requires a saturated solution, as, for instance, one teaspoonful of the powder to a cup of water stirred until dissolved.

Sponges and plugs can be recommended as perfectly safe, if followed by an antiseptic douche before the removal of the plug or sponge, thus preventing the sperm from entering the womb. The problem is: to kill the male sperm upon entering the vagina, or to wash it out or to kill it directly afterwards. A weak solution of alum may also be used for cotton plugs and sponges, *also carbolated vaseline on plugs.*

Vaginal Suppositories

Suppositories are becoming more generally used in U.S.A. than any other method of prevention.

These may be found at any reliable pharmacy. The majority of them are made from cocoa butter or gelatine, which makes it necessary that they be deposited in the vagina several minutes before the act, in order for them to melt. Special ingredients negate the effect of the male seed.

Any reliable druggist will make this up for you:

Boric acid, 0.6 grams
Salicylic acid, 0.12 grams
Chinosol, 0.12 grams
Glycerine gelatine, 6.0 grams
Allow twenty minutes for melting

Another form of suppository, which was recommended by a physician who charged a fee of $10 for the prescription, is the following:

Boric acid, 10 grains
Cocoa butter, 20 grains

Another suppository, which is the same as the well-known Aseptikon, is the following:

Salicylic acid, 2 grains
Boric acid, 10 grains
Quin, purol (alkal), 1 grain
Chinosol, 2 grains
Cocoa butter, 90 grains
M. f. supos. Glob No. 1
(Introduce into vagina three minutes before act.)
Still another found reliable is:
Boric acid, 10 grains
Salicylic acid, 2 grains
Quinine bisulphate, 3 grains
Cocoa butter, 60 grains

Practically all vaginal suppositories act as preventives but the most commonly used is the Aseptikon, manufactured by the Chinosol Company. They are to be secured at any reliable druggist's upon demand. They should be kept in a cool place. They are not poisonous and cause no injury to the membranes.

They are distributed into a box costing 85 cents. The prescription quoted above can be made up more cheaply however.

It is interesting to note that in the rural districts in France the peasant women make up their preventive suppositories themselves, placing them carefully away in glass jars. This is one of the recipes which has been used:

Gelatine, 1 part
Water, 2 parts
Glycerine, 5 parts
Bisulphate of Quinine – one-half a part

Make this into a paste. Allow to spread out and solidify, then cut into pieces of 2 grammes each, wrap separately and put in a cool place (air-tight).

I have given in the foregoing pages the most commonly known means of prevention. Personally I recommend every woman to use a well fitted pessary and learn to adjust it.

Birth control, or family limitation, has been recommended by some of the leading physicians of the United States and Europe. The movement can no longer be set back by setting up the false cry of 'obscenity.' It has already been incorporated into the private moral code of millions of the most influential families in every civilized country. It will shortly win full acceptation and sanction by public morality as well.

In cases of women suffering from serious ailments, such as Bright's disease, heart disease, insanities, melancholia, idiocy, consumption, and syphilis, all a physician is allowed to do is to tide these women through their pregnancies if possible. Even though the life of the woman is positively endangered, he cannot relieve her without calling a colleague in consultation. Therefore, the mortality of mothers suffering from these diseases and their infants is very high, and premature births common.

To conserve the lives of these mothers and to prevent the birth of diseased or defective children are factors emphasizing the crying need of a sound and sane educational campaign for birth control.

[Source: *Family Limitation*, 5th ed. (1914; repr. 1916), 2–16. History of Women microfilm, reel 9989, Gale International, Ltd.]

Madeleine Pelletier (1874–1939) was the first French woman to take the exam to become a psychiatrist, and the first to work in asylums as an intern. A feminist and a socialist, Pelletier helped *La Solidarité des femmes* (Women's Solidarity) become one of the most radical feminist organizations of its day.

Pelletier also co-founded the French Socialist Party, and often represented it at international meetings. Pelletier wrote about women's education and dress, abortion and birth control, and religion, among other topics. Not one to preach without practising, Pelletier wore her hair short and was known for her cross-dressing. After travelling to the Soviet Union, she returned to France to join first the communist then the anarchist movements. Though she was partially paralyzed by a stroke in her later years, Pelletier continued to practise abortion, for which she was eventually arrested.

Madeleine Pelletier

From *L'Émancipation sexuelle de la femme* (1911)

A Single Moral Code for Both Sexes

Depending on whether one is a man or a woman, the word 'decent' means something different. A decent man is one who does not wrong his peers; a woman, for her part, can wrong others and still be considered decent, because hers is a very special order of decency: it consists in subscribing to the law of man.

There is no independent existence for the young woman living under the guardianship of her parents. She awaits a husband. A single duty comprises all the others for her. Indeed, the others do not even exist except in light of it: the young woman must remain a virgin for the man she will marry. To ensure the preservation of virginity, primitives confined young women just as they did married women to ensure their fidelity. Civilization has removed the bars, but moral prescriptions, indeed material arrangements, accomplish the same goal.

Among the French bourgeoisie, the young woman hardly goes out without a chaperon. She knows little of life because her experience is limited to parental relationships. She only knows the outside world through novels that she often must read in secret. In the middle classes and the working classes, the young woman may go out alone, but she is far from enjoying a freedom equal to that of the young man. If she is not followed to the office or the workshop, her time is calculated in such a way that she can hardly be free without liberating herself completely. Often, independently of her parents, her brother will watch over her conduct. He satisfies without constraint his own sexuality, but he believes just the same that it is his right to take his sister to task for the least deviation, and the parents, far from rebuking him for it, congratulate him for fulfilling his brotherly duty. The young woman, moreover, raised as she is for slavery, would hardly know how to make use of her liberty. She emancipates herself from the guardianship of the family only to fall under the yoke of her husband [...]

Men do everything they can to lead women to transgress the law of man. In this respect, as in many others, the interest of the individual is in conflict with the interest of the collective. Marriage, which puts a woman in the care of a guardian, binds a man at least to a certain degree. He also understands that he is able to satisfy his desires largely outside of it. Through seduction, ruses, intimidation, sometimes through violence, man leads woman into illegitimate love. On this point, conventional morality reprimands him, but real morality excuses and even glorifies him. Given that woman is considered less a person than an object to be consumed, the reputation of seducer equals that of the happy man who is successful in life.

But if to seduce is praiseworthy, to be seduced is on the contrary shameful. The disrepute that the seduced girl suffers is fundamentally a material depreciation; through the loss of her virginity she falls to the level of a second-hand object; she is a young woman with a stain, 'spoiled merchandise difficult to dispose of.'

Thus, 'decency' for the young woman is her virginity. For the married woman, decency is fidelity; the decent woman is the one who does not betray her husband. Just as society erects all sorts of barriers to protect the young woman's virginity, so it erects social barriers to guard the fidelity of the wife [...]

Even more than the young single woman, the married woman is incited by men to transgress sexual morality for their benefit, but while adultery is permissible for the husband, if not exactly by law at least by public sentiment, a woman's adultery is practically a crime. The man does not really believe himself constrained to practice conjugal fidelity; public opinion even makes it a woman's duty to pardon her adulterous husband, and the one who refuses courts blame. But the adulterous woman is treated as the real culprit. The husband who pardons her, far from being lauded, is ridiculed, while the husband who kills the adulterous wife is considered both by public opinion and by jury to be exercising his right.

This inequality in attitudes toward the same act, depending on whether it is committed by one or the other sex, is justified by traditionalists from the point of view of the prospective child.

The man takes fierce pride in his paternity. If he has doubts about his paternity, founded or not, he believes he has the right to make the life of the child he suspects of not being his unbearable, and despite habitual compassion toward children, the public excuses him. Meanwhile, fatherly sentiment is far from strong. The newborn hardly appears more than a 'package of red flesh' to the father, to use the contemporary journalistic expression. If it is a boy, the man is proud to have reproduced his sex, the superior sex; if one assures him the child resembles him, he is flattered. True affection only develops as an effect of cohabitation. There is also, at the heart of paternal pride, a feeling of ownership. The man, sovereign master over his wife, keeps for himself alone the right to give her children; an outside paternity strikes him as a robbery committed against him.

Even from the point of view of the barbarian, male adultery ought not to be more excusable than female adultery. If the adulterer brings no bastards into his own household, he brings them into another, unless he weighs down some poor single girl with the burden of maternity. But current morality does not take account of these eventualities. Man is considered to have the right to draw as he pleases from the female herd. If another man is thereby wronged, too bad; he should have watched better over the women who, as wives, sisters, or daughters, depended on him: 'My roosters are on the loose, watch your hens.'

Thus, the reason for the double moral standard has to do with woman's dependence on man. Like most causes, this one is ignored by most of the interested parties. The mother raises her daughter according to the principles by which she was raised, and only what is good for the man is considered by women to be an absolute good.

The spinster who lives alone in chastity has no husband or jealous lover to fear, her virginity because of her age having ceased to have value and yet she hardly behaves differently than a woman under a man's authority. If she is delayed outside the home, she quickly returns. What will the concierge say, what will the neighbours think if she returns to the house *at an unwarranted hour*? What would they say especially if she were to stay out all night? It would be nothing less than a scandal. And yet in this lodging no-one awaits her; she has no children, no elderly parents who require her care; alone in life, she has no dependents. That means nothing. Just as though she were not on her own, her life is regulated. She portions out her outings, and takes care that they are not too frequent for fear that she be rebuked for *never being at home*. Her methodically empty existence is like a cult rendered to the masculine sex whose authority weighs even on her.

Were she to emancipate herself from her neighbours, moreover, this spinster would hardly know what to do with her liberty. Society in its entirety would remind her every instant that she belongs to the enslaved sex. In the street, she is subject to masculine insults. If she is young and pretty, men hail her with obscene words, filthy propositions; sometimes they add gestures to the words, the smutty touch. If she is unattractive, she suffers gibes from passersby. The ugly man passes unnoticed, but a woman has no right to be ugly. If she is old, she is insulted for her age. In England, women are more respected and not snubbed in this way, but in France customs have not changed in this respect since the times of the barbarians. Police regulations protect men from solicitations, but woman, no doubt because she is weaker, is left to the mercy of those who accost her. In streets she helps to maintain through her financial contributions, she moves as though in enemy territory, hurrying along [...]

I fully expect to be rebuked by 'decent' people in claiming for women the freedom to go to cafés. They will cry that I am claiming the right to debauchery. It is all the same to me. Going to a café does not necessarily mean one is debauched or a drunkard. As long as there is no other place where one may see people, read newspapers, listen to music, or meet people without the complicated formalities of an invitation, the café will have its use. If men are in general better informed than women it is partly thanks to the café, which permits them to rub shoulders with others; however intelligent the woman, she remains in the inferior condition of one who is isolated. But it is clear that the freedom of the café cannot be the object of a law; it is up to women themselves to preserve its unfettered quality by rejecting the prejudices that keep them away. For a long time to come, to be sure, women will not feel entirely at ease in cafés, but one only triumphs over public hostility with courage. Besides, men are beginning to grow accustomed to seeing women coming in to quench their thirst; eventually they will cease to be surprised at the sight of women gathering in cafés as they do themselves. It is this direction that feminists must go; they will serve the cause better in this way than by installing, as they do, 'homes' for women that only serve to preserve women's original timidity.

Once woman has won the right to political life, her emancipation from custom will proceed more rapidly. The special virtues demanded of her will no longer have a place, and the equality of the sexes in matters of love will be acknowledged. Will man suffer from this emancipation? Quite the contrary. Montaigne, in his *Essays*, said that the sexual tie would be the sweetest of all if it were possible to add the union of mind to that of the body.

Currently, the law of morality that obliges the woman who wants to remain honourable to be chaste condemns the young man to venality. To satisfy their desires, intelligent and cultivated men are reduced to the company of ignorant and unintelligent women. They must endure insipid chatter, pretend to take an interest in tedious gossip. Either sex could only gain if to be worthy of the title of decent woman it sufficed to perform the social duties of a decent man.

[Source: *L'Émancipation sexuelle de la femme* (Paris: M. Giard & E. Brière, 1911), 1–2, 3–4, 5–9, 9–11. Trans. M. Moynagh. Available through the Gerritsen Collection.]

Stella Browne (1880–1955) was an English feminist, socialist, and campaigner for women's reproductive rights. More radical than mainstream suffrage feminists, Browne served as a link between early-twentieth-century sex reformers and the women's movement. Browne helped to found the Abortion Law Reform Association in 1936.

F.W. Stella Browne
Studies in Feminine Inversion (1923)

What I have to put before you to-day are only very fragmentary data, and suggestions on a peculiarly obscure subject. They have, however, this validity; that they are the result of close and careful observation, conducted so far as I am consciously aware, without any prejudice, though they would probably be much more illuminating had they been recorded by an observer who was herself entirely or predominantly homo-sexual [...]

The cases which I will now briefly describe to you are all well-known to me; they are all innate, and very pronounced and deeply rooted – not episodical. At the same time – though I am sure there has been, in some of them at least, no definite and conscious physical expression – they are absolutely distinguishable from affectionate friendship. They have all of them, in varying degrees, the element of passion [...]

Case A. Member of a small family, but numerous cousins on both sides. The mother's family is nervous, with a decided streak of eccentricity of varying kinds, and some of its members much above the average in intelligence. The father's family much more commonplace, but robust. She is of small-boned frame, but childish rather than feminine in appearance, certainly not in the least masculine. (Throughout this paper, I use the adjectives masculine and feminine, only as referring to the pitch of the voice and outline of the body as modified by greater or less development of the secondary sexual characteristics; *not* to mental or emotional qualities.) Quick and deft in movement, neat and rather dainty about her appearance. Much manual dexterity and indefatigable motor energy and activity. Never happy unless occupied in some fairly strenuous way, though she will not, of course, admit this, and derives great moral satisfaction from the consciousness of her own industry. Unfortunately many of these activities seem, to an unprejudiced observer, to be petty and irrelevant, and a subconscious way of finding a vent for frustrated emotional force. A good organizer, but with too little sense of proportion or breadth of view for a position of supreme control. Strong sense of responsibility and capacity for detail. Methodical. Mentally very positive, emotionally shy, reserved, proud and extremely jealous. Some musical talent and keen appreciation of music. Can be extremely generous and devoted where her affections are stirred. Is virtually an agnostic, without having at all thought out the implications of that position. An absorbing devotion to a woman relative; a devotion of an unmistakably, though I believe unconsciously, passionate kind completely dominates her life; it has almost all the manifestations of a really great love; intense interest, idealisation, unremitting care, joy in service, and unsparing sacrifice of her own comfort and of the happiness of third parties. Has had some very long and close friendships with other women, into which the same element entered, to a much slighter extent; notably one with a cousin, a smart, shrewd, worldly little person, who did not lose by it. She is fond of children and has a gift for dealing with them, and very sympathetic and tender to animals [...] Has an instinctive horror of men [...] and also quite a definite antagonism to them socially [...] As a rule, criticises even the most harmless or upright and well-intentioned men, unsparingly.

I consider that this woman's unconsciousness of the real nature of the mainspring of her life, and the deprivation of the liberating and illuminating effect of some definite and direct physical sex-expression, have had, and still have, a disastrous effect on a nature which has much inherent force and many fine qualities. Her whole outlook on life is subtly distorted and dislocated, moral values are confused and a false standard of values is set up. The hardening and narrowing effect of her way of life is shown in a tremendous array of prejudices on every conceivable topic: caste-prejudices, race-prejudices, down to prejudices founded on the slightest eccentricity of dress or unconventionality of behaviour; also in an immense intolerance of normal passion, even in its most legally sanctioned and certificated forms. As to unlegalised sex-relationships, they are of course considered the very depth alike of depravity and of crass folly. And all the while, her life revolves round a deep and ardent sex-passion, frustrated and exasperated through functional repression, but entirely justified in her own opinion as pure family affection and duty! Though the orthodox and conventional point of view she takes on sex-questions, generally, would logically condemn just *that* form of sex-passion as peculiarly reprehensible.

Case B. Also the member of a small family though with numerous cousins, paternal and maternal. Family of marked ability – on both sides, especially the mother's. Of very graceful and attractive appearance, entirely feminine, beautiful eyes and classical features, but indifferent to her looks and abnormally lacking in vanity, self-confidence and animal vitality generally, though no one is quicker to appreciate any beauty or charm in other women. I think she is a pronounced psychic invert whose intuitive faculties and bent towards mysticism have never been cultivated. Keen instinctive delicacy and emotional depth, enthusiastically devoted and generous to friends; much personal pride (though no vanity) and reserved. Too amenable to group suggestions and the influences of tradition. Artistic and musical tastes and a faculty for literary criticism which has lain fallow for want of systematic exercise. Rather fond of animals and devoted to children, especially to young relatives and the children of friends. Has done good philanthropic work for children, but is essentially interested in *persons* rather than in theories, or institutions. Is a devout Christian and I think gets much support and comfort from her religious beliefs. A distaste, even positive disgust, for the physical side of sex, which is tending more and more to manifest itself in conventional moral attitudes and judgments. General social attitude towards men less definitely *hostile* than that of Case A, but absolutely aloof. Devoted to women friends and relatives, yet has had no full and satisfying expression of this devotion. This inhibition of a whole infinitely important set of feelings and activities has weakened her naturally very sound judgment, and also had a bad permanent effect on her bodily health.

Case C. The sixth, and second youngest of a large and very able and vigorous family. Tall, and of the typical Diana build; long limbs, broad shoulders, slight bust, narrow hips. Decidedly athletic. Voice agreeable in tone and quite deep, can whistle well. Extremely energetic and capable, any amount of initiative and enthusiasm, never afraid to assume responsibility; very dominating and managing, something of a tyrant in practise, though an extreme democrat in theory, and most intolerant towards different emotional temperaments. Scientific training; interested in politics and public affairs; logical and rationalistic bent of mind. Emotionally reserved, intense, jealous and monopolistic. Will always try to express all emotion in terms of reason and moral theory, and is thus capable of much mental dishonesty, while making a fetish of complete and meticulous truthfulness. An agnostic and quite militant and aggressive. The episode in her life which I observed fairly closely was a long and intimate friendship with a young girl – ten years her junior – of a very attractive and vivacious type, who roused the interest of both men and women keenly. Cleverness and physical charm in girls appealed to her, but she instinctively resented any independent divergent views or standard of values. For years she practically formed this girl's mental life, and they spent their holidays together. When the girl fell in love with and impulsively married a very masculine and brilliantly gifted man, who has since won great distinction in his special profession, C's agony of rage and desolation was terrible and pitiable, though here again, she tried to hide the real nature of her loss by misgivings as to the young man's 'type of ethical theory' – her own phrase! I cannot for a moment believe that she was ignorant of her own sex-nature [...] She is a very strong personality, and a born ruler. Her attitude towards men was one of perfectly unembarrassed and equal comradeship.

Case D. Is on a less evolved plane than the three aforementioned, being conspicuously lacking in refinement of feeling and, to some extent, of habit. But is well above the average in vigor, energy and efficiency. A decided turn for carpentry, mechanics and executive manual work. Not tall; slim, boyish figure; very hard, strong muscles, singularly impassive face, with big magnetic eyes. The dominating tendency is very strong here, and is not held in leash by a high standard of either delicacy or principle. Is professionally associated with children and young girls, and shows her innate homosexual tendency by excess of petting and spoiling, and intense jealousy of any other person's contact with, or interest in the children. I do not definitely know if there is any physical expression of her feelings, beyond the kissing and embracing which is normal, and even, in some cases conventional, between women or between women and children. But the *emotional tone* is quite unmistakable; will rave for hours over some 'lovely kiddy,' and injure the children's own best interests, as well as the working of the establishment, by unreasonable and unfair indulgence [...]

Case E [...] Two assistant mistresses at a girls' boarding-school were completely inseparable. They took all their walks together, and spent all their time when they were 'off duty' and not walking, in one another's rooms – they occupied adjoining rooms.

One of them was a slim, graceful, restless, neurotic girl with a distinct consumptive tendency; quick in perception and easy in manner, but it seemed to me then, and it seems still, decidedly superficial and shallow. The other partner was an invert of the most pronounced physical type. Her tall, stiff, rather heavily muscular figure, her voice, and her chubby, fresh-coloured face, which was curiously eighteenth-century in outline and expression, were so like those of a very young and very well-groomed youth, that all the staff of the school nick-named her 'Boy,' though I do not believe any of them clearly realised what this epithet, and her intimacy with a woman of such strongly contrasted type, implied. 'Boy' was extremely self-conscious and curiously inarticulate; she had musical tastes and played rather well – not in the colourless and amateurish style of the musical hack. I think music was an outlet for her. She was also fond of taking long walks, and of driving, and of dogs and horses. Beyond these matters I don't think I ever heard her express an opinion about anything [...] There was some idealism in the relationship, at least on 'Boy''s side [...]

I know of two modern English novels in which the subject is touched on with a good deal of subtlety, and in both cases in association with school life. *Regiment of Women* by Clemence Dane – a brilliant piece of psychology, and a novel by an Australian writer, cruder and shorter, but unmistakably powerful, *The Getting of Wisdom* by Henry Handel Richardson [...]

I would draw your attention to one quality which two of my cases have in common, and to a very marked degree: the maternal instinct. Two of the most intensely maternal women I know are cases A and B, both congenital inverts [...]

This problem of feminine inversion is very pressing and immediate, taking into consideration the fact that in the near future, for at least a generation, the circumstances of women's lives and work will tend, even more than at present, to favour the frigid, and next to the frigid, the inverted types. Even at present, the social and affectional side of the invert's nature has often fuller opportunity of satisfaction than the heterosexual woman's, but often at the cost of adequate and definite physical expression. And how decisive for vigor, sanity and serenity of body and mind, for efficiency, for happiness, for the mastery of life, and the understanding of one's fellow-creatures – just this definite physical expression is! The lack of it, 'normal' and 'abnormal,' is at the root of most of what is most trivial and unsatisfactory in women's intellectual output, as well as of their besetting vice of cruelty. How can anyone be finely or greatly creative, if one's supreme moral law is a negation! Not to *live*, not to *do*, not even to try to understand [...]

I think it is perhaps not wholly uncalled-for, to underline very strongly my opinion that the homo-sexual impulse *is not in any way superior* to the normal; it has a fully equal right to existence and expression, it is no worse, no lower; *but no better.*

By all means let the invert – let all of us – have as many and varied 'channels of sublimation' as possible; and far more than are at present available. But, to be honest, are we not too much inclined to make 'sublimation' an excuse for refusing to tackle fundamentals? The tragedy of the repressed invert is apt to be not only one of emotional frustration, but complete dislocation of mental values.

Moreover, our present social arrangements, founded as they are on the repression and degradation of the normal erotic impulse, artificially stimulate inversion and have thus forfeited all right to condemn it. There is a huge, persistent, indirect pressure on women of strong passions and fine brains to find an emotional outlet with other women. A woman who is unwilling to accept either marriage – under present laws – or prostitution, and at the same time refuses to limit her sexual life to auto-erotic manifestations, will find she has to struggle against the whole social order for what is nevertheless her most precious personal right. The right sort of woman faces the struggle and counts the cost well worth while; but it is impossible to avoid seeing that she risks the most painful experiences, and spends an incalculable amount of time and energy on things that should be matters of course. Under these conditions, some women who *are not innately or predominantly homosexual* do form more or less explicitly erotic relations with other women, yet these are makeshifts and essentially substitutes, which cannot replace the vital contact, mental and bodily, with congenial men.

[Original source: *Journal of Sexology and Psychoanalysis* 1 (1923): 51–8; repr. in *Sexology Uncensored: The Documents of Sexual Science*, ed. Lucy Bland and Laura Doan (Chicago: University of Chicago Press, 1998), 61–6.]

Nazira Zain al-Din (1905–?) was born in Lebanon, the daughter of a distinguished religious scholar who schooled her at home in Islamic thought. Her book *Unveiling and Veiling*, published in Beirut in 1928, argued that all Muslims, including women, were free to interpret religious texts. She wrote at a time when veiling was still pervasive in most countries of the Middle East, but Zain al-Din cited the Qur'an and other religious texts in support of her claim that veiling was not ordained by Islam.

Nazira Zain Al-Din
Unveiling and Veiling: On the Liberation of the Woman and Social Renewal in the Islamic World (1928)

Two Views: One View on the Unveiled World and the Other on the Veiled World

Ladies and Gentlemen, in the beginning I compared opposites, the numbers of the veiled and the unveiled. I found that the veiled are not more than a few million Muslims living in towns. Those in the villages of the Islamic world and more than one thousand seven hundred million in other nations are not veiled. They have rejected the veil that they had previously worn. I have noticed that the nations that have given up the veil are the nations that have advanced in intellectual and material life. Such advancement is not equalled in the veiled nations. The unveiled nations are the ones that have discovered through research and study the secrets of nature and have brought the physical elements under their control as you see and know. But the veiled nations have not unearthed any secret and have not put any of the physical elements under their control but only sing the songs of a glorious past and ancient tradition. With such singing they sleep in stagnation.

I have seen many intellectuals of the nations where women are still veiled advocating unveiling, but I haven't seen anyone in the unveiled nations advocating or preferring the veil. That is, I haven't seen anyone who has tried unveiling and then has preferred the veil. Even if some westerner in his hypocritical words makes the veil appear in a favourable light, he is only pleased with the beauty of the oriental veil while at the same time he would reject the veiling of his mother, wife, sisters, and daughters because of the harm in the veil he favours for others.

I cannot imagine that in the advanced nations which have discovered the secrets of nature and harnessed its powers, which have not let anything pass without examining it to the fullest, where the struggle between right and wrong is continuous until right becomes victorious, nations which have produced works on social subjects we view as masterpieces of literature and sociology, have neglected to study veiling and unveiling to understand the benefits and disadvantages. I cannot think that our own ignorance can bring us any greater understanding of what honour is than the unveiled nations possess in learning nor that our conduct is superior to theirs, nor that their women going outside unveiled and enjoying their freedom is evidence of their lower conduct and corrupt morals.

Yes, I looked into all that and I could not but consider it evidence of their superior education and elevated conduct. When our esteemed ladies who wear the veil go to a western country, they take off the veil and the men accompanying them do not prevent them from doing this the way they do when they are at home or after they return. This is because we have more faith in the conduct of westerners than in our own conduct. The conduct of western men has been influenced by mingling with women and thus western men have based their habits and morals on logic and reason looking to benefits and positive results while our conduct and morals are based on our customs whatever they may be.

I shall never forget a conversation between an eastern man advocating the veil and an unveiled western woman who enjoyed her freedom and independence. The easterner said to the westerner, 'Our nature cannot accept your customs. Our customs are more noble than yours and our men support our women. The man according to his right walks in front of his wife but in your country the woman walks in front of the man as if she were the provider.'

The western woman said, 'If you really want to protect your wife please let her go in front of you so that you can watch out for her the way our men do, rather than letting her walk behind you so that she would misuse her freedom and get hurt.'

The eastern man paused and said, 'Truly, westerners ground their customs in reason. Reason alone should dictate custom.'

It is not fitting for us to say that we who are only a few million, most of whom are not advanced, are more honourable than the one and a half billion people (in the world) most of whom are more advanced than we are.

It is not honourable for us to deny our shortcomings and believe we are perfect and claim that our customs are the best customs for every time and place. This conceit and false presumption is a barrier to the reform we seek. When the nation feels its shortcomings that is the first step in its advancement.

It is inconceivable that we claim to be defenders of honour while the veil is our strongest shield. We must understand as everyone else does that honour is rooted in the heart and chastity comes from within and not from a piece of transparent material lowered over the face.

We have to realise, as the advanced unveiled world does, that good behaviour and honour come from sound upbringing grounded in noble principles and virtues. We are shortsighted if we think that the veil keeps evil away from women and that those in the rest of the world exceeding one and a half billion are all in the wrong while we are in the right.

He Who Bears Falsehood to the People Has to Provide Evidence to Them

I have mentioned the above, Ladies and Gentlemen, fearful that I might be confronted by someone who does not use logic and reasoning to make his points, but relies on untruths concerning the advanced unveiled nations. He may look where vice is but he does not wish to rise up to see where virtue resides. He might have seen their baser women and generalises from them, subsuming the noble and honourable in his generalisation, and hurls accusing arrows of untruths at them even though human beings should not be like flies pouncing on tails (of animals) and ignoring their heads.

He does not dare to lord scientific and industrial knowledge over the unveiled nations because these are tangible matters. Therefore he accuses them of lack of morals and good conduct because these are not tangible. Thus he is overwhelming in this even though his accusation is false.

You know, gentlemen, nations are like trees whose rotten fruits fall to the ground and vermin, humans and animals go after them. Those who are wise and advanced look only to the good and ripe fruits, by which the tree is identified.

My antagonist seems to be ignorant of that or is playing the role of the ignorant. He wants to know the tree by the fallen fruits he sees beneath it. Moreover, he does not want to recognise that in every nation, however advanced, there is a lower class overcome by corruption whose morals and conduct have deteriorated because they did not have the chance to be educated and to develop so that they could reach the higher level in the nation.

Gentlemen, we should do our best to see to it that the majority in our nation are able to have an education and the means to develop. Then it would be possible for us to be proud before our nations ...

We should not believe everything we hear and take our evidence from falsehood, especially evidence that brings great evil to the nation by obstructing reform and maintaining continual backwardness.

We should abstain from hurling lies and falsehoods at others, which is alien to morality and decent debate and only brings down those who lie. Instead we should subscribe to truth, sound reasoning, unbiased knowledge, and correct behaviour. In accordance with the will of God almighty and the will of His Prophet, may God bless him ... (She quotes from the Quran and Hadith.)

How Men Should Support Women

Gentlemen, you have heard the response of the western woman to the Eastern man who was proud to support his woman and to walk in front of her. Yes, let men support women in principle. Every man supports his own wife spending money on her, but he has no authority over any other woman. An *aya* from the Quran was sent by God about this in relation to Saad ibn al-Rabi from al-Naqba and his wife Habiba; the words are related specifically to husband and wife. Men should know that authority is limited by the benefit deriving from it. Therefore, men should attain high moral development as God wants and society requires. This would make women strong and self-dependent, for when people have virtue, dignity, and honour they turn away from evil, not out of fear of punishment, nor because of reward, nor because of an immovable obstacle, but because evil is ugly and such a person would not allow herself to engage in lowly acts.

The Prophet, God bless him, said, 'I was sent to help you attain the highest morality.' Does not the highest morality come from the soul? Pieces of cloth over faces shall never be a measure of morality.

The Veil (Niqab) Is an Insult to Men and Women

It is not beneficial to men and women that men should just support women physically and financially, nor is it beneficial that man rule over those whom the *Sharia* did not give him the right. It greatly harms the two sexes that every man continues to insult his mother, daughter, wife, and sister, suspiciously accusing them of bad morals and keeping them confined to a cage, as the venerable Qasim Amin said, 'With their wings cut off, heads bent down, and eyes closed. For him (man) is freedom and for them (women) enslavement. For him is education and for them ignorance. For him is sound reasoning and for them inferior reasoning. For him is light and open space and for them darkness and imprisonment. For him are orders and for them obedience and patience. For him is everything in the universe and for them part of the whole he has captured.'

May God be merciful to Qasim and bless his pen about which 'The Poet of the Two Countries' has said, 'He tears down the ugly and builds the beautiful, returning to the Sunna of the Drawer. He sheds light even when he writes with the dark water of the night.'

Unfortunately, if the veil (*hijab*) implies the inability of the woman to protect herself without it, it also reveals that man, however well brought up and in spite of supporting the woman, is a traitor and a thief of honour; his evil should be feared and it is better that the woman escapes from him.

You, Man, the Supporter

If some women, because of the ignorance into which you have cast them, have not recognised the insult to them and to men by the veil, is it easy for you, the man who has kept himself free seeking perfection and good conduct, to bear this insult that comes to you and to your mother, daughter, wife, and sister?

Does the woman who escapes from you, or approaches you lowering the veil over her face, or turns her back on you, confirm your high status, as she might think and say and you might think and say, or is it a great insult? Does this constitute the woman's decorum, chastity and modesty? If so, then men should not be without these precious attributes; let them wear veils and let them meet each other and meet women lowering veils over their faces the way women do.

[Source: *Opening the Gates: A Century of Arab Feminist Writing*, trans. Ali Badran and Margot Badran, ed. Margot Badran and Miriam Cooke (Bloomington and Indianapolis: Indiana UP, 1990), 272–6.]

F.W. Stella Browne
The Right to Abortion (1929)

The Ethical Theory

From a practical standpoint, the essential requisite for sexual reform on a scientific and humanist basis is the power to separate the fulfilment of the sexual impulse from the procreation of children, except and unless the latter are desired. Both practically and ethically, the possibility and the discussion of Birth Control by contraception have made an enormous difference to the climate of opinion in these matters. But British public opinion has not faced the further logical implication of the humanist point of view – the full right of free motherhood, as it is claimed by Left Wing feminism and socialism on the Continent, and as I have ventured to express the demand for this right in lectures to Labour and Secularist audiences, and in the *Malthusian*, the *New Generation*, and the publications of Dr W. J. Robinson since the middle of the War years, and in the B[ritish] C[ommonwealth] Conference in 1922.

Our comrades from Central and Eastern Europe and from France will no doubt give an absorbing account of the progress of this demand in their countries. As to the history of the concept of abortion as a crime, I would refer you to Dr Havelock Ellis's sixth volume of *Studies in the Psychology of Sex*, and to the admirable monograph in German 'Fort mit der Abtreibungsstrafe' ('Away with the Penalty on Abortions') by Dr Stoecker, Dr Stabel, and Herr S. Weinberg.

I will confine myself to a few remarks on the present situation in England and to stating the case for the absolute freedom of choice on the woman's part in the early months of pregnancy.

The Legal Position

By the Offences Against the Person Act of 1861 (cl. 100, section 58), the unlawful administration of drugs or use of instruments by a pregnant woman to herself, or (whether she be with child or not) by any person to her, with intent to procure miscarriage, is a felony punishable by penal servitude or by imprisonment at the discretion of the Courts. Section 59 makes the unlawful procuring of such drug or instrument a misdemeanour, whether the pregnancy is actual or imaginary. Thus a woman may be convicted of conspiracy to procure her own miscarriage. The *lawful* procurement of miscarriage can only take place by qualified physicians in specific and established cases of danger to the woman's health and life, as in cases of contracted pelvis and certain forms of heart and kidney disease, and is hedged round with difficulties.

In 1924 an attempt was actually made to extend the scope of this merciless Act, in Clause 2 of the Children and Young Persons Protection Bill – a Private Members' Bill. This Clause – a legal and grammatical curiosity – would have made it possible to change an indictment from homicide to procuring abortion; and would have made the penalty penal servitude for any term less than ten years or more than three, or imprisonment with or without hard labour for not less than two years.[1]

Fortunately it was possible to organize enlightened opinion against this Clause and to bring such pressure to bear that the Bill was dropped. But the possibilities of Puritan reaction are by no means exhausted.

The recent Bill in the House of Lords for the Penalizing of Infanticide during Birth is an example!

Some Illogicalities

Now with the sacramental or traditional point of view on Abortion, as on all Sex questions, Birth Control, Marriage, Divorce, Abnormality – it is impossible to really argue. One can only realize it, and submit or fight it. But with the half-hearted, who profess and practise birth control, but express abhorrence of abortion, it is possible to come to grips. For, firstly, in the early stages of pregnancy, nothing we can recognize as a living human being is extinguished. And secondly, the present position of our contraceptive knowledge and technique indicates very clearly that an absolutely 100 per cent reliable and otherwise acceptable preventive is not only as yet undiscovered, but possibly in many cases *undiscoverable*. I would refer doubters to the excellent Second Report of the International Committee on Birth Control, which quite frankly faced the probability that in many cases abortion was the only possible method of preventing increase. (Abortion, N.B. by new, endocrinological methods.)

Every worker in our cause knows that for every one case of poor women demanding contraceptive knowledge and help, there are at least three (some say eight of ten) who swallow poisons or fatally injure themselves with hatpins,

---

1 Children and Young Persons Bill, 1924.

There is the Clause 2, paragraph 1: –

(1) 'If a person commits any acts which, if it had caused the death of a person would have rendered him liable to be prosecuted and punished for criminal homicide, and by such act causes the death of an unborn child, he shall be guilty of felony and shall be liable upon conviction or indictment to be *kept in penal servitude for ten years or any shorter term not less than three years, or be imprisoned with or without hard labour for any term not exceeding two years.*'

The second paragraph provides that no such indictment is to be tried at Quarter Sessions; the third defines the 'unborn child' to mean the child wholly *in utero*. The fourth paragraph runs: 'If upon the trial of an indictment for homicide the jury are not satisfied that the accused person is guilty of the offence charged in the indictment, *but* are satisfied that he is guilty of an offence under this Section, *they may acquit him of the offence charged in the indictment, and find him guilty of that other offence*, and in that case he shall be liable to be punished as though he had been convicted on an indictment for that other offence.'

– From *The New Generation*, November 1923.

knitting needles and even meat-skewers (!!) in the effort to procure miscarriage. Or they achieve an incomplete operation, which by their very ignorance and its incompleteness becomes septic. Every hospital, every nurse, every doctor knows of such cases, where the help that can be given is asked too late.

No Necessary Danger

Let this be cried from the house-tops. The sacrifice of women is unnecessary. A miscarriage is not necessarily fatal or permanently injurious. The statistics of the great Russian experiment prove that very clearly, even apart from the possible extension of methods by endocrine injections.

The old-fashioned ignorance – which some birth controllers seem willing to uphold – was quite needless. Women have been sacrificed where there was *no* need, though here, too, there is great individual variation.

The Case for Complete Freedom

An apparently plausible case may be made for restricting the right to an abortion in the early months to cases where the mother is unmarried, or to cases of rape. The situation of the deserted girl, pregnant and alone, is extraordinarily poignant and worthy of all consideration, but I think it would be a mistake on principle to confine the right to abortion to such cases as this. For it would be making the institution of marriage, which some of us regard as obsolete, or at any rate as only one among many equally justifiable and excellent ways of life and love, the Criterion; and marriage was made for humans, not humans for marriage. The position of many married women who are unwilling expectant mothers in the slums of our large towns, or lonely villages, overcrowded, underfed, with unemployed husbands and swarms of starving children, is equally hideous and even more deadly hopeless, though without the especial emotional agony of Gretchen or Hetty Sorel. (Too often agony has given place to numb apathy.) It would be a tragic mistake to limit our demand to the unmarried mother. The women's need and wish, not a ring or a scrap of paper, should be the test. Secondly, in cases of enforced motherhood due to rape, a particularly ghastly and brutal injustice is perpetrated. But I think that it would be an equal mistake to ask for relief to unwilling motherhood in the case of rape only. To begin with, such cases are notoriously difficult to prove, and it is admitted by sexologists that many false accusations of this crime are made. To limit the right to abortion to such cases would be to place a premium on such accusations. Is that wise or just? Moreover, it is probable that the vast majority of unwilling and enforced conceptions take place within the marriage tie. This is no reason for refusing relief, but it is a reason against legal quibbling and pettifogging. It would be just as foolish to refuse relief from unwanted motherhood to women whose general (not sexual) character and ethics were contemptible. Do we want to perpetuate cads' stock? Is a child to be inflicted as a punishment?

Eugenic Considerations

On the racial damage caused by unwilling maternity and pregnancy, I hold a very strong view. I am aware that this view cannot be scientifically proved, as yet, but such an authority as e.g. Professor F. A. E. Crew has admitted its force.

I pass on to two final considerations in favour of free right to abortion (by skilled doctors) up to the fourth month, if the woman desires it.

Psychic Effect of Pregnancy

It is accepted that the physical processes of gestation have tremendous effects on mind and emotions. Many women who have conceived a child unwillingly, or, at least, unintentionally, soon become entirely reconciled to the prospect. The new life with its powerful fermentations in their nerves and veins lulls their resistance to sleep and conquers them. If at the end of three months this has not happened, and the woman's refusal is still definite and passionate, I submit that the case for relief is overwhelming – both for the sake of the mother and the unborn. Do we want more nervous wrecks, more embittered, and yet half-hearted mortals?

Abortion Erotically Preferable

Again, in many cases all known forms of contraception are inadequate and unsatisfactory, in that they destroy or impair pleasure. This is largely a matter of individual constitution, and is of course an added reason for further research in contraceptive methods. But it is also a reason for *extending the area of living*, and the *art of living*, and for making it possible for e.g. women in whom the portio vaginalis and the cervix are as nervously sensitive and active as the clitoris – for as Dr Van de Velde pointed out in 1925, there are these distinct types, and a tremendous register of genital diversity – to enjoy and benefit by normal inter-course, without enforced motherhood. In many cases, if the habit of early abortion is once established it becomes automatic. Health may be fully preserved by the resources of modern science. I note that one distinguished doctor in one of the Maternal Mortality and Official Futility Conferences was chiefly concerned lest the possibility of safe and healthy abortions should become known to women. Slaves are safer!

Against that attitude I protest and rebel.

The new demand for free motherhood is going to be the next step in feminism.

Finally, before I close, may I express my thanks, and appreciation, too, of the work of those Russian and German pioneers who have made this cause practical politics in their countries, and to the little group of medical and social workers – Dr Eden Paul, Dr Binnie Dunlop, and Dr W. J. Robinson, and the Editors of the *Malthusian* and *New Generation* – who have not been afraid to support women's right to freedom of choice, or, at least, to allow the case to be put? In the name of the mothers I have known, I thank them. And I thank those here who believe that knowledge, freedom, and honesty are preferable to ignorance, terror, blood-poisoning; and an enormous amount of safe and secret blackmail.

In this matter I would quote one of our dead leaders:

Over our face a web of lies is woven,
Laws that are falsehoods bind us to the ground.

Who will help in this fight? Not abortion, but forced motherhood, is the crime.

Paulina Luisi (1875–1950) was a leader of the feminist movement in Uruguay. She was the first woman in the country to obtain a medical degree (1909) and was a keen supporter of women's rights, representing Uruguay in international women's conferences and lending support to feminists across Latin America. She founded the Consejo Nacional de Mujeres (National Women Council), the Alianza de Mujeres para los Derechos Femeninos (Alliance of Women for Women's Rights), and the Uruguayan and Argentine branches of the International Abolitionist Federation. In 1922, the Pan-American Conference of Women named her honorary vice-president of the conference. Luisi was the first Latin American woman to serve as a government representative at the League of Nations.

Paulina Luisi

International Woman Suffrage Alliance: Committee on an Equal Moral Standard and Against the Traffic in Women – from the Report of the Chairman (1926)

III

Sociological and health experts are at the present moment fully preoccupied with the closely allied questions of how best to combat venereal disease, the traffic in women and the regulation of prostitution. The formation by the League of Nations of a Committee to deal with these questions has brought them within the sphere of practical action, by Governments in the first place, and in the second by all those who, having made a thorough study of the matter, are capable of giving effective co-operation, either directly or by unofficial measures, or lastly by means of propaganda. It is in this way that the Geneva Convention of 1921 against Traffic in Women has come to be ratified by many of the States Members of the League, and that further progress will yet be made. Having myself the honour to be a member of this Committee as the Delegate of my Government, I may have occasion (as has already been the case) to put forward and support the woman's point of view on questions which touch her so nearly, provided such action falls within my sphere as a national representative.

Of all the laws, rules and regulations which down the centuries have helped to place women in a position of inferiority, none has been so powerful in creating in the spirit of men and peoples a sentiment of scorn and contempt for our sex as the degrading idea of a double standard of morals. It is from this that there has sprung that worst attack on women's dignity, the regulation of prostitution. For many, many years enlightened women have fought against this infamous system, which in spite of their efforts, still persists in many countries. At the present day, the continuance of such a doctrine and of the laws which are founded on it, is a shameful anachronism unworthy of our civilisation.

The acid tests to which we have been submitted during the second decade of this century, have disproved once and for all the inferiority of women. How then can we at this present day submit to regulations, more or less legal, which transform a woman into a mere chattel, a piece of tainted merchandise? Just so long as women are submitted to this degrading system of regulation, so long as the double standard of morals continues to exist, not only in law but in the spirit of our moral code, will the emancipation of women have failed to achieve its full object. It is, therefore, essential that the women of all the countries of the world should unite in one supreme effort to put an end for all time to this hideous survival from the barbarous past.

If this united effort is to gain its end, we need first of all a common programme, and then a carefully studied plan of action. At Rome we obtained agreement to the principle, not of course on the general lines which had long been accepted, but on certain secondary questions on which differences of opinion had existed. At this Congress, we must agree upon a common plan of action in order to achieve a complete practical realisation of our ideals.

In every country our doctrine meets the same obstacles, which, from time to time, come to life even in countries where the shameful system has been abolished once but where efforts are made to re-establish it in a form which still leaves the woman to bear alone the blame and the punishment. We shall need all our energy and all our courage in this unresting fight, but we have the will to win and we are determined to gain our end. For every enlightened woman throughout the world, this is a duty: for those who are yet unenfranchised, within the limits of their power; for those who have already won their political rights, with the full strength of their power as active members of the civic life of their countries. The duty is ONE: to throw the whole weight of our energy into this struggle, in which are involved the morale of our people, the dignity of our sex, and the future of our children and our race.

IV

For the work of the present Congress, a questionnaire was sent to all the national members on the Committee and to the Presidents of the Auxiliaries, in accordance with the usual practice of the Alliance; the Secretariat in London kindly undertaking this work [...]

In preparing the questionnaire for the present Congress, I was guided by the above considerations, and on these lines (submitted for the approval of the Board at its meeting in May 1924) I have drawn up the questionnaire in three parts.

PART I

In order to acquire an exact knowledge of the facts based on enquiries conducted by women, which are not always quite in agreement with official enquiries, I put in an *evidential section* dealing with both countries where regulation still exists and those where it has been abolished. We cannot, however, ignore the fact that the question of regulation wears many aspects, and that many people who claim to be abolitionists are in fact regulationists or neo-regulationists, that is to say they admit ordnances, laws or regulations which appear to be equal as between the sexes, but are inapplicable or applicable only to women, and which in consequence would re-impose a double standard of morals. Others do not differentiate between questions which relate to health, morals or public order. I have therefore thought it desirable that the questionnaire should demand such detailed information as would allow of these different questions being clearly separated.

I have not forgotten, moreover, that certain countries having done away with state regulation of prostitution, consider themselves as abolitionist, while maintaining in matters of public health special regulations affecting prostitutes, which from the point of view of a single moral standard, leave them still among the upholders of regulation.

In considering the different replies received, our Committee is in a position to take a clear view of this subject.

Finally, since it is claimed that certain special ordnances applying to women only are necessary for the public health and their abolition is refused on the grounds of Professor Fournier's famous argument to 'common sense,' I have added in the third paragraph of the questionnaire an enquiry as to regulations dealing with unnatural vice, which is unfortunately sufficiently common to be considered along with prostitution as a source of contagion and dissemination of venereal disease. Are there in fact health measures to deal with such cases, whose exponents are quite as likely to spread contagion as is the woman prostitute?

If it is claimed that the necessities of public health justify the existence of special laws for prostitutes, do not these necessities equally call for measures to deal with men who follow the same profession? It is precisely in order to have yet one more proof of the one-sided laws which offend against the doctrine of a single standard of morals that I have thought it of use to obtain evidence on this point. It is not enough merely to know what laws exist, we must also study their application and the form in which they are drawn. This is a matter of the first importance for women in the claim for equality in all fields, and particularly in that of the moral standard, which we desire shall be a high one, uncompromising towards vice and debauchery, the same for both the halves of the human race.

Where the law is different, injustice is obvious. But where the law is *in appearance* equal between the sexes, is it so in fact? Here is another point of great importance which is dealt with in paragraph 4 of Section A of the questionnaire.

Women who have given careful study to these difficult problems are asked to give us their observations on the results obtained by such laws and regulations in their countries, and also what modifications they consider necessary (Paragraphs 5 and 6 of Section A of the questionnaire), in order to secure the realisation of the Resolution passed at the last Congress of the Alliance in Rome, 1923, namely:

The abolition of the regulation of prostitution and the suppression of the traffic in women and children.

The establishment of an equal moral standard and a consequent equality of the sexes before the law.

PART II

The second section of the questionnaire deals with the progress gained in the period between our last Congress and the present Congress.

The first question is concerned with adhesion to or ratification of (in the case of countries which require to ratify) the Geneva Convention of 1921 against Traffic in Women. Secondly, we deal with any new laws for the suppression of commercialised vice; and thirdly we ask for information as to progress made during the period towards an equal moral standard either by administrative measures, or by public health measures.

The replies received show that there has been real progress in the realisation of our ideals, and I am very happy to be able to state the fact.

The questionnaire also asked for information as to progress achieved in regard to the questions raised at the Rome Congress. In this connection I may point out: –

For the first question, 'Compulsory declaration of venereal disease,' opinions differ, but show a certain leaning in favour.

For the second question, 'Free treatment,' the replies show that in every country there is genuine anxiety to deal with the prevention of venereal disease otherwise than by mere regulation of prostitution. The Cause is marching to victory.

For the third question, 'Marriage certificates,' the position is about the same as in 1923.

For the fourth question, 'Sex education,' although the introduction of this subject into the curricula of schools is not much further advanced than in 1923, the idea and unofficial experiments have advanced considerably. We may affirm that the idea is spreading and that before long we shall see it definitely accepted.

Finally, I think, I may add to the sum of work done and progress accomplished, the steps taken and the proposals made by me to the Advisory Committee against the Traffic in Women and Children of the League of Nations, in my capacity as Government Delegate of Uruguay and with the consent of my government.

The first very serious question arose with regard to the formulations of suggestions to be submitted to the Council regarding the protection of girl and women immigrants for presentation to the International Diplomatic Conference at Rome for the preparation of an International Convention on Immigration. Several useful and necessary proposals for the protection of women immigrants against the traffic in women were made to the Advisory Committee by members. But these proposals, while protecting women, were also a menace to their liberty and equality of rights in all countries. Under the proposals made, the woman immigrant became liable to be considered as a minor, and the legal measures asked for threatened to become infringements of her liberty: they might indeed have meant the abrogation of many of those rights to full adult status which we have already won in many countries. Woman would have thus become once again the 'eternal minor,' under legal restrictions even greater than those to which she is still submitted in many places.

The resolution submitted was not accepted without difficulties, but with the support of the Danish delegate, Dr Estrid Hein, was finally accepted and submitted by the council to the Diplomatic Conference in Rome, which accepted it. This resolution, which was communicated to you at the time, reads as follows:

> The recommendation is made to the Governments that measures passed with a view to protecting women immigrants against traffic in women shall be drafted in a form which shall not interfere with the personal liberty of adult women. Legal measures taken with regard to such women shall not differ from those taken with regard to all immigrants without regard to sex.

In a communication from the Board dated the 19th May 1924, your attention was again called to this resolution, since it is our duty to ensure that all laws or regulations regarding the protection of women against this traffic shall accord with this resolution which is a guarantee of the liberty and legal emancipation of our sex. We must guard jealously every step won in the emancipation of women, which in the domain of morals even more than in others, are easily lost again under this pretext of protection against the traffic in women. This is why I call your attention once more to this particular item in our work, and I submit it for your approval as I have included it among the resolutions to be submitted by our Committee to the Congress.

Two other questions equally important have been submitted by me to the Advisory Committee, also with the approval of my Government and in accordance with suggestions made to the Alliance Board. These questions have been adopted by the Committee for study and therefore I suggest that they should be also adopted for study by our Alliance Committee during the period before us; they are: –

(1) The age of consent in connection with sex offences.
(2) Child marriage from the point of view of morals, health and commercialised vice.

To come back to our questionnaire and to the progress achieved since our last Congress, a summary of the replies received has been made and is submitted for your consideration in the following pages [...]

PART III

The third section of the questionnaire is devoted to subjects for study at this present congress. I have put forward two questions, the first of which may be made, if desired, to cover the whole field.

I have in fact asked what administrative measures should be put forward in order to advance our views in a country where regulation still obtains, from the point of view of public morals, street order, etc., and from the point of view of measures needed for public health.

In the course of my studies and in the discussions of various medical and scientific congresses which I have attended, having moreover been asked to collaborate in preparing a bill for the Parliament of my own country, I have found that well meaning legislators are full of hesitation and uncertainty as to the practical form to adopt in applying our principles, while taking into account the grave problems of prophylaxis and hygiene.

I thought it would be very interesting to learn the opinion and have the advice of women in the different countries as to how such reforms should be drafted, by asking them to consider themselves in the position of members of Parliament and to draft bills on such a supposition. For those countries which still adhere completely to the principle of regulation, and in others which still do so in reality though they may have adopted the outward form of the freedom we advocate, the true abolitionist should find a mainspring of ideas and suggestions in a study made by suffragists as to the practical application of the doctrine of abolition.

We know well the arguments on which the partisans of regulation base the maintenance of their vicious system, the replies received should have given us the fruit of the reflection and study of each of our colleagues.

I have made a summary of the replies received referring solely to measures proposed in the various replies, grouped in different categories, in order to facilitate discussion.

Finally, I have proposed as Resolutions from our Committee some of the most important measures proposed in the replies received to this first question.

The Congress will discuss these measures and afterwards we shall be able to give a summary of the resolutions which have obtained most support and which may be taken as representing the suffrage view and thus form a scheme for our future programme for combatting venereal disease by methods in accordance with our views.

If the replies received have not been very numerous, they are nevertheless extremely interesting and instructive. They show that on the main points, all women, whether enfranchised or unenfranchised, hold the same point of view. They have all declared in favour of:

THE ABOLITION OF REGULATION OF PROSTITUTION FROM THE POINT OF VIEW OF ADMINISTRATION.
FROM THE HEALTH POINT OF VIEW, THE PROVISION OF DISPENSARIES FOR FREE AND SECRET TREATMENT.

[Source: *International Woman Suffrage Alliance: Committee on an Equal Moral Standard and Against the Traffic in Women – from the Report of the Chairman* (1926), 7–8, 9–13, 18–19. Pamphlet. Women's Library, London Metropolitan University]

When colonial authorities threatened to introduce forced vaginal examinations of black women in Namibia, eight women from the town of Keetmanshoop wrote a collective letter of protest. Each woman signed on behalf of the women in the area in which she resided. The letter was originally written in Afrikaans, which was the mother tongue of many southern Namibians.

Katrina Stephanus, Sofia Labau, Magdalena Vries, Katrina Skeier, Emmillie Adams, Sofia Kloete, Katrina de Klerk, and Lissie Kisting
Letter from Keetmanshoop (1939)

30 June 1939

Your Excellency, Honourable Sir

We have been informed of Government notice No 152 of October 1, 1938, regarding the examination of every female, but this law caught us unawares. Therefore, on the 27th of June, we pleaded in all humility with the local magistrate, in writing and in person, to please repeal or change the law, or leave the matter to us, because we have never experienced something of this nature. Now, according to this notice, all women must be examined on July the third 1939, without knowing why. We all know that we must go to a doctor when we are ill; we have always done that, without fail. It is therefore very difficult for us to understand that we are forced to do this, and that we shall be prosecuted by the law if we fail to do so. We saw such medical examinations in the time of the German government, but only on the women who needed them, or for whom the law deemed this necessary. One of those women, by the name of Anna Velskoendraer, is still alive and living in the Keetmanshoop location. She can make a statement, if necessary, about the treatment they had to suffer. All of them stopped getting their periods and they are all infertile, sickly or handicapped. Those who died suffered the most terrible deaths.

Honourable Sir! We trust that Your Excellency will understand how difficult it is for us to be subjected to something we don't understand and have never experienced. We are already afraid, and don't want to offend the doctor at his work or make his work difficult for him on the third of July by someone or other not co-operating. Such action will surely be a violation of the law and will be prosecuted. Because this matter is very urgent, we are turning to Your Excellency in the hope and confidence that Your Excellency will have sympathy and will help us before things go that far.

Because we know, where there is a will there is a way. We would also want to apologise to Your Excellency for any mistake that might be in this letter.

With high regard Your Excellency
Your humble women
Katrina Stephanus
On behalf of all the women in A location
Sofia Labau of B location
Magdalena Vries of C and B location
Katrina Skeier of D Location
Emmillie Adams of E location
Sofia Kloete of G Location
Katrina de Klerk
Lissie Kisting of F location

[Source: 'Letter from Keetmanshoop,' trans. Renee Lotter, in *Women Writing Africa: The Southern Region*, ed. M.J. Daymond et al. (New York: Feminist Press at the City University of New York, 2003), 220–1.]

PART SEVEN
Work

From the first half of the nineteenth century, social reformers addressed the conditions under which women and children worked and agitated for legislative protections. While the link these reforms made between women and children later came to be a bone of contention for feminists, the gendering of labour laws was one of the central themes of international organizing within the women's movement. Protective labour legislation was particularly sought by working-class and some socialist women, or by middle-class women on behalf of working women, while middle- and upper-class women were keen to address access to professions and 'respectable' positions; maternity allowances and labour laws governing married women attracted interest across class lines. Nitza Berkovitch points out that much of the effort directed at establishing international labour laws was undertaken by state officials, partly in order to offset the perceived threat of the international labour movement.[1] Yet socialist women and other women's groups organized to influence this international legislation, and to oppose some of the measures, including the restrictions on the kinds of employment women could undertake and restrictions on night work.

The mid-nineteenth-century laws aimed at protecting women governed only women in industrial occupations. As the broadsheet advertising a mass meeting organized by the Working Women's Society of New York reveals, this legislation did nothing to ameliorate working conditions for women in retail services, or many of the other areas in which women were employed. Organizations like the Working Women's Society or the Women's Employment Defence League in the UK emerged in an effort to give working women a public voice about the legislation that sought to 'protect' them. From national associations like these the trajectory led inevitably to international organizing. In 1907 the first International Conference of Socialist Women took place Stuttgart, Germany. Socialist women were already active internationally by virtue of their participation in the Socialist Internationals, but they also began meeting formally as women in the early twentieth century. When they met in 1915 in Berne, Switzerland, they were, quite understandably, preoccupied with the war. The First International Congress of Working Women was held in Washington, DC in 1919, and adopted resolutions on a variety of questions from the eight-hour day to maternity insurance, night work, unemployment, and hazardous occupations. Taka Kato addressed the International Congress of Working Women in Vienna in 1923, pointing out that in Japan women were still employed in mining and in other dangerous trades from which they were 'protected' elsewhere. She addressed other nationally specific concerns as well, presumably with the aim of securing support internationally for Japanese women workers in the struggle to improve their working conditions.

In 1920 the First Congress of the Peoples of the East took place in Baku, Azerbaijan, bringing together those active in socialist, communist, and anti-imperialist movements in the East. Among the delegates invited to address the 'woman question' was Najiye Hanım of Turkey, who offered a critique of bourgeois feminists who were, in her estimation, unduly focused on veiling rather than on the more pressing issues faced by women in Eastern countries. Socialist and communist feminists, while they saw their emancipation bound up with the emancipation of working people irrespective of gender, were also aware of women's gender-specific needs and possibilities. For Alexandre Kollontai, whose resolution on the role of working women was submitted to the Congress of Communist International States in 1919, the Communist party was in need of the participation of women workers if it was to achieve its goals – an argument about the contribution women could make as 'citizens' that was not fundamentally different from the claims of many bourgeois feminists in other contexts; the difference lay rather in the conception of citizenship itself.

Working men's and working women's interests were at times opposed. While socialist women generally agreed that men also needed protection from hazardous occupations and exploitative conditions, some socialist feminists made the case that as long as women had fewer opportunities for unionizing, protective legislation should be supported. Yet, another group that began as a national organization but then became international was one that opposed protective legislation that distinguished between men and women on the basis of gender. The Open Door Council was founded in England in May of 1926, partly in response to pressure from the Labour government, which was planning to extend gender-specific protective legislation. The aim of the organization was to ensure that women's employment conditions and opportunities were the same as those of men. An international committee was formed almost immediately, and it organized an international conference in Berlin in June 1929 for women concerned with equality in the workplace. The Open Door International was constituted out of this conference, and counted twenty-one countries among its members. Established international women's organizations like the IAW also undertook to address issues related to women's employment. At its Rome Congress in 1923, for instance, the IAW adopted several resolutions on equal pay for equal work, a key theme of feminist organizing around work to this day.

Middle- and upper-middle-class women, by contrast, were concerned about access to employments suited to their class and their education. Isabel Thorne advocated the admission of women into medical fields like midwifery, which she studied herself. As she points out in her letter to the editor of *The Englishwoman's Review*, women who worked as midwives in this period did not have official accreditation. Thorne herself was one of the seven women who enrolled in medicine at the University of Edinburgh, and then was prevented from graduating. She transferred to the newly created London School of Medicine for Women, where she served as an administrator. Her daughter May graduated as a surgeon from LSMW in 1908. In the twentieth century the admission of women into non-traditional occupations continued to occupy feminists. Amelia Earhart, while she addresses a range of options for women in the field of aviation apart from the role of pilot, points out that far more women could enter this field than were serving in it at the time she wrote.

The colonial divide is once again evident when it comes to the question of labour. Sarojini Naidu's impassioned address at a conference in Allahabad in 1917 on the subject of indentured labour is a case in point. The problem of indentured Indian labour in British colonies is the problem of slavery carried into twentieth century. Naidu is particularly concerned with the vulnerability of women to sexual harassment and rape at the hands of their 'employers' ('masters' may be the more appropriate term) under the conditions of indenture, and she appeals to the 'honour' of the Indians in the audience to redress the international exploitation of Indian women and men in the colonies of the Caribbean. Naidu frames this transnational problem as one for nationalists to address, making it part of the movement for independence but also imagining diasporic linkages as part of the nation-to-be.

NOTE

1 Nitza Berkovitch, *From Motherhood to Citizenship: Women's Rights and International Organizations* (Baltimore and London: Johns Hopkins UP, 1999), 21, 50.

You are earnestly requested to attend a

MASS MEETING

TO BE HELD UNDER THE AUSPICES OF

The Working Women's Society

OF 27 CLINTON PLACE,

CHICKERING HALL,

Fifth Avenue and Eighteenth Street.

On Tuesday, May 6th, at 8 P. M.

THE SPEAKERS WILL BE:

REV. DR. HUNTINGTON	Grace Church
REV. DR. ALEXANDER	Tenth Street Presbyterian
REV. FATHER ELLIOTT	Paulist Fathers
REV. DR. FAUNCE	Fifth Avenue Baptist
REV. DE SOLA MENDES	Shaarai Tefilla
REV. DR. McCHESENEY	Madison Avenue Methodist

The following Clergymen have expressed their sympathy and desire to co-operate with the Working Women's Society in calling this meeting, the object of which is: The consideration of the conditions of employment in the large Retail Dry Goods Stores of this city; the seeking of a remedy for improving such conditions, and your relation to the subject:

Rev. Dr Morgan Dix
Rev. Father Deshon
Rev. Dr P.H. Mendes
Rev. Dr Huntington
Rev. Dr Geo. Alexander
Rev. Dr Faunce
Rev. Dr Howard Crosby
Rev. Dr M.H. Hains
Rev. Dr Stanger
Rev. Dr C.D. W. Bridgeman
Rev. Dr O.A. Brown
Rev. Father Ducey
Rev. Dr Van De Water
Rev. Joachim Elemendorf
Rev. Dr H. Mottett
Rev. Dr J.W. Brown
Rev. Leighton Williams
Rev. Dr Morehouse
Rev. Dr H. Olson
Rev. Dr Theodore C. Williams
Rev. Sturges Allen
Rev. F. de Sola Mendes
Rev. Dr Mellvane
Rev. Dr De Costa
Rev. Dr Tipple
Rev. Dr T.A. Hyland
Rev. Dr J.A. Locke
Rev. Dr P.A.H. Brown
Rev. Dr O. Riddell
Rev. Dr S.M. Hamilton
Rev. Dr F.E. Edwards
Rev. Dr E. Acheson
Rev. Dr W.T. Crocker
Drv. Dr T.W. Chambers

Rev. Dr C.S. Hanover
Rev. Dr J.M. Philiputt
Rev. Dr G.A. McCrew
Rev. Dr R. Booth
Rev. Dr J.W. Shackleford
Rev. Dr J.M. Worrall
Rev. Dr J.W. Ashworth
Rev. Dr Rob't Colyer
Rev. Dr T.M. Brown
Rev. Dr H.S. Jacobs
Rev. Dr Wm. Vaughan
Rev. Dr E. McCheseney
Rev. Father Elliott
Drv. Dr Arthur Brooks
Rev. Dr Richard Harlan
Rev. Dr Leny
Rev. Dr J.T. Patey
Rev. Dr Burtsell
Rev. Dr Duryea
Rev. Walter Rauschenbusch
Rev. Dr C.C. Tiffany
Rev. Dr Brainard Ray
Rev. Father Phelan
Rev. Dr R.F. Sample
Rev. Dr J.W. Johnston
Rev. Dr C.H. Parkhurst
Rev. Dr J.W. Hill
Rev. Henry Meissner
Rev. J.O.S. Huntington
Rev. Dr H. Bauman
Rev. Dr Wm. Westerfield
Rev. Dr B.B. Tyler
Rev. Dr F Gleak
Rev. H. Le Grand Ernard

Rev. Dr A.W. Wittmeyer

Rev. Dr J.C. Lamphior

Rev. Dr C.H. Eaton

Rev. Dr F.D. Soddell

Rev. Dr S.S. Seward

Rev. Dr. Chas. A. Jones

Rev. Dr Dwight M. Hodge

Rev. Dr D. Odell

Rev. Dr Newton Perkins

Rev. Dr K. Junor

Rev. Dr Chas. L. Thompson

Rev. Dr K Kohler

Rev. Edward Kenney

Rev. Dr T.O. Hughes

ALICE L. WOODBRIDGE, Secretary

[Source: *Broadsheet: The Working Women's Society Mass Meeting* (The John Crerar Library). Available through the Gerritsen Collection.]

Isabel Thorne (1834–1910) was an early campaigner for medical education for women in England. In the late 1860s she started midwifery training at the Female Medical College in London, and then responded to Sophia Jex-Blake's advertisement calling for women to join her in an attempt to qualify as doctors at Edinburgh University. Despite winning first prize in an anatomy examination, Thorne was prevented from graduating along with the six other women who had enrolled in medicine. Thorne, Jex-Blake, and some of the others then organized the London School of Medicine for Women, and Thorne gave up her own ambition to qualify as a physician in order to run the school.

Isabel Thorne
Employment for Educated Women (1867)

To the Editor of the 'Englishwoman's Review'

Madam, – Finding that the letter you kindly inserted in your last number has attracted some attention amongst your readers, may I ask if you will grant me some more of your valuable space. Every journal of the present day speaks of the great difficulties experienced by women of the educated classes, when endeavouring to procure an honourable livelihood, should the misfortune or death of their male relative throw them unprovided on the world.

The *Saturday Review*, in a recent article on literature as a profession, speaks very ably on this subject, and the *British Medical Times*, of 17th August, mentioned in feeling terms the distress of many gentle-women, who are obliged to seek their own subsistence. The Society for the Employment of Women is pre-eminently calculated to sound the depths of this difficulty, in consequence of the vast numbers who apply to it for help. The stagnation of commerce, which still exists, causes the class of those ladies to increase who desire to assist in the maintenance of their families, so that besides the ordinary numbers of gentle-women seeking employment, there are hundreds who have up to this time been moving in good society, and are now thrown on their own resources.

The mass of course become governesses, for there is scarcely any other position they can take which does not entirely degrade them in the social scale. A few, specially gifted, may find in literature or in arts the means of subsistence, while others with sufficient courage and intelligence may meet with not only a lucrative employment, but also a wide field for their energies and sympathies in the objects promoted by the Female Medical Society, viz. – the practice of midwifery and the treatment of the diseases of women and children. Mid-wifery has been entirely monopolized by men, but from the fact of its female practitioners not being required to possess any proofs of their competency, not to pass through any definite training, they have become degraded and without legal status. Now the prospect is brightening. Educated women see before them the possibility of pursuing a career which will widen their sympathies, increase their intellectual capacities, and make them honoured and useful members of society.

Women are particularly fitted for attendance on the sick; they have proved themselves for ages the best nurses; but it is, above all, as accoucheuses and consultants on diseases of their own sex that skilled gentlewomen are required. Many Englishwomen are so accustomed to call in a medical man, that they do not suffer from the shrinking which others feel to such an intense degree that the operations of nature are hindered and fearful risks run. To the latter female practitioners are an immense boon, and ladies while qualifying themselves as accoucheuses are really conferring immense benefits on their own sex, and at the same time opening out for themselves a remunerative career. Some will doubtless attain distinction in this branch of the profession; just as Mesdames Lachapelle and Boivin did in France, and the fact that there is one profession open to women will have an elevating effect upon the whole sex.

Marriage is looked upon by many as the only object of a woman's life. If we take this for granted, what is to become either of the large surplus (some half million) of our female population, or of those who when married find that their prospects are not what they were; or who by the death of the father, the bread winner, are left with small means to bring up a young family.

Terrible are the struggles gone through by such an one, in her efforts to main-tain her own position and to rear her children fitly. At a moderate expense, and in a comparatively short time, ladies may qualify themselves as accoucheuses, and find a wide and ever increasing field for the exertion of their talents. I am not speaking of an hypothetical possibility, but of a proved fact. Certificated students of the college have been in practice for some time, and their success is undoubted, and shows that there is a vast and as yet almost unbroached field for the professional employment of gentlewomen.

I shall be happy to give any information on the subject of the working of the college, and of the extension of its operations, to those who may apply to me.

I am, Madam, yours faithfully,

Isabel Thorne

18, Charles Street, Grosvenor Square. W.

[Source: *The Englishwoman's Review of Social and Industrial Questions* 1, no. 5 (1867): 312–13. Available through the Gerritsen Collection.]

Anonymous

The Women's Employment Defence League (1896)

The Association held their annual meeting on Wednesday, December 2nd. Mrs Charles Greenwood presided, and the report was read by Miss Whyte, hon. Secretary. The Association was formed a few years back for the purpose of watching, and if necessary opposing legislative measures or Trades' Union regulations likely to affect injuriously the position of women in the labour market. The meeting was held at the Cadogan Club, which was opened by the Countess of Cadogan, after whom it was named. Here at their fortnightly meetings, women enjoyed opportunities hitherto denied to the female portion of the wage-earners, of discussion on proposed restrictions, and careful consideration of their effects.

The League does not believe in the opinion of women being taken second-hand, but considers that the workers themselves should, even if they cannot vote, speak out when their power to earn their bread is being interfered with. Twice the League has assisted working women to appear before the Home Secretary, and speak for themselves. Until the first of these deputations in 1895, no purely working women's deputation, with only working women speakers, had ever before visited the House of Commons. The result of this action was that, whereas Mr Asquith told them then, that 'the whole of factory legislation was based on *treating women like children*,' later on Mr Russell in receiving a similar deputation premised his remarks by saying, 'the government did not wish to treat women as children, nor to limit their freedom by unnecessary restrictions.'

The adoption of the report was proposed by Miss Jean Grieve, who has earned a grand reputation for helping on the movement whenever necessary, and the adoption was seconded by Miss Ada Heather-Bigg, who devotes much time and energy to the cause. The following resolution was put by a member in the audience, 'That this League affirms the necessity of clubs for working women, and urges all present to join either the Cadogan, the Jersey or the Boucherett Clubs.' This was seconded and carried unanimously.

Mrs Charles Greenwood then told of her experiences in enquiring into the conditions of the pit brow girls, in Lancashire, this being one of the threatened industries. She said:

'I was lately present at a debate at the Pioneer Club when Mr Slevelding, who is one of the gentlemen who kindly served on our Committee, spoke with convincing force and vigour against the legal and parliamentary restrictions which have been placed in the past on women's labour. In reply a lady, criticizing his speech, said she thought he was not up to date in alluding to the pit brow women. Well, ladies, I wonder whether that lady knew that the pit brow women were wished to be interfered with as late as July in this year when the 'Miners' International Congress' advocated the prohibition of female labour at the pit brow?

'Doubtless in some instances it was wished for by men who really desired the good of the women, but they always forget, I notice, one thing in these questions, that is, that we have tongues and can speak for ourselves; we can't vote, but we can speak; perhaps if we could vote, we should not do so much talking!

'I am very much interested in these pit brow ladies, and when I was staying in Lancashire this autumn I went to see them coming out from their work, and a fine set of young women they were, I can assure you. Now I made enquiries about them, because I had heard talk against them; I was not afraid, I knew I should find out nothing but what was good, but I own I was surprised at one or two things; one was, that these girls, whom you will hear some people describe as so unsexed by their work, were so fond of working for people poorer than themselves that a lady told me, who had just been calling at house after house to get new members for her needlework guild, that forty were members, and that she had greatly offended one woman because she had not called there.

'Now I tell you this not because *I* think every woman is unsexed and unwomanly because she is not able to use her needle, any more than I should think every man who is unable to wield a sword unmanly; we allow men to choose their occupations, and we take it quite meekly when they choose apparently unsuitable ones, such as when a young man has to stretch a stocking over our hands, although you might think it perhaps more suitable if women's stockings and under-garments were served to them in the shops by women. No, depend on it some of us are destined to become mothers, and others to remain single, and have to work for our daily bread, and therefore let us fight to the bitter end any legislation likely to interfere with women's own choice of life.

'Another person I visited on the same day, said to my sister, "I did not quite agree with what you said in your article about the pit girls as servants, you said they would probably not make good servants; now I know to the contrary, I have had several of them come to me, and although I am an invalid and easily upset, I have never had better servants in my house."

'So you see this much-repeated assertion that women lose much of their womanliness at this occupation is entirely without foundation. When we hear all this talk about protection of women, I feel what they really want to be protected from is their protectors.'

A concert followed which afforded hearty enjoyment for all, after which the audience dispersed.

[Source: *Shafts: A Magazine of Progressive Thought* 4, no. 12 (1896): 162–3. Available through the Gerritsen Collection.]

Freedom of Labour Defence

Employment of Women at Night and Use of White Phosphorus; Women and the Dangerous Performances Bill (1906)

Employment of Women at Night and Use of White Phosphorus

The International Conference on the Employment of Women at Night, and on the use of white phosphorus in the manufacture of matches, which opened at Berne on September 17, concluded its sittings on Thursday the 27th. The States represented were Austria, Belgium, Denmark, France, Germany, Holland, Hungary, Italy, Luxembourg, Portugal, Spain, Sweden, Switzerland, and the United Kingdom. The principal result of the Conference was the signature of a Convention on the subject of the employment of women at night, whereby the signatory States bind themselves to ensure a *minimum* period of eleven hours' repose, to include the time from 10 p.m. to 5 a.m., to women employed in all industrial enterprises where there are more than ten workers of both sexes. Certain exceptions are allowed for perishable goods, unforeseen contingencies, and 'season' trades; and provision is made for the subsequent adhesion of the Colonies or possessions of the signatory States. This Convention was signed by all the delegates to the Conference, and is to take effect in two years' time. A Convention to prohibit the use, importation, or sale of matches made with white phosphorus was signed by seven out of the fourteen States, namely, Denmark, France, Germany, Holland, Italy, Luxembourg, and Switzerland. To the first of these Conventions is appended a resolution in favour of the establishment of a standing International Commission, consisting of representatives of the signatory States, for the purpose of giving an opinion, when requested to do so by one or more of those States, on any doubtful points arising out of the Convention, and of serving as a medium for the exchange of preliminary views between the signatory States with regard to future industrial conferences. This resolution was adopted by ten out of the fourteen States represented, the States abstaining being Austria, Belgium, Germany, and Hungary, and it concludes with a request to the Swiss Government to invite the adhesion to the resolution of those four States, with a view to its being then transformed into a Convention. The signature of the first of these Conventions involves only one or two minor alterations in the law of this country. For the most part the regulations in force in the United Kingdom on the subject of the employment of women at night are stricter than those prescribed by the Convention.

Women and the Dangerous Performances Bill

A letter from Lady Frances Balfour appeared in the *Westminster Gazette* of July 21, protesting against the insertion of the word 'Woman' in the Dangerous Performances Bill, the object of which is to embody 'legislation passed in the interests of those not yet come to years of discretion.' A meeting was held by 'lady performers,' who feared that their profession would be endangered 'by the introduction of a word which gives the Bill a new meaning and scope.' Several thousand women gain an honest livelihood by acrobatic and athletic performances, and they fear lest 'under the wide powers given in this Act, and the vague wording of the Bill, few managers will care to run the risk of employing women in performances which are only dangerous to the unskilled and untrained.' 'No one,' adds Lady Frances Balfour, 'desires that performances whose only merit is their danger should be permitted. Whether it be a man or a woman, it is equally inexpedient ... that such performances should be permitted. But it is an act of gross injustice to insert the word "woman" in a Act which rightly protects those who are entering a professional life at an age too young to be their own guardians in their particular training.' In the meantime the Bill has been blocked.

[Source: *The Englishwoman's Review of Social and Industrial Questions* 37, no. 271 (1906): 257–8. Available through the Gerritsen Collection.]

International Conference of Socialist Women
Women of the Working People! (Berne, March 1915)

Where are your husbands? Where are your sons?

For eight months they have been at the front. They have been torn from their work and their homes: youths, the support and the hope of their parents, men in the prime of life, men with graying hair, the providers of their families. They all wear uniforms, live in the trenches, and are ordered to destroy what industrious labor has created.

Millions already lie in mass graves. Thousands upon thousands lie in the hospitals – with mangled bodies, with shattered limbs, with blinded eyes and destroyed minds, seized by epidemics or prostrated from exhaustion.

Burned villages and towns, demolished bridges, destroyed forests, and cratered fields form the trail left by their deeds.

Proletarian women! They told you that your husbands and sons departed to defend you, the frail women, your children, your hearth, and your home. What is the reality? A double burden has been heaped on the shoulders of you 'weak' women. Defenseless, you have been delivered up to grief and misery. They threaten to take the roof from over your head. Your children starve and freeze. Your hearth is cold and empty.

They spoke to you of one great brotherhood and sisterhood between the noble and the humble, of a 'civil peace' between poor and rich. But the 'civil peace' now shows its true face. The boss lowers your wages, the merchant and unscrupulous speculator increase prices, and the landlord threatens to put you out onto the street. The state is miserly toward you and bourgeois charity sets up its soup kitchens while advising you to be thrifty.

What is the purpose of this war which brings you such dreadful suffering? They say it is for the well-being and the defense of the fatherland. But what is the well-being of the fatherland? Should it not be the well-being of the many millions? The well-being of the millions whom the war turns into corpses, into cripples, into unemployed, into beggars, into widows, and into orphans?

Who endangers the well-being of the fatherland? Is it the men of other countries in different uniforms who wanted the war just as little as did your husbands and who know just as little why they should murder their brothers? No! The fatherland is endangered by all those who derive their wealth from the misery of the broad masses and who base their rule upon oppression.

Who benefits from the war? In every nation it is only a small minority, above all, the manufacturers of rifles and cannon, armor plate and torpedo boats, the owners of the docks, and the suppliers of the army. To feed their profits they aroused nationalist hatred among the peoples and so contributed to the outbreak of war. Moreover, the war benefits the capitalists in general. Has not the labor of the disinherited and exploited masses accumulated goods that are denied to those who created them? Denied to them, of course, because they are poor. They cannot pay for them! The sweat of the workers created these goods and now the blood of the workers must conquer new export markets for them abroad. Foreign lands must be colonized where the capitalists can rob the earth of its treasures and exploit the cheapest labor power.

Not the defense of the fatherland, but its expansion is the purpose of this war. Such are the requirements of the capitalist order, for without the oppression and exploitation of one human being by another, it cannot exist.

The workers have nothing to gain from this war but everything to lose – all that is dear to them.

Women of the working class! The men of the belligerent countries have been brought to silence. The war has dulled their consciousness, paralyzed their wills, and deformed their entire beings.

But you women who endure misery and deprivation at home, in addition to the gnawing concern for your loved ones at the front, why should you hesitate to voice your desire for peace, to raise your protest against the war? Why do you recoil? Until now you have endured for the sake of your loved ones. Now it is time to act for the benefit of your husbands, for the benefit of your sons.

Enough of the slaughter! This cry resounds in all languages. Millions of proletarian women sound this call. It echoes back from the trenches where the conscience of the sons of the people rebels against the slaughter.

Women of the laboring people! In these difficult days Socialist women from Germany, England, France, and Russia have come together. Your misery, your suffering have touched their hearts. For the sake of the future – yours and that of your loved ones – they call upon you to work for peace. Just as the will of Socialist women is united across the battlefields, so you in all countries must close ranks in order to raise the call – peace, peace!

The World War has imposed the greatest sacrifice upon you. It robs you of your sons to whom you gave birth in pain and suffering and whom you have raised with effort and worry. It robs you of your husbands who are your companions in life's hard struggle. In comparison to these sacrifices all others are small and insignificant. All of humanity looks to you, proletarian women of the belligerent countries. You must become the heroines, the deliverers!

Unite in one will and in one action! Proclaim a millionfold that which your husbands and your sons cannot yet assert.

The working people of all countries are brothers. Only the united determination of the people can stop the slaughter. Socialism alone is the future peace of humanity!

Down with capitalism, which sacrifices untold multitudes of humanity to the wealth and power of the propertied!

Down with the war! Onward to socialism!

[Original source: *Dokumente und Materialien zur Geschichte der deutschen Arbeiterbewegung* (Berlin [GDR]: Dietz Verlag, 1958), series 2, vol. 1, 125–7; repr. in *The Communist International in Lenin's Time: Lenin's Struggle for a Revolutionary International. Documents: 1907–1916, The Preparatory Years*, ed. John Riddell, 2nd ed. (New York: Pathfinder Press, 1986), 277–9.]

Sarojini Naidu
Indentured Labour (1917)

At the meeting on Indentured Labour, held at Allahabad, on the 19th January, 1917, Mrs Sarojini Naidu delivered the following speech:

Citizens of India, I think we represent almost every province here to-night. The words that you have heard from the previous speakers must have made your hearts bleed. Let the blood of your hearts blot out the shame that your women have suffered abroad. The words that you have heard to-night must have kindled within you a raging fire. Men of India, let that be the funeral pyre of the indenture system. (*Applause.*) Words from me to-night! No, tears from me to-night, because I am a woman, and though you may feel the dishonour that is offered to your mothers and sisters, I feel the dishonour offered to me in the dishonour to my sex. I have travelled far, gentlemen, to come to you tonight only to raise my voice, not for the men, but for women, for those women whose proudest memory is that Sita would not stand the challenge to her honour but called upon mother earth to avenge her and the earth opened up to avenge her. I come to speak on behalf of those women whose proudest memory lies in this, that Padmini of Chittore preferred the funeral pyre to dishonour. I come to speak on behalf of those women who, like Savitri, have followed their men to the gates of death and have won back, by their indomitable love, the dehumanised soul of their men in the colonies abroad. I come to speak to you in the name of one woman who has summed up in her frail body all the physical sufferings the women of India have endured abroad – in the broken body, the shattered health, of Mrs Gandhi. (*Applause.*) I ask you to witness the suffering, the starvation and the indignities that have been suffered by the women because they loved their men and their men suffered for a cause. These women shared with their husbands the martyrdom and the personal sorrow rather than prefer their own comfort while their men suffered for the sake of national honour and self-respect. I ask you in the name of that murdered sister, that sister of whom Mr Andrews told us, that found in death the only deliverance from dishonour. I ask you in the names of those two brothers who preferred to save the honour of their family and the religion in the blood of their sister rather than let her chastity be polluted.

National Honour

Do you think – you who are clamouring for self-government today – do you think, you who are dreaming dreams of territorial patriotism, you are patriots if you cannot stop the agony that is sending its echoes to you night and day – night and day from those men who are in no way better than dogs, from those women who are growing worse than brutes? Self-Government shriek – for whom? And for what? For men whose hands are folded while their women shriek, whose voices are silent even in the face of the most terrible insult that can be offered to man? Wealth! What is wealth to us? What is power to us? What is glory to us? How shall the wealth and power and glory of a nation be founded save on the immutable honour of its womanhood? Are we going to leave to posterity a wealth got with dishonour? Are we going to leave to the unborn generations a sorrow and shame that we have not been able to wipe out? Men of India, rather the hour of doom struck than that after to-night you should live to say: 'We heard the call for help, but we had not the courage. We felt in our hearts the challenge to our national honour and yet we were cowards kept still, for fear of punishment that might be given.' If after tonight, men of India, if after tonight, I say, it is possible for the most selfish interests to use the humanity of India to enrich, almost as a manure, the sugar plantations of the colonies, if it is possible, I say, to let the forces of the greatest evil on earth to daunt you in this campaign, you are not only unworthy and degenerate sons of our mother whose name stood for glory in the past, but we are the murderers, the suicides of national honour and national progress. You discount the future, nay, you slay the future. There can be no future for a nation whose present men and women do not know how to avenge their dishonour. Does it matter that you, as one of the speakers said, could sleep in your beds, with the thought that your daughters are safe, that your wives are safe and that your mothers are set upon a pedestal? Are not those wives and mothers, are not those virgins that might have been honoured mothers, citizens of India? What are they gentlemen? What are they but the refuse that even fire will not care to burn? I have come today to speak, but I think the fire within me is so strong that it bids me be silent, because words are so weak. I feel within me today the anguish that has been from year to year the lot of those women who had better be dead. I feel within me the shame, the inexpressible, the immeasurable, the inalienable shame, gentlemen, that has been the curse of this indenture system of labour. And who are responsible men of India, for this that our men should go abroad for bread? Why is not your patriotism sufficient to have resources enough to give bread to them who go to seek bread abroad? Why is not your patriotism so vigilant, so strong and so all-comprehensive that you are able to guard the ignorance of them, that go abroad, not merely to death – for death, gentlemen, is tolerable – but dishonour which it is not within the province of self-respecting manhood to endure. Ours has been the shame, because ours has always been the responsibility, but we were asleep or we were dreaming of academic powers, we were discussing from platforms the possibilities in the future, but we were not awake to the degradation of the present. Therefore, the shame is ours in a measure that can never be wholly wiped out either by our tears or by the blood of those who have endured the dishonour for the sake of material profit and wealth. So to-night if our patriotism means more than the curiosity to come by thousands to hear a few speakers, if it means more than the hysteria of the moment, if it means more than the impulse to pity, then I charge you, men of India – I do not appeal to you, I charge you, I lay upon you this trust, I entrust you with this burden, on behalf of those, suffering women, on behalf of every woman in this audience, on behalf of every woman from the Punjab to Malabar; I entrust you with this mission, to wipe out the dishonour that lies on our name. It is we who suffer, gentlemen, not those degraded people – it is the honour of the women in your homes, who cannot show their faces. That mark of crime is written here on us because we have no destiny apart from our sisters. Our honour is indivisible, so must be our dishonour. That is, our destiny is one, and whether for glory or for shame, we share alike. And we women who give our sons to the country, we cannot endure our sons to think that their mothers belong to a generation part of whose womanhood was dishonoured.

When a Nation Grows Bitter

Have I not said enough to stir your blood? Have I not said enough to kindle within you such a conflagration that must not merely annihilate the wrongs of the indenture system but recreate in the crucible a new stirring, a new purpose, a new unity of self-respect that will not sleep, that will not rest, that will be a sword to avenge, that will be a fire to burn, that will be the trumpet call to liberty that only comes when a nation grows bitter, that only comes when a nation says, 'the health within me is rotten.' It is the bitterness that comes when we hear these wrongs abroad. It is the bitterness that comes when we feel that we have let ourselves sleep. It is when we have that indignation against the wrong-doer in our homes that we shall be able to see that we have felt the spirit of Sri-Krishna reborn within ourselves for re-establishing our national righteousness. Is national righteousness possible when the chastity of your womanhood is assailed? Is national righteousness possible when the men of India sit still and see such crimes? Is national righteousness possible til every man amongst you becomes a soldier of the cause, a devotee, a fanatic, everything and anything which means destruction of the wrong and triumph of the right? Gentlemen, it is a stormy sea in a crowded boat that may or may not stand the burden of our sorrow, but like Khusru of old shall we not say, even when the night is dark, when the waves are high, when there is a rush in the boat, when there is no pilot with us, shall we not say –

Nakhuda dar kashteeay ma gar na bashad gu ma bash.
Makhuda dareem ma ra nakhuda darkar nest.

What though there be no pilot to our boat? Go, tell him, we need him not. God is with us, and we need no pilot.

[Source: *Speeches and Writings of Sarojini Naidu* (Madras: G.A. Natesan, 1918), 121–9.]

The International Congress of Working Women (ICWW) was founded by Margaret Dreier Robins, a wealthy, progressive Republican who was passionate about women's labor issues and was president of the Women's Trade Union League (WTUL). The first meeting of the ICWW in 1919 brought together representatives from nineteen countries to discuss the reform of labour laws for women.

International Congress of Working Women

Resolutions Adopted by First International Congress of Working Women, Washington, USA, 28 October to 9 November 1919

Preliminary

The First International Congress of Working Women requests the First International Conference of Labor of the League of Nations:

That *Article Three* concerning the representation of each country at the International Labor Conference be amended to read as follows:

The Conference shall be composed of six representatives of each of the high contracting parties; viz.,

Two delegates representing the Government, one of whom shall be a woman;
Two delegates representing Labor, one of whom shall be a woman;
Two delegates representing the Employers.

1. Eight Hour Day and Forty-four Hour Week

The First International Congress of Working Women requests the First International Conference of Labor of the League of Nations that an international convention establish:

1 For all workers a maximum eight hour day and a forty-four hour week.
2 That the weekly rest period shall have an uninterrupted duration of at least one day and a half.
3 That in continuous industries a minimum rest period of one-half hour shall be accorded in each eight hour shift.

2. Child Labor

The First International Congress of Working Women requests the First International Conference of Labor of the League of Nations that an international convention establish:

EMPLOYMENT OF CHILDREN

(a) Minimum age:
No child shall be employed or permitted to work in any gainful occupation unless he is 16 years of age, has completed the elementary school and has been found by a school physician or other medical officer especially appointed for that purpose to be of normal development for a child of his age and physically fit for the work at which he is to be employed.

No young person under 18 years of age shall be employed in or about a mine or quarry.

The legal work day for young persons between 16 and 18 years of age shall be shorter than the legal work day for adults.
(b) During the night:
No minor shall be employed between the hours of 6 p.m. and 7 a.m.
(c) Unhealthy processes:

Prohibition of the employment of minors in dangerous or hazardous occupations or at any work which will retard their proper physical development.

ADMINISTRATION

(1) Work permits: A yearly medical inspection by medical officer appointed for that purpose by the authorities, records of which inspection shall be kept.
(2) Lists of employed minors with their hours of work shall be posted in all workrooms in which they are employed
(3) The number of inspectors, and especially women inspectors, employed by the factory or labor commission shall be sufficient to insure regular inspection of all establishments in which children are employed and such special inspections and investigations as are necessary to insure the protection of the children.
(4) We further recommend compulsory continuation schools for minors until the age of 18.

3. Maternity Insurance

MAJORITY REPORT

The First International Congress of Working Women requests the First International Conference of Labor of the League of Nations that an international convention establish:
1 The method of administration of maternity benefits shall be left to the individual nations to determine.
2 No woman shall be employed for six weeks before or six weeks after child birth.
3 Every woman shall be entitled during maternity to free medical, surgical and nursing care, either in a hospital or at home, and also to a monetary allowance.
4 The monetary allowance given to mothers shall be adequate for the full and healthy maintenance of mother and child during the aforesaid period.
5 In each country government commissions shall be created to study the best methods of maternity and infant care, and to devise and put in operation effective methods of securing such care.
6 A bureau shall be established in the labor office of the League of Nations to collect information on the best methods of maternity and infant care, said information to be furnished countries represented in the Labor Conference.

MINORITY REPORT

1 The following countries voted to change clause three (3) to read: 'Every wage-earning woman or the wife of a wage earner shall be entitled during maternity to free medical, surgical and nursing care, either in a hospital or at home, and also to a maternity allowance.'
Belgium
Czecko-Slovakia
Poland
Italy
Canada
2 The following countries voted to change clause four (4) to read: 'The indemnity given to mothers shall be based on the living wage in the district.'
Belgium
Czecko-Slovakia
Poland
Italy

4. Night Work

The First International Congress of Working Women requests the First International Conference of Labor of the League of Nations that an international convention establish:
– This Congress adheres to the Berne Convention of 1906 prohibiting night work for all women in industrial employment;
– It further urges that night work shall be prohibited by law for men except in so far as it may be absolutely necessary through the special nature of, or the continuity of, the occupation or in the case of essential public service.
– Night work shall be defined as the hours between 9 p.m. and 6 a.m.

5. Unemployment

The First International Congress of Working Women requests the First International Conference of Labor of the League of Nations that an international convention establish:
Whereas, The problem of unemployment is such that it can not be viewed in isolation from wage standards as a whole nor separated from the social and industrial organizations at present prevailing in all countries, and
Whereas, The causes of unemployment have been obscured and remedies

obstructed by lack of adequate governmental and international research and control, and

Whereas, Unemployment today results in unwarranted poverty, disease, child labor, incompetency, expense to the State, and unrest; and

Whereas, the problems of unemployment are closely allied with the fluctuations of commerce between nations, therefore be it

Resolved: That the first International Congress of Working Women adopt the following recommendations:

1 That a special Bureau of Employment be established in the International Labor Office to act as the International Bureau of Information between nations on all matters relating to employment and unemployment.

2 That the International Labor Conference recommend to each nation in the League of Nations the establishment of a free employment service in all cities and industrial towns in the nation; and that a system of unemployment insurance be made effective in each country in co-operation with the Labor Unions.

3 That the International Labor Office shall coordinate the research work to be undertaken by the National Labor Departments into the possible causes of unemployment, including maldistribution of raw material, migration, labor turnover and bad management. The results of such research to form the basis of International law for the prevention of unemployment.

4 That with a view to the prevention of unemployment each Nation be required to provide for the allocation of public contracts in such a way as to minimize protracted periods of unemployment for both men and women.

5 That no propaganda of misrepresentation for the exportation of foreign labor be carried on by transportation companies of private corporations.

6 That in the International Labor Office and in the national and local labor offices there must be a woman as director of the departments specifically relating to women.

6. Hazardous Occupations

The First International Congress of Working Women requests the First International Conference of Labor of the League of Nations that an international convention establish:

1 Prohibitions of home work in occupations involving the use of poisonous material.

2 No exception of small factories from the regulations governing the industry.

3 Prohibition of the employment of women only in trades which cannot be made healthy for women as potential mothers.

4 An international inquiry to be instituted in order to ascertain the scope of measures which have been adopted in different countries to control dangerous occupations and to publish the results with the object of making clearly known which countries fall short of the standards already established in the more advanced countries.

5 The appointment of a committee including women under the League of Nations, international in personnel, to coordinate the work of national research in the dangerous trades, with a view to eliminating poisonous substances through the substitution of non-poisonous, and where this is impossible to devise new and efficient methods of protection.

7. Emigration

The First International Congress of Working Women requests the First International Conference of Labor of the League of Nations that an international convention establish:

Whereas emigration is a direct consequence of employment; and

Whereas it is in the highest interests of the workers of all countries that emigration be regulated and protected;

Therefore Be It Resolved, that every nation interested in this question should base its legislation on the subject in conformity with the following principles:

1 Emigration, regulated by Labor Treaties, through agreements between the governments concerned and the trade unions.

2 Equal rights for the foreign workers and his family as far as social labor legislation is concerned.

3 Equal rights for foreign and native born workers.

4 Right of nations whose citizens emigrate to appoint officials to the country to which they emigrate for their assistance and protection.

5 Agreement between the Trade Unions of the several countries for the organization of the immigrant workers and for securing exchange of information of their respective labor movements.

8. Distribution of Raw Materials

The First International Congress of Working Women requests the First International Conference of Labor of the League of Nations that an international convention establish:

1 To ask the League of Nations to appoint a Committee to consider and plan for the equal distribution of the raw materials existing in the world, as well as the international control of maritime transports which determine the increase of price of the raw materials.

9. Russian Blockade

Whereas neither the United States nor any of the Allied and Associated powers is officially at war with Russia; and

Whereas, the blockade of the greater part of Russia, in Europe, is in effect directed against millions of women and children, and has brought in its train starvation, disease, and death, to countless victims; therefore be it

Resolved, that we, the delegates to the First International Congress of Working Women in congress assembled, at Washington, hereby protest against this blockade, and we demand the removal of all restrictions upon the shipment of food and other necessities to the people of Russia.

10. A Permanent Bureau

For the purpose of calling another Congress, be it resolved, that there be a Provisional Committee elected by this Congress consisting of a president, five vice-presidents and a secretary-treasurer, and that the present members of the executive committee, or alternates nominated by trade union groups of the various nations, be corresponding members of this Provisional Committee.

1 The basis of representation for the next Congress shall be the same as the basis for this Congress.
2 That the officers be empowered to transact any necessary business.
3 That the International Office be in the United States.

[Source: *Resolutions Adopted by First International Congress of Working Women Washington, U.S.A. October 28 to November 6, 1919* (Chicago: National Women's Trade Union League of America, 1919).]

Alexandre Kollontai (1872–1952) was a leading Russian Communist revolutionary, first as a Menshevik, then from 1914 on as a Bolshevik. She became People's Commissar of Social Welfare under Lenin. The most prominent woman in the Soviet administration, and a well-respected socialist feminist, Kollontai founded the Zhenotdel or 'Women's Department' in 1919. In 1923 she was appointed

Soviet Ambassador to Norway, partly in an effort to remove her from spheres of influence in the party in light of her many criticisms of the Communist Party. She fulfilled a series of diplomatic roles for the remainder of her career.

Alexandre Kollontai
Resolution on the Role of Working Women (submitted by A. Kollontai) (1919)

The Congress of the Communist International states that the success of all the tasks it has set itself, as well as the final victory of the world proletariat and the final abolition of the capitalist system, can be ensured only through the common joint struggle of working men and women. The enormous increase in female labor in all branches of the economy; the fact that at least half of the wealth in the world is produced by female labour; in addition, the important part, recognized by all, which women workers play in the construction of the new communist living conditions, in the reform of family life and in the realization of a socialist, community education for children, the goal of which will be to turn out hard-working citizens, imbued with the spirit of solidarity, for the Council republic – all that imposes on all parties adhering to the Communist International the pressing duty to stretch all their forces and energies in order to win working women to the Party and to use every means in order to educate them in the meaning of the new society and to apply communist ethics to social and family life.

The dictatorship of the proletariat can be achieved and maintained only with the energetic and active participation of working women.

[Source: *Theses, Resolutions and Manifestoes of the First Four Congresses of the Third International*, ed. Alan Adler (London: Inks Links; Atlantic Highlands, NJ: Humanities Press, 1980), 46–7.]

At its second congress, the Communist International called for a special conference to forge an anti-imperialist and pro-communist alliance with the peoples of central Asia. The First Congress of the Peoples of the East was held in Baku, Azerbaijan, in 1920. Among the participants were approximately fifty-five women, and the struggle for women's liberation was a topic the conference addressed several times. Three women were unanimously elected to the Presiding Committee, and two delegates addressed the gathering about the struggle of women of the East. One of those women was Najiye Hanīm, a Turkish communist delegate to the conference. Her impassioned address, delivered in Turkish, was translated to the assembly in Baku by another woman delegate, Shabanova of Azerbaijan.

Najiye Hanīm

Comrade Najiye's Address to the First Congress of the Peoples of the East (1920)

Chairman: The Presiding Committee has decided also to call upon a representative of the women, Comrade Najiye. (*Applause.*)
Najiye: (*speaks in Turkish. Her speech is interrupted by applause.*)
Chairman: I call upon Comrade Shabanova to translate.
Shabanova: Comrades, Comrade Najiye said: The women's movement beginning in the East must be looked at not from the standpoint of those frivolous feminists who are content to see woman's place in social life as that of a delicate plant or an elegant doll. This movement must be seen as a vital and necessary consequence of the revolutionary movement taking place throughout the world. The women of the East are not fighting merely for the right to walk in the street without wearing the chador, as many people suppose. For the women of the East, with their high moral ideals, the question of the chador, it can be said, comes last in priority. If the women, who form half of every community, are set up against the men and do not enjoy the same rights, obviously it is impossible for society to progress; the backwardness of Eastern societies is irrefutable proof of this.

Comrades, you can be sure that all your efforts and labors to realize new forms of social life, however sincere and however vigorous your endeavors may be, will be fruitless unless you summon the women to become real helpers in your work.

In Turkey, owing to the conditions caused by the war, women have been obliged to quit the home and the household and take on the performance of a variety of social duties. Women have had to take over the responsibilities of the men who have been called up for military service. What is more, in roadless localities of Anatolia that are inaccessible even to pack animals, women have been dragging artillery equipment for the troops. This fact cannot, of course, be called a step forward in the conquest of equal rights for women. People who view the fact that women are making up with their labor for the shortage of beasts of burden as a contribution to the cause of equal rights for women are unworthy of our attention.

We do not deny that at the beginning of the 1908 revolution some measures were introduced for women's benefit. In view, however, of the ineffectiveness and inadequacy of these measures, we do not regard them as highly significant.

The opening of one or two schools of elementary and higher education for women in the capital and in the provinces, and even the opening of a university for women, does not accomplish a thousandth of what still needs to be done. Of course, more fundamental or serious measures on behalf of women held in bondage cannot be expected from the Turkish government, whose actions are based on the oppression and exploitation of the weaker by the stronger.

But we also know that the position of our sisters in Persia, Bukhara, Khiva, Turkestan, India, and other Muslim countries is even worse. The injustice done to us and to our sisters, however, has not remained unpunished. Proof of this is to be seen in the backwardness and decline of all the countries of the East. Comrades, you must know that the evil done to women has never gone and will never go without retribution.

Because this conference of the Congress of the Peoples of the East is drawing to a close, lack of time obliges us to refrain from discussing the position of women in the various countries of the East. However, the comrade delegates are entrusted with the great mission of taking back to their homelands the noble principles of the revolution. Let them not forget that all the efforts they devote to winning happiness for the peoples will remain fruitless unless there is real help from the women.

In order to deliver us from all calamities, the Communists consider it necessary to create a classless society, and to this end they declare relentless war against all the bourgeois and privileged layers. The women Communists of the East have an even harder battle to wage because, in addition, they have to fight against the despotism of their menfolk. If you, men of the East, continue now as in the past to be indifferent to the fate of women, you can be sure that our countries will perish, and you and we together with them. The alternative is for us, together with all the oppressed, to begin a bloody life-and-death struggle to win our rights by force.

I will briefly set forth the women's demands. If you want to bring about your own emancipation, listen to our demands and render us real help and cooperation.

1 Complete equality of rights.
2 Ensuring to women unconditional access to educational and vocational institutions established for men.
3 Equality of rights of both parties to marriage. Unconditional abolition of polygamy.

4 Unconditional admission of women to employment in legislative and administrative institutions.
5 Establishment of committees for the rights and protection of women everywhere, in cities, towns, and villages.

There is no doubt that we are entitled to raise these demands. In recognizing that we have equal rights, the Communists have reached out their hand to us, and we women will prove their most loyal comrades. True, we may stumble in pathless darkness, we may stand on the brink of yawning chasms, but we are not afraid, because we know that in order to see the dawn one has to pass through the dark night.

[Source: *The Communist International in Lenin's Time: To See the Dawn: Baku, 1920 – First Congress of the Peoples of the East*, ed. John Riddell (New York: Pathfinder Press, 1993), 204–7.]

International Woman Suffrage Alliance / International Alliance of Women

Resolutions Adopted at the Rome Congress: Equal Pay and Right to Work (1923)

IV. Equal Pay and Right to Work

That this Congress, realizing that economic necessities and the desire and right of women to work and secure for themselves the means of life has made them important and irreplaceable factors in production; and believing that it is essential that all avenues of work should be open to women, and that the sole consideration in regard to work should be the physical and intellectual suitability of the workers, declares

1 That education for professions and trades should be equally available for women as for men.
2 That all professions and all posts in the Civil Service in all its functions, administrative, judicial and executive, should be open to women as to men, and that advancement to all higher posts should be equally open for both sexes.
3 That women should receive the same pay as men for the same work, and that the only interpretation of the expression 'Equal Pay for Equal Work' which is acceptable to the Alliance is that men and women shall be paid at the same

rate, whether this be computed by time or by piece, in the same occupation or grade.

4 That the right to work of all be recognized, and no obstacle placed in the way of married women who desire to work; that no special regulations for women's work, different from regulations for men, should be imposed contrary to the wishes of the women concerned; that laws relative to women as mothers should be so framed as not to handicap them in their economic position, and that all future labour regulations should tend towards equality for men and women.

[Source: *Jus Suffragii: International Women Suffrage News* 17, no.9 (1923): 150. Available through the Gerritsen Collection.]

Taka Kato (1887–1979) was a Japanese Christian who contributed to the founding of the Tokyo YWCA, an organization she continued working with until her retirement in 1944. In 1937 she spent six months working in the head office of the International YWCA in Geneva. In 1928 she became the president of the Surugadai Women's Academy, while she was still active with the YWCA. She was also chair of the International Labour Organization's Women's Labour Committee and worked to improve the working conditions of women workers in mines and mills.

Taka Kato

Working Women in Japan: Address to the International Congress of Working Women (1924)

During the last half-century Japan has made a record for a rapid progress in its transformation from a feudal system into a new industrial and commercial nation. As a result she has to face many Labour problems. One of the burning questions of the day is how to better the conditions existing among the women workers.

Besides the usual problems in industrial occupations, as known in other countries, there are some complications peculiar to Japan. These are three in number:–

(1) Employment of women at hard labour-mining, building, etc.

(2) Employment of women and young girls in immoral occupations licensed by the government. (Mr Kagawa, the leading Christian Labour leader in Japan, says that one girl in every seventeen becomes either a 'geisha' or a regular prostitute. The total number is over 107,000.)

(3) The dormitory system for housing women factory employees.

How many women are employed in Japan? Statistics are difficult to compile accurately, but Mr B. Suzuki, president of the General Federation of Labour of Japan, roughly estimates the number as 12,820,000, of whom 100,000 are working in mines.

Somewhere about 60,000 women work along with men in the pits of the coal mines in a temperature of ninety degrees. Men and women are naked, with loin-cloths only. It is extremely hot and damp. The men dig coal, and the women carry the coal, in two shallow baskets suspended from a crosspiece, each basket holding about 25 lb. Miners have their own peculiar disease, such as lung trouble, as a result of coal dust filling the lungs, and intestinal difficulties. The whole condition is inhuman.

The number of factories of all kinds where women are employed is 1,250,000. The ratio of female to male workers in the factories is as 60 to 40. In the textile industries alone 25 per cent of the employees are men and 75 per cent are women. In the spinning factories there are 700,000 women workers. Of the women textile employees 80 per cent are housed in large dormitories, and have been brought in from village life under contracts for at least three years. They sleep in alternate shifts (day and night workers), each one being allowed an average of one and a half mats (6 ft. by 3 ft.) in the dormitory room. Wages are shockingly low. Hours are long. They are allowed only one day out of every ten days.

The equipment in some factories is very up to date, and the girls do good work, but the employers do not treat girls as human beings.

In the agriculture industries, of every 100 people employed, 46 are women and 54 men. The agrarian problem is most pressing and urgent. A Farmers' Union has been started recently, but most of its members are uneducated, a circumstance which has its dangers.

Unfortunately, the age admission for children into industry is very low. Thousands of children at twelve years are actually listed in Government reports, and there are few or no inspectors to note the little children of ten or fewer years who are employed in the mines and other industries. Many abuses of the Child Labour Law, such as women working with babies on their backs, are found in the sweated industries and in many factories in the country districts where the number of employees is less than ten. It is significant that 87 per cent of all women employees are under twenty years of age.

Literacy in Japan is probably as high as in any country in the world, but notwithstanding this we have thousands of river-boat children unregistered, and illegitimate children who will never attend school at all, and are not included in Government educational reports because officially they do not exist. Some of our Japanese reformers are trying hard to raise the standard of educational requirements in order to help control this child-labour problem.

While schools are very up-to-date as to buildings, equipment, etc., conditions for the teachers, especially women teachers, are very bad, their wages being very low as compared to those in other countries. Many are married women, but their hours are long and their classes too large. Increasingly, however, the standards and opportunities for women teachers are improving. Each year more Japanese girls go abroad to study.

Wages for all women workers are very low and living prices high. Last year Kobe was said to be the most expensive city in the world to live in. A leading economist in the Tokyo Imperial University stated in 1919 that not more than 40 per cent of all the workers could afford proper nourishment. Mr Sherwood Eddy, of the American Y.M.C.A., who has travelled much in the East, states that that 90 per cent of all the Japanese people are trying to live on less than 500 yen (about £50) a year. So it is natural that the workers' state of health is very shocking. The dormitory system helps to increase the death rate from tuberculosis, which is the highest of any country publishing statistics. The factory physician estimates that one-third of all employees in Osaka have trachoma, a contagious disease. A Tokyo newspaper says that 80 per cent of 60,000 telephone operators fall victims to tuberculosis.

As to the Trade Unions in Japan, Mr Suzuki made a small beginning for women in Tokyo in 1916, but it was not successful. Mr Kagawa's wife in the South tried to start a Women's Union, but there are actually very few members. A number of small Women's Unions for Typists, etc., and Business Girls' Clubs have been formed, but at present they are uninformed as to their own limitations, and incapable of organising themselves for protection or progress. Certainly, we all realise that we need more active women leaders for our social betterment, and especially do we need leaders among the workers themselves.

What is the Government doing to better these conditions? The rather newly organised Bureau of Home Affairs is very active, and doing some constructive as well as much remedial work. The International Labour Office in London reports that the Japanese Government has ratified the convention, making fourteen years the minimum age for the employment of children.

We are especially happy to be blessed with a new Juvenile Law Court, of which the eight judges are Christians, and the chief probation officer is a woman. Miss Mary Dingman and I had an interview with one of the officials for Home Affairs in Tokyo on the subject of night work and working hours, and gathered that within three years at most the Government will try its best to reform matters by legislation.

Japan has been from the first an enthusiastic member of the League of Nations, and we are very proud that Dr Omazo Nitobe is still working as the third member of the original Secretariat in Geneva.

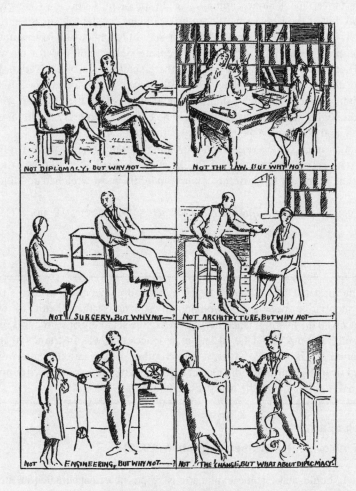

[Source: *International Women's News: Jus Suffragii* 25, no. 5 (1931): 73. Image published with permission of ProQuest; further reproduction is prohibited without permission.]

Some cities are especially progressive in their social work; Tokyo and Osaka have advanced clinics, vocational guidance bureaux, employment agencies, working men's restaurants, maternity hospitals, and very up-to-date social centres in the most congested factory sections.

The Government alone cannot solve the problem. Good laws are greatly needed, but at the same time there must be plans for their adequate enforcement. It is absolutely necessary that there should be organisations to stimulate the people's desire along the line of securing right conditions for all workers. There is also an insistent call that there shall arise women leaders from among the workers themselves who will educate the workers towards their own improvement, and who shall lay great emphasis on the idea that women are equal with men, and shall no longer be considered merely the belongings of men, and no longer expect conditions to right themselves.

Women must get vision, education, and a burning zeal to fight; if not for their own sakes, for the sake of the Japanese women and children who are doing the necessary work of the country under the most wretched conditions.

[Source: *Jus Suffragii: International Women Suffrage News* 18, no. 5 (1924): 77.]

Amelia Earhart (1897–1939) was a US aviation pioneer and women's rights advocate. Earhart was the first woman to fly solo across the Atlantic, for which she received the Distinguished Flying Cross. She set many other records, wrote best-selling books about her flying experiences and was instrumental in the formation of The Ninety-Nines, a women pilots' organization. Earhart disappeared over the central Pacific Ocean during an attempt to make a circumnavigational flight in 1937. She was declared dead in 1939.

Amelia Earhart

The Employment of Women in Aviation (1932)

I feel I should make some explanations of possible inaccuracies in the following text by saying it is very difficult to get up to date statistics on women in aviation. There are apparently several reasons for this lack, not the least of which is the numerical unimportance of the group. Even though the industry be expanded to include such occupations as are found in the aircraft divisions of precision instrument manufactures, for instance, the total number of women employed therein is still small. So far as I can find there is no agency following up the subject specially nor any one which has complete information. The Labor Bureau Statistics I have been able to obtain are not quite of today. However, they show some interesting facts which are unchanged in the main and I shall quote them as published. They apply, of course, only to factory work. Flying and special positions I shall discuss separately.

In all airplane occupations the proportion of men to women is about 44 to 1. Only 24 of the 66 concerns reported employ women at all in any capacity, yet there are listed 16 possible occupations. The average earnings for men are about 70 cents an hour, for women 38 cents. Sometimes this difference in pay obtains for the same type of work, and apparently depends solely upon whether the worker is a man or a woman. I myself have seen evidence of this in one factory visited. There, the vice-president boasted about the excellence of the women's work as compared with that of men on the same job. When I asked about the pay he admitted the scale was as above, and added, 'Well, the women will work for less so you can't blame the factory manager for cutting his costs any way he can.' The Department of Labor shows the full time hours of women in aviation to be 47.3 as compared to 47.9 for men, so that discrepancy cannot be accounted for through lost time on the women's part. Most of the feminine labor is used in the wing departments for sewing the fabric used in wing covering, or doing the lightest wood work. There are, however, several women welders and some inspectors in engine plants. The Naval Aircraft Factory in Philadelphia lists several women employees, and in building the dirigibles, the Shenandoah and the Akron, women were employed in the construction of the gas cells and in the application of gold beater's skin to them. There are a few one-of-a-kind factory jobs, existing usually because of an individual's especial ability and as long as the worker offers almost no threat to men's employment. These jobs are uncatalogued and I hesitate to mention any, as my knowledge is hearsay or based on unauthenticated news releases.

As I have indicated before, the aircraft divisions of rubber, petroleum and instrument companies, to mention only a few of the ramifications of the industry, utilize women in various capacities.

Closely allied to aviation, as a useful parasite perhaps, is the manufacturing of parachutes. There women almost exclusively cut and sew the fabric used, but men pack the finished products into covers – at least, in every instance I have noted.

Outside factory work there is clerical help to consider. As in all industries, much of it is now designated definitely 'women's work,' and so wherever filing, stenography, etc., are necessary, women are found. The offices where they work are not always in town. Often they are on or adjacent to an airport or testing field where the staff can see something of actual flying activities.

It seems necessary to make a distinction between the occupations I have mentioned on the one hand, and flying and special jobs on the other. In the first place many people think of aviation as composed almost entirely of pilots. They overlook the great non-flying group of workers who are necessary to build the planes, and keep them running. With increasing air travel on the part of the public, an army of traffic men, ticket sellers, accountants, and mechanics, all under trained heads, besides pilots, are needed to operate the country's great network of airlines. In this group, as well as in factories and executive offices, women play their part, but their part is almost without exception a clerical one. In fact, if I were to count only pilots, there would be not one woman discovered in the cockpit of any scheduled airplane. (By scheduled I mean operated according to time-table, i.e., the regular service of aircraft leaving a port at a given time to arrive at another similarly.)

However, there are women who do earn their living by flying. They sell airplanes, they ferry plans about the country, they carry passengers, they instruct, they fly in the promotion department of a few companies who use airplanes for advertising and for transporting their executives.

As to special positions, there are a number worthy of mention. Several women own or manage airports; several conduct schools, alone or with their husbands, several hold traffic positions of varying importance, one designs the interior of passenger airlines. There is one woman examiner in the medical staff of the Department of Commerce, Aeronautics Branch. (Pilots, you know, have to undergo a physical examination every six months and individuals are not granted permits for learning to fly until they pass prescribed physical tests.) A number of women are associated with the journals of the trade. One conducts a special page, another is assistant editor, others write articles for use inside and outside this special field. There is one woman publicity director, and of course, many touch aviation through advertising. One of the most able and accurate artists on drawing aircraft for advertising (or any other outlet, for that matter) is a woman. Two airlines employ women as hostesses on their large cabin planes. Everyone is familiar with the number of women who manage travel bureaus throughout the country. Most of these now handle air-line tickets and there is one with a feminine owner which caters only to air travelers.

To return to pilots, there are 472 licensed women in the United States. Of these about fifty hold the transport of highest grade. This license alone permits its holder to fly the regular passenger or mail lines for hire or to give instruction. Four hundred and seventy-two seems a large number when it is remembered there were but 12 women licensees in January, 1929. However, it shrinks to about 1 in 37 in the face of the entire pilots' listing, which is 17,226 strong.

Taking into consideration only the 50 transport licenses, for none other can really be counted as offering commercial possibilities, the number of potential candidates for available jobs, if any, is seen to be exceedingly small.

Despite these figures, there are more women flyers in commercial aviation in the United States than in all the rest of the world. Nearly all feminine records, as homologated by the international sporting body, the Fédération Aeronautique Internationale, are claimed by American flyers. The categories for men and women, by the way, are separate. However, a world record may be made by either, equipment and ability permitting.

An interesting commentary on women's earning capacity in contest flying is given by the results of the National Air Races of last September. The sweepstakes in the handicap derby for men and women were won by a woman. Her prizes throughout the meet certainly totalled more than $4,000, not including a Ford car. A Springfield entrant won the largest single prize for women in the closed course events by coming in first in the Aerol Trophy Race. She received a beautiful cup for a year, and $3,750 to keep.

I should like to mention one more aspect of women's flying before I draw a conclusion. In the Women's Speed Classic I mentioned only a moment ago, the winning time was 187 m.p.h. This was only a little less than 15 miles slower than that of the corresponding men's event of last year.

Probably nothing has done more to demonstrate women's flying ability than such outstanding performances in the air. Because they could not point to much in the way of flying well done heretofore, women have been handicapped when applying for the simplest flying positions. However, it must be admitted that some prejudice is not without foundation. Not only have women had fewer opportunities to obtain instruction than men (the army and navy don't accept them yet for instance), but they have had fewer opportunities to gain experience after they soloed. Without proper training and wide experience no pilot can hope to find a position in transport work. Officially women face such odds in both these cases that it is a wonder to me they have succeeded as they have. For instance, courses of instruction are still, to a greater or lesser degree, founded on men's background of education – which after all is very different from their sisters'. Airplanes are still made for men in some details. Jobs where tuition could be partly earned are harder for girls to obtain than for boys. (Nobody wants a girl grease monkey that I know of.)

Despite the fact that there is no sex distinctions made in Federal licenses, as in some countries, there is at least one locality with the laws restrictive to women. In New Jersey, for instance, women cannot race in a closed course event unless they go simply round the required turns for a comparison of their elapsed times. No sort of trial of skill is held either for men or women, but women, because they are such, are tacitly adjudged incompetent to be in the air together in regular racing forms. Perhaps making accomplishment as difficult as any of these is the voice of Tradition still echoing loudly, 'Women can't.'

With such handicaps it will be some time before women generally achieve experience enough to be qualified for all flying positions. Although there are a few women who are entirely equal to becoming airline pilots now, many, many more must win their wings before individual ability can obliterate sex lines. By the time such is the case the air traveling public will have no prejudice, nor need to have, against women in aviation.

[Source: *The National Woman's Party*, 4 June 1932, 139–40. Available through the Gerritsen Collection.]

PART EIGHT
Peace

European and North American women became involved with peace movements on both a national and international basis in the first half of the nineteenth century, although these peace organizations were not specifically feminist.[1] It was with the creation of a feminist and pacifist weekly, *La Paix des Deux Mondes*, by the French activist Eugénie Niboyet and the founding in Geneva of l'Association Internationale des Femmes by Marie Pouchoulin-Goegg in 1868 that women began to define peace work as their purview. At the end of the century international feminist organizations began more concertedly to participate in the peace movement from a feminist perspective. The WCTU began actively pursuing peace in the 1880s, urging arbitration rather than war as a means of settling imperialist disputes, despite the often contradictory imperialist impulses of WCTU national sections.[2] In the 1890s the ICW created a committee for International Peace and Arbitration; and the International Peace and Arbitration Association issued a call soliciting the participation of women at its 1885 Berne congress. As M.E. Phillips reports in *The Woman's Signal*, the British Women's Temperance Association, perceiving a link between temperance and peace in the financing of armaments through alcohol sales, sent delegates to the Peace Congress in Antwerp in 1894.

New feminist organizations with a specifically pacifist orientation also came to be created in the period. In 1895 the Union Internationale des Femmes was created in France following a visit by a delegate of the British Peace Society, Ellen Robinson, who brought an appeal signed by English women.[3] Princess Gabrielle Wiszniewska founded the Ligue des Femmes pour le Désarmement in 1896, an organization that changed its name to the Alliance des Femmes pour la Paix in 1899. In the article translated and published in the *Australian Woman's Sphere*, Wiesniewska focuses on education as the primary method for working towards abolishing war, advocating among other specific recommendations international exchanges of pupils and teachers so as to create transnational bonds and undo national prejudice founded on ignorance. Women also demonstrated internationally for peace, as May Wright Sewall indicates in her article in *The Woman's Exponent*. Sewall describes the meetings held by women around the world on 15 May 1899, organized by the German pacifist-feminist Margerethe Lenore Selenka and timed to precede by a few days an important peace conference at the Hague on 18 May of that year. Sometimes known as the Czar's peace conference, that meeting established a permanent court of international arbitration. In 1901, Sewall called for women throughout the United States to organize meetings on the anniversary of that conference to further the cause of peace.

The outbreak of the First World War brought more women still into the peace movement. The manifesto issued by the IWSA describes women as the 'mothers of the race' and urges arbitration as a means of averting the horrors of the war that is threatened – this despite the fact that Millicent Garrett Fawcett, one of the signatories on behalf of the IWSA, was not a pacifist. Lucy Thoumaian's call to women to meet weekly during the war and to petition their respective governments to pursue arbitration as a means of bringing a speedy end to the war also refers to women as the 'mothers of humanity.' Olive Schreiner elaborates on this maternalist pacifism that characterized much of the discourse of women's peace organizations, including the Women's Peace Party and the International Committee of Women for Permanent Peace which later became the Women's International League for Peace and Freedom (WILPF).[4] Not all the women engaged in pacifism during the First World War believed in such a natural link between women and peace, however. Jane Addams, one of the key organizers of the International Congress of Women at the Hague from 28 April to 1 May 1915 out of which emerged the International Committee of Women for Permanent Peace, disputed the theory that women were naturally pacifist, yet made the case for women contributing to internationalism and promoting peace. She was part of the delegation of women selected to tour European capitals over the month or so following the meetings at the Hague to attempt to mediate between belligerent parties and bring about an end to the war. Socialist women like Adelheid Popp and Sylvia Pankhurst found still other reasons to argue for peace: the common exploitation of workers across national boundaries and 'enemy' lines by the bourgeoisie who profited from war.

If the outbreak of war compelled some women to direct their organizing towards pacifist causes, other feminist work was interrupted by the conflict and many of the feminists involved with international organizations engaged in patriotic support of their respective nations. The work of the International Council of Women and of the International Women's Suffrage Alliance was effectively halted, although the existence of *Jus Suffragii* at least enabled the members of the IWSA to stay in touch.[5] Following the First World War, members of the Alliance began to take up the cause of peace, calling on its members to participate in a study conference on the subject in Amsterdam in 1927. Even though the war had given birth to new international feminist organizations working specifically on peace, pre-eminently the WILPF, the Alliance felt it had a role to play as well.

International work on peace encountered many of the same impediments to transnational solidarity as other aspects of the women's movement, not the least of which was the structural prejudice of international organizations and international law in favour of nation states. As Sandi Cooper puts it, 'The problem for peace congresses – be they pre-war or the 1915 Hague women's meeting – was that the international law formulations on which they all depended so completely were meaningless for peoples who had no nations.'[6] Thus, for Palestinian feminist Matiel Mogannam, peace was very much linked with acquiring national rights. Similarly, Egypt's dependent nation status in relation to Britain prompted disagreements over the WILPF position on the question of disarmament, as the exchange of letters between WILPF vice-president Clara Ragaz and Alice Jacot of the Egyptian section makes evident. Another kind of tension emerges between imperialist powers like the United States and its Latin American neighbours in Josephine Schain's account of the resentment and distrust directed towards the United States that she noticed when she attended a conference initiated by a group of women in Buenos Aires who aimed to 'banish war from the Western hemisphere.'

In the late 1930s, as fascism was on the rise and Mussolini invaded Ethiopia, Franco took up arms against the republican government in Spain, Japan invaded China, and Hitler began annexing Austria and part of Czechoslovakia, women again took a stand against war and tyranny. Virginia Woolf published *Three Guineas* at least partly in response to the Spanish Civil War, arguing that the 'daughters of educated men' could not be expected to support war given their political and civil positions as women. Margery Corbett Ashby, by contrast, urged women to fight against tyranny and in the name of freedom and democracy. The All-India Women's Conference of 1939, with an eye to recent and on-going conflicts around the world in the months leading up to the Second World War, issued a resolution against war and appealed to women around the world to promote non-violence.

NOTES

1 See Sandi E. Cooper, 'Women's Participation in European Peace Movements: The Struggle to Prevent World War I,' in *Women and Peace: Theoretical, Historical*

and Practical Perspectives, ed. Ruth Roach Pierson (London, New York, Sydney: Croom Helm, 1987), 51–75.

2 Ian Tyrell, *Woman's World, Woman's Empire: The Woman's Christian Temperance Union in International Perspective, 1880–1930* (Chapel Hill, London: U of North Carolina P, 1991), 170, 178, 183.

3 Cooper, 'Women's Participation,' 56–7.

4 See Susan Zeiger, 'She Didn't Raise Her Boy to Be a Slacker: Motherhood, Conscription, and the Culture of the First World War,' *Feminist Studies* 22.1 (Spring 1996): 6–39.

5 Leila Rupp, *Worlds of Women: The Making of an International Women's Movement* (Princeton: Princeton UP, 1997), 26.

6 Cooper, 'Women's Participation,' 67.

Anonymous

The International Arbitration and Peace Association (1884)

The International Arbitration and Peace Association propose to hold an International Conference, at Berne, next August, and an appeal for help has been sent to all their supporters. This appeal is specially directed to women. 'It is a work,' they say, 'in which women, as well as men, may everywhere take part,' and again –

> This is especially a woman's question, for the evil and brutalizing influence of armies and of war comes home to them as mothers and wives. Their clearer perception of the need of humanizing influences, and their natural comprehension of the truth that all progress depends on the principle of love, as the only regenerating force of mankind, will make them feel it to be a sacred duty to deliver the world from this source of terror and wrong. To maintain these proposed societies, to meet the expense of supplying literature, the employment of lecturers, and other means – funds will not be wanting – for women can always, by their patience and perseverance, obtain money for a good cause. Their fidelity to great principles, unwearied and unresting, will always prevail. Therefore to women we appeal for co-operation, for suggestions, and for help to enable us to carry out this good work. We shall be glad to enroll women of every class, creed, and country as our adherents to correspond with them respecting detailed plans of action and to obtain their aid in laying the foundation of a mighty confederation in the cause of Human Progress. Here is a field in which every woman may do something towards bringing about a new era for humanity. It depends on the extent to which men and women everywhere in their several spheres of influence, in cottage and in hall, in village and in city, will work for this sacred cause – how soon shall it find its triumph?

But our legislators tell us that women are not concerned in foreign politics and questions of peace and war. Are we to believe them?

[Source: *The Englishwoman's Review of Social and Industrial Questions* 15, no. 134 (1884): 293–4. Available through the Gerritsen Collection.]

M.E. Phillips (?–?) was a member of the British Women's Temperance Association, was Honorary Treasurer of the New Society for the Sale of Ladies

Work in the 1870s, and Honorary Secretary of the Ladies School for Technical Needlework in the 1880s.

M.E. Phillips
The Peace Congress at Antwerp (1894)

The Peace Cause is dovetailed into that of Temperance by the fact that the enormous cost of the armaments of Great Britain is mainly defrayed out of the revenue derived from the sale of intoxicating drinks, while the same love that prompts [women] to work for the deliverance of humanity from the evils of intemperance must also be in sympathy with efforts to do away with the curse of war.

This sentiment found expression at the last executive committee of the B.W.T.A., in the appointment of a delegate to the Sixth Annual Peace Congress to be held at Antwerp from August 29th to September 1st.

The municipality of Antwerp kindly placed the Rand Hall of the Athenaeum at the disposal of the Peace Bureau. There gathered on the opening day of the Congress about 150 delegates from 53 different societies, representing the nationalities of Belgium, France, Germany, Switzerland, Austria, Italy, Denmark, Sweden, Portugal, America, and England. Among these were M. Frede Passy, ex-member of the French Chamber of Deputies, M. Fredc. Bayer, deputy to the Danish Parliament, M. Moneta, editor of the Italian paper, *Il Secolo*, President Trueblood, from America, and Mme Frost Ormsby, of the W.W.C.T.U., who, on their behalf, presented a bell to the bureau, Mme La Baronne Suttner, the talented authoress of 'Die Waffen Nieder' (Lay Down Your Arms), a book which, in Austria and Germany has had much the same effect in creating a public opinion against the military system that 'Uncle Tom's Cabin' had against slavery.

The Congress was presided over by M. de la Haye, deputy to the Belgian Parliament, who was supported by M. Le Baron Moreau, ex-Foreign Minister of Belgium.

Letters of regret at inability to attend were read from many eminent persons, as well as a telegram, expressive of the approval of and interest in the Congress felt by the king, who at a later period courteously received at Brussels several of the leading members of the Congress. The Burgomeister of Antwerp also gave a reception to all the members of the Congress in the Hotel de Ville, and addressed them in terms that betokened his unity with and appreciation of the efforts of the Bureau de la Paix.

The President's opening address betokened a man of statesmanlike ability, coupled with deep humanitarian sympathies. It ended with a vivid account of the horrors he had himself witnessed on the battlefield of Sedan. This was followed by speeches from the representatives of the different nationalities, each giving an account of the work for the cause of Peace carried on in his or her own country. Almost all reported a growing public opinion against the military system.

The work of the Congress was arranged by two separate committees, the one taking charge of the numerous resolutions which had been sent up proposing various methods of propaganda. Under this head women were encouraged to realize their responsibilities both as mothers and citizens. The former were exhorted, instead of giving their children warlike toys and dressing them in soldier-like clothes, to seek to instill into their young minds peace principles. Much was said on the need of substituting for school books, which make wars the chief incidents in history, those which represent the far more potent and true causes of the development of civilised races. The importance of enlisting the interest of the working class in the Peace Movement formed also the subject of a resolution. The other committee devoted itself to the resolutions suggesting ways for establishing courts of arbitration for the settlement of international disputes.

Amongst the resolutions brought before the Congress, and carried unanimously, was the following: –

'Every sovereign state, large and small, weak or strong, shall be considered the equal of all others, and have right to the same consideration as the strongest nation,' etc., thus giving to Right the place hitherto held by Might.

Another important resolution was passed in like manner, urging that efforts be made to induce the different governments to meet in Congress to consider a process of mutual reduction of armaments. Some of these resolutions were specially recommended to the consideration of the Interparliamentary Congress about to be held at The Hague by invitation of the Dutch Government.

Despite the difficulties naturally arising from the different languages spoken, the debates were carried on with earnestness and mutual consideration, and all felt that the intercourse this afforded was a helpful element towards a mutual understanding between different nations, and *au revoir* was the farewell spoken on every hand. A pleasant excursion on the River Scheldt, a banquet, and a public meeting at which a splendid oration was made by M. F. Passy, were amongst the incidents of the Congress.

Thus closed the Peace Congress. Antwerpen (Handwerfen) derives its name from a legend which tells of a tyrant who levied a toll on every vessel which passed his castle on the river. Captains who were caught evading this imposition had their hands amputated and thrown into the river. The severed hands appear on the Antwerp coat of arms, and as this device formed a conspicuous ornament on the beautiful carved mantelpiece of the room in which we held our last meeting, I thought of a future when men should regard the militarism of to-day in much the same light as the acts of the tyrant of Antwerp are regarded by the present generation. A happy, peaceful Sabbath followed, when over thirty of the delegates gathered to return thanks to God for the blessings of the past weekend, and to re-commit themselves and the cause to the guidance of the Prince of Peace.

[Source: *The Woman's Signal*, 1894, 154. Available through the Gerritsen Collection.]

May Wright Sewall
In the Interest of Peace (1901)

On May 15, 1899, a universal demonstration in behalf of peace was undertaken by an international committee of women. Through the indefatigable labors of this committee numerous meetings were held in eighteen different countries. The chairman of the entire committee, Frau Margerethe Lenore Selenka, Munich, reported the results of this demonstration [at] the peace conference at its opening session at the Hague, which took place on May 18th of that year.

Notwithstanding the discouraging conditions of the intervening years, and the many pessimistic jeers at the Czar's conference at the Hague, it is certainly a matter for grateful consideration that as a result of that conference the permanent court of international arbitration will convene at the Hague on the second anniversary of the conference. To celebrate this event, to show that their zeal for peace, instead of being cooled by wars and rumors of wars, is only by these events excited to greater ardor, the same international committee has undertaken another demonstration by women to be held on May 18th, 1901. The demonstration will be simultaneous with the opening of the court of international arbitration.

By the authority of the international committee, including distinguished women of Germany, England, Austria, Canada, Belgium, Denmark, Spain, France, Holland, Roumania, Hungary, Italy, Norway, Russia, Servia, Sweden, Switzerland and Japan, as the representatives on the committee in the United States, the undersigned hereby urges women throughout the United States to arrange for meetings, large and small, in behalf of international peace and arbitration.

Wherever local councils exist, it is recommended that such organizations as they include should take the initiative in making arrangements for such meetings.

In 1899, with less than a month's notice, there were held in the United States on May 15th, in twenty-one different States, 163 meetings, at which there were reported to be present 73,921 women. With that precedent the same length of time should enable the women of our country to double the number of meetings to be held on May 18th, and to proportionately increase their attendance.

The taste of war which has been so bitter upon our lips should, and surely does, increase the desire of women everywhere to strengthen public sentiment for peace and to increase public faith in the possibility of ultimate arrival at a condition of universal peace, where war will no longer be tolerated by enlightened nations more than personal combat is now tolerated by enlightened individuals.

Let all women to whose notice this call comes feel the appeal to be an individual one to aid in a local demonstration.

Where local councils do not exist women's clubs, temperance unions, educational associations and college leagues are all appropriate agencies through which arrangements may be made for local demonstrations.

Mary Wright Sewall,
Representing the United States of America on the International Peace Committee of Women.

[Source: *Woman's Exponent* 29, no. 24 (1901): 103. Available through the Gerritsen Collection.]

Gabrielle Wiszniewska (?–?), founder of the Ligue des Femmes pour le désarmement (1896), an organization that subsequently became the Alliance des femmes pour la Paix in 1899.

Princess Gabrielle Wiszniewska
Women's Universal Alliance for Peace (1904)

We print below the translation of an article by the Princess Wiszniewska on the aims of the new alliance, whose object is the abolition of war by the means of education. This is work which is already being carried on by the International Council of Women with its nineteen affiliated National Councils. The world-wide organization of this body gives it a great advantage in undertaking such a campaign.

This society perceived from its foundation that it was premature and useless to talk of disarmament – which should be regarded as the result and not as the means of universal peace – and it drew up a new programme, which has borne fruit, and made it one of the most powerful agencies for peace. It determined to form societies of women in all the countries of the world, and to promote acts of friendship between nations. The society has now more than five millions of adherents. These acts of friendship have been the precursors of the entente cordiale just formed between France and England. In Spain, Her Royal Highness the Infanta Eulalia offered on her own initiative to become honorary president of the Alliance, thus setting a fine example to the ladies who are holding aloof from the peace movement, which all women, rich and poor, throughout the world, ought to join.

1   The next object of the Universal Alliance is Peace by Education, which was unfolded with all its details at our Congress in the Paris Exposition of 1900, and this new teaching has spread all over the world. The principal resolutions passed at Congress were:

2   That the cultivation of the pacific ideal should be the particular care of mothers, of governesses, and of tutors.

3   That the young should not be allowed to witness any spectacle tending to excite the instincts of cruelty or of oppression of the weak.

4   That the teaching of history establishes the difference between the modern age, which is one of science and work, and the ancient, which was one of conquest and war.

5   That the principles of International Arbitration should be taught in all schools; and that, for the teaching of languages, teachers should be exchanged from the schools of various countries.

6   That libraries of books on Peace and Arbitration should be installed in all schools.

7   That, where possible, there should be frequent changes of batches of pupils between schools of different nations, in order to bring together the youth of varying nationalities, and thus help to efface international hatreds.

The Women's Universal Alliance invites all schoolmasters and teachers, as well as all women, rich and poor alike, to join the Alliance, and use their influence to prevent hatred and fratricidal strife between men. Woman is particularly fitted for such a mission. She it is who, under the halo of her tenderness and strength of will, can inaugurate this education by pouring into the hearts of children the sweetness of Christian morality, and by inspiring men to noble thoughts. Such is a brief outline of the principles propagated by the Alliance in all countries, for it is only by education that universal peace can be realized.

(Of the resolutions passed at the first Congress of the Alliance, the sixth would at first seem to be one of the most difficult to carry into practice, but it is already being carried out between England, France and Germany. – Ed., *Woman's Sphere*.)

[Source: *Woman's Sphere* 3, no. 41 (1904): 395–6. Available through the Gerritsen Collection.]

Olive Schreiner (1855–1920) was a South African author, pacifist, and political activist. In 1881 she travelled to England with the ambition of enrolling in medical studies, but was prevented by ill health from pursuing formal training. Instead, she devoted herself to socially conscious writing. She joined the Progressive Organization, a group of radical thinkers who debated politics and philosophy. In 1889 she returned to South Africa and began to get involved in Cape politics. During the lead-up to the Boer War, she attempted to deter South African officials from pursuing war, and she published *The South African Question by an English South African* in an effort to influence English popular opinion. Unsuccessful at averting the conflict, she turned to writing *Woman and Labor*, in which she returned to the theme of war.

Olive Schreiner

From *Woman and War* (1911)

But, it may be said: 'What then of war, that struggle of the human creature to attain its ends by physical force and at the price of the life of others: will you take part in that also?' We reply: Yes; more particularly in that field we intend to play our part. We have always borne part of the weight of war, and the major part. It is not that in primitive times we suffered from the destruction of the fields we tilled and the houses we built; it is not that later as domestic laborers and producers, though unwaged, we, in taxes and material loss and additional labor, paid as much as our male towards the cost of war; it is not that in a comparatively insignificant manner, as nurses of the wounded in modern times, or now and again as warrior chieftainesses and leaders in primitive and other societies, we have borne our part; nor is it even because the spirit of resolution in its women, and their willingness to endure, has in all ages, again and again largely determined the fate of a race that goes to war, that we demand our controlling right where war is concerned. Our relation to war is far more intimate, personal, and indissoluble than this. Men have made boomerangs, bows, swords, or guns with which to destroy one another; we have made the men who destroyed and were destroyed! We have in all ages produced, at an enormous cost, the primal munition of war, without which no other would exist. There is no battlefield on earth, nor ever has been, howsoever covered with slain, which it has not cost the women of the race more in actual bloodshed and anguish to supply, than it has cost the men who lie there. *We pay the first cost on all human life.*

In supplying the men for the carnage of a battlefield, women have not merely lost actually more blood, and gone through a more acute anguish and weariness, in the long months of bearing and in the final agony of child-birth, than has been experienced by the men who cover it; but, in the long months of rearing that follow, the women of the race go through a long, patiently endured strain which no knapsacked soldier on his longest march has ever more than equalled; while, even in the matter of death, in all civilized societies, the probability that the average woman will die in child-birth is immeasurably greater than the probability that the average male will die in battle.

There is, perhaps, no woman, whether she have borne children, or be merely potentially a child-bearer, who could look down upon a battlefield covered with slain, but the thought would rise in her, 'So many mothers' sons! So many young bodies brought into the world to lie there! So many months of weariness and pain while bones and muscles were shaped within! So many hours of anguish and struggle that breath might be! So many baby mouths drawing life at women's breasts; – all this, that men might lie with glazed eyeballs, and swollen faces, and fixed, blue, unclosed mouths, and great limbs tossed – this, that an acre of ground might be manured with human flesh, that next year's grass or poppies or karoo bushes may spring up greener and redder, where they have lain, or that the sand of a plain may have a glint of white bones!' And we cry, 'Without an inexorable cause, this must not be!' No woman who is a woman says of a human body, 'It is nothing!'

On that day when the woman takes her place beside the man in the governance and arrangement of external affairs of her race will also be that day that heralds the death of war as a means of arranging human differences. No tinsel of trumpets and flags will ultimately seduce women into the insanity of recklessly destroying life, or gild the willful taking of life with any other name than that of murder, whether it be the slaughter of the million or of one by one. And this will be, not because with the sexual function of maternity necessarily goes in the human creature a deeper moral insight, or a loftier type of social instinct than that which accompanies the paternal. Men have in all ages led as nobly as women in many paths of heroic virtue, and toward the higher social sympathies; in certain ages, being freer and more widely cultured, they have led further and better. The fact that woman has no inherent all-round moral superiority over her male companion, or naturally on all points any higher social instinct, is perhaps most clearly exemplified by one curious very small fact: the two terms signifying intimate human relationships which in almost all human languages bear the most sinister and antisocial significance are both terms which have as their root the term 'mother,' and denote feminine relationships – the words 'mother-in-law' and 'step-mother.'

In general humanity, in the sense of social solidarity, and in magnanimity, the male has continually proved himself at least the equal of the female. Nor will women shrink from war because they lack courage. Earth's women of every generation have faced suffering and death with an equanimity that no soldier on a battlefield has ever surpassed and few have equalled; and where war has been to preserve life, or land, or freedom, rather than for aggrandisement, and power, unparasitised and laboring women have in all ages known how to bear an active part, and die.

Nor will woman's influence militate against war because in the future woman will not be able physically to bear her part in it. The smaller size of her muscle, which might severely have disadvantaged her when war was conducted with a battle-axe or sword and hand to hand, would now little or not at all affect her. If intent on training for war, she might acquire the skill for guiding a Maxim or shooting down a foe with a Lee-Metford at four thousand yards as ably as any male; and undoubtedly, it has not been only the peasant girl of France, who has carried latent and hid in her person the gifts that would make the great general. If our European nations should continue in their present semi-civilized condition a few generations longer, it is highly probable that as financiers, as managers of the commissariat department, as inspectors of provisions and clothing for the army, women may probably play a very leading part; and that the nation which is the first to employ women may be placed at a vast advantage over its fellows in time of war. It is not because of woman's cowardice, incapacity, nor, above all, because of her general superior virtue, that she will end war when her voice is fully and clearly heard in the governance of states – it is because, on this one point, and on this point almost alone, the knowledge of woman, simply as woman, is superior to that of man; she knows the history of human flesh; she knows its cost; he does not.[1]

[Source: *Woman and Labor* (New York: Frederick A. Stokes Company Publishers, 1911), 173-179.]

---

1 It is noteworthy that even Catherine of Russia, a ruler and statesman of a virile and uncompromising type, and not usually troubled with moral scruples, yet refused with indignation the offer of Frederick of Prussia to pay her heavily for a small number of Russian recruits in an age when the hiring out of soldiers was common among the sovereigns of Europe.

Millicent Garrett Fawcett and Chrystal Macmillan
International Manifesto of Women (1914)

Drawn up by the International Woman Suffrage Alliance and delivered on July 31st at the Foreign Office and Foreign Embassies in London.

We, the women of the world, view with apprehension and dismay the present situation in Europe, which threatens to involve one continent, if not the whole world, in the disasters and horrors of war. In this terrible hour, when the fate of Europe depends on decisions which women have no power to shape, we, realizing our responsibilities as the mothers of the race, cannot stand passive by. Powerless though we are politically, we call upon the Governments and Powers of our several countries to avert the threatened unparalleled disaster. In none of the countries immediately concerned in the threatened outbreak have women any direct power to control the political destinies of their own countries. They find themselves on the brink of the almost unbearable position of seeing all that they most reverence and treasure, the home, the family, the race, subjected not merely to risks, but to certain and extensive damage which they are powerless either to avert or assuage. Whatever its result the conflict will leave mankind the poorer, will set back civilization, and will be a powerful check to the gradual amelioration in the condition of the masses of the people, on which so much of the real welfare of nations depends.

We women of twenty-six countries, having banded ourselves together in the International Women's Suffrage Alliance with the object of obtaining the political means of sharing with men the power which shapes the fate of nations, appeal to you to leave untried no method of conciliation or arbitration for arranging international differences which may help to avert deluging half the civilized world in blood.

Signed on behalf of the International Woman Suffrage Alliance,

> Millicent Garrett Fawcett,
> > First Vice-President.
> Chrystal Macmillan
> > Recording Secretary.

[Source: *Jus Suffragii: International Women Suffrage News* 8, no. 13 (1914): 1. Available through the Gerritsen Collection.]

Lucy Thoumaian (1890–1940), also known as Lucie Thoumaian-Rossier, was an Armenian exile living in London. She and her husband, Garabed Thoumaian, participated in the First Universal Races conference in London in 1911, where they made the symbolic gesture of formally embracing the Turkish delegates. Thoumaian was among the women who participated in the conference of women at the Hague in 1915.

Lucy Thoumaian

A Manifesto to Women of Every Land (1914)

The 'Every Woman' International Movement for Arbitration at the Hague.
To the Editor and to Women of Every Land.

Dear Sisters of Every Land. – Whilst our respective soldiers go bravely to the front, and whilst we at home do what we can for the wounded and the distressed, there is something else still more important to do, of which no one seems to think and which is very specially suited also to the soothing and loving influence of woman. It is the *preventing* our beloved soldiers to become wounded! It is to work, and this *internationally*, in the interest of the future peace of Europe. It is whilst the human mind is proving the evils of war that it is best disposed to consider the advisability of peace for the present time and for all time.

To this effect and to *women everywhere* we advise to hold, *in every land*, in towns and villages and centres, *weekly women's meetings*, which will go on till we have secured peace. Though begun by prayer, they will continue in work, in results, this being the only efficacious, legitimate, and logical way, were only individuals as well as nations willing to understand it! *I shall be pleased to hear of any hall or large room in London to be had weekly for this purpose*, if possible free of charge; *and from any well-accredited woman of every land who wishes to join the London Committee and to help the movement in any way.*

Whilst being heart and soul with our devoted soldiers at the front, whilst we tend them everywhere, nurse and comfort them, we will then also, in peace and in love, we *women of all nations*, consider matters week by week, call out together – 'each to our God' and each to our own Governments, to shorten the *intolerable evil and sin*, and to resort to *arbitration*, now and at all times, it being the only possible means to disentangle the present tangle of Europe, which, far from heading us towards peace, is leading us straight away to further hatred and spirit of revenge, hence to further wars.

War begets war: it has done so from the beginning, and will forever do so.

But love and peace and kindness beget love and peace and kindness. We will meet without distinction of party, creed, or nationality – we will do so all over the world. We will do so without 'nagging' at any nation, whether ours or any other. They all need all our sympathy and help. We will do so as mothers of humanity – as sisters of the whole human race. We will do so as mothers, sisters and wives of our beloved ones of all nations who are now being ruthlessly murdered on the battlefields. We will do so as true women, and that is enough! This will forward our cause better than anything else. We will believe and we will know that we *shall* succeed, and we shall thank God and man in anticipation! We women cannot afford to allow this madness of war to go on, neither now nor at any future time; we have had enough of it! And it rests on our honour with posterity that we see to this. – Your *Sister in Every Land*,
Lucy Thoumaian, R. de V. (Mme)

[Source: *Jus Suffragii: International Women Suffrage News* 8, no.13 (1914): 170. Available through the Gerritsen Collection.]

Jane Addams (1860–1935) was a pioneer social worker in the United States, a feminist, and an internationalist. In 1889 she and Ellen Gates Starr co-founded Hull-House in Chicago, Illinois. Its main purpose was to provide social and educational opportunities for working-class people (many of them recent immigrants) in the surrounding neighbourhood. At its height, Hull-House was visited each week by around two thousand people. Addams was also a founding member of the American Civil Liberties Union and the NAACP. In 1911, she became the first vice-president of the National American Women's Suffrage Association. In 1919, she was elected the first president of the Women's International League for Peace and Freedom. In 1931 Addams became the first American woman to receive the Nobel Peace Prize.

Jane Addams
Women and Internationalism (1915)

The group of women from five of the European nations who, under the leadership of Dr Aletta Jacobs of Amsterdam, convened the International Congress of Women at The Hague, were confident that although none of the existing international associations had met since the beginning of the war, the women, including those from the belligerent nations, would be able to come together in all sobriety and friendliness to discuss their common aims and the perilous stake they all held in the war.

The women who attended the Congress from the warring countries came from home at a moment when the individual, through his own overwhelming patriotism, fairly merges his personal welfare, his convictions, almost his sense of identity, into the national consciousness. It is a precious moment in human experience, almost worth the price of war, but it made the journey of the women leaving home to attend the Congress little short of an act of heroism. Even to appear to differ from those she loves in the hour of their affliction has ever been the supreme test of a woman's conscience.

For the women who came from neutral nations there were also great difficulties. In the Scandinavian countries women are enfranchised and for long months had been sensitive to the unusual international conditions which might so easily jeopardize the peace of a neutral nation and because in a large Congress an exaggerated word spoken, or reported as spoken, might easily make new complications, they too took risks and made a moral venture.

The fifteen hundred women who came to the Congress in the face of such difficulties must have been impelled by some profound and spiritual forces. During a year when the spirit of internationalism had apparently broken down, they came together to declare the validity of the internationalism which surrounds and completes national life, even as national life itself surrounds and completes family life; to insist that internationalism does not conflict with patriotism on one side any more than family devotion conflicts with it upon the other.

In the shadow of the intolerable knowledge of what war means, revealed so minutely during the previous months, these women also made solemn protest against that of which they knew. The protest may have been feeble, but the world progresses, in the slow and halting manner in which it does progress, only in proportion to the moral energy exerted by the men and women living in it; advance in international affairs, as elsewhere, must be secured by the human will and understanding united for conscious ends.

The delegates to the Congress were not without a sense of complicity in the war, and so aware of the bloodshed and desolation surrounding them that their deliberations at moments took on the solemn tone of those who talk around the bedside of the dying. It was intimated on the floor of the Congress that the time may come when the exhausted survivors of the war may well reproach women for their inaction during this year. It is possible they may then say that when a perfervid devotion to the ideal of patriotism drove thousands of men into international warfare, the women refused to accept the challenge for the things of the spirit and in that moment of terror they too failed to assert the supreme sanctity of human life. We were told that wounded lads, lying in helpless pain and waiting too long for the field ambulances, call out constantly for their mothers, impotently beseeching them for help; of soldiers who say to their hospital nurses: 'We can do nothing for ourselves but go back to the trenches so long as we are able. Cannot the women do something about this war? Are you kind to us only when we are wounded?' There is no one else to whom they dare so speak, revealing the heart of the little child which each man carries within his own even when it beats under a uniform.

The belief that a woman is against war simply because she is a woman and not a man cannot of course be substantiated. In every country there are women who believe that war is inevitable and righteous; the majority of women as well as men in the nations at war doubtless hold that conviction. On the other hand, quite as an artist in an artillery corps commanded to fire upon a beautiful building like the *duomo* at Florence would be deterred by a compunction unknown to the man who had never given himself to creating beauty and did not know the intimate cost of it, so women, who have brought men into the world and nurtured them until they reach the age for fighting, must experience a peculiar revulsion when they see them destroyed, irrespective of the country in which these men may have been born.

Perhaps the most pathetic women we met, either at the Congress or later, were those who had sent their sons and husbands into the war, having themselves ceased to believe in it. I remember one mother who said: 'Yes, I lost my son in the first three months of the war and I am thankful he died early before he harmed the son of any other woman called an enemy.' To another woman, who as well as her husband was a pacifist, I said, 'It must be hard for you and your husband to have lost a son in battle,' and she replied quickly: 'He did not die in battle; I am happy to say he never engaged in battle. He died of blood poisoning in one of the trenches, but we have reason to believe there had been no active engagement where he was stationed.' The husband of another woman had gone to the front, telling her that under no circumstances would he be driven to kill a fellowman. One night he met a sentry from whom she believes he might have defended himself but he lost his life rather than put another man out of existence.

It was also said at the Congress that the appeals for the organization of the world upon peaceful lines may have been made too exclusively to reason and a sense of justice, that reason is only a part of the human endowment; emotion and deep-set racial impulses must be utilized as well – those primitive human urgings to foster life and to protect the helpless, of which women were the earliest custodians, and even the social and gregarious instincts that we share with the animals themselves. These universal desires must be given opportunities to expand and to have a recognized place in the formal organization of international relations which, up to this moment, have rested so exclusively upon purely legal foundations in spite of the fact that international law is comparatively undeveloped. There is an international commerce, a great system of international finance and many other fields in which relationships are not yet defined in law; quite as many of our most settled national customs have never been embodied in law at all. It would be impossible to adjudicate certain of the underlying economic and social causes of this war according to existing international law and this might therefore make more feasible the proposition urged by the Women's Congress at The Hague, of a conference of neutral nations composed of men who have had international experience so long and so unconsciously that they have come to think not merely in the terms but in the realities of internationalism and would therefore readily deal with the economic and human element involved in the situation. Such a conference would represent not one country or another, but human experience as it has developed during the last decades in Europe. It would stand not for peace at any price, but would seriously and painstakingly endeavor to discover the price to be paid for peace, which should if possible be permanent as well as immediate. The neutral nations might well say: 'Standing outside, as we do, refusing to judge your cause, because that must be left to the verdict of history, we beg of you to remember that as life is being lived at this moment on this planet of ours, difficult and complicated situations must in the end be decided and adjudicated by the best minds and the finest good will that can be brought to bear upon them. We who are outside of this fury of fighting agree that you have all proven your valor, you have demonstrated the splendor of patriotism and of united action, but we beg of you, in the name of the humane value of life, in the name of those spiritual bonds you once venerated, to allow us to bring in some other method for ending the conflict. We believe that only through help from the outside will this curious spell be broken. Great and wonderful as the war has been in certain aspects, it cannot commend itself to the people of neutral nations who are striving to look at life rationally. It is certainly possible to give powers of negotiation to some body of men who, without guile and without personal or nationalistic ambitions, will bend their best energies to the task of adjudication.'

A survey of the situation from the humane and social standpoint would consider for instance the necessity of feeding those people in the southeast portion of Europe who are pitifully underfed when there is a shortage of crops, in relation to the possession of warmwater harbors which would enable Russia to send them her great stores of wheat. Such harbors would be considered not in their political significance, as when the blockade of the Bosphorus during the Tripolis War put a stop to the transport of crops from Odessa to the Mediterranean, not from a point of view of the claims of Russia nor the counterclaims of some other nation, but from the point of view of the needs of Europe. If men of such temper, experience, and understanding of life were to make propositions to the various Governments, not in order to placate the claims of one nation and to balance them against the claims of another, but from the human standpoint, there is little doubt but that the international spirit would again reassert itself and might eventually obtain a hearing. If the purely legalistic aspects were not overstressed, such a raising of the international standard would doubtless be reinforced in many ways. For centuries Europe has not been without a witness to the spiritual unity of nations. Pope Benedict XV, who gave our delegation an audience of half an hour, and Cardinal Gaspari, in an extended interview, made it evident that the men with religious responsibility fear keenly the results of this war; while the statesmen see in it a throwback to civilization, the great international Church views it as a breeder of animosities, which will tear down and rend to pieces the work of years.

We also met in several countries the representatives of Protestant Churches organized into World Alliances or International Friendships, and countless individuals who could scarcely brook the horror of Jew fighting against Jew, Christian against Christian.

The International Congress of Women at The Hague passed a resolution to hold a meeting 'in the same place and at the same time as the Conference of the Powers which shall frame the terms of the peace settlement after the war, for the purpose of presenting practical proposals to that Conference.'[1] We recalled the fact that at the Congress of Vienna, held in 1815, in addition to determining by treaty the redistribution of the territory conquered by Napoleon, the slave trade was denounced and declared to be 'contrary to the principles of civilization and human rights,' although of course abolition of slavery was a matter for each state to determine for itself.

Within the borders of every country at war there is released a vast amount of idealism, without which war could never be carried on; a fund which might still be drawn upon when the time for settlement arrives. If the people knew that through final negotiations Europe would be so remade and internationalized that further wars would be impossible, many of them would feel that the death of thousands of young men had not been in vain, that the youth of

---

1 The reader is referred to the official report of the International Congress of Women at The Hague for a fuller account of this resolution and the organization already effected for carrying out its provisions.

our generation had thus contributed to the inauguration of a new era in human existence. It is, therefore, both because of the precedent in 1815 and at other times of peace negotiations, when social reforms have been considered, and because idealism runs high in the warring nations, that the women in the Hague Congress considered it feasible to urge a declaration that 'the exclusion of women from citizenship is contrary to the principles of civilization and human right,' as one of the fundamental measures embodied in their resolutions for permanent peace.

But perhaps our hopes for such action are founded chiefly upon the fact that the settlement at the end of this war may definitely recognize a fundamental change in the functions of government taking place in all civilized nations, a change evoked as the result of concrete, social, and economic conditions, approximating similarity all over the world. The recent entrance of women into citizenship coming on so rapidly not only in the nations of Europe and America, but discernible in certain Asiatic nations as well, is doubtless one manifestation of this change, and the so-called radical or progressive element in each nation, whether they like it or not, recognize it as such. Nevertheless, there are men in each of these countries even among those who would grant the franchise to women in city and state, to whom it is still repugnant that women should evince an interest in international affairs. These men argue that woman's municipal vote may be cast for the regulation of contagious disease, her state vote for protection of working children, and that war no longer obtains between cities or even between states; but because war is still legitimate in settling international difficulties, and because international relations are so much a matter of fortified boundaries and standing armies, that it is preposterous for women who cannot fight, to consider them. Furthermore, when war was practically man's sole occupation, no one had a voice in the deliberations of the nation save those responsible for its defence, the king, the nobles, the knights. In the succeeding centuries, as other tests of social utility have been developed and the primitive test of fighting has subsided, the electorate has been steadily enlarged, the *bourgeoisie*, the workingman, and last the women, each group largely following its own interests as government took them over – the regulation of commercial relations, of industrial conditions, of the health and education of children. Only in time of war is government thrown back to its primitive and sole function of self-defence, belittling for the moment the many other real interests of which it is the guardian. War moreover has always treated the lives of men and women broadly, as a landscape painter who suppresses all details – 'The man bold, combative, conquering; woman sympathetic, healing the wounds that war has made.'

But because this primitive conception of the function of government and of the obsolete division between the lives of men and women has obtained during the long months of the European war, there is obviously great need at the end of the war that women should attempt, in an organized capacity, to make their contribution to that governmental internationalism between the nations which shall in some measure approximate the genuine internationalism already developed in so many directions among the peoples. In normal times, moreover, all modern Governments with any living relation to the great developments in commerce, industry, sanitary science, or a dozen other aspects of contemporary life, are coming to realize that the current type of government implies the frequent subordination of an isolated nationalism to general international interests. It is hoped that this new approach to international relationships, typified by the international postal system and a hundred other semi-governmental regulations, will be vital enough to assert itself at the end of this war as over against the militaristic and 'armed peace' relationships.

An organized and formal effort on the part of women would add but one more to that long procession of outstanding witnesses who in each generation have urged juster and more vital international relations between Governments. Each exponent in this long effort to place law above force was called a dreamer and a coward, but each did his utmost to express dearly the truth that was in him, and beyond that human effort cannot go.

This tide of endeavor has probably never been so full as at the present moment. Religious, social, and economic associations, many of them organized since the war began, are making their contributions to the same great end. Several of them are planning to meet at 'the Conference of the Powers which shall frame the terms of the peace settlement after this war,' and such meetings are not without valuable precedent.

A federation or a council of European powers should not be considered impossible from the very experience of the nations now at war. The German Empire, Consolidated Italy, or the United Kingdom have been evolved from separate states which had previously been at war with each other during centuries; the response to the call of imperialistic England, during the last months, for more troops has shown that patriotic emotion can be extended to include the Boers of South Africa and the natives of India; certain of these great federated states and empires have again formed alliances with each other and are fighting together against a common enemy.

Is it too much to hope that the good will and the consciousness of common aims and responsibilities can be extended to include all the European nations and that devices for international government can be provided, able to deal in the interests of the whole with each difficult situation as it arises? The very experience of this war should demonstrate its feasibility and the analogy inevitably suggests itself that as the states of Germany and Italy came together under the pressure of war, possibly this larger federation may be obtained under the same sense of united effort.

Out of the present situation, which certainly 'presents the spectacle of the breakdown of the whole philosophy of nationalism, political, racial, and cultural,' may conceivably issue a new birth of internationalism, founded not so much upon arbitration treaties, to be used in time of disturbance, as upon governmental devices designed to protect and enhance the fruitful processes of cooperation in the great experiment of living together in a world become conscious of itself.

[Source: *Women at the Hague: International Congress of Women and Its Results* (New York: Macmillan, 1915), 124–41. Available through History of Women microfilm, Gale International Ltd, reel 7158.]

Adelheid Popp (1869–1939) was a socialist feminist who founded the proletarian women's movement in Austria. In 1889 she joined the Viennese Association for the Education of Working Women. As a member of the Austrian Social Democratic Workers Party, she became editor-in-chief of the *Arbeiterinnenzeitung* (*Women Workers' Newspaper*) in 1892. In 1893 she organized the first strike of women garment workers in Vienna. Popp created the Association of Social-Democratic Women and Girls in 1902. She was elected to the municipal council of Vienna in 1919 and also to the Austrian parliament, where she served until 1934. Popp succeeded Clara Zetkin as chair of the Second International's Women's Committee.

Adelheid Popp

An Appeal to Women from Austrian Socialist Women (1915)

Dear Comrades:

In our hearts, and I think I have the right to speak in the name of all Socialist working women of Austria, the longing is alive to see the end of this terrible war.

The blood of our relatives, friends, and comrades is being shed on the battlefields, and we do not call only the workers of Austria and Germany our own. The workers of Britain, Belgium, France, Russia and Servia are just as dear to us, and we know they have, just as our slaughtered workers have, mothers, wives and children who weep for them. Nothing can separate us from the working class of other nations but the frontiers. We are conscious, even if we speak in different tongues, that we must take joint action, because the working class of all countries have to suffer from the same fate. It appears to us that one of the most terrible consequences of the war is the fact that the communications between the working men and women of all countries have been cut off. But, nevertheless, we cannot despair! We are conscious that the fraternization of the peoples is a historical need and that it is even more necessitated by the miseries of daily life.

We cannot doubt that the Socialist International will be restored, and we are convinced that those Socialists who defend their country with rifle and sword are longing like us for the time when they will again be able to press the hands of the 'enemy'!

We women, although we are not at war, daily witness the terrible consequences of the war, and when we look at our returning soldiers we consider it our duty to work hard in order to prevent estrangement and national hatred hindering the future action of the working class International. The command of Christ, 'Thou shalt love,' has been taken over by the Socialists. We are proud that feelings of international sympathy and friendship have so strongly taken root, and we consider it the duty of all Socialists to do all in their power to see that these feelings are not extinguished. And, therefore, I am glad to have the opportunity to speak to the comrades of Britain and to tell them that the Socialist women of Austria have not a moment forgotten their ideals.

We are deeply longing for the end of this war! We have no greater wish than to be able to co-operate again in fastening strongly and indestructibly the tie which unites all peoples.

> Adelheid Popp, Leader of Socialist Women of Austria
> Vienna, January, 1915.

[Source: *A Group of Letters from Women of the Warring Nations*; repr. by the Woman's Peace Party, Chicago, 1915. Library and Archives of Canada.]

Sylvia Pankhurst (1882–1960), daughter of Emmeline Pankhurst and sister of Christabel, began by working for suffrage within the Women's Social and Political Union founded by her mother. Sylvia was also drawn to the labour movement, however, and believed in organizing among working-class women. In 1914 she broke with the WSPU and formed the East London Federation of Suffragettes, eventually the Workers' Socialist Federation, and founded the organization's newspaper, the *Women's Dreadnought*. Pankhurst also attended meetings of the Third International and of the Italian Socialist Party.

Sylvia Pankhurst
Our Equal Birthright (1915)

Do you believe that if all the wealthy landowners, merchants and manufacturers, all the great financiers the world over, had been told that their incomes would be cut down to a bare subsistence level if war were declared, and so long as war should last, that they would have agreed to war?

Do you believe that they would have agreed to war, if they had known that they would have to starve and stint as you do?

Do you believe that any Kaiser, Czar, or Emperor, could cause war, alone, without the help of the financiers and the people?

Do you know that the great armament firms are international, that they have directors, who are both British and German, and that they have supplied arms to both sides in the war, and that Great Britain is paying a royalty to Krupps of Germany for every fuse we fire?

Do you not think it is dangerous to give the right to supply armaments to any private firm? If a man sells tea, he tries to make you want to drink it, if he sells guns, he tries to make you shoot.

Do you not want to get behind the armament firms that flourish by our fighting, and the merchants and shippers, who in their desire to open markets, consider the people between them and their trading only as pawns in the game?

Do you remember that when the Russian people were fighting for their freedom against an oppression more terrible than anything we know, the financiers of Great Britain lent money to the Czar and his Ministers to crush them down?

Do you remember that when the British dockers were striking, the German dockers sent money to them to help them to hold out?

Do you not want to get behind the financiers, to the workers of the other nations, in order that you may discover together *why* it is that you should fight, and together solve the differences that arise?

Do you remember that on Christmas Day there was a truce between the English and the German soldiers?

How was it that the men who had been murdering each other for months past were able to want this truce and enjoy it together? It was because they were human beings with minds of the same sort, who had lived the same sort of lives, and Christmas had for them all the self same memories. The religious ideal of Christmas, as drawing together all mankind in peace and goodwill as children of one family in the sight of God, and the intimate tender home memories with which it was interwoven in all the soldiers' hearts, accomplished a miracle indeed! It enabled them to cast out fear – the strongest of our masters – fear of the men of the opposing armies concealed in the opposite trenches, fear of the officers beside them, armed with the frequently exercised power of life and death over those who disobey.

What Christmas did in some portions of the opposing lines, a greater catastrophe than war would also do. If God should send a rain of fire from heaven, or if tremendous floods or an earthquake should arise, immediately the opposing troops would cease their fighting, and as poor bewildered human fugitives, would rush to each other for sympathy and aid.

Deep down beyond all race and class distinctions we are human beings, with the same needs and instincts, and this is revealed to us when we are threatened by great catastrophes arising from non-human things.

We are suffering now, both nationally and internationally, from our imperfect social organisations, and the mistakes and difficulties that come from fear or suspicion of each other. It is because the people of the various countries fear each other that they are prevailed upon to fight. It is because they fear to trust to their equal birthright as human beings that they allow evil social conditions to prevail at home.

Those who are afraid to trust to the possibility of there being enough for everyone, in a state of society in which equal opportunities should be given to all, strive to maintain things as they are.

We must rid ourselves of the idea that there are any *real* class distinctions. The only essential differences that there are between us, as human beings, are to be found amongst the individuals in every social class. The class distinctions that we know at present are due to the system of allowing one individual to benefit by the toil of others, and that of putting money out to interest, under which a sum of money is never spent by its owner, but always remains intact, and enables him to exact an unending toll of the things that other people work to produce. The war loan is a striking example of this.

These things are defended on the ground that production must be organised, but the capitalist is not necessarily an organiser, and we must work towards a state of society in which the person who undertakes the, to him, congenial work of organising, shall not be given a larger share of the general benefits produced, than those who are responsible for other forms of labour.

During the war it has been demonstrated very clearly that production organised by competing individuals, each striving for his own private benefit is inefficient in the extreme.

It is because the inefficiency has been very glaring that the Ministry of Munitions has been instituted. Yet still the Government refuses to take the making of munitions out of private hands and even extends the practice, so that such firms as Bryant and Mays, the match makers, are given facilities for becoming munition makers to the Government, and can get a share of the munition profits; although if munitions had been nationalised, war profits would have been saved. It is universally admitted that shippers, coal owners, and those who deal in wheat, meat and other forms of food, have been making enormous profits out of the war; but the Government refuses to prevent these powerful interests from preying upon the consumers.

There is no doubt that the Government is sacrificing the interests of the people to those of the financiers at the present time. Do you believe that you can trust the Government not to do so when the terms of peace come to be decided?

Do you consider it is safe at any time to allow the foreign policy of the nation to be hidden from the people?

You will be told that it is useless to try to democratise our British foreign policy, because the foreign policies of the other Powers are autocratic and, therefore, our own regard for the welfare of the peoples of the world could do nothing to prevent wars.

Do not believe that. With certainty believe that there are people in every nation whose faith is built on the brotherhood of mankind and those men and women, though they are unknown to us, are striving even as we strive. Every success of ours makes their fight less difficult. Social reforms initiated in one country spread across the world just as scientific discoveries and the developments in music and painting do.

Before the war, during the war, after the war is done, the old striving for more perfect human development continues and will continue for all time.

As we take our part in the struggle let us determine that we will not want for ourselves more of the world's material goods than the common average for all, but that that common average shall be a high and abundant one for all the people of the world.

[Original source: *The Woman's Dreadnought*, 14 August 1915; repr. in *A Sylvia Pankhurst Reader*, ed. Kathryn Dodd (Manchester: Manchester UP, 1993), 70–3]

International Alliance of Women for Suffrage and Equal Citizenship
Announcement of Study Conference (1927)

Committee for Peace and the League of Nations
(Commission de la Paix et de la Société des Nations –
Ausschuss für Frieden und Volkerbund)

Officers:
President: Carrie Chapman Catt
Chairman: Ruth Morgan
Vice-Chairman: Frances M. Sterling
Hon. Secretary: Rosa Manus

Correspondence to
Rosa Manus, Keizersgracht 580, Amsterdam, Holland
Telegrams, 'Romanus-Amsterdam'
Telephone 37574

Study Conference
On action possible to women as citizens in support of Peace and the League of Nations
Colonial Institute, Amsterdam, November, 17–18–19, 1927

A committee for Peace and the League of Nations has been formed by the International Alliance, in pursuance of instructions given by the Congress sitting in Paris in 1926.

This committee, in conjunction with the Board of the Alliance, has sought for the best contribution which the Alliance can make towards this great object. It is clearly undesirable in any way to duplicate work being done by many existing societies, but it is also clear, as the Congress felt, that a body of women, drawn from different countries, of all political parties, organized as citizens or would-be citizens but working politically beyond the limits of party or nationality, should be able to use their power and unity to good effect.

It is abundantly clear that there are certain underlying causes of war not easy to discern, still less easy to remove, and which governments and politicians may even fight shy of discussing; nevertheless, until these questions are deeply studied and discussed, that advance in public opinion in all countries, without which governments cannot act, will not take place. If we are to hope to affect public opinion we must first learn ourselves.

The Peace Committee therefore calls upon the auxiliaries to send their best, ablest and most expert women to a Study Conference, to be held in Amsterdam at the Colonial Institute on 17th, 18th and 19th November, 1927, at which it is proposed to deal with some of these fundamental questions.

Selection has been difficult, but the subjects have been grouped under two general heads: Economic and Political; in each there are matters ripe for Government action and others barely yet recognized as fundamental.

We cannot hope in the short space of three days to advance far along our chosen path, but we may survey the ground to be covered and be able to select the more detailed work next to be undertaken.

The highest world experts obtainable have been invited to address the meetings at which, besides our own delegates, it is hoped that representatives of older Peace organizations will be present.

It may be that on some matters so general an agreement will be arrived at, that it may be possible to pass resolutions expressing that agreement. Such resolutions, carried back by the delegates each to her own country, will form the basis of further work within the auxiliary, guided by all that the delegation has learned at the conference. Each auxiliary will then be able to decide what action (often in conjunction with other Peace organizations) can be taken in its own country, towards affecting public opinion.

It is intended to hold at least two more Study Conferences before the next Congress of the Alliance in 1929, and by that time we hope that some important matters connected with World Peace will be ripe for action by that Congress.

Each auxiliary will be entitled to send TWELVE delegates, of whom THREE will speak and vote, and visitors will also be admitted to the Sessions.

Further particulars and forms of application for tickets are enclosed, together with a draft programme.

In conclusion, we would urge all peace-loving women within our Alliance to do all in their power to make this, our first Study Conference, a success worthy of the cause it is intended to serve.

> Ruth Morgan, Chairman.
> Frances M. Sterling, Vice-Chairman.
> Rosa Manus, Hon. Secretary.

Programme

FIRST DAY. NOV. 17. 10 a.m.   Opening addresses. The subjects to be dealt with will fall under two heads:
A. Economic Causes of International Unrest
B. Political Causes of International Unrest

11–12 & 2–5	A. (Economic Causes)
	1. Resolutions of economic conference, the action of States upon them and other relevant matters arising during the assembly of the League.
	2. Raw materials and the necessaries of life; possibilities of international control.
SECOND DAY. NOV. 18	B. (Political Causes).
10–12.30 & 2–5	1. Security and arbitration: recent developments.
THIRD DAY. NOV. 19	2. Armaments. Their general limitation and their relation to peace and economic stability.
10–12.30 & 1.30–4.30	3. Regional disarmament.
	Closing speeches, findings, votes of thanks.

[IAWSEC] Notes. – Proposed, that should the conference prove to be almost unanimous on any conclusions regarding any subject, any resolution passed by at least a ¾ majority should be recorded; it being clearly understood to be the opinion of the conference, not of the Alliance. Such resolutions would form the basis of further study by the auxiliaries and might be adopted later by next congress, should the Alliance so desire.

[Source: *Jus Suffragii: International Women Suffrage News* 21, no.1 (1927): 2. Available through the Gerritsen Collection.]

Matiel E.T. Mogannam
Arab Woman's Bid for Peace (1937)

Palestine is, perhaps, the only country which is designed to inspire a message of peace. It is held in deep veneration by followers of the three Great Faiths. From it many a prophet gave his message to the world. To many millions of the Christian faith in the East and West Palestine is considered as the most precious of all religious sanctuaries. It contains the Holy Sepulchre and the Church of the Nativity and many other places of sanctity with which the name of Jesus Christ is associated. By the Moslems it is held in no less veneration. It contains the second of the three great mosques in Islam, and the faces of the faithful are turned to it in prayer five times a day.

A country with such characteristics should serve as a centre of culture and knowledge and inspire peace amongst all men. It is unfortunate that this unique position by which Palestine is blessed has been a cause of continual unrest to its population. For centuries Palestine was the subject of competition between European Powers, each one endeavouring to obtain wider concessions or more liberal privileges from the Sultan. It is this position perhaps, amongst other factors of strategic importance, which moved the Allies during the Great War to organize a special campaign for its deliverance from the Turks which ended with its occupation.

But has such occupation and the Administration which was set up thereafter under the British Mandatory assisted in securing the maintenance of peace in the Holy Land? It would be a repetition to state the reasons which have made Palestine a scene of continual unrest and repeated disturbances. It suffices here to say that during a period of less than eighteen years since the British Occupation no less than four sweeping riots have taken place, the last of which, in April, 1936, culminated in considerable loss to life and property. Indeed, in no other land in the world does one feel so unsafe or insecure as in Palestine, not owing to the insufficiency of forces to maintain public security, for such exist in large numbers, but because a riot is liable to take place for the smallest reason and might be accompanied by acts of violence on either side, irrespective of the consequences.

This state of uncertainty derives its origin from the peculiar circumstances under which the country is now placed. It is due in no small measure to the attempts which are being made to establish a National Home for an alien race in a country which is already populated.

The contribution made by the Arab women to the disclosure of the evils of such policy has not been insignificant. Their efforts to secure an undisturbed future have been continuous. They directed their endeavours to one end: to remove all causes of unrest and bloodshed, and in that they made their message quite clear.

In their appeal for peace and the protection of the rights of their nation they wish to rely upon the unfailing support and co-operation of the true citizens of all nations, so that this Holy Land will be once again the birthplace of everything that is good and noble.

[Source: *The Arab Woman and the Palestine Problem* (London: Herbert Joseph, 1937), 101–2.]

In preparation for the WILPF Luhacovice conference, the Egyptian Section proposing to affiliate with the WILPF prepared a series of propositions, the second of which concerned the WILPF's goal of 'total and universal disarmament.' Alice Jacot, representing the Egyptian Section, sent this document to Clara Ragaz, one of three vice-presidents of the WILPF. Ragaz reacted strongly to the Egyptian position on disarmament and an exchange of letters followed. The second proposition of the Egyptian section reads: 'Disarmament in Egypt cannot be envisaged as it is everywhere else from the fact that Egypt is disarmed; on the contrary, it must arm itself by all means not in anticipation of aggressive acts, but for the defence of its continually coveted territory. Egypt cannot cease to arm itself until its sovereignty is inviolable, until it can be assured of that materially and effectively, and not by words that prove invariably to be vain, but by actions and deeds. We imagine that the Near East in its entirety as well as peoples who have not yet obtained their independence are absolutely in the same position as Egypt. Let us repeat one more time: there can be no stable peace unless people have an assured and sustained freedom.'

Clara Ragaz and Alice Jacot
Exchange of Letters on Disarmament (1937)

Clara Ragaz to Alice Jacot, 12 May 1937

Dear Madame,

To my considerable regret, I am only managing today to send you some reflections that came to me in reading your letter of the 15th of April and, above all, the second paragraph of the 'Propositions' that your Section intends to present at the Luhacovice Congress. It was the passage concerning disarmament, or rather, declaring your country's necessity of armaments that struck me.

You say in your letter that for Egypt there can be no question of disarmament since it is a disarmed country, but that it is the duty of your people to arm themselves 'to the teeth' to defend their newly acquired and still threatened liberty. In paragraph two of your 'Propositions,' the same idea of the absolute necessity of an army to defend the liberty of your country is expressed.

I do not blame you for the frankness with which you present your ardent love for the independence of your country and I am prepared to share your burning desire to preserve it. For me, the only questions that arise are:

a) Can people really expect to ensure the security of their countries with armed force?

b) Is it not, rather, in relying on ideas of justice and the rule of law on a national and international basis that they lay a secure foundation for the liberty of their countries?

c) Above all, how can a section of the WILPF, or a group aspiring to be accepted as a national section, place itself in contradiction with fundamental principles of the League which, from its founding, has been against *all* war, whether a defensive war or a war of aggression.

I admit that it is difficult these days to preserve one's faith in the strength of ideas and that one is often tempted to have recourse to ordinary and traditional means of defence through arms. I also admit that we pacifists are often obliged to let pass in silence what we should, according to our principles, condemn publicly. But at least we should not demand what our principles condemn.

Once again, I do not mean to reproach you. I merely point out that if you make yourselves advocates of armament, you are not in accord with the principles of the League, and I see neither the possibility nor the point in your affiliation with the League. That is what I would have liked to write you as soon as I learned of your attitude to this question. I was prevented from doing so until now, but I could not fail to do so today. I am sending a copy of my letter to my two colleagues who are the two other vice-presidents of the League, Madames Baer and Ramondt, who, I am sure, share my point of view. You still have, naturally, the right to bring the question of your admission or non-admission before the Congress and we will all be happy to see you and to discuss with you the problem in question. I also hope that even if we cannot work together under the rubric of the League, you will not entirely abandon the work you are doing for peace and that we will meet in other organizations such as, for example, the R.U.P. [Rassemblement Universel pour la Paix] to which the League also belongs.

In concluding I ask that you believe in my very sincere support.

Signed, Clara Ragaz
Vice-President

Alice Jacot to Clara Ragaz, 22 May 1937

Dear Madame Ragaz,

We have just received your letter of May 12th and understand your apprehension on the subject of certain passages in our letter and our 'propositions' of the 28th of March. We are nonetheless certain that it is a question of a misunderstanding, precipitated perhaps by the terms used in our letter which were, we admit, neither very concise nor sufficiently clear for those of you who live so far from our country. Also contributing to misunderstanding is the fact that we have not yet had the opportunity to discuss the various aspects of the problem of peace and freedom face to face with you and your colleagues. We are therefore particularly happy that the Luhacovice Conference will present the opportunity to exchange our points of view more directly.

Allow us to return today to the three questions you have posed in your letter and to try to clarify our thoughts, beginning with your comment c). We are convinced our point of view is not in contradiction with the principle of total and universal disarmament, nor with the other fundamental principles of the WILPF.

It seems to us that 'total and universal disarmament' does not mean in all cases unilateral disarmament in each country without consideration as to whether it is a weak or strong country, free or oppressed, aggressive or pacifist. Besides, have you not yourselves more than once made certain distinctions of this kind?

In the case of Spain, for example: you did not demand the disarmament of Republican Spain. Not even an unconditional withdrawal of foreign volunteers fighting on the side of the government! On the other hand, you demanded very energetically the immediate withdrawal of the foreign rebel elements, and it was only after such a withdrawal that you proposed to invite democratic governments to call home the republican volunteers (letter of December 23, 1936 to various governments). In that case you evidently did not place a war of aggression and a defensive war on the same footing!

Concerning question b): We have always very clearly taken a position in favour of ideas of justice and international law, and we have even insisted on this position, despite the discouraging experiences of our neighbour Ethiopia, which suffered the most cruel and barbarian war – she who was completely disarmed and had no defence other than her confidence in international justice! We have in no way wished to express a distrust of the establishment of an international order of law and justice, able to safeguard the independence and liberty of all peoples. These are the very principles we want to defend with all our strength. (We remind you of our demonstrations in favour of the League of Nations and the entry of Egypt into that organization, etc.; see also paragraph 3 of our 'propositions').

Finally, concerning point a), we are certainly not among those who demand security by means of armaments. It is, on the contrary, in the collaboration of all peoples precisely in the establishment of a system of justice and law that we see as the only way to realise the aspirations to liberty of all countries like ours.

But to explain in depth our attitude toward the Egyptian army, we have to enter into some of the details of the political situation in Egypt.

1. *The Anglo-Egyptian Treaty*. The Treaty signed last year with England

stipulates that imperial troops withdraw, after a transition period, as soon as and on the condition that the protection of Egyptian territory and the Suez Canal can be assumed by the Egyptian army that is to be created. Without approving the Treaty in all points, it is nonetheless the case that to oppose the creation of the Egyptian army would mean *de facto* the maintenance of British troops in Egypt. You see how the situation presents itself. Whether we approve of it or not, we have to take it into account. And we cannot cease to take a position in a brave and above all realistic manner in favour of the complete independence of our country. This principle we can never renounce if we want to fight for peace and liberty in a country like ours, even if this principle obliges us, in a very specific case, to approve national armaments.

And it does not seem to us that the proper course to follow currently is to attack the Treaty, despite clauses that impose on Egypt the creation of an army, etc., since that would be to oppose Egypt's development toward the emancipation that is necessary and that is certainly in the final analysis a development toward peace and liberty. It would also be to make the game too easy for other powers, no less imperialist than England, who are waiting on the doorstep of our country.

2. *The Italian threat.* World opinion is not yet sufficiently informed about the military preparations of Italian fascism in Tripoli and on the Egyptian frontier. Vast aerodromes, military routes, etc. are under construction and constitute, together with propaganda and obscure intrigues among the nomad populations of the region, a very serious threat to the security and independence of our country. Moreover, the Duce's claim to be the 'defender of Islam' is also significant.

Are you of the opinion that in the face of this Italian threat Egypt should remain disarmed like Ethiopia did? and expect that the League of Nations, such as it is at the moment, ensure the independence of our territory?

This is the situation that makes the establishment of an international order able to guarantee the independence of peoples without their having to have recourse to national armaments seem urgent to us.

But currently we certainly cannot consent to struggle blindly against armaments without being able to replace them with a pacifist mechanism capable of preventing our country from becoming an Ethiopia or a Spain.

Were such a mechanism to exist, we would be against armaments, and the entire Egyptian populace would be with us. Armaments constitute an enormous financial burden for the country, and we desire that pacifist methods be employed for the resolution of international conflicts.

But we are for armaments 1. to the extent that they currently are a condition of the evacuation of foreign troops from Egypt (under the Treaty); and 2. to the extent that they replace the British troops that at this time protect Egyptian territory from foreign threats (and they did so successfully during the Italo-Ethiopian war), although they exploit this privilege in favour of British interests.

We are certain that this letter will dissipate at least partly the misunderstanding and firmly hope that we will reach complete agreement when we have the opportunity to discuss these matters in person.

In any case we thank you sincerely for the forthrightness with which you have posed these questions and we hope soon to receive an equally clear response to this letter.

We beg of you to transmit the enclosed copies of this letter to Madames Baer and Ramondt, and to accept, dear Madame Ragaz, our sincere fraternal greetings.

Signed, Alice Jacot.

[Source: WILPF papers. Microfilm reel 3 [French]. Trans. M. Moynagh.]

Josephine Schain (1886–1972) began her career as a social worker in Minneapolis, and worked as a settlement house worker on New York's East Side from 1918 to 1924. Schain was also active in the suffrage and peace movements. She served as director of the Department of International Relations for the National League of Women Voters 1924–8, and chaired the National Committee on the Cause and Cure of War 1936–41, the Peace and Disarmament Committee of the Women's International Organizations 1933–8, and the Pan-Pacific Women's Association 1949–55. Schain was also a member of the International Alliance of Women for Suffrage and Equal Citizenship 1933–8.

Josephine Schain

Peace in the Americas (1937)

With swiftness and precision unprecedented in international conferences, the Inter-American Conference for the Maintenance of Peace held in Buenos Aires, Argentina, wound up its work in order to adjourn before Christmas. The Conference was called to banish war from the Western hemisphere. It left behind it concrete results in the form of a series of conventions which provide for collective security, non-intervention which in reality gives the Monroe Doctrine a multilateral character, and neutrality on a basis which recognizes commitments which many of the countries have made under the League of Nations.

Committees were set to work under six headings: Organization of Peace, Neutrality, Limitation of Armaments, Juridical Problems, Economic Problems and Cultural Relations. I attended a number of the committee meetings as well as plenary sessions. Among the delegates there was an unmistakable spirit of cooperation and desire to secure real results. To Mr Hull must go a large share of the credit for the spirit in which the work was carried on. He dissipated the old animosity which has characterized the attitude of South American representatives toward the United States in so many conferences.

A pact providing for collective security was the first to be agreed upon. It was presented in the name of all twenty-one of the countries represented in the Conference. Those who feel that there is no idealism left in the international world would have been inspired by the almost consecrated attitude of the men at the meeting when this document was received. The treaty calls for consultation in case the peace of the American republics is menaced in order that they may work out methods of cooperation for preventing armed conflict from breaking out. It provides also for collaboration in event of war between any of the American states or in event of international war outside the Americas which might affect these republics, in order that peace in this continent may be preserved.

A non-intervention convention was agreed to by which any unfriendly act by any one of the powers will be construed to affect all of them. Such an act would provide the basis for proceeding under the collective security provisions. Thus common defense is provided against any power that intervenes in the internal affairs of another American state. Provision is made for conciliation and arbitration of questions which can not be settled by diplomatic means. This treaty in reality means that all of the countries accept the responsibility which formerly the United States alone carried under the Monroe doctrine. When this treaty is ratified we shall no longer take action alone but only after consultation and in cooperation with the other American states.

The five treaties now in existence among the states are coordinated in one instrument. These include the Gondra Treaty To Avoid and Prevent Conflict between the American States, passed in 1923, the Kellogg-Briand Pact, for the renunciation of war as an instrument of foreign policy, the Inter-American Conciliation Convention, signed in 1929, the Inter-American Arbitration Treaty, signed in 1929, and the Argentine Anti-War pact which was fathered by Saavedra Lamas.

This treaty deals with the matter of neutrality – one of the most thorny of the questions that confronted the Conference. The states that had commitments because of their membership in the League of Nations were hesitant to sign anything that might be interpreted to conflict with these obligations under the League. Dr Lamas was the one in particular who held back until he felt sure that the provisions of the treaty would not drive a wedge between the Argentine and its world associates. He presided over the Assembly of the League of Nations last September and, as Minister of Foreign Affairs, is anxious to see his country take an important place in world affairs.

The provisions finally agreed upon stated that in the event of the out-break of hostilities between any two states, the others would adopt a common and solidary attitude of neutrality. Each nation is left free to decide its own domestic policy regarding an embargo on arms and loans. The commitments of nations members of the League of Nations are specifically recognized.

No international conference which Mr Hull had a hand in directing would be complete without a consideration of tariff barriers. He feels strongly that the free flow of trade is fundamental as a basis for peace, because peace is dependent on the economic well-being of peoples. Resolutions were passed urging the reduction of tariffs and equality of trade opportunities. Many matters which come under the heading of moral disarmament met with favorable consideration. Mrs Burton Musser of the United States delegation secured a provision for interchange of professors and students. Other ideas which met with favor in the Conference were teaching of peace in the schools, exchange of educational motion pictures and art exhibits and similar plans for intellectual cooperation. A resolution was passed urging the countries which have not already done so to extend political and civil rights to women.

Several of the countries had sent in proposals for the formation of an American League of Nations. This question was left for the next Pan-American Conference to struggle with at Lima in 1938. There is little likelihood that any such scheme can win unanimous cohesion of all Central and South American countries because of their loyalty to the principle of an association of powers on a world basis.

The whole experience was to me a fascinating and inspiring adventure. Early on the morning of Friday, the thirteenth of November, I took my seat in an airplane at Brownsville, Texas, and away I went on the modern magic carpet. I flew over the plains of Mexico, over mountain ranges and cities. Distance no longer had a meaning. In six days I was seated in the parlor of a hotel in Buenos Aires talking with a group of Argentine women. Formalities were soon dispensed with and together we were off on a mental magic carpet planning how war might be done away with, what steps might be taken to overcome antagonisms, and how trade and intercourse might be developed between the two continents.

I had gone to Buenos Aires with a group of other women from the United States to attend the Conferencia Popular [para] La Paz de America. We represented the National Committee on the Cause and Cure of War as well as the National Council of Women, the National Congress of Parents and Teachers, the Women's International League for Peace and Freedom and the Peoples Mandate – organizations that had joined together for this particular gathering. The conference was initiated by a group of women in Buenos Aires and invitations had been sent to organizations interested in international affairs in both North and South America, men as well as woman being included. In this respect the organizing committee had followed the Brussels Conference plans.

There were ninety-one organizations from South America represented in the Conference. Among these were the League of Nations Association, the cooperatives, the Federation of Labor, the Methodist Church, the Argentine Circle for Peace, organizations of writers and artists, women's clubs, libraries and a long list of cultural groups. Neither the extreme right nor left was represented, but this did not mean that the meetings lacked color. Political refugees from many countries and men who had fought in the Chaco saw to it that the dramatic quality was not missing.

In the Call to the Conference three points had been stated as the basis of the meetings: to maintain the status quo in armaments; to gradually re-establish free trade between American countries; to permit the free circulation of men and ideas throughout the American countries. The women's organizations from the United States had not accepted these points as stated, but did accept them as a basis for discussion with the recommendation that armaments, through international agreement, be reduced to the level sufficient to repel invasion and to maintain internal order, and that peaceful and friendly relations between the nations of the western continents be stimulated still further by continuing the reduction of tariffs through reciprocal trade agreements.

To an Anglo-Saxon the outline submitted seemed simple and the subjects for discussion very definite. The dominant group in the conference, however, was Latin, which meant lengthy discussions on details that we generally settle by common consent. As a result, when the time for adjournment came, the findings for the Conference had to be referred to a committee to be formulated later.

There were outside influences that also added to the confusion. The Mayor of Buenos Aires was opposed to the holding of a popular conference. To understand why, one must go back into the history of South America, the long years of oppression and the more recent years of fighting for what we in North America term civil liberties. The present government in the Argentine represents a minority group and stays in power only because it has the army on its side. The

Mayor is appointed by the federal government. The situation in the Argentine is duplicated, more or less drastically, in practically all of the South American countries. Those in control are afraid of popular conferences because they do not believe in free speech. It is only natural, therefore, that the people who are working for international understanding can not separate the issue of free speech from that of peace, because they have to fight first for the right to hold a meeting without interference from the police.

Granted the confusion and difficulties, granted the lack of concrete results. I believe this Conference served a very constructive purpose and that definite results will follow. I believe the peace forces in South America now realize that they have to begin to build a more solid foundation for their movement. Organization for peace is not as simple a matter as they believed it to be. They now know the strength of those who are defending the old order. As a result of some of the more belligerent speeches made at the Conference, we from the United States have more of an appreciation of the fear and suspicion of our country that exists. It may be that the antagonism is fanned by those who have a motive in so doing, but as long as it does exist, we have a task in overcoming it.

In the light of this experience, one can better appreciate what Mr Roosevelt's visit has done toward improving relations between the two Americas. It was a dramatic historical event to have witnessed. By his message to the Inter-American Conference for the Maintenance of Peace he swept away any basis for future suspicions of 'The Colossus of the North.' By his challenging defense of democracy, he helped to reinforce those who are struggling against such terrific odds to safe-guard the rights of the great masses of the South American people.

The Inter-American Conference was opened by Mr Roosevelt. It was indeed a dramatic session. He was at his best. Again and again he was applauded and after he started to leave the dais he turned and smiled his broadest smile to the galleries. And how the galleries did respond! He was 'simpatico,' everyone said.

At the end of the second plenary session the Peoples Mandate was presented to the delegates. Mrs Elise Musser, as a member of the congress, spoke on behalf of the women from the United States who had come with over a million signatures asking for disarmament and peaceful settlement of disputes. Mrs Rosalinda Miller, the other woman delegate to the conference, joined the women from North America in voicing the longing of the women of Brazil for peace. Mrs Caroline O'Day presented the mandate to the delegates saying:

Since Government is a contrivance of human wisdom to provide for human wants, we, the people, are presenting to our governments a mandate. Through this mandate we voice our conviction that there is no problem affecting humanity that can not be settled without recourse to war. That war must be abolished. National honor can be attained by strengthening the good neighbor policy which had already brought about the warm friendship that exists between Latin America and my own country.

Never before have women shown such interest in Pan American conferences. There were large numbers of them from the United States, Paraguay, Uruguay, Brazil and Chile, and a scattering from the other countries. The Buenos Aires women were untiring in their effort to entertain the delegates. The guests were invited to teas and various social affairs and there was a constant whirl of visits to social service and public institutions.

If we can start now to work for a well-informed delegation of women, vitally interested in Pan American affairs, to the Lima Conference in 1938 we shall contribute much toward helping to further friendly relations between the Americas.

[Source: *National Business Woman* 16, no. 1 (1937): 4–5, 29–30. Available through the Gerritsen Collection.]

Margery Corbett Ashby (1882–1981) became a member of the National Union of Women's Suffrage Societies and secretary of the Constitutional Suffrage Movement while attending Cambridge University. Though she passed her examinations, because she was a woman, Cambridge refused to grant Ashby a degree. After a brief career as a teacher, Ashby became involved in the International Woman Suffrage Alliance, and in 1923 was elected president of the IWSA, a post she would hold until her retirement in 1946. In 1932 she was the British delegate to the Geneva Disarmament Conference, but she resigned from this position in 1935 in protest at the British government's refusal to support any practical scheme for mutual security and defence. In 1937 Ashby was one of the signatories of a declaration in the press asserting that war could be avoided if the League of Nations took positive action.

Margery I. Corbett Ashby
The Women's Movement and Democracy (1938)

The shocks of the last few weeks when Europe was brought to the brink of war and when a gallant and free people were betrayed by their friends into bondage have created in the hearts of all women a feeling of despair. We seem to have so little influence on the course of events. We have worked and spoken for 20 years on international friendship, on support of the League of Nations, on the value of personal responsibility. Now are we quietly to submit as Europe returns to the barbarism of the Middle Ages? Let us at least fight for freedom. Women must not allow themselves to be satisfied with home duties or with even the widest and deepest of social movements for the prevention and cure of suffering. We must join and work for the political parties who stand against dictatorship or tyranny in any form. Women have wasted 20 years of political opportunity: we have not used the machine which controls us. Let us awake and determine that women shall enter the machine to direct it for the defence of democracy. Let us awake before it is too late.

[Source: *Jus Suffragii: International Women Suffrage News* 33, no. 2 (1939): 9. Available through the Gerritsen Collection.]

All-India Women's Conference
Resolution on War (1939)

Conscious of the gravity of the situation today in the world and believing that a new order is an imperative need, we wish to stress once more our abhorrence of war as a solution of any problem. We declare ourselves in utter and eternal opposition to all oppression and exploitation. We have been pained and horrified at the betrayal of Austria and Czechoslovakia, at the abetment from outside and continuance of the internal strife in Spain, at the merciless persecution of the Jews, at the deplorable interference and cruelties in Palestine and at the unjustifiable aggression in China. The inability of the so-called great powers of the world to put an end to all this woe and misery is proof enough of the futility of their methods of approach [...] We appeal to the women of the world to unite on the platform of non-violence and actively demonstrate that by this power alone can the forces of hatred and the desire for possession be brought under control and a real and lasting peace established.

[Source: *All-India Women's Conference Thirteenth Session* (Bombay: Malini-bai Sukthankar, Hon. General Secretary AIWC, 1939), 35.]

Index

STUDIES IN GENDER AND HISTORY

General editors: Franca Iacovetta and Karen Dubinsky